THE REAL GUIDE:

VENICE

REAL GUIDE CREDITS

Series Editor: Mark Ellingham
Editorial: Martin Dunford, John Fisher, Jack Holland, Jonathan Buckley, Greg Ward
US Text Editor: Jamie Jensen
Production: Susanne Hillen, Kate Berens, Gail Jammy
Typesetting: Andy Hilliard
Series Design: Andrew Oliver

ACKNOWLEDGEMENTS

Both authors thank Andy Hilliard, Susanne Hillen and Kate Berens for their hard work and advice, Barry Curtis for sharing his knowledge of Venice's recent past, and Brenda Keatley for tips on the Verona region. Individually we'd like to thank:

Jonathan: Baldessare de'Gaspari, Luigi and Maria-Luisa Benedetti, Katharine Buck and Linda Riley.

Hilary: Louise Schwartz and Mick Hargreaves for hospitality (and Mick again for info on Verona); Franco Donaggio for insights into life on the lagoon; Roberto Longo for enthusiastic exposés of Venice and good company; Matteo, Sandro and the rest of the drummers for entertainment during the Carnevale; Gabriella Balbinot; and Sandro Sartori.

And special thanks to Mark Ellingham, for guidance and constant good humor.

Published in the United States and Canada by
Prentice Hall Press
A division of Simon & Schuster Inc.
15 Columbus Circle
New York, NY 10023

Prentice Hall Press and colophons are registered trademarks of Simon & Schuster Inc.

Typeset in Linotron Univers and Century Old Style.
Printed in the United States by R.R. Donnelley & Sons.

352pp.
Includes index.

THE REAL GUIDE

VENICE

WRITTEN AND RESEARCHED BY

JONATHAN BUCKLEY
AND
HILARY ROBINSON

Edited by Jonathan Buckley

with Mark Ellingham

PRENTICE HALL PRESS

NEW YORK LONDON TORONTO SYDNEY TOKYO SINGAPORE

HELP US UPDATE

We've gone to a lot of effort to ensure that this edition of the Real Guide: Venice is completely up-to-date and accurate. However, things do change—hotels and restaurants come and go, opening hours are notoriously fickle, and there's the ever-present danger of monuments being closed for long periods while under restoration. Any suggestions, comments, or corrections toward the next edition would be much appreciated. We'll credit all contributions, and send a copy of the new book (or any other Real Guide, if you prefer) for the best letters. Send them along to:

Jonathan Buckley, The Real Guides, Prentice Hall Press, A Division of Simon and Schuster Inc., 15 Columbus Circle, New York, NY 10023.

CONTENTS

Introduction

VENICE

S. Michele

Miracoli

S.S. Giovanni e Paolo

S. Francesco della Vigna

S. Maria Formosa

CASTELLO

S. Marco

PIAZZA SAN MARCO

Palazzo Ducale

Pieta

Arsenale

S. Pietro di Castello

EASTERN DISTRICTS

Salute

RCO

S. Giorgio Maggiore

Giardini Pubblici

S. Elena

INTRODUCTION

N obody ever sees Venice for the first time. Depicted and described so often that its image has become part of the collective consciousness, the city can initially create the slightly anticlimactic feeling that everything looks exactly as it should. The Gothic palaces along the **Canal Grande** are as impressive a sight as the brochure photographs made them out to be, just as the panorama across the water from the Palazzo Ducale is as dazzling as Canaletto painted it. Then details of the scene catch the attention—a strange carving high on a wall, a boat being maneuvered round an impossible corner, a window through which a painted ceiling can be seen—and the sense of familiarity begins to fade. And the longer you look, the stranger and more intriguing the city becomes.

Founded fifteen hundred years ago on a cluster of mudflats in the center of the lagoon, Venice rose to become Europe's main trading post between the West and the East, and at its height controlled an empire that spread north to the Dolomites and over the sea as far as Cyprus. As its wealth increased and its population grew, the fabric of the city grew ever more dense. Very few parts of the hundred or so islets that compose the historic center are not built up, and very few of its closely-knit streets bear no sign of the city's long lineage. Even in the most insignificant alleyway you might find fragments of a medieval building embedded in the wall of a house like a fossil remains lodged in a cliff face.

The melancholic air of the place is in part a product of the discrepancy between the grandeur of its history and what the city has become. In the heyday of the Venetian Republic, nearly 200,000 people lived in Venice, not far short of three times its present population. Merchants from Germany, Greece, Turkey, and a host of other countries maintained warehouses here; transactions in the banks and bazaars of the **Rialto** dictated the value of commodities all over the continent; in the dockyards of the **Arsenale** the workforce was so vast that a warship could be built and fitted out in a single day; and the **Piazza San Marco** was perpetually thronged with people here to set up business deals or report to the Republic's government. Nowadays it's no longer a living metropolis but rather the embodiment of a fabulous past, dependent for its survival largely on the people who come to marvel at its relics.

The monuments which draw the largest crowds are the **Basilica di San Marco**—the mausoleum of the city's patron saint—and the **Palazzo Ducale**—the home of the doge and all the governing councils. Certainly these are the most dramatic structures in the city: the first a mosaic-clad emblem of Venice's Byzantine origins, the second perhaps the finest of all secular Gothic buildings. Every parish rewards exploration, though—a roll-call of the **churches** worth visiting would feature over fifty names, and a list of the important paintings and sculptures they contain would be twice as long. Two of the distinctively Venetian institutions known as the **Scuole** retain some of the outstanding examples of Italian Renaissance art—the **Scuola di San Rocco**, with its sequence of pictures by Tintoretto, and the **Scuola di San Giorgio degli Schiavoni**, decorated with a gorgeous sequence by Carpaccio.

Although many of the city's treasures remain in the buildings for which they were created, a sizable number have been removed to one or other of Venice's

museums. The one that should not be missed is the **Accademia**, an assembly of Venetian painting that consists of virtually nothing but masterpieces; other prominent collections include the museum of eighteenth-century art in the **Ca' Rezzonico**, and the **Museo Correr**, the civic museum of Venice—but again, a comprehensive list would fill a page.

Then, of course, there's the inexhaustible spectacle of the streets themselves, of the majestic and sometimes decrepit palaces, of the hemmed-in squares where much of the social life of the city is conducted, of the sunlit courtyards that suddenly open up at the end of an unpromising passageway. The cultural heritage preserved in the museums and churches is a source of endless fascination, but you should discard your itineraries for a day and just wander—the anonymous parts of Venice reveal as much of the city's essence as the highlighted attractions. And equally indispensible for a full understanding of Venice's way of life and development are expeditions to the **northern and southern islands** of the lagoon, where the incursions of the tourist industry are on the whole less obtrusive.

Venice's hinterland—the **Veneto**—is historically and economically one of Italy's most important regions. Its major cities—**Padua**, **Vicenza**, and **Verona**—are all covered in Part Three of the guide, along with many of the smaller towns located between the lagoon and the mountains to the north.

When to go

Venice's tourist season is very nearly an all-year affair. **Peak season** is from **April to October**, when hotel rooms are very hard to come by; if possible give the central part of this period a miss, and at all costs don't try to stay in July and August, when the crowds are at their fullest and the climate becomes oppressively hot and clammy. Venice at these times is best visited on day trips from outside the city. The other two popular spells are the **Carnevale** (leading up to Lent) and the weeks on each side of **Christmas**; again, hotels tend to be well booked, but the authentic life of the city isn't submerged during these festive periods, as it is by the summer inundation.

For the ideal combination of comparative peace and pleasant climate, the two or three weeks **immediately preceding Easter** is perhaps the best time of year. The days should be mostly mild—though the weather can be capricious—and finding accommodation won't present insuperable problems. Climatically the months at the end of the high season are somewhat less reliable: some **November** days are so clear that from the top of the Campanile the Dolomites seem to start on the edge of the mainland, while others bring fogs that make it impossible to see from one bank of the Canal Grande to the other. However, the desertion of the streets in winter is magical, and the sight of the Piazza under floodwater is unforgettable. If you want to see the city at its quietest, **January** is the month to go—take plenty of warm clothes, though, and be prepared to spend a while looking for a room, as many of the cheaper hotels close down for the really slack period.

THE VENETIAN CLIMATE		
	Average Temp °C (°F)	Average Rainfall mm (in)
January	3.8 (38)	58 (2)
April	12.6 (54)	77 (3)
July	23.6 (74)	37 (1)
October	15.1 (59)	66 (3)

PART ONE

THE
BASICS

GETTING THERE

While flying is by far the simplest and cheapest way to get to Venice, direct flights from the USA are few and far between, and you'll very likely have to make a connection somewhere en route.

DIRECT FROM THE USA

Most flights from the USA stop in either London, Frankfurt, or Milan before connecting to Venice. Conditions of purchase attached to tickets are the same for most airlines; usually you have to book 30 days prior to departure, with a minimum stay of seven days and a maximum stay of three weeks to three months. The prices quoted here are the non-refundable fares. If you want to book a ticket that you can change at a later date, expect to pay anywhere between $100–200 extra.

Alitalia (☎800/223-5730), the Italian national airline, have flights connecting major US cities to New York before flying out to Venice. In terms of cost they beat the American operators hands down, with midweek fares ranging from as little as $650 in the low season to around $1000 in high season. *Pan Am* (☎800/221-1111) offer the most competitive prices after *Alitalia* with fares ranging from $750 in the low season to around $1100 high season. *TWA* (☎800/892-4141) are pricey in comparison with fares ranging from $856 in low season to around $1300 high season, but are more likely than the other airlines to offer flexibility over changing tickets.

FROM CANADA

There are no direct flights from Canada to Venice and most flights stopover in London, Frankfurt, Amsterdam, Rome, or Milan. It may be worth taking a cheap flight to New York and then connecting onto one of the above mentioned flights, as this could well represent a saving. *Canadian Airlines* (☎800/426-7000) have flights from Montreal, Vancouver, and Toronto that range from $908 in low season to a hefty $1428 high season. As an alternative, you might do well to look into package deals offered to major cities in Italy, ditch the accommodation option and travel overland to Venice. If you're not too bothered about getting there in a roundabout fashion, you'll save money.

VIA GREAT BRITAIN

If you decide to travel via Britain, there's a wider range of travel options available. **Flying** is the most straightforward, with daily flights on *Alitalia* and *British Airways* from London Heathrow to Marco Polo airport, 13km from the center of Venice. The best available deals on both airlines are the **APEX** fares, which work out less expensive even than the student fares. For discount and/or charter flights, check the London magazines *Time Out* or *LAW*, or for reliable agents try *STA* (74 Old Brompton Rd, London SW7; ☎071/937 9921) and *Campus Travel* (52 Grosvenor Gardens, London SW1; ☎071/730 3402).

If you're interested in seeing more of Europe en route to Venice, traveling **by train** may be more appealing, though be prepared for prices comparable to airfares if you're over 26, and a shortest possible journey time of 24 hours. If you're under 26 however, a range of youth fares is available, including **BIJ youth tickets** (which discount standard fares by 20–35 percent and allow any number of stopovers along a pre-specified route), and **Explorer** tickets (similar to a pass but on a set route). The **InterRail pass** gives a month's unlimited European rail travel, but is only available to those resident in Europe for six months—otherwise invest in an American **Eurail** pass before leaving home (an under-26 pass is currently $320 for one month, $470 for those over 26).

COUNCIL TRAVEL IN THE US

Head Office: 205 E. 42nd St., New York, NY 10017;
☎212/661-1450

CALIFORNIA
2486 Channing Way, Berkeley, CA 94704; ☎415/
848-8604
UCSD Price Center, Q-076, La Jolla, CA 92093;
☎619/452-0630
1818 Palo Verde Ave., Suite E, Long Beach, CA
90815; ☎213/598-3338
1093 Broxton Ave., Suite 220, Los Angeles, CA
90024; ☎213/208-3551
4429 Cass St., San Diego, CA 92109; ☎619/270-
6401
312 Sutter St., Suite 407, San Francisco, CA
94108; ☎415/421-3473
919 Irving St., Suite 102, San Francisco, CA 94122;
☎415/566-6222
14515 Ventura Blvd., Suite 250, Sherman Oaks, CA
91403; ☎818/905-5777

COLORADO
1138 13th St., Boulder, CO 80302; ☎818/905-5777

CONNECTICUT
Yale Co-op East, 77 Broadway, New Haven, CT
06520; ☎203/562-5335

DISTRICT OF COLUMBIA
1210 Potomac St., NW Washington, DC 20007;
☎202/337-6464

GEORGIA
12 Park Place South, Atlanta, GA 30303; ☎404/
577-1678

ILLINOIS
1153 N. Dearborn St., Chicago, IL 60610; ☎312/
951-0585
831 Foster St., Evanston, IL 60201; ☎708/475-
5070

LOUISIANA
8141 Maple St., New Orleans, LA 70118; ☎504/
866-1767

MASSACHUSETTS
79 South Pleasant St., 2nd Floor, Amherst, MA
01002; ☎413/256-1261
729 Boylston St., Suite 201, Boston, MA 02116;
☎617/266-1926
1384 Massachusetts Ave., Suite 206, Cambridge,
MA 02138; ☎617/497-1497
Stratton Student Center MIT, W20-024, 84
Massachusetts Ave., Cambridge, MA 02139;
☎617/497-1497

MINNESOTA
1501 University Ave. SE, Room 300, Minneapolis,
MN 55414; ☎612/379-2323

NEW YORK
35 W. 8th St., New York, NY 10011; ☎212/254-
2525
Student Center, 356 West 34th St., New York, NY
10001; ☎212/643-1365

NORTH CAROLINA
703 Ninth St., Suite B-2, Durham, NC 27705;
☎919/286-4664

OREGON
715SW Morrison, Suite 600, Portland, OR 97205;
☎503/228-1900

RHODE ISLAND
171 Angell St., Suite 212, Providence, RI 02906;
☎401/331-5810

TEXAS
2000 Guadalupe St., Suite 6, Austin, TX 78705;
☎512/472-4931
Exec. Tower Office Center, 3300 W. Mockingbird,
Suite 101, Dallas,TX 75235; ☎214/350-6166

WASHINGTON
1314 Northeast 43rd St., Suite 210, Seattle, WA
98105; ☎206/632-2448

WISCONSIN
2615 North Hackett Avenue, Milwaukee, WI;
☎414/332-4740

STA IN THE US

BOSTON
273 Newbury St., Boston, MA 02116; ☎617/266-
6014

HONOLULU
1831 S. King St., Suite 202, Honolulu, HI 96826;
☎808/942-7755

LOS ANGELES
920 Westwood Blvd., Los Angeles, CA 90024;
☎213/824-1574
7204 Melrose Ave., Los Angeles, CA 90046; ☎213/
934-8722

2500 Wilshire Blvd., Los Angeles, CA 90057;
☎213/380-2184

NEW YORK
17 E. 45th St., Suite 805, New York, NY 10017;
☎212/986-9470;☎ 800/777-0112

SAN DIEGO
6447 El Cajon Blvd., San Diego, CA 92115; ☎619/
286-1322

SAN FRANCISCO
166 Geary St., Suite 702, San Francisco, CA 94108;
☎415/391-8407

TRAVEL CUTS IN CANADA

Head Office: 187 College St., Toronto, Ontario M5T 1P7; ☎416/979-2406

ALBERTA

1708 12th St. NW, Calgary T2M 3M7; ☎403/282-7687. 10424A 118th Ave., Edmonton T6G 0P7; ☎403/471-8054

BRITISH COLUMBIA

Room 326, T.C., Student Rotunda, Simon Fraser University, Burnaby, British Columbia V5A 1S6; ☎604/291-1204. 1516 Duranleau St., Granville Island, Vancouver V6H 3S4; ☎604/689-2887. Student Union Building, University of British Columbia, Vancouver V6T 1W5; ☎604/228-6890 Student Union Building, University of Victoria, Victoria V8W 2Y2; ☎604/721-8352

MANITOBA

University Centre, University of Manitoba, Winnipeg R3T 2N2; ☎204/269-9530

NOVA SCOTIA

Student Union Building, Dalhousie University, Halifax B3H 4J2; ☎902/424-2054. 6139 South St., Halifax B3H 4J2; ☎902/424-7027

ONTARIO

University Centre, University of Guelph, Guelph N1G 2W1; ☎519/763-1660. Fourth Level Unicentre, Carleton University, Ottawa, K1S5B6; ☎613/238-5493. 60 Laurier Ave. E, Ottawa K1N 6N4; ☎613/238-8222. Student Street, Room G27, Laurentian University, Sudbury P3E 2C6; ☎705/673-1401. 96 Gerrard St. E, Toronto M5B 1G7; ☎ (416) 977-0441. University Shops Plaza, 170 University Ave. W, Waterloo N2L 3E9; ☎519/886-0400.

QUÉBEC (Known as *Voyages CUTS*)

Université McGill, 3480 rue McTavish, Montréal H3A 1X9; ☎514/398-0647. 1613 rue St. Denis, Montréal H2X 3K3; ☎514/843-8511. Université Concordia, Edifice Hall, Suite 643, S.G.W. Campus, 1455 bd de Maisonneuve Ouest, Montréal H3G 1M8; ☎514/288-1130. 19 rue Ste. Ursule, Québec G1R 4E1; ☎418/692-3971

SASKATCHEWAN

Place Riel Campus Centre, University of Saskatchewan, Saskatoon S7N 0W0; ☎306/343-1601

NOUVELLES FRONTIÈRES

In the United States

NEW YORK 19 W. 44th St., Suite 1702, New York, NY 10036; ☎212/764-6494

LOS ANGELES 6363 Wilshire Blvd., Suite 200, Los Angeles, CA 90048; ☎213/658-8955

SAN FRANCISCO 209 Post St., Suite 1121, San Francisco, CA 94108; ☎415/781-4480

In Canada

MONTREAL 1130 ouest, bd de Maisonneuve, Montréal, P.Q. H3A 1M8; ☎514/842-1450

QUEBEC 176 Grande Allée Ouest, Québec, P.Q. G1R 2G9; ☎418/525-5255

STUDENT AND DISCOUNT FLIGHTS

Student fares are not ubiquitous and restrictions apply, but if you meet the conditions (under 26, student, etc) high season fares can be found for as little as $690 round-trip from New York to Venice, and $1000 from Los Angeles. See the boxes above and opposite for *STA* and *Council Travel* offices in the US. If you're not a student, one way of picking up a discount flight is to check the Sunday travel sections of the *New York Times* and *Los Angeles Times* for discount/charter flights. Discount flights are a little cheaper than scheduled ones, and some companies offer genuine bargains if you are able to be flexible in your travel plans. *Nouvelles Frontières*, *Access International* (☎800/TAKE-OFF), and *McTravel* (☎800/330-3335) are all worth calling

to check out the latest deals. There are also many **discount travel clubs**, which charge an annual fee for membership and sell unsold airline tickets at discounts ranging from fifteen to sixty percent. Travelers call a hotline number for information on what's available. However, precise dates and destinations cannot be guaranteed—instead you tell them what range of days you want to fly on and where you want to fly to, and a few days prior to your specified departure time you will be offered a choice of flights.

Naturally this form of travel is very uncertain—while you're almost sure to leave when you wanted, it can't be guaranteed that you'll fly to your chosen destination. It should also be remembered that discount ticket availability is very sensitive to seasonal demand, and some travel clubs close down over peak vacation periods.

RED TAPE AND VISAS

U.S. and Canadian citizens can enter Venice and stay for up to three months simply on production of a valid passport.

Legally you're required to register with the police within three days of entering the country.

This will be done for you if you're staying in a hotel, but if you're not you should register at the *Questura* (headquarters of the state police)—it's on the Fondamenta San Lorenzo, to the east of Santa Maria Formosa. It used to be the case that nobody bothered with this formality, but after recent scares about terrorism some policemen have begun to pay more attention to backpacking types in Venice. So if you think you might look like the sort of person a Venetian policeman might deem undesirable, get registered.

For stays longer than three months you'll need to contact an Italian embassy for information about a student or working visa. For students the procedure is fairly straightforward, but for a working visa you'll need a letter from an Italian employer stating that you have a definite job offer—though be warned that even this will not guarantee your visa application success. Either way, allow a good three months before your departure date to make such arrangements.

ITALIAN EMBASSIES AND CONSULATES

Los Angeles 12400 Wilshire Boulevard, #3300, CA 90025 (☎213/820-0622).
New York 320 Park Avenue, NY 10022 (☎212/737-9100).
Chicago 500 North Michigan Avenue, Ill 60611 (☎312/467-1550).

San Francisco 2590 Webster Street, CA 94115 (☎415/931-4924).
Boston 100 Boylston Street, MA 02116 (☎617/542-0483).
Philadelphia 421 Chestnut Street, PA 19106 (☎215/592-7329).

COSTS, MONEY, AND BANKS

There is no getting round the fact that Venice is an expensive city, second in Italy only to Milan. A vacation trip need not break the bank, but you may have to exercise a degree of self-restraint every now and then.

COSTS

If you're on the least luxurious of expeditions—camping, hitchhiking, cooking your own food—it should just about be possible to get by on around $20 a day. Assuming, though, that you stay in a simple hotel, eat out in the evenings, and go to a gallery or museum each day, the bare minimum would be over twice that amount. Even in the dead of winter there are no more than a handful of double rooms in Venice costing less than $25, and a strict diet of coffee and croissant in the mornings, bread and cheese at lunchtime and pizza in the evening will account for around $20 at least. Add onto this the cost of the odd entrance fee and vaporetto ticket, and you've passed the $35 mark before you know it. Allowing for small extravagances and the occasional excursion onto the mainland, it's reasonable to budget for a basic outlay of $45 per day.

In winter it's sometimes possible to negotiate for a room at a price lower than the listed out-of-season rate, but after Easter most hotels shift to a higher price scale, and none have difficulty filling their rooms. The summer inflation varies from 5 percent to an exorbitant 50 percent—the good news being that the smaller relative increases are more common at the lower end of the price range. Venice's high-season minimum for a double room is around $30. As ever, costs are higher for the person traveling alone: for single rooms, you'd be doing well to find anything around $20 out of season or around $25 in the summer. (See "Finding a Place to Stay" at the start of *The City*.)

Eating out in Venice is proportionately costly, but it is possible to eat well for under $20 a head, including wine. (See Chapter 10.)

If you're between 16 and 27, you can get hold of a **Carta Giovani**, a sort of discount card issued by Venice's tourist authorities between late spring and autumn (the dates are variable). The card comes with a booklet listing hotels, restaurants, shops, movie theaters, and museums where cardholders qualify for reductions; just turn up at the San Marco tourist office with a passport-size photo and proof of your age, and you'll be issued one on the spot.

MONEY AND BANKS

The Italian unit of **money** is the *Lira* (plural *Lire*), always abbreviated as L: the rate right now is around L1260 to the US dollar. You get notes for L1000, L2000, L5000, L10,000, L50,000, and L100,000; and coins for L50, L100, L200, and L500. Smaller denomination coins are still floating around and you might be given them as change.

The easiest and safest way to carry your money is as **travelers' checks**, available for a small commission (one percent of the amount ordered) from most American banks and some savings and loans, whether or not you have an account. You'll usually—though not always—pay a small commission, too, when you **exchange money** using travelers' checks, around L2000 each time. The major **credit cards**—*Visa* and *American Express*—are accepted in most places in return for goods or cash; *Mastercard* comes a poor third, at least as far as getting cash advances from banks is concerned. It's a good idea to have at least some Italian money for when you first arrive, and you can buy Lire in advance from currency exchanges in most American airports, but are limited to taking in no more than L400,000 in cash (around $320).

Banks in Venice are collected in two main areas—**Campo S. Bartolomeo** (near the Rialto bridge) and **Calle Larga XXII Marzo** (near the Piazza). A useful bank in the northern part of the city is in **Campiello dell'Anconetta**, between Rio Terrà S. Leonardo and Rio Terrà della Maddalena. All have similar commission and exchange rates. **Banking hours** are generally Mon–Fri 8:30am–1:30pm and 3–4pm.

The **American Express** office in Salizzada S. Moisè (a couple of minutes' walk from the Piazza), is useful for changing cash or travelers' checks out of office hours (Mon–Sat 8am–8pm). There are clusters of **exchange bureaus** (*cambio*) where tourists gather—near San Marco, the Rialto, and the train station. Open all week and late at night, they can be useful in emergencies, but their rates of commission and exchange tend to be steep.

HEALTH AND INSURANCE

An Italian **pharmacy** (*farmacia*) is well-qualified to give you advice on minor ailments, and to dispense prescriptions. A rota of *Farmacie di Turno* ensures that there's always one open all night: listings are given in *Un Ospite di Venezia*, and every *farmacia* should display the address of the nearest night pharmacy on its door (or phone ☎192 for information). If you get **seriously ill**, or are involved in an accident, get to the hospital in Campo Santi Giovanni e Paolo and go to the *Pronto Soccorso* (emergency) section, or phone ☎13 and ask for *ospedale* or *ambulanza*.

INSURANCE

Travel insurance can buy you peace of mind as well as save you money. Before you purchase any insurance however, check what you have already, whether as part of a family or student policy. You may find yourself covered for medical expenses and loss, and possibly loss of or damage to valuables, while abroad. Bank and charge **accounts** (particularly *American Express*) often have certain levels of medical or other insurance included, as do **homeowners' or renters'** insurance.

SPECIALIST INSURANCE

Only after exhausting these possibilities might you want to contact a specialist travel insurance company; your travel agent should be able to recommend one—*Travelguard* and *The Travelers* are good policies.

Travel insurance offerings are quite comprehensive, anticipating everything from charter companies going bankrupt to delayed (and lost) baggage, and sundry illnesses and accidents. **Premiums** vary widely—from the very reasonable ones offered primarily through student/youth agencies (though available to anyone), to those so expensive that two or three months of coverage will probably equal the cost of the worst possible combination of disasters.

A most important thing to keep in mind—and a source of major disappointment to would be claimants—is that *none* of the currently available policies insures against **theft** of anything while overseas. North American travel policies apply only to items lost from, or damaged in, the custody of an identifiable, responsible third party, i.e. hotel porter, airline, luggage consignment, etc. Even in these cases you still have to contact the local police to have a complete report made out so that your insurer can process the claim.

It's also worth remembering that all policies work by reimbursing you once you return home, so it's essential to keep all your receipts from doctors and pharmacists. Any thefts should be reported immediately to the police and a police report obtained—no report, no refund.

INFORMATION AND MAPS

Before you leave, it's worth dropping in at the Italian State Tourist Office (ENIT) to pick up some maps and brochures. Don't overload yourself, though—not only can most of the material be picked up in Venice, but the practical information such as accommodation prices is often out of date in the offices outside Italy.

TOURIST INFORMATION

In the **US**, ENIT offices can be found in New York (630 5th Ave., NY 10111; ☎212/245-4822), San Francisco (Suite 801, 360 Post St., CA 94108; ☎415/392-6206), and Chicago (500 N. Michigan Ave., IL 60611; ☎312/644-0990). In **Canada** they are located at 3 Place Ville Marie, 56 Plazaz, Montreal, Quebec, H3B 2E3 (☎514/866-7667).

In Venice, *Ente Provinciale per il Turismo* (EPT) offices are at: **Piazzale Roma** (8am–8pm in **summer** only; ☎5227404), the **train station** (8am–8pm; ☎715016), and on the corner of **Calle dell'Ascensione**, under the archways at the far end of the **Piazza** from the Basilica (Mon–Sat 8:30am–7pm in summer, shorter hours in winter; ☎5226356.) The first two can help arrange accommodation by phone, taking a deposit of L10,000 against your bill. (The small tourist information office at **Marco Polo airport** also offers this service.) On the **Lido**, there's an office in Gran Viale Santa Maria Elisabetta (Mon–Sat 9am–2pm).

The San Marco EPT is the best for information about all events—cultural and otherwise. An additional source is *Un Ospite di Venezia*, a free Italian-English magazine which also gives other practical information such as up-to-date boat timetables. This is produced weekly in summer and monthly in winter, and can be picked up at the EPT or at the receptions of larger hotels. Alternatively, most newspaper stalls sell the budget-oriented *Venezia in Jeans* (L1000), and the glossier *Marco Polo*, which comes out every month.

MAPS

If you're going to explore Venice in depth, a really comprehensive map is a must. The tourist office's free map is useful for general orientation, but omits too many alleyways and buildings to be of any use as a serious navigational aid. The **most accurate map of Venice** is that produced by the *Touring Club Italiano:* consisting of a large-scale foldout map, a larger-scale mini-atlas of the city, and a directory of street names, it comes in a neat plastic folder and will cost you around $15, though it can be difficult to obtain outside Venice. Equally clear, and almost as reliable, is the *Hallwag* 1:5500 plan of the city, which has the distinct advantage of costing around a third of the *TCI*'s price. If you don't want the fuss of unfolding and refolding a large single sheet every time you inadvertently stray into a cul-de-sac, the ingeniously designed *Falkplan* is very handy, its only drawback being its unavoidably small scale. The map published by *Litografia Artistica Cartografica* includes a detailed plan of the islands of the northern lagoon; as a map of the city itself, though, it's inferior to the *Hallwag* and *TCI* productions. For these and other maps, try the *Rand McNally* chain of travel stores.

MAIL, PHONES, AND THE MEDIA

Venice's main post office is in the Fondaco dei Tedeschi, near the Rialto bridge. Any poste restante should be addressed to Fermo Posta, Fondaco dei Tedeschi, 80100 Venezia; it can be collected Mon–Sat 8:15am–1:45pm—take your passport with you. Stamps are on sale Mon–Sat 8:15am–7pm; the telegram service operates round the clock. The principal branch post offices are in Calle dell'Ascensione (Mon–Fri 8:10am–1:25pm, Sat 8:10am–noon) and at Záttere 1406 (same hours). Stamps can also be bought in tabacchi, as well as in some gift shops; post cards are L550, letters L650.

Public **telephones** come in various forms, usually with clear instructions printed on them (in English, too). For the most common type, you'll need L100 or L200 coins, or a token known as a *gettone* (L200), available from *SIP* offices (the state telephone company), *tabacchi*, bars and some newsstands—they're also in common use as currency. Some phones also take L500 coins. **Phone cards** (*schede telefóniche*), too, are available for L2000, L5000, and L10,000 from *tabacchi* or news-stands; they'll soon be accepted in all phone booths. Bars too will often have a phone you can use, though these often take *gettoni* only: look for the yellow phone symbol.

Although virtually all Venice's public phone booths are marked *interurbano* (which means you can make international calls), to **phone long distance** it's best to go to the two main *SIP* offices, where you can dial direct and be charged afterwards, rather than pump coins into the box every few seconds. The offices are at Piazzale Roma (8am–9:30pm daily) and in the main post office building (8am–8pm daily). The same service is offered by the larger hotels, but they normally charge 25 percent more. To make an **international collect** call, dial the international operator (☎176) and ask for a call *cárico a destinatario* (for America, say *Vorrei telefonare all'America, cárico a destinatario*).

> For direct **international calls**, dial the country code (given below), the area code (minus its first 0), and finally the number.
> US: ☎001
> CANADA: ☎001
> AUSTRALIA: ☎0061
> UK: ☎0044
> Venice's city code is ☎**041**.

You'll find the main **national newspapers** on any newsstand: *La Repubblica* is middle-to-left with a lot of cultural coverage; *Il Corriere della Sera* is authoritative and rather right-wing;

L'Unità is the Communist Party organ; and *Il Manifesto*, a more radical and readable left-wing daily. Venice's **local papers** are the *Gazzettino* and *Nuova Venezia* (good for listings). More widely read than any, however, is the pink *Gazzettino dello Sport*, essential for the serious sports fan. **American newspapers** can be found for around L2000 at the railroad station, by the Calle dell'Ascensione post office and at various stands throughout the city—usually a day or two late.

If the opportunity arises, take a look at Italian **TV** to sample the pros and cons of deregulation in television. The three state-run channels, *RAI 1, 2*, and *3*, controlled by the *DC*, *PSI*, and local networks respectively, have got their backs against the wall in the face of the massive independent onslaught, led by the Euromogul Berlusconi. The output is generally pretty bland, with a heavy helping of American sitcoms and films, and ghastly Italian cabaret shows, though the *RAI* channels have less advertising and mix some good reporting in among the dross. The situation in **radio** is even more anarchic, with the FM waves crowded to the extent that you can pick up a new station just by walking down the corridor. Again, the *RAI* stations are generally more professional, though daytime listening is virtually undiluted non-stop dance music.

HOURS, HOLIDAYS, AND MUSEUMS

Basic hours for most shops and businesses are Monday to Saturday from 8am–9am to around 1pm, and from around 4pm to 7pm–8pm, though some offices work to a more standard European 9am–5pm day. Everything closes on Sunday except bars and restaurants and a few pasticcerie which stay open until lunchtime.

Other disrupting factors are **national holidays**. Everything, except bars and restaurants, will be closed on the following dates:
1 January
6 January (Epiphany)
Good Friday
Easter Monday
25 April (Liberation Day and St. Mark's Day)
1 May (Labor Day)
15 August (Assumption of the Blessed Virgin Mary)

1 November (*Ogni Santi*; 'All Saints')
8 December (Immaculate Conception of the Blessed Virgin Mary)
25 December
26 December

In addition, many shops and businesses close or work shorter hours for the local festival of the *Salute* (Nov 21: see p. 14).

CHURCHES AND MUSEUMS

The rules for visiting **churches** are much as they are all over the Mediterranean. Dress modestly, which usually means no shorts, and covered shoulders for women—and don't wander around during a service. Many churches open in the early morning, around 7–8am for mass, and close around noon, and open again at 4–5pm, closing at 7pm; more obscure ones will only open for early morning and evening services; some only open on

VENICE MUSEUMS CHECKLIST

Accademia ☎5222247; 9am–2pm (9am–1pm); closed Mon; L4000.

Aquarium di Venezia ☎5207770; 9am–7pm (9am–7pm); closed Tues; L1500 (children under 10: L1000).

Ca' d'Oro/Galleria Franchetti ☎5238790; 9am–2pm (9am–1pm); L2000.

Campanile di San Giorgio ☎5289900; 10am–12:30pm & 2:30–6pm (10am–12:30pm & 2:30–6pm); L1000.

Campanile di San Marco ☎5224064; 9:30am–8pm (9:30am–8pm); L3000.

Cattedrale di Torcello ☎730084; 10am–12:30pm & 2–5:30pm (10am–12:30pm & 2–5:30pm); L1000 (L500).

Cini Collection ☎5210755; 2–7pm (2–7pm); closed Mon; L4000.

Frari 9:30am–noon & 2:30–6pm (3–5:30pm); L800, free Sun & holidays.

Galleria d'Arte Moderna (Ca' Pésaro) ☎721127; 10am–4pm (9:30am–12:30pm); closed Mon; L3000.

Guggenheim Collection ☎5206288; noon–6pm (noon–6pm), Sat noon–9pm; closed Tues; L5000 (L3000), Sat 6–9pm free.

Monastero Mekhitarista (San Lazzaro degli Armeni) ☎5260104; Thurs & Sun 3–5pm; donation.

Museo Archeologico ☎5225978; 9am–2pm (9am–1pm); L2000.

Museo Correr ☎5525625; 10am–4pm (9am–12:30pm); closed Tues; L3000 (L1500).

Museo Comunità Israelitica (Museum and Synagogues) ☎715359; 10:30am–1pm & 2:30–5pm; closed Sat, Sun pm & Jewish holidays; L2000.

Museo del '700 Venezia (Ca' Rezzonico) ☎5224543; 10am–4pm (9am–12:30pm); closed Fri; L5000 (L3000).

Museo Diocesiano di Arte Sacra ☎5229166; 10:30am–12:30pm (10:30am–12:30pm); free.

Museo Dipinti Sacra Bizantini (San Giorgio dei Greci) ☎5226581; 9am–1pm & 2–5pm (9am–1pm); closed Tues; L3000.

Museo dell'Estuario, Torcello ☎730761; 10am–12:30pm & 2–5:30pm (10am–12:30pm & 2–5:30pm); closed Mon; L2000.

Museo Fortuny ☎5200995; 9am–7pm (9am–7pm); closed Mon; L5000.

Museo Goldoni ☎5236353; 8:30am–1:30pm; free.

Museo Orientale (Ca' Pésaro) ☎5241173; 9am–1:30pm (9am–12:30pm); closed Mon; L2000.

Museo di Storia Naturale ☎5240885; 9am–1:30pm (9am–1pm) closed Mon; L3000 (L1500).

Museo Storico Navale ☎5200276; Mon–Fri 9am–1pm, Sat 9am–noon; L1000.

Museo Vetrario di Murano ☎739586; 10am–4pm (9am–12:30pm); closed Wed; L3000 (L1500).

Palazzo Ducale ☎5224951; 8:30am–6:30pm (8:30am–6:30pm); L8000 (L4000).

Pinacoteca Querini-Stampalia ☎5225235; 10am–12:30pm (10am–12:30pm); closed Mon; L5000.

San Francesco del Deserto ☎528683; 9–11am & 3–5:30pm (9–11am &3–5:30pm); donation.

San Marco: Pala d'Oro e Tesoro ☎5225697; 9:30am–5:30pm (2–5:30pm); L1000 & L2000.

Scuola dei Carmini ☎5289420; 9am–noon & 3–6pm; L2000.

Scuola Grande di San Rocco ☎5234864; 10am–1pm & 3:30–6:30pm (10am–1pm & 3:30–6:30pm); L5000 (L3000).

Scuola dei Merletti di Burano ☎730034; 9am–6pm (10am–4pm); closed Tues; L2000 (L1000).

Scuola di San Giorgio degli Schiavoni ☎5228828; 10am–12:30pm & 3:30–6pm (10am–12:30pm); L3000 (L2000).

Torre dell'Orologio ☎5231879; 9am–noon & 3–6pm (9am–noon) closed Mon. (Closed for restoration.)

Sunday and on religious holidays. Wherever possible, the hours of churches are given in the guide.

One problem you'll face is that many churches and monuments are either completely or partly **closed for restoration** (*chiuso per restauro*): At any one time dozens of projects are in progress all over the city (see *Contexts*), and it's impossible to predict which buildings will be under wraps in the near future—all that can be said with any degree of certainty is that you'll find restorers at work in parts of the Basilica di San Marco and the Palazzo Ducale.

It's equally impossible to compile an absolutely accurate guide to the opening hours and times of Venice's **museums**, so frequent are the changes to both; the list above represents the latest high-season details for the major museums and those churches where an entrance fee is payable. Opening times in brackets indicate Sunday and holiday hours—no brackets means it's closed on those days. Any price in brackets indicates concessionary tickets; where avalable you'll need to show a student card or similar—no bracket, no reduction.

ART AND FILMS

In addition to those permanent museums which hold one-off exhibitions from time to time, Venice has numerous venues that specialize in temporary shows. Look in *Un Ospite di Venezia* for details (see "Tourist Information"), or take note of posters and banners advertising shows.

The Fiat-owned **Palazzo Grassi** holds the most impressive in terms of sheer no-holds-barred presentations, the scale and style of the displays making the Royal Academy's mammoth productions look very dull and dusty. The other major venues are as follows.

Palazzo Ducale: art history/ethnology/ archaeology.

Museo Correr: specifically Venetian exhibitions in the main part of the building; other art shows—eg *Matisse in Italy*—in the *Ala Napoleonica*.

Ca' Pésaro: modern art.

Fondazione Cini: art history.

Fortuny: design and photography.

Scuola Grande di San Teodoro: generally modern and applied art (often tacky).

Querini-Stampalia: art history.

Scuola Grande di San Giovanni Evangelista: photography, video, technology as applied to the arts.

Archivio di Stato: Venetian history.

Guggenheim: modern art (in winter).

Contemporary private galleries in Venice are generally timorous affairs; again, look in *Un Ospite* for their latest offerings. Three stand out against a background of dross:

Cavallino, Frezzeria;

Santo Stefano, Campo Morosini;

Traghetto, Campo Santa Maria del Giglio.

THE BIENNALE

The Venice Biennale was set up in 1895 as a show-piece for international contemporary art, and is held every even-numbered year from June to September.

The Biennale's permanent site in the Giardini Pubblici has pavilions for about forty countries (the largest for Italy's representatives), plus space for a thematic international exhibition. Supplementing this central part of the Biennale is the *Aperto* ("Open"), a mixed exhibition showing the work of younger, or less established artists—often more exciting than the main event. The *Aperto* takes over spaces all over the city: the salt warehouses on the Záttere, for instance, or the Corderie in the Arsenale. Over and above this, various sites throughout the city host fringe exhibitions, installations, and performances, particularly in the opening weeks.

Financial and administrative difficulties have been rife in recent years, and in 1988 a new co-ordinator was brought in to cobble the whole thing together just a couple of months before the opening date. There are people who say that the Biennale has been surpassed by Kassel's seven-yearly Dokumenta show, and it's undeniable that the central part of the show has become less a meeting ground for artists than a benefit for the international dealers. If you have an interest in contemporary art, though, you'll get something out of the Biennale, particularly the *Aperto* and other less institutionalized shows.

Tickets for the whole Biennale cost L10,000, but it's possible to buy tickets for individual parts of the show. Exhibits from earlier years, plus a fabulous collection of magazines and catalogues from all over the world, are kept in the **archive** in the Palazzo Corner della Regina (close to Ca' Pésaro); entrance is free. The San Marco tourist office should be able to give you all the information you need, but if not try the Biennale administrative headquarters, in the Ca' Giustinian (Calle Vallaresso).

THE FILM FESTIVAL

The Venice Film Festival, the most important in Europe after Cannes, is held on the Lido in late August and early September. It was closed in 1968, when the youth movements declared the *Leon d'Oro* (the Golden Lion, the Festival's equivalent of an Oscar) to be an insult to the workers of Venice and a symbol of the commercial degeneration of the film industry. In the late 1970s the communist general secretary of the Biennale, Carlo Lizzani, reinstated the Festival under the auspices of the Biennale; more recently the *Leon d'Oro* has been reinstated too. It always seems to be surrounded by rows between directors of differing political persuasions and vehement disputes over the programming. All good stuff, and reported with relish in the local papers. Go and look at the beautiful people at play on the Lido, then line for a ticket (no advance sales) for the Palazzo del Cinema or one of the fringe showings. If you are a student or young person, the *Carta Giovani* will get you a discount (see "Costs"). Posters advertising the Festival's schedule appear weeks in advance, and the tourist office again is a good source of information. (For a list of Venice's movie theaters, see Chapter 10.)

VENETIAN FESTIVALS

Venice celebrates with enthusiasm a number of holidays (*feste*) either not observed elsewhere in Italy, or, like the *Carnevale*, celebrated to a lesser extent. Although they have gone through various degrees of decline and revival, the form they take now is still related very strongly to their traditional character.

CARNEVALE

John Evelyn wrote of the 1646 Carnevale: "all the world was in Venice to see the folly and madness ... the women, men and persons of all conditions disguising themselves in antique dresses, & extravagant Musique & a thousand gambols." Not much is different in today's Carnevale, for which people arrive in such numbers that the causeway from the mainland has sometimes had to be closed because the city has been too packed.

The origins of the Carnevale can be traced in the word itself: *carne vale*, a *farewell to meat* before the strictures of Lent—the same origin as the tamer British custom of eating pancakes on Shrove Tuesday. The medieval European carnival developed into a period when the the world could be turned over—a time of license for those normally constrained by rank, and a means of quelling discontent by a ritualized relinquishing of power. Venice's Carnevale can be related to the surrender of power on a wider scale, as the eighteenth-century heyday of the festival coincided with the terminal decline of the Republic. The eighteenth-century Carnevale officially began on December 26, lasting for nearly two months until Shrove Tuesday; aspects of it, such as the wearing of masks, stretched into the rest of the year, until Carnevale unofficially continued for six months.

Today's Carnevale is limited to the **ten days leading up to Lent**, finishing on Shrove Tuesday with a masked ball for the glitterati, and dancing in the Piazza for the plebs. It was revived spontaneously in the late 1970s, and after three years gained support from the city authorities, who now organize various pageants and performances. (Details from the San Marco tourist office.) Apart from these events, Carnevale is very much a case of see and be seen. During the day people don costumes and go to the Piazza to be photographed; parents dress up their kids; businessmen can be seen doing their shopping in the classic white mask, black cloak, and tricorne hat. In the evening some congregate in the remoter squares, while those who have spent literally hundreds of pounds on their costumes install themselves in the windows of *Florian's* and pose for a while before making an exit with an adoring entourage. But you don't need to spend money or try to be "traditional" in your disguise: a simple black outfit and a painted face is enough to transform you from a spectator into a participant.

Masks are on sale throughout the year in Venice, but new mask and costume shops suddenly appear during Carnevale, and Campo San Maurizio sprouts a marquee with mask-making demonstrations and a variety of designs for sale. For the best permanent stockists, see the "Shopping" section of Chapter 10.

LA SENSA

The feast of **La Sensa** happens in May on the Sunday after Ascension Day—the latter being the day on which the doge enacted the wedding of Venice to the sea (see "The Lido," in the *Southern Islands* chapter). The ritual has recently been revived—a distinctly feeble procession which ends with the mayor and a gang of other dignitaries getting into a present-day approximation of the *Bucintoro* (the state barge) and sailing off to the Lido.

Of more interest is the **Vogalonga** (long row), held on the same day. Open to any crew in any class of rowing boat, it covers a 32km course from the Bacino di San Marco out to Burano and back; the competitors arrive at the bottom of the Canal Grande anywhere between about 11am and 3pm.

SANTA MARIA DELLA SALUTE

Named after the church of the Salute, this centuries-old feast day is a reminder of the plague of 1630–31 which killed a third of the lagoon's population. The church was built in thanks for deliverance from the outbreak, and every November 21 since then the Venetians have processed over a pontoon bridge across the Canal Grande to give thanks for their good health, or to pray for the sick. It offers the only chance to see the church as it was designed to be seen—with its main doors open, and with hundreds of people milling up the steps and round the building.

THE REDENTORE

Another plague-related festival, this time to mark the end of the epidemic of 1576. Celebrated on the third Sunday in July, the day is centered on Palladio's church of the Redentore, which was built by way of thanksgiving for the city's escape. A bridge of boats across the Giudecca canal allows the faithful to walk over to the church, and on the Saturday night hundreds of people row out for a picnic on the water. The night ends with a fireworks display, after which it's traditional to make for the Lido to watch the sunrise.

THE REGATA STORICA

Held on the first Sunday in September, the **Regata Storica** is the annual trial of strength and skill for the city's gondoliers and other expert rowers. It starts with a procession of richly decorated historic craft along the Canal Grande course, their crews all decked out in period dress. Bystanders are expected to join in the support for the contestants in the main event, and may even be issued with appropriate colors. Other *regate* are held throughout the year in various parts of the lagoon, the main ones being the **Regata di S. Zanipolo** (June), the **Regata di Pellestrina** (Aug), and the **Regata di Burano** (Sept).

GAY VENICE AND SEXUAL POLITICS

Venice's **gay scene** is not very conspicuous, with no exclusively gay bars or meeting places. **Ai Canottieri** has a regular gay clientele, as does **Paradiso Perduto** (see Chapter 10 for details); **Al Teatro**, in Campo San Fantin, and **Haig's**, in Campo Santa Maria del Giglio are also worth a try. Meeting points on the streets include the Accademia bridge and the Giardinetti Reali. For the latest information, contact **ARCI-gay**; part of the youth division of the PCI (*Partita Communista Italia*). Any PCI office should put you in touch, but attitudes among them differ: Sezione di Vittorio Cannaregio, off Fondamenta della Misericordia, is particularly sympathetic (☎719907).

For **HIV testing and AIDS counseling**, contact **Centro Dermoceltico**, on Fondamenta dell'Abbazia (☎5221942).

The PCI is also a good contact for any **women's groups**. The women's movement in Italy is fragmented, with groups coming and going, but the PCI has strong women's sections (though they avoid the word feminist). Contact the section mentioned above for Venetian activities; the Mestre section is particularly active too—Via S. Girolamo 16, Mestre.

Although the streets of Venice are safer than those of any other major city in the country,

sexual harassment is still a problem for a woman traveling on her own. The Venetian male may not be as aggressive in his attentions as some of his compatriots, but he can still be a pain in the neck. Walking alone at night at anything less than a determined pace, the odds are that you'll be approached at least once. A mouthful will often deter, but if he persists, the following phrases should see him off: *che rompiscatole* ("what a pain in the ass"); *lasciàtemi in pace* ("leave me alone"); *sei fesso?* ("are you stupid?"); and, the last resort, *va fan culo* ("fuck off") or *va a fartì fottere* ("go fuck yourself").

DISABLED TRAVELLERS

Venice presents problems for anyone who is not able-bodied. The islands that make up the city are joined by stepped bridges, and getting in and out of the water buses can be hazardous if the water level is low or the canals are choppy, despite the helpfulness of the conductors. Wheelchair users should avoid the *motoscafi*—lines 2, 4, and 5—as they have just a small platform around the pilot's cabin, the main passenger area being below deck level, down steep steps.

Two organizations that may be worth contacting before arriving in Venice are **ANFAS** (Frari, San Polo 3080/N; ☎719020), which is a

charitable organization for the disabled, and **Progetto "Veneziapertutti"** (Università d'Architettura, Tolentini, Santa Croce), which is staffed by a team of disabled architects and planners. "Veneziapertutti" ("Venice for All") has produced a map grading the accessibility of different islands of the city—it's on display on some of the major vaporetto stops (train station, Rialto, Accademia and San Marco) and at the information office at Piazzale Roma. Lists of tour operators specializing in holidays for the disabled are available from the Italian State Tourist Office.

DIRECTORY

ADDRESSES Usually written as the street name followed by the *sestiere* (district), followed by the number—eg Calle Vallaresso, San Marco 1312. Sometimes, though, the *sestiere* is placed before the street, and sometimes the street name is omitted altogether—making the place impossible to find for the outsider.

AIRLINES *Alitalia*, Salizzada San Moisè, San Marco 1463 (☎5200355); *British Airways*, Riva degli Schiavoni, Castello 4191 (☎5285026); *TWA*, Salizzada San Moisè, San Marco 1475 (☎5203219).

AIRPORT INQUIRIES Marco Polo airport; ☎661111.

AIRPORT TAX Invariably included in cost of the flight.

BARGAINING Not really on in shops and restaurants, though you'll find you can get a "special price" for some rooms and cheap hotels if you're staying a few days in the quieter periods.

BEACHES The Lido has two public beaches, at the northern and southern extremities of the island. The southern is the less crowded; better still, go down to Sottomarina, in the south of the lagoon (see Southern Islands chapter).

BUS INQUIRIES For *ACTV* land buses dial ☎5287886; for information on city water buses, call ☎700310.

CAMPING GAZ Easy enough to buy for small portable camping stoves, either from hardware stores (a *ferramenta*) or camping/sports shops. You can't carry canisters on airplanes.

CAR RENTAL The major companies have offices at Marco Polo and Piazzale Roma. Expect to pay upwards of L60,000 per day, excluding gas.

CIGARETTES You buy cigarettes (and tobacco) in shops called *tabacchi*, which distinguish themselves by a sign outside with a T on it. Historically, tobacco and salt were both state monopolies, sold only in *tabacchi*—salt's no longer deemed so important, but cigarettes are still hard to track down anywhere else. You'll be able to buy sweets and stamps in a *tabacchi* too.

CONSULATES Great Britain—Palazzo Querini, Accademia, Dorsoduro 1051, ☎5227207. The nearest US consulate is in Milan (☎02/652841); travelers from Australia, New Zealand and Canada should contact their Rome consulates.

CONTRACEPTION Rubbers (*profilático*) available over the counter from all pharmacies and some supermarkets; the Pill (*la píllola*) on prescription only.

ELECTRICITY The supply is 220V, but anything requiring 240V will work. Most plugs are two round pins: a travel plug is useful.

EMERGENCIES For all emergency services (police, ambulance and fire) dial ☎113. Alternatively, dialling ☎112 puts you straight through to the *Carabinieri* (police) and 115 goes straight to the *Vigili del Fuoco* (fire brigade).

HOSPITAL *Ospedale Civile*, Campo Santi Giovanni e Paolo (☎5205622).

KIDS Children can get fatigued easily in Venice. If the various squares don't appeal as playgrounds, you could try the Giardini Pubblici or the Lido's beaches. A long boat trip often works wonders too, as does a visit to the city's aquarium (see the list of museums). Hotels normally charge around 30 percent extra to put a bed or cot in your room.

LAUNDROMATS There's one on Fondamenta Pescaria, off Rio Terrà San Leonardo, in the Cannaregio district (Mon–Fri 8:15am–12:30pm and 3–7pm; Sat morning only). Be discreet about washing clothes in your hotel room—it's usually forbidden.

LUGGAGE CONSIGNMENT Train station luggage desk open 24hr; L1000 per item.

LOST PROPERTY If you lose anything on the train or at the station, call ☎716122 (ext. 3238); on the vaporetti call ☎780310; and anywhere in the city itself call ☎ 5208844 (the town hall).

PASSPORTS In the event of a lost passport, notify the *Questura* (see p.6) and then your consulate.

PHOTOGRAPHIC FILM More expensive than in the US both to buy and have developed.

PUBLIC SHOWERS For L4000 you can have the use of a shower cubicle at an *Albergo Diurnale*—there's one off Calle dell'Ascensione and one at the train station (both open 9am–7:30pm). For a wash-basin and toilet the charge is L500.

PUBLIC TOILETS At the train station, at Piazzale Roma, on the west side of the Accademia bridge, by the Giardinetti Reali, off Campo San Bartolomeo, and a few other places; the charge is around L200. Toilets are to be found in all the city's bars as well—it's diplomatic to buy a drink before availing yourself of the facility, but it's not a legal requirement.

TAMPONS From pharmacies and supermarkets everywhere; slightly more expensive than in Britain.

TIME Italy is six hours ahead of Eastern Standard Time, and nine hours ahead of Pacific Standard Time.

TRAIN INQUIRIES ☎715555.

VACCINATIONS None required.

PART TWO

THE
CITY

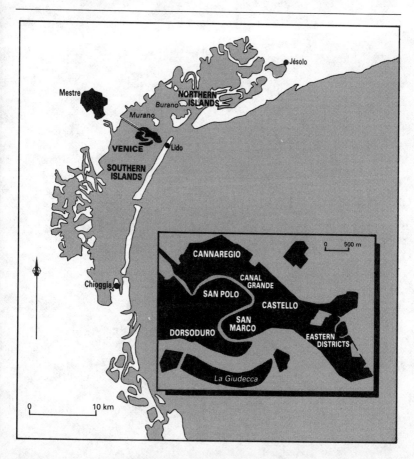

POINTS OF ARRIVAL

BY AIR

If you are arriving **by air**, you'll touch down either at **Treviso**, 30km inland from Venice, or at **Marco Polo** airport, on the outskirts of Venice itself. The former is used by charter companies, many of whom provide a bus link from the airport into Venice. If such a service isn't provided, take the #6 bus from right outside the arrivals building into Treviso, from where there are regular bus and train connections to Venice. Tickets cost L600, and must be bought before you get onto the bus—the bar across the road sells them. All scheduled flights and some charters arrive at Marco Polo. Motor launches are conveniently timed to meet incoming scheduled flights, and if you're on a package tour the cost of travel to the city center might already be covered. If it's not, don't take to the water: the launches are expensive, while the water-taxis that hang around touting for trade charge exorbitant rates—around L80,000. There's a prominent desk for the **ATVO** bus company inside the airport building; their service is fairly regular and costs L4000. The cheapest way to travel from Marco Polo, however, is to take the **ACTV** (*Azienda del Consorzio Transporti Veneziano*) **bus #5**, which runs hourly and costs just L600 (plus a small supplement for each large piece of luggage). *ACTV* tickets can be bought from the exchange booth in the entrance area—look out for the yellow *ACTV* sticker, with the bus/boat logo.

BY CAR

People arriving **by car** must leave their vehicle either on the mainland or try for the parking lots of Venice itself—either at **Piazzale Roma** or at the ever-expanding **Tronchetto**, the largest parking lot in Europe. Piazzale Roma is well-connected with the main water bus services (see below), while three services run from Tronchetto: the #34 and the summer-only #3 to San Marco, plus the #17 to the Lido. Prices at these two vary with the time of year, the length of stay and the size of car, but it's never a cheap option (from around L14,000 per day), and in summer the tail-backs can be horrendous. Best to use the **San Giuliano** parking lot at Mestre or the one at **Fusina**; both are open-air, and operate only in summer, at Easter, and during the Carnevale. In summer the #24 boat goes from San Giuliano to Fondamente Nuove (there's also a bus to Piazzale Roma), and the #16 connects Fusina with the Riva degli Schiavoni.

BY TRAIN OR BUS

Arriving **by train or bus**, you get off at the end of the line. The **Piazzale Roma** (bus station) and **Santa Lucia** (train station) are five minutes' walk from each other, at the top of the Canal Grande, and both well served by vaporetto services to the city center (see below). The **luggage consignment** at the train station charges L1000 per item, per 24 hours; there's also a separate consignment for larger items, at the station.

GETTING AROUND

Venice has two interlocking street-systems—the canals and the sidewalks—and contrary to what you might expect, you'll be using the latter for most of the time. The network of waterways is largely the province of gondolas, water-taxis, delivery vessels, and small private boats; the public transit boats operate along just two of the city's canals—the Canal Grande and the Rio Nuovo–Rio Ca' Fóscari (which cuts through to the Canal Grande from Piazzale Roma). Otherwise they skirt the city center, connecting points on the periphery and the outer islands. So, unless you want to nip across the Canal Grande and are a long way from one of its three bridges (see below), or you want to get from one end of the city

TRANSPORT SERVICES

0   500 m

To: S. Giuliano
24

S. Alvise
5

Madonna
dell'Orto
5

Ponte Tre Archi
5

San Marcuola
1, 2

Ponte Guglie
5

Ferrovia
1, 2, 4, 5

Riva di Biasio
1

San Stae
1

Ca d

Tronchetto
3

Tronchetto
17, 34

San Silvestro
1

Piazzale
Roma
1, 2, 4, 5, 34

San Toma
1, 4

Sant'Angelo
1

ACTV Office

S. Marta
5, 8

Ca Rezzonico
1

S. Samuele
2

S. M. del Giglio

S. Basilio
5, 8

Accademia
1, 2, 4

Zattere
5, 8, 9

Sacca Fisola
5, 8

S. Eufemia
5, 8

Giudecca
8, 9

Redentore
5, 8

To: S. Clemente
S. Lazzaro
S. Servolo
La Grazia
10, 20

To: Alberoni
S.M. Del Mare
Pellestrina
Chioggia
11

To: Murano 5, 12, 13, 18
    Mazzorbo 12
    Burano 12
    Torcello 12
    Treporti 12
    Vignole 13
    Isola di S. Erasmo 13

All year service

— 1
— 2
— 5
— 6
— 8
— 34
— 9
— 10,20
— 11
— 12
— 13
— 17

Summer only

•••••••••• 3
— — — 4
▲▲▲▲▲▲ 15
•••••••••••• 16
◆◆◆◆◆◆ 18
○○○○○○○○○○ 21
22
•••••••••••• 24

Winter only

---------- 14

Isola S.
Michele
5

Fondamente
Nuove
5, 12, 13, 18, 24

Ospedale
Civile
5

Celestina
5

Campo della Tana
5

Rialto
1, 2, 4

San Zaccaria
1, 2, 4, 5, 8

Riva Schiavoni
6, 10, 11, 14,
15, 16, 21,

Arsenale
1

San Marco
1, 2, 3, 4, 34

Giardini Esposizione
1, 4, 21

S. Giorgio
Maggiore
5, 8

Zitelle
5, 8

Sant'Elena
1, 2, 14, 21

To: Fusina
16

To: Lido (S.M.E.)
1, 2, 4, 6, 11, 14

To: Lido (S. Nicolo)
14, 17, 21

To Punta Sabbioni
14, 15, 17

to the other, the speediest way of getting around is **on foot**. Distances between major sights are extremely short (you can cross the whole city in an hour), and once you've got your general bearings you'll find that navigation is not as daunting a prospect as it seems. And anyway, getting lost within a space smaller than a soccer pitch is one of the pleasures of a stay in Venice.

THE TRANSPORTATION SYSTEM

A **water-bus** can be the quickest way of getting between two points, though, and even in cases where it would be quicker to walk, a canal trip is often the more pleasant way of covering the distance. The lack of clear numbering on many of the boats is confusing at first, and the *ACTV* map of the lagoon network system seems at first glance to resemble the wiring diagram of a telephone exchange, but in fact the routes are pretty straightforward.

There are two basic types of boat: the **vaporetti**, which are the lumbering workhorses used on the Canal Grande stopping service and other slow routes, and the **motoscafi**, smaller vessels employed on routes where a bit of speed is needed. The **most useful services** for visitors are as follows.

#1, the so-called *accelerato*, is perversely the slowest of the water buses; it starts at the Piazzale Roma, stops at all but one of the stops on the Canal Grande, works its way along the San Marco waterfront to Santa Elena, then goes over to the Lido. It returns by the same route.

#2, known as the *diretto*, is the second-quickest way to get between San Marco and Piazzale Roma or the train station (see #34). Goes both clockwise and counter-clockwise on the following loop: train station, Piazzale Roma, Rio Nuovo/Rio Fóscari, San Marco, Lido. So, if you get on a #2 from the Lido at San Marco, check which way it's going: some will go up the Canal Grande via Rialto, others take the Rio Fóscari. It stops only five times along the Canal Grande, compared to the #1's fourteen stops.

#4, known as the *turistico*, is a limited-stop summer service along the Canal Grande and across to the Lido.

#5, the *circolare*, comes in two forms. The **destra** goes from the Fondamente Nuove, through the Arsenale to San Zaccaria, zig-zags between La Giudecca and the Zattere, goes up to Piazzale Roma and the station, along the Canale di Cannaregio, back to the Fondamente Nuove, then

over to the cemetery and Murano. The **sinistra** does the same in reverse—so if you jump on a #5, make sure you know which way round the city it's going. Be warned that the #5 sometimes shoots off up the Canal Grande instead of heading over to San Giorgio Maggiore and La Giudecca; called the *barrato*, this version of the service is more common in winter—look for the sign on the side of the boat reading "Diretto—Piazzale Roma".

#8 shuttles between the Riva degli Schiavoni, San Giorgio, La Giudecca and the Zattere.

#12 takes off to the northern islands from the Fondamente Nuove.

#34, the *turistico*, is an express service that stops only at the Tronchetto parking lot, Piazzale Roma, the train station, and San Marco.

Tickets (*biglietti*) are available from most landing stages and from shops displaying the *ACTV* sign. In the remoter parts of the city, though, you may not be able to find anywhere to buy a ticket (particularly after working hours); as tickets bought on board are subject to a surcharge, and the spot-fine for not having a valid ticket is L15,000, it's a good idea to buy a block of ten (*un blochetto*). Flat-rate fares apply for each service— L2500 for the #2, #4, and other motoscafi, L1800 for the rest—which means that the #5's circumnavigation costs the same as a two-minute hop.

A *Biglietto Turistico* gives you unlimited travel for a 24-hour period, but as it costs L10,000 you'd have to spend a hell of a lot of time on the boat to make it cost effective. If you think you'll be making more than half a dozen trips, it's worth investing in a **Carta Venezia**, which is also valid on all *ACTV* road buses. This also costs L10,000, and entitles you to travel for L700 per journey (L800 on the motoscafi)—and it's valid for three years. Take a small photo and your passport to the **ACTV office** in Corte dell'Albero (Mon–Sat 8:30am–1pm), near the Sant'Angelo stop on the Canal Grande.

Timetables are posted at each stop, and details of the more important lines are included in each issue of *Un Ospite di Venezia* (see "Tourist Information," in *Basics*). The city center services run through the night, at greatly reduced frequency after about 1am.

As there are only three bridges across the Canal Grande—at the train station, Rialto, and Accademia—the **traghetti** (ferries) which cross it can be useful time-savers. Costing just L400, they are also the only cheap way of getting a ride on a gondola—though it's *de rigeur* to stand in a *traghetto* rather than sit. In summer most of the Canal Grande *traghetti* run from early morning to around 7–9pm daily. The *traghetti* routes vary from season to season and from year to year, but the most frequent gondola *traghetto* services are marked on all our maps.

In addition to these, some *vaporetti* and *motoscafi* operate as *traghetti* across the Canal Grande and over to the nearer islands: for example, if you want go from San Zaccaria over to San Giorgio Maggiore, you need only pay the L1000 *traghetto* fare (L300 with a *Carta Venezia*). If your journey is a single-stop trip across a body of water, check if a *traghetto* fare applies—it'll be shown on the tariff list on the ticket booth.

Gondolas are no longer a form of transport but rather an adjunct of the tourist industry. To rent one costs L50,000 for 50 minutes for up to five passengers, then L25,000 for every additional 25 minutes; between 8pm and 8am the rate goes up to L60,000. Even though the tariff is set by the local authorities, it's been known for some gondoliers to try to extort a little more. If you do decide to go for a voyage, be sure to establish the charge before setting off. For a list of current gondola stands, consult a copy of *Un Ospite*.

FINDING A PLACE TO STAY

If you arrive with nowhere to stay and don't want to spend your first hours hunting for a bed, there are plenty of **booking offices**: at the **train station** (8am–9pm daily); on the **Tronchetto** (9am–8pm); at **Piazzale Roma** (9am–9pm); at **Marco Polo airport** (winter noon–7pm; summer 9am–7pm); at the **autostrada's Venice exit** (8am–8pm). They only deal with hotels (ie no hostels) and take a L10,000 deposit, deductible from your first night's bill.

High season is approximately from **mid-March to late October**, plus two weeks around **Christmas and New Year** and the period of the **Carnevale** (the ten days in February up to Shrove Tuesday). At any time during the high season it's wise to reserve a hotel room well in advance, and for July and August it's virtually obligatory. During the winter it's possible to bargain for a reduced-rate room (see "Costs" in *Basics*), but many hotels close down from November to February, so you might have to put in a bit of leg-work before finding somewhere.

Breakfast should be optional, but many hotels get around this regulation by saying that the price of the room includes breakfast. If it's at all possible, get a room without breakfast, as even in the humblest places a jug of coffee and a puny croissant can put L9000 on your bill. Your money is better spent joining the locals in a nearby café.

Any **complaints** should be put to the *Dipartimento Turismo* of the *Giunta Regionale del Veneto*, at Lista di Spagna 168 (☎792638). Don't hesitate if you feel ripped off.

HOTELS

Below is a list of one-star hotels, costing up to L60,000 for a double room. The prices quoted are the **minimum** for a double, excluding the cost of breakfast, which you might not be able to avoid. In the peak season, expect to pay at least ten percent more. The sub-headings correspond to the chapter areas in which the hotels are found, while the addresses given are the full postal addresses. For the explanation as to how a place can be in the Dorsoduro district but not in the Dorsoduro chapter, see the box at the end of this section.

SAN MARCO

Al Gambero, Calle dei Fabbri, San Marco 4687, ☎5224384. A very short distance off the north side of the Piazza. L40,000.

Casa Petrarca, Calle delle Colonne, San Marco 4394, ☎700430. With doubles from L32,000, the cheapest near the Piazza—but call first, as they only have six rooms. Extremely hospitable, with English-speaking staff.

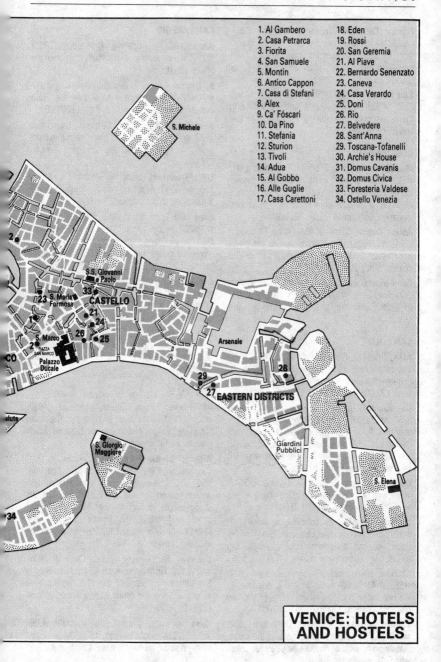

1. Al Gambero
2. Casa Petrarca
3. Fiorita
4. San Samuele
5. Montin
6. Antico Cappon
7. Casa di Stefani
8. Alex
9. Ca' Fóscari
10. Da Pino
11. Stefania
12. Sturion
13. Tivoli
14. Adua
15. Al Gobbo
16. Alle Guglie
17. Casa Carettoni

18. Eden
19. Rossi
20. San Geremia
21. Al Piave
22. Bernardo Senenzato
23. Caneva
24. Casa Verardo
25. Doni
26. Rio
27. Belvedere
28. Sant'Anna
29. Toscana-Tofanelli
30. Archie's House
31. Domus Cavanis
32. Domus Civica
33. Foresteria Valdese
34. Ostello Venezia

S. Michele

S.S. Giovanni e Paolo

CASTELLO

S. Maria Formosa

S. Marco

PIAZZA SAN MARCO

Palazzo Ducale

Arsenale

EASTERN DISTRICTS

S. Giorgio Maggiore

Giardini Pubblici

S. Elena

VENICE: HOTELS AND HOSTELS

Fiorita, Campiello Nuovo, San Marco 3457, ☎5234754. Just nine rooms, so again it's important to book. Welcoming management, and there's a nearby *traghetto* across the Canal Grande. L32,000.

San Samuele, Piscina S. Samuele, San Marco 3358, ☎5228045. Another friendly place, with rooms distinctly less shabby than some at this end of the market. L37,000.

DORSODURO

Montin, Fondamenta di Borgo, Dorsoduro 1147, ☎5227151. Famed for its restaurant, recommended by everyone who stays there, though the food is on a different price-scale than the accommodation. Only seven rooms. L35,000.

Antico Capon, Campo S. Margherita, Dorsoduro 3004, ☎5285292. Situated on one of the city's most atmospheric squares, in the heart of the student district. L38,000.

Casa di Stefani, Calle Traghetto San Barnaba, Dorsoduro 2786, ☎5223337. Very handily placed for getting over the Canal Grande into the San Marco area. L40,000.

SAN POLO

Alex, Rio Terrà Frari, S. Polo 2606, ☎5231341. Decorated in Sixties' style, but bearably so. Supermarket in front is useful for picnic preparations. L37,000.

Ca' Fóscari, Calle della Frescada, Dorsoduro 3888, ☎5225817. Tucked away in a micro-alley near San Tomà, near the university. Quiet, well decorated and relaxed. Despite its size (10 rooms), you can sometimes find a room even when all others are booked solid. L33,000.

Da Pino, Crosera S. Pantalon, Dorsoduro 3942, ☎5223646. Very close to the place above, in the area's main shopping street. L40,000.

Stefania, Fondamenta Tolentini, S. Croce 181, ☎5203757. A few minutes from the Piazzale Roma, so has an international clientele. Big rooms, some with bizarre murals. L32,000.

Sturion, Calle del Sturion, S. Polo 679, ☎523.62.43. Needs to be booked in advance, as it's popular with Italian families. One of the few bargains along the Canal Grande. L30,000.

Tivoli, Crosera S. Pantalon, Dorsoduro 3638, ☎5237752. The biggest cheap hotel in the immediate vicinity, with 24 rooms—so often has space when the rest are full. L36,000.

CANNAREGIO

Adua, Lista di Spagna, Cannaregio 233/a, ☎716184. Appalling decor but fairly humane prices. L35,000.

Al Gobbo, Campo S. Geremia, Cannaregio 312, ☎715001. Rather more genteel than the Adua, and correspondingly more expensive. L39,000.

Alle Guglie, Rio Terrà S. Leonardo, Cannaregio 1523, ☎717351. Minuscule place, with one bathroom per four rooms; the cheapest around. L22,000.

Casa Carettoni, Lista di Spagna, Cannaregio 130, ☎716231. By a long way the most comfortable one-star in the vicinity. L40,000.

Eden, Rio Terrà Maddalena, Cannaregio 2357, ☎720228. In a more salubrious part of town than the Lista di Spagna; one to try if you're traveling alone, as it has singles from L20,000. Doubles from L30,000.

Rossi, Calle delle Procuratie, Cannaregio 262, ☎715164. In a quiet back-street near the Lista; rather characterless but pleasant enough. L40,000.

San Geremia, Campo S. Geremia, Cannaregio 290, ☎716245. Another one to try if you're on your own—singles from L22,000, doubles L32,000.

CASTELLO

Al Piave, Ruga Giuffa, Castello 4838, ☎5285174. Not the most picturesque of places, but clean; frequented mainly by Italians, which must mean something. L 38,000.

Albergo Bernardi Semenzato, Calle dell'Oca, Cannaregio 4366 (off Campo SS. Apostoli), ☎5227257. The owners speak good English, and are concerned for the welfare of impecunious young people visiting the city. Nice bars in the street and round the corner. Singles from L19,000, doubles from L30,000—around L2000 extra for shower.

Caneva, Ramo della Fava, Castello 5515, ☎5228118. On the approach to the busy Campo San Bartolomeo, yet very peaceful; has a private inner courtyard and overlooks the Rio della Fava. L28,000.

Casa Verardo, Ruga Giuffa, Castello 4765, ☎5286127. Thought by many to be the best deal in the district; all rooms have a bath or shower. L40,000.

Doni, Fondamenta del Vin, Castello 4656, ☎5224267. Behind San Marco, heading towards San Zaccaria; most of the eleven rooms look over the Rio del Vin or over the courtyard. Cozy, with wooden floors instead of the usual stone.

Rio, Campo SS. Filippo e Giacomo, Castello 4356, ☎5234810. A couple of minutes' walk from the Piazza, so a bit of a bargain in the circumstances. L35,000.

EASTERN DISTRICTS

Belvedere, Via Garibaldi, Castello 1636, ☎5285148. Far from the crowds, and usually with a room or two available, except in the height of summer. L35,000.

Sant'Anna, Corte del Bianco, Castello 269, ☎5286466. Good for families with children, as it has rooms for three or four people and is fairly near the Giardini Pubblici. Although it's in one of the remotest parts of the city, beyond the far end of Via Garibaldi, it's been discovered in recent years—so book well in advance. L32,000.

Toscana-Tofanelli, Via Garibaldi, Castello 1650, ☎5235722. Spartan, but a terrific site, and with a very good trattoria. One of the best deals for someone traveling alone, with singles at L18,000; doubles from L32,000.

HOSTELS

Venice's hostels, most of which are run by religious foundations, are generally comfortable, well-run, and inexpensive—moreover, even in the high season they will have a place or two to spare. Each year the tourist office produces a simple typed list of all hostel accommodation in the city; if the places listed below are full up, ask for a copy of it at the San Marco branch.

Archie's House, Rio Terrà S. Leonardo, Cannaregio 1814/b, ☎720884. A cross between a hostel and a pensione, and a favorite of US college kids. Archie himself is easy-going but runs a tight ship: no-one under 21, no rowdy behavior, and payment in advance. Communication is never a problem, as he speaks six European languages well, and six others adequately. Prices variable depending on the size of the group, the time of year, and the number of nights you stay. Expect to pay L13,000–17,000. No breakfast.

Domus Cavanis, Rio Terrà Foscarini, Dorsoduro 912, ☎5287374. On the street going down the left of the Accademia. Catholic-run (ie separate male

and female rooms); open June–Sept; single, double, and triple rooms. Clean, but not the cheapest: L27,000 each for the double rooms. Full dinners L8000.

Domus Civica, Calle Campazzo, S. Polo 3082, ☎721103. A student house in winter, open to women travelers June–July & Sept–Oct. Close enough to the station, but a little awkward to find in the dark: it's off Calle della Lacca, which lies to the west of San Giovanni Evangelista. Most rooms are doubles with running water; showers free; no breakfast; reception 7:30am–11:30am; 11:30pm curfew. Around L22,000 per person.

Foresteria Valdese, S. Maria Formosa, Castello 5170, ☎5286797. Go east from the Campo Santa Maria Formosa along Calle Lunga, over the bridge forking right at the end, and it's in front of you— a real palace with flaking frescoes and a large salon. Run by Waldesians, it's principally a hostel for grown-ups, with occasional school groups. Two large dorms, and a couple of rooms for two to four people. There is also a self-catering apartment for three to six people, usually heavily booked—worth checking out, as it's one of the most pleasant low-cost places to stay. Hostel open for registration 11am–1pm and 6–8:30pm. L20,000 per person for a room; L16,000 for a dorm, including breakfast and shower.

Ostello Venezia, Fondementa delle Zitelle, Guidecca 86, ☎5238211. Superb location looking over to San Marco from the island of Giudecca. The only youth hostel in town, run with a certain briskness—notices demand "perfect sobriety and cleanliness". Oct–May you can phone to reserve on the answerphone from 1–6pm; June–Sept personal reservations only. The waiting room opens at noon in summer and 4pm in winter for the 6pm registration, and it's a good idea to get there early. Curfew at 11:30pm, checking-out time 9am. Gets so busy in July–Aug that written reservations must be made by April. If it's full, don't panic: they use a local school with camp-beds as an annex. L12,000 includes breakfast and sheets (remember to add the expense of the boat over to Giudecca); no kitchen, but full (and excellent) meals for L8000. IYHF card necessary, but you can join on the spot.

CAMPING

There are no inexpensive campgrounds in the immediate area of Venice, but perhaps the most convenient are the pair on the road from the airport: the *Marco Polo* (L20,000 per person per night) and the friendlier *Leone di San Marco* (L16,000). The surroundings are nobody's idea of bucolic bliss, but at least there's a regular bus to get you into the historic center. All the other sites require boat rides or convoluted bus journeys.

The **Litorale del Cavallino**, stretching from the Punta Sabbioni to Jésolo, has sites with a total of around 60,000 places, many of them quite luxurious. The vaporetto #14, from the Riva degli Schiavoni to the Punta, stops close to *Marina di Venezia* (Via Montello 6; ☎966146; April–Sept; minimum stay 3 days) and *Miramare* (Lungomare Dante Alighieri 29; ☎966150; April–Sept). The coastal setting is attractive, but most of the sites along the Cavallino shore are inexcusably expensive—typically L15,000 per night for the site plus L5000 per person. When you've added on the fare for the forty-minute boat trip into the city you're not left with an economical proposition.

The **Lido** is a shorter ride away, but its **San Nicolò** site, at Riviera San Nicolò 65 (☎767415), has only 150 places; an International Camping Card is necessary.

There's an all-year campground back on the mainland at **Fusina** (Mestre Fusina, Via Moranzani, ☎969055), the catch here being that the direct vaporetto (#16) only operates in the summer; at other times you have to get the bus to the Mestre and change there. It has 1000 places.

SLEEPING OUT

Self-sufficient travelers used to spread their sleeping bags on the forecourt of the train station in summer, an practice that was banned in 1987. At that point the Scuola San Caboto (Cannaregio 1104/f; ☎716629) opened its doors to take in the displaced *saccopelisti*, as they're called. The school charges L5000 for sleeping under the stars in its garden, L8000 with your tent, L6500 with their tent, L10,000 dorm-style in the school buildings. It's open 7pm–midnight, and you have to be out by 9am. Follow the signs from the Ponte delle Guglie, on the Canale di Cannaregio.

Recently there's been a resurgence of the *saccopelisti*, but the camping-ground has shifted to the opposite bank of the canal, next to San Simeone Piccolo. The situation changes each year—the tourist office at the station will tell you if San Caboto has been joined by other refuges for sleeping-baggers.

The 118 islands of central Venice are divided into six districts known as *sestieri*, three on each side of the Canal Grande. The *sestiere* of **San Marco** is the zone where the majority of the essential sights are clustered, and is accordingly the most expensive and most crowded district of the city. On the east it's bordered by **Castello**, and on the north by **Cannaregio**—both of which become more residential, and poorer and quieter, the farther you go from the center. On the other bank the largest of the *sestieri* is **Dorsoduro**, which stretches from the fashionable quarter at southern tip of the canal to the docks in the west. **Santa Croce**, named after a now demolished church, roughly follows the curve of the Canal Grande from Piazzale Roma to a point just short of the Rialto, where it joins the smartest and commercially most active of the districts on this bank—**San Polo**.

Within each *sestiere* the buildings are numbered in a sequence that makes sense solely to the functionaries of the post office—you'll find houses facing each other across an alleyway which have numbers separated by hundreds. To the uninitiated, the boundaries of the *sestieri* can seem just as perplexing, and they are of little use as a means of structuring a guide. So, although in most instances this guide uses the name of a *sestiere* to indicate broadly which zone of the city we're in, the boundaries of our sections have been chosen for their practicality and do not, except in the case of *San Marco*, follow the city's official divisions.

CHAPTER ONE

SAN MARCO

Right at the start of Venice's existence, when the city's founders decamped from the coastal town of Malamocco to settle on the safer islands of the inner lagoon, the area now known as the **Piazza San Marco** was established as the nucleus of Venice. It was here that the first rulers built their citadel—the **Palazzo Ducale**—and here that they established their most important church—the **Basilica di San Marco**. Over the succeeding centuries the Basilica evolved into the most ostentatiously rich church in Christendom, and the Palazzo Ducale grew to accommodate and celebrate a system of government so well equipped with checks and balances that it endured for longer than any other republican regime in Europe. Meanwhile, the setting for these two great edifices developed into a fittingly dignified public space, a process that was rounded off in the course of the sixteenth century with the construction along the Piazza's sides of the administrative buildings known as the **Procuratie**, and the completion of the **Libreria Sansoviniana** in the Piazzetta.

Enclosed by the lower loop of the Canal Grande, the *sestiere* (district) of San Marco—a rectangle smaller than 1000m by 500m—is where the big money is spent. The plush hotels are concentrated here, the most elegant and exorbitant cafés spill out onto the sidewalk from the Piazza's arcades, and the swankiest shops in Venice line the Piazza and the streets radiating from it—interspersed with dozens of hugely profitable souvenir suppliers. And yet, small though this area is, it harbors plenty of refuges from the assaults of commerce. The Renaissance church of **San Salvatore**—only a few minutes' walk from the Piazza—and the Gothic **Santo Stefano** are both magnificent buildings and both comparatively neglected, while **San Moisè**, **Santa Maria Zobenigo** and the **Scala del Bovolo** rank among the city's most engaging oddities. On the fringes of the *sestiere* you'll find two of Venice's major exhibition spaces: the immense **Palazzo Grassi**, where the city's prestige art shows are now held, and the rickety **Museo Fortuny**, which as well as staging special events also contains a permanent collection of work by the designer Mariano Fortuny.

THE PIAZZA AND AROUND

Just half of Venice's visitors stay for more than one day, the rest making a beeline for the Piazza. Dazzled by the scenery around the Basilica and the views from the waterfront, and perhaps daunted by the city's geography, a good proportion of them never stray far from the Piazza and the main drag connecting it to the Rialto district—which means that in high season it can be a tricky business getting an uninterrupted look at the buildings. You'll see the best of the Piazza by rising with the lark and staying up late, and you'll enjoy the interiors of the Basilica and the Palazzo Ducale more if you're at the head of the morning's

Rialto Market

R. D. FONTEGO D. TEDESCHI

PONTE DI RIALTO

Fondaco d.
Tedeschi
(Post Office)

Rialto
1, 2, 4

S. Lio

CAMPO DI
SANTA MARIA
FORMOSA

S. Maria
Formosa

S. Bartolomeo

C. D. STAGNER

R. DELLA FAVA

SAL. DI S. LIO

raghetto

CAMPO
S. SALVADOR

S. Salvatore

S. Maria
della Fava

Palazzo Loredan
(Municipio)

MER. DI S. SALVADOR

R. DELLA GUERRA

Palazzo
Querini-
Stampalia

alazzo
arsetti

Teatro
Goldoni

C. DE L'OVO

R. G. BARBETTIER

R. DELLA GUERRA

CAMPO
S. LUCA

S. Giuliano

MER. DEL CAPITELLO

uca

O MANIN

R. DELLE COLONNE

C. FIUBERA

R. DEL CAPELLO

C. LARGA SAN MARCO

Torre
dell'Orologio

Scala del
Bovolo

R. DEI FUSERI

C. FREZZERIA

R. DE CAVALETTO

P. DEI LEONCINI

San
Marco

R. D. PALAZZO

neo
eto

CAMPO
S. GALLO

R. DEI CAVALLETTI

Prigioni

CAMPO S. FANTIN

FREZZERIA

BACINO
ORSEOLO

Procuratie
Vecchie

Campanile

PIAZZA SAN MARCO

PIAZZETTA

Fenice

R. DE VESTE

C. DE L'ASCENSION

Procuratie
Nuove

Post Office

C. DEL'ASCENSION

S. Moisè

R. DE L'ALBARON

SAL. S. MOISÈ

EPT

R. DELLE ZECCA

Libreria
Sansoviniana

MOLO

Palazzo
Ducale

C. VALLARESO

Zecca

Ponte dei
Sospiri

CAMPO
S. MOISÈ

C. LARGA XXII MARZO

C. DO PISTOR

Giardinetti
Reali

S. Marco Giardinetti
3

DI S. MOISÈ

Palazzo
Giustinian

S. Marco Vallaresso
1, 2, 4, 34

Salute
1

Dogana di Mare

Salute

SAN MARCO

line. There are, though, two places within the Piazza where the crowds shouldn't be a problem: the civic museum of Venice—the **Museo Correr**—is rarely busy, and the **Museo Archeologico** never.

The Piazza

The **Piazza San Marco** is the center of gravity of the city's social life. Contrary to first appearances, the customers at *Florian* and *Quadri* are almost as likely to be Venetians as they are to be outsiders, and the square is the main stage for the evening *passeggiata*. Wander through at midday and there'll be clusters of friends taking the air and chatting away their lunch hour; come down at midnight and you'll almost certainly see a few groups rounding off the evening with a stroll across the flagstones. (This is the only *piazza* in Venice, by the way—all other squares are *campi* or *campielli*.)

"The finest drawing-room in Europe" was how Napoleon described the Piazza, but less genteel phrases than Napoleon's might seem appropriate on a summer afternoon, as your ears are battered by the competing café orchestras blasting out selected melodies from the Lloyd-Webber oeuvre, and your sightlines are repeatedly blocked. You can take some consolation from the knowledge that the crowds and the racket are maintaining a long tradition. The Piazza has always been crowded, and foreigners have always made up a sizable proportion of the crowds—long before the tourist industry got into its stride, the swarms of foreign merchants and travelers in the Piazza were being cursed as "the monsters of the sea," to quote one disgruntled native.

A note on the ubiquitous **pigeons**—you can choose between three improbable stories about their origins: either they came here with the refugees from Attila's army; or they're the descendants of caged birds given to a doge's wife in an attempt to cheer her up; or they're the distant relatives of pigeons released by successive doges during Holy Week, in a ceremony commemorating the return of Noah's dove. Whatever their ancestry, the Venetians appear to cherish the beasts, and until fairly recently they were fed daily by a council official.

Market Stalls and Coffee Houses

If anything, life on the Piazza is less diverse nowadays than it used to be. From the foundation of the city, this area was used by traders (until the end of the ninth century the slave market was here) and as the city grew, so the range of activities taking place on the Piazza multiplied: by the end of the fifteenth century butchers and grocers had established their pitches, moneylenders and notaries had set up kiosks nearby, and makeshift stages for freak shows and masques were regular additions to the scene.

By the eighteenth century the Piazza might have become a touch more decorous, but it was certainly no emptier. One English visitor characterized the throng as "a mixed multitude of Jews, Turks, and Christians; lawyers, naves, and pick-pockets; mountebanks, old women, and physicians; women of quality, with masks; strumpets barefaced; . . . a jumble of senators, citizens, gondoleers, and people of every character and condition." Jugglers, puppeteers, sweet-sellers, fortune-tellers and a host of other stallholders seem to have been almost perennial features of the landscape, while Venetian high society passed much of the day in one or other of the Piazza's dozen coffee houses.

During the Austrian occupation of 1814–66 the coffee houses were drawn into the social warfare between the city's two hostile camps. Shops used by the occupying troops were shunned by all patriotic Venetians—*Quadri* became an Austrian coffee house, whereas *Florian* remained a Venetian. Certain prominent Venetians even went to the length of shunning the Piazza whenever the Austrian band was playing, a policy that entailed a thrice-weekly withdrawal from the center of the city.

Florian and *Quadri* are the only eighteenth-century coffee houses to have survived and they're the most expensive in Venice, predictably enough; just one small *expresso* at the former will set you back L5000, plus a L3000 supplement for the privilege of listening to the racket made by the band. The equally intimidating *Lavena* is a nineteenth-century place, and was the favorite haunt of Richard Wagner.

Festivities, Fairs, and Rebellions

The Piazza's brightest splash of color comes from the **Carnevale**. Though gangs of masked and wildly costumed revelers turn every quarter of the city into a week-long open-air party, all the action tends to drift towards the Piazza, and the grand finale of the whole proceedings is a huge Shrove Tuesday ball in the square, with fireworks over the Bacino di San Marco.

Mass entertainments used to be far more frequent, taking over the Piazza on feast days and whenever a plausible excuse could be found. From the twelfth century onward pig-hunts and bullfights were frequent spectacles, but from around the beginning of the seventeenth century the authorities became increasingly embarrassed by these sanguinary pursuits, and they were relegated to other squares in the city. The bloodsports were succeeded by gymnastic performances known as *Labors of Hercules*, in which teams of young men formed human pyramids and towers on platforms that were often no more than a couple of planks resting on a pair of barrels. Military victories, ducal elections and visits from heads of state were commonly celebrated with tournaments and pageants—a three-day tournament was held in the Piazza in 1364 after the recapture of Crete (with guest appearances by a gang of English knights on their way to create bedlam in the Holy Land), and in 1413 the election of Doge Tommaso Mocenigo was marked by a a tournament that was watched by 70,000 people. (Mocenigo also initiated the postelectoral ritual of carrying the new doge shoulder-high round the Piazza while he distributed coins to the populace.)

The major religious festivals were the occasion for lavish celebrations, the most spectacular of which was the **Procession of Corpus Domini**, a performance meticulously recorded in a painting by Gentile Bellini in the Accademia. Regrettably, not all of Venice's holy processions achieved the solemn dignity captured in Bellini's picture—in 1513 one stately progress went wrong when a row broke out over which group had the right to enter the Piazza first, a disagreement that rapidly escalated into an almighty punch-up.

But no festivities were more extravagant than those of **Ascension Day**, and it was in the wake of Ascension that the Piazza most closely resembled the modern tourist enclave. From the twelfth century until the fall of the Republic, the day itself was marked in Venice by the ceremony of **The Marriage of Venice to the Sea** (see entry on "The Lido"), a ritual which inaugurated a short season of feasts and sideshows in the Piazza, culminating in a trade fair called the **Fiera della Sensa** (*Sensa* being dialect for Ascension). The Fiera began in 1180, when, as a result of Pope Alexander III's proclamation that an indulgence would be granted to anyone who prayed in San Marco during the year, the city was flooded with pilgrims. Before long it became a cornucopia of luxury commodities, and by the last century of the Republic's existence it had grown into a fifteen-day shindig that filled the Piazza with temporary wooden shops and arcades.

The Buildings of the Piazza

When the first Palazzo Ducale was built, in the ninth century, much of the area now occupied by the Piazza was covered by the orchard of the nuns of San Zaccaria, and was divided by a canal that connected the waterways to the north with the Bacino di San Marco. It was in the late twelfth century, under the direction of **Doge Sebastiano Ziani** (often known as the Architect Doge), that the land was transformed into a public space—the canal was filled in, the ancient church of San Geminiano, which stood on the bank, was demolished (a plaque close to the Campanile marks where it stood) and a replacement built at the far end. The general shape of the Piazza hasn't changed much since Ziani's scheme, but most of the buildings you see today (excluding San Marco itself and the Campanile) date from the great period of urban renewal which began at the end of the fifteenth century and went on for much of the following hundred years.

The Campanile and Loggetta

The **Campanile** (opens daily 9:30am, closes between 3:30 and 8pm, depending on season; closed Dec 25 and all Jan; L3000) began life as a combined lighthouse and belltower in the early tenth century (when what's now the Piazzetta was the city's harbor) and was modified continually up to 1515, the year in which Bartolomeo Bon the Younger's rebuilding was rounded off with the positioning of a golden angel on the summit. Each of its five bells had a distinct function: the *Marangona*, the largest, tolled the beginning and end of the working day; the *Trottiera* was a signal for members of the Maggior Consiglio to hurry to the council chamber; the *Nona* rang midday; the *Mezza Terza* announced a session of the Senate; and the smallest, the *Renghiera* or *Maleficio*, gave notice of an execution.

The Campanile played another part in the Venetian penal system—"persons of scandalous behavior" ran the risk of being subjected to the *Supplizio della Cheba* (Torture of the Cage), which involved being stuck in a crate which was then hoisted up the south face of the tower; if you were lucky you'd get away with a few days swinging in the breeze, but in some cases the view from the Campanile was the last thing the sinner saw. A more cheerful diversion was provided by the *Volo dell'Anzolo* (or *del Turco*—Flight of the Angel or Turk), a stunt which used to be performed each year at the end of the Carnevale, in which an intrepid volunteer from the Arsenale would slide on a rope from the top of the Campanile to the first-floor loggia of the Palazzo Ducale, and there present a bouquet to the doge.

To the people of Venice, the Campanile's most significant contribution to the history of the city was made on 14 July 1902, the day on which, at 9:52am, the tower succumbed to the weaknesses caused by recent structural changes, and fell down. (At some postcard stalls you can buy faked photos of the very instant of disaster.) The collapse was anticipated and the area cleared, so there were no human casualties; the only life lost was that of an incautious cat called

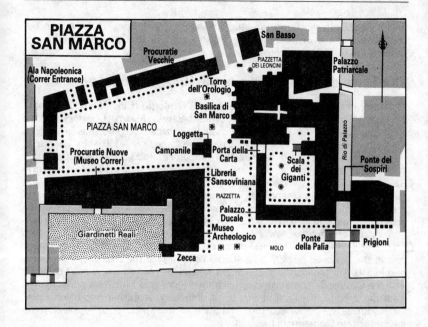

Mélampyge (named after Casanova's dog, apparently). What's more, the bricks fell so neatly that San Marco was barely scratched and the Libreria lost just its end wall. The town councillors decided that evening that the Campanile should be rebuilt "dove'era e com'era" (where it was and how it was), and a decade later (St Mark's Day 1912) the new tower was opened, in all but minor details a replica of the original.

At 99m, the Campanile is the tallest structure in the city, and from the top you can make out virtually every building, but not a single canal—almost as surprising as the view of the Dolomites, which on clear days seem to be in Venice's back yard. Among the many who have marveled at the panorama are Galileo, who demonstrated the telescope from here; Goethe, who had never before seen the sea; and the Emperor Frederick III, whose climb to the top was achieved with a certain panache—he rode his horse up the tower's internal ramp. The ready access granted to the tourist is a modern privilege—the Venetian state used to permit foreigners to ascend only at high tide, when they would be unable to see the elusive channels through the lagoon which were crucial to the city's defense.

The collapse of the Campanile of course pulverized the **Loggetta** at its base, but somehow it was pieced together again, mainly using material retrieved from the wreckage. **Sansovino**'s design was for a building that would completely enclose the foot of the Campanile, but only one quarter of the plan was executed (in 1537–1549). Intended as a meeting place for the city's nobility, it was soon converted into a guardhouse for the *Arsenalotti* (workers from the Arsenale) who patrolled the area when the Maggior Consiglio was sitting, and in the last years of the Republic served as the room in which the state lottery was drawn. The bronze figures in niches are also by Sansovino (Pallas, Apollo, Mercury, and Peace), as is the terracotta group inside (although the figure of St John is a modern facsimile);

the three marble reliefs on the attic are, as ever, allegories of the power and beneficence of the *Serenissima* (the Most Serene Republic): Justice = Venice, Jupiter = Crete, Venus = Cyprus.

The Torre dell'Orologio and the Piazzetta dei Leoncini

The other tower in the Piazza, the **Torre dell'Orologio** (Clock Tower) was built between 1496 and 1506, the central portion being by **Mauro Coducci** and the wings possibly by **Pietro Lombardo**. (The three ornate **flagstaff bases** between the Campanile and the Torre were made at the same time—1505—by **Leopardi**, the sculptor who finished the Colleoni monument.) A gruesome popular tale relates that the makers of the clock's elaborate mechanism, Paolo and Carlo Rainieri, slaved away for three years at their project, only to have their eyes put out so that they couldn't repeat their engineering marvel for other patrons. In fact the Venetians were suitably grateful and gave the pair a generous pension— presumably too dull an outcome for the city's folklorists.

A staircase within the tower leads up to the terrace on which stand the two bronze wild men known, because of their dark patina, as "The Moors"; they were cast in the Arsenale in 1497. The stairs take you past the innards of the clock; horologists will probably find the climb worthwhile, but the view can't compete with the Campanile's, and you can watch the Moors strike the hour perfectly well from the ground. If you're in Venice on Epiphany or during Ascension week, you'll witness the clock's star turn—on the hour the Magi, led by an angel, troop out and bow to the figure of the Madonna.

To your right as you face the Torre is the **Piazzetta Giovanni XXIII**, familiarly known as **dei Leoncini**, after the two eighteenth-century marble lions—if you can't see them immediately, it's because they're smothered in children. Facing San Marco's flank is **San Basso**, a deconsecrated church now used for exhibitions, and at the far end is the nineteenth-century **Palazzo Patriarcale**, home of the Patriarch of Venice. The Palazzo contains the banqueting hall in which the doge used to entertain official guests and, once a year, the *Arsenalotti*; a corridor, now demolished, ran from the hall, through San Marco and into the Palazzo Ducale.

The Procuratie, Ala Napoleonica, and Museo Correr

Away to the left, from the Clock Tower, stretches the **Procuratie Vecchie**, once the home of the **Procurators of San Marco**, whose responsibilities included the upkeep of San Marco and the administration of the other government-owned properties. Never numbering more than nine, the procurators were second in position only to the doge, who himself was generally drawn from their ranks. With the doge and the Grand Chancellor—the head of the civil service—they shared the distinction of being the only state officials to be elected for life.

From the time of Doge Ziani, the procurators and their attendant bureaucracies were installed on this side of the Piazza, but the present building was begun around 1500 by **Coducci**, continued after a fire in 1512 by **Bartolomeo Bon the Younger** and completed c.1532 by **Sansovino**. Much of the block earned rents for the city coffers, the upper floors housing some of the choicest apartments in town and the ground floor being leased to shopkeepers and craftsmen.

Within a century or so, the procurators were moved across the Piazza to new premises. Sansovino, who had only recently completed the old offices, proposed a development that involved knocking down a pilgrims' hospice, along with the unsightly shacks around it. The **Procuratie Nuove** were eventually built between 1582 and 1640, first to designs by **Scamozzi**, and then under Longhena's control. Napoleon appropriated the quarters for use as a royal palace, and then discovered that the accommodation lacked a ballroom. His solution had the true, gossamer Napoleonic touch to it: he demolished Sansovino's church of San Geminiano, which had taken up part of the third side of the Piazza, and connected the Procuratie Nuove and Vecchie with a wing containing the essential facility. Generally known as the **Ala Napoleonica**, the building is topped by a gallery of Roman emperors—there are no prizes for guessing whose effigy was meant to fill the gap in the middle.

The Museo Correr

The majority of the rooms in the Ala Napoleonica and Procuratie Nuove have been occupied since 1923 by the **Museo Correr**, the civic museum of Venice (10am–4pm, Sun 9am–12:30pm; closed Tues; L3000, reductions L1500). An immense triple-decker collection which nobody could digest in its entirety, it incorporates a picture gallery that more than makes up for the duller stretches.

The second floor is given over to the **historical collection**, only sporadically enlightening unless your Italian is reasonably good or you have a pretty wide knowledge of Venetian history already. The collection of Venetian coins from the ninth century to the end of the Republic is impressive, as are some of the pieces of ducal regalia and depictions of state ceremonies, but you might find yourself in agreement with those who complain that the only colorful aspects of Venetian history are the costumes. Qualitatively, this part of the Correr is downhill all the way once you're past the pieces by **Canova** in the first couple of rooms—including the group that made his name, *Daedalus and Icarus*, sculpted at the age of 21. The figures of *Orpheus and Eurydice*, placed just outside the door to room 1, were created even earlier.

Things improve sharply on the floor above, where you come to the **Quadreria** (Picture Gallery). It may be no rival for the Accademia's collection, but it sets out clearly the evolution of painting in Venice from the thirteenth century to the sixteenth (though not all of its pictures are by Venetians), and does contain some gems. Ones to seek out are the *Pietà* by **Cosmè Tura** (room 7), the *Transfiguration* and *Dead Christ Supported by Angels* by **Giovanni Bellini** (room 13), a couple of **Carpaccio**s—the *Portrait of a Young Man in a Red Hat*, and the painting of two terminally bored women that is usually known as *The Courtesans* (room 15). The subjects of this last picture are in fact a couple of late fifteenth-century bourgeois ladies dressed in a style at which none of their contemporaries would have raised an eyebrow. Their perilous platform shoes (*Ciapine*) served a double function: they kept the silks and satins out of the mud, and they enabled the wearer to circumvent the sumptuary laws, which naively attempted to limit the volume of expensive materials used in dresses by forbidding trailing hems.

At room 19 the Quadreria turns into a display of ceramics, most of them hideous, but in the very last rooms (often closed) there's a more appealing exhibition of small bronzes, household objects and other examples of the applied arts in Venice, featuring pieces by **Tullio Lombardo**, **Riccio** and **Vittoria**, and the original blocks, plus a print, of **Jacopo de'Barbari's** astonishing **aerial view of Venice**, engraved in 1500. The final part of the Correr, the **Museo del Risorgimento** (also on the second floor) is rarely open, a fact which should grieve only worshippers of **Daniele Manin**—five of its fifteen rooms are given over to the brief rebellion he led against the Austrians. (See "North of the Piazza"—"Campo Manin.")

The Piazzetta

For much of the Republic's existence, the **Piazzetta**—the open space between San Marco and the waterfront—was the area where the councillors of Venice would gather to scheme and curry favor; the name by which it was known locally—the *broglio*—is the probable source of the English word imbroglio. But as well as being a sort of open-air clubhouse, the Piazzetta played a crucial part in the penal system of Venice.

Those found guilty of serious crime by Venice's courts were often done away with in the privacy of their cells; for public executions the sidewalk between the two granite columns on the waterfront (the Molo) was the usual site. Straightforward hanging or decapitation were the customary techniques, but refinements were available to certain offenders, such as the three traitors who, in 1405, were buried alive, head downward. Even this was mild by comparison with a form of execution that goes some way to explaining the reputation for barbarity that the Venetian system had abroad: the victim was taken to a raft over in the west of the city, where he was mutilated and burned until almost dead, then tied to a horse and hauled through the streets to the columns, where he was at last given the *coup de grâce*. The last person to be executed here was one Domenico Storti, condemned to death in 1752 for the murder of his brother. Superstitious Venetians avoid passing between the columns.

Sometimes the heads of freshly dispatched villains were mounted on the **Pietra del Bando**, the stump of porphyry at the other end of the Piazzetta, against the corner of San Marco; a more benign service was done on the day the Campanile collapsed, when it stopped the avalanche of bricks from hitting the church. Its routine use was as one of the two stones from which the laws of the Republic were proclaimed (the other is at the Rialto). The stone was brought back from Acre in 1256, following Venice's victory over the Genoese there; the two square pillars near to it—Syrian works dating from the fifth century—were filched from Constantinople during the **Fourth Crusade** of 1204.

The **columns** should have a companion, but the third one fell off the barge on which they were being transported and has remained submerged somewhere off the Piazzetta since c.1170. The columns themselves were purloined from the Levant, whereas the figures perched on top are bizarre hybrids. The statue of **Saint Theodore**—the patron saint of Venice when it was dependent on Byzantium—is a modern copy; the original was a compilation of a Roman torso, a head of Mithridates the Great (first century BC) and miscellaneous bits and pieces. The **winged lion** on the other column is a chimera from Syria, Persia or China, with added wings and a book shoved under his paw—it was partly recast in the nineteenth century, to rectify damage done when the French dragged it off to Paris.

The Libreria Sansoviniana and Museo Archeologico

The Piazzetta is framed by two outstanding buildings—the Palazzo Ducale on one side and the **Libreria Sansoviniana** (or *Biblioteca Marciana*—the Library of St Mark) on the other. Sansovino's contemporaries regarded the Libreria as one of the supreme designs of the era: Palladio remarked that it was "perhaps the richest and most ornate building to be created since the times of ancient Greece and Rome." Venice had an opportunity to establish a state library in the fourteenth century, when Petrarch left his priceless collection to the city— but the the beneficiaries somehow mislaid the legacy, which gives you some idea of the importance of literature in Venetian culture. In the end, the impetus to build the library came from the bequest of Cardinal Bessarion, who left his celebrated hoard of classical texts to the Republic in 1468. Bessarion's books and manuscripts were housed in San Marco and then the Palazzo Ducale, but finally it was decided that a special building was needed.

Sansovino got the job, and in 1537 the site was cleared of its hostels, slaughter-house and bakery, thus turning the Campanile into a freestanding tower. Construction was well advanced when, in December 1545, the project suffered a minor setback: frost got into the vaulted ceiling of the main hall and brought it crashing down. Charged with incompetence, Sansovino was thrown into prison, and it took some determined pleading by his cronies—Titian among them—to get him out. Upon being allowed back on the job he took notice of conventional wisdom, which argued that vaults really weren't a terrific idea in a place where the land keeps shifting, and stuck a flat ceiling in its place, with a wooden vault attached, to keep up appearances. The library was finished in 1591, two decades after Sansovino's death.

The **main hall** of the original library, one of the most beautiful rooms in the city, is covered with paintings by **Veronese**, **Tintoretto** and others; the anteroom has a **Titian** ceiling panel. (Items from the library's collection—such as the *Grimani Breviary* of 1500, and Fra Mauro's 1459 map of the world, are sometimes displayed, but the rooms are currently being rearranged.) Permission to see the hall, and the grand **staircase** stuccoed by **Vittoria**, can be obtained from the director's office at the main library (no. 13a), though you'll have to convince the people on the front desk that you're no idle tourist, and be prepared to come back at a time convenient to the library. It's worth the effort.

The Museo Archeologico

The entrance to the **Museo Archeologico** (Tues–Sat 9am–2pm, Sun 9am–1pm; L2000) is also in the loggia of the Libreria, at no. 17. The core of the museum is Cardinal Domenico Grimani's bequest of Greek and Roman sculpture, which was given to the city in 1523 and exercized a powerful influence on the artists of Renaissance Venice. His collection of fourth- and fifth-century BC statues, including an amazing *Persephone*, is the highlight of the visit. Of the Roman pieces, the second-century bust presumed to be of Vitellius is the most striking. In many cities a collection of classical works as comprehensive as this one would merit the strongest recommendation; but in Venice it's hard to feel guilty about leaving it for a rainy day. At some point in the future the museum will be uprooted and transported over to the Grimani palace at Santa Maria Formosa, but the shift doesn't seem to be imminent.

The Zecca and the Giardinetti Reali

Attached to the Library, with its main facade to the lagoon, is Sansovino's first major building in Venice, the **Zecca** (Mint). Constructed in stone and iron to make it fireproof (most stonework in Venice is just skin-deep), it was built between 1537 and 1545 on the site occupied by the Mint since the thirteenth century, when it was moved from a factory near the Rialto bridge. Part of the finance for the project was raised by selling freedom to slaves on Cyprus. By the beginning of the fifteenth century the city's prosperity was such that the Venetian gold ducat was in use in every European exchange, and Doge Tommaso Mocenigo (he of the big handout in the Piazza) could look forward to the day when the city would be "the mistress of all the gold in Christendom." In later years the ducat became known as the *zecchino*, source of the word sequin. The rooms of the Mint are now part of the library.

Beyond the Zecca, and behind a barricade of postcard and toy gondola sellers, is a small public garden—the **Giardinetti Reale**—created by Napoleon on the site of the state granaries as part of his improvement scheme for the Procuratie Nuove. It's the nearest place to the center where you'll find a bench and the shade of a tree, but in summer it's about as peaceful as a school playground. On the far side of the gardens is that rare thing in Venice—a public toilet.

The Basilica di San Marco

San Marco is the most exotic of Europe's cathedrals, and it has always provoked strong reactions. To Herman Melville it was beautiful and insubstantial—as though "the Grand Turk had pitched his pavilion here for a summer's day"; Mark Twain adored it for its "entrancing, tranquillizing, soul-satisfying ugliness"; Herbert Spencer found it loathsome—"a fine sample of barbaric architecture"; but to John Ruskin it was the most gorgeous of holy places, a "treasure-heap ... a confusion of delight." The Basilica is certainly confusing, increasingly so as you come nearer and the details emerge, but some knowledge of the building's background helps bring a little order out of chaos.

Although San Marco is open from 6:30am on most days, tourists are asked to observe the following hours: Mon–Sat 9:30am–5:30pm, Sun & hols 2–5:30pm. Admission fees totalling L5000 are charged for certain parts of the church. Sections of the Basilica will almost certainly be under restoration; current long-term projects include the Cappella Zen and Baptistery.

San Marco and Venice's Destiny

All over Venice you see images of the lion of Saint Mark holding a book on which are carved the text "Pax tibi, Marce evangelista meus. Hic requiescet corpus tuum" ("Peace be with you Mark, my Evangelist. Here shall your body rest"). These supposedly are the words with which Saint Mark was greeted by an angel who appeared to him on the night he took shelter in the lagoon on his way back to Rome. This **legend of Saint Mark's annunciation** was adopted as fact in order to overcome the discrepancy between the first Venetians' notion of their

THE BASILICA DI SAN MARCO

Sacristy

Pala d'Oro

Cappella di San Clemente

Madonna of Nicopeia

Sarcophagus of St. Mark

Rood screen

Pulpit

Pulpit

Cappella di Sant'Isidoro

Cappella della Madonna dei Mascoli

Il Capitello

Treasury

Porta dei Fiori

PIAZZETTA DEI LEONCINI

To the Museo & Horses

Baptistery

NARTHEX

Cappella Zen

Porta di Sant'Alipio

Porta di San Clemente

PIAZZA SAN MARCO

spiritual pedigree—as successors of the shattered Roman empire and as the first state to be founded as a Christian community—and the inglorious fact that the settlement of the lagoon islands had begun as a scramble to get out of the path of Attila the Hun. Having thus assured themselves of the sacred ordination of their city, the proto-Venetians duly went about fulfilling the angelic prophecy. In **828** a pair of merchants called Buono Tribuno da Malamocco and Rustico da Torcello **stole the body of Saint Mark** from its tomb in Alexandria, and (so the story goes) having smuggled the corpse past the Muslim guards by hiding it in a consignment of pork, brought it back to Venice and presented it to the doge.

Work began immediately on a shrine to house the relic; modeled on Constantinople's Church of the Twelve Apostles, it was consecrated in **832**. In 976 a riot provoked by the tyrannous Doge Pietro Candiano IV reduced the Palazzo Ducale to a pile of ashes and ruined the Basilica too; its replacement was in turn superseded by a **third church in 1063–94**. It is this third Basilica, embellished by the succeeding centuries, that you see now.

The combination of ancient structure and later decorations is, to a great extent, what makes San Marco so bewildering: for example, the Gothic pointed arches and carvings on the roofline of the main facade (mostly early fifteenth-century) are not what you'd expect to see on top of squat, rounded Byzantine arches, and the garish seventeenth- to nineteenth-century mosaics that dominate this front must be the worst aesthetic mismatch in all Italy. But the picture is made yet more complicated by the addition of ornaments which were looted from abroad, are sometimes older than the building itself and in some cases have nothing to do with the Church. Into the last category fall two of the most famous features of the exterior: the porphyry figures of the **Tetrarchs** and the **horses of San Marco**. (More about both later.)

The reason for the presence of these seemingly profane decorations is simple: the doge was the lieutenant of Saint Mark, as the pope was the lieutenant of Saint Peter—therefore anything that glorified Venice was also to the greater glory of the Evangelist. Every trophy that the doge added to the Basilica was proof of Venice's secular might and so of the spiritual power of Saint Mark. Conversely, the saint was invoked to sanctify political actions and rituals of state—the doge's investiture was consecrated in the church, and military commanders received their commissions at its altar.

As can be imagined, the Venetians' conception of their city as the state with the purest lineage, and the often cynical use they made of this self-image, was not conducive to good relations with the Vatican. "They want to appear as Christian before the world," commented Pope Pius II, "but in reality they never think of God and, but for the state, which they regard as a deity, they hold nothing sacred." The Basilica is an emblem of the city's maverick position, because at no time in the existence of the Venetian Republic was San Marco the cathedral of Venice—it was the doge's chapel, and only became the cathedral in 1807, when the French moved the Patriarch of Venice here from San Pietro di Castello. Until the eighteenth century it was common practice for the doge to advertise his proprietorship by hanging his coat of arms on the front of the building.

In effect, the Venetians ran a semi-autonomous branch of the Roman Church: the Patriarch of Venice could convene a synod only with the doge's permission, bishops were nominated by the Senate, priests were appointed by a ballot of the parish and had to be of Venetian birth, and the Inquisition was supervised by the Republic's own, less draconian, doctrinal office. Inevitably, there were direct clashes with the Papacy; for the story of the most serious, the Interdict of 1606, see Chapter Four.

The Exterior of the Basilica

Shortly after becoming the architectural custodian (*Proto Magister*) of San Marco in 1529, Jacopo Sansovino set about strengthening the building and replacing some of its deteriorating decoration, a procedure that resulted in the removal of around thirty percent of the church's mosaics. On the main facade, the only mosaic to survive this and subsequent restorations is the scene above the **Porta di Sant'Alipio** (far left)—*The Arrival of the Body of St Mark*. Made in c.1260, it features the earliest known image of the Basilica. In the lunette (recess) below the mosaic are fourteenth-century bas-reliefs of the symbols of the Evangelists; the panels composing the door's architrave are fifth-century; and the door itself dates from 1300. The next door is from the same period, and the reliefs on the arch are thirteenth-century; the mosaic of *Venice Worshipping St Mark*, however, is an eighteenth-century effort.

The worst and the best aspects of the facade are to be found above the **central entrance**: the former being the nineteenth-century mosaic of the *Last Judgement*, the latter the **Romanesque carvings** of the arches. Begun with the innermost arch in the 1220s and completed about a century later, these are among the outstanding sculptural works of their time, but about one visitor in a thousand spares them a glance, despite their recently restored sparkle. **Inner arch**: under face—animals, Earth and Ocean; outer face—fighting figures (the savage antithesis of Venetian civilization?). **Middle arch**: under—the months and signs of the Zodiac; outer—Virtues and Beatitudes. **Outer arch**: under—the trades of Venice; outer—Christ and Prophets. The carved panel in the lunette, *The Dream of St Mark*, is also thirteenth-century, but the door (known as the **Porta di San Clemente**) is 700 years older, and is thought to have been a gift from the Byzantine emperor Alexius Comnenus.

The fourth portal follows closely the model of the second; the mosaic of the fifth is similarly an eighteenth-century job, but the marble decoration is a mixture of eleventh- to thirteenth-century carvings, except for the architrave panel of *Christ Blessing*, a remnant of the second Basilica, built after the 976 fire.

Of the six marble panels between the entrance arches, only the Roman bas-relief of *Hercules and the Erymanthean Boar* isn't a twelfth- or thirteenth-century piece. The terrace running across the facade above them was the spot from which the doge and his guests watched the festivities in the Piazza; the mosaics on this level all date from the early seventeenth century, and the peculiar blank window was occupied by a Byzantine screen until a fire in 1419 destroyed everything except the four half-columns. The encrustation of Gothic pinnacles, kiosks, figures and ornamental motifs was begun in 1385 under the direction of the **Dalle Masegne** family, the leading sculptors in Venice at that period, and was continued through the early part of the following century by various Tuscan and Lombard artists, of whom **Nicolo Lamberti** and his son **Pietro** were the most proficient. To see the real **horses of San Marco** you have to go into the church—these are modern replicas.

The North and South Facades

In the 1860s–70s an extensive and controversial **restoration** of the Basilica was undertaken, a scheme which would probably have finished with the rearrangement of the main facade. An international protest campaign, supported by Ruskin, forced the abandonment of the project soon after it had reached the Piazzetta corner of the west front, and the damage caused to that section was largely reversed in later years. The **north and south facades**, though, were altered irrevocably by the restorers, who replaced the old polychromatic marble panels with badly fitted sheets of gray stone, creating an effect which was described by an English stonemason in 1880 as resembling "a dirty lime wash on a white plastered wall."

The **north side** of San Marco, the last to be completed (in the first half of the thirteenth century), is studded with panels from a variety of sources—they include a seventh- or eighth-century relief showing the Apostles as twelve lambs, and a tenth-century piece illustrating Alexander the Great's mythical attempt to reach heaven by harnessing a pair of griffons to his chariot. The entrance on this side, the **Porta dei Fiori**, is thirteenth-century (the tomb of **Daniele Manin** is a bit farther on); and most of the sculpture on the upper part is by the **Lamberti**.

Jutting out between the **south facade** and the entrance to the Palazzo Ducale is the wall of the Treasury, thought by some to be a remnant of the **first palace of the doges** and the chamber in which the body of Saint Mark was first placed after its arrival in Venice. The screen fragments (*plutei*) set into the walls date from the ninth to the eleventh century. A number of tales center on the group of figures set into the angle of the Treasury. Thomas Coryat tells a version in which four Albanian brothers plot against each other for the possession of the cargo their ship is carrying, and end up poisoning each other. But the most popular version turns them into a gang of Saracens who raided the Treasury and then contrived to murder each other in a squabble over the spoils. Hence, like the figures on the Torre dell'Orologio, they're often nicknamed "The Moors"; but more properly they're known as the **Tetrarchs**, as in all likelihood they're a fourth-century Egyptian work, depicting Diocletian and the three colleagues with whom he ruled the unraveling Roman Empire—peculiar adornments for a church, bearing in mind Diocletian's prowess as a persecutor of Christians.

The Narthex

From the Piazza you pass into a vestibule called the **narthex**, which once, before the partitioning of the Baptistery and the Cappella Zen, bracketed the entire west end of the church. The stonework of the narthex **floor** is mostly eleventh- and twelfth-century, and one fragment of it is especially significant: the small white lozenge set into the floor in front of the main entrance is said to mark the spot on which the Emperor Frederick Barbarossa knelt before Pope Alexander III on 23 August 1177. Prior to this, the Empire and the Papacy had been at each other's throats, and this symbolic reconciliation in the portal of San Marco clinched one of Venice's greatest diplomatic triumphs.

Most of the **mosaics** on the domes and arches constitute a series of **Old Testament scenes** which complements the New Testament iconography in the main body of the church. (As with the mosaics inside, this account is necessarily incomplete; if you want a thorough guide, go for *The Mosaics of St Mark's* in the Electa Artistic Guides series, which is available in many of Venice's bookshops.) Predominantly thirteenth-century, the mosaics were begun in the dome on the far right, with scenes from *Genesis* (c.1230 but much restored, as indicated by the inset red lines), and executed in a continuous series right round the narthex. The *Genesis* dome is followed by: **first arch**—*Noah and the Flood* (note the preferential treatment handed out to the lion); in the **bay in front of main door**—double tier of niches containing the **oldest mosaics in San Marco**, a group showing *The Madonna with Apostles and Evangelists* (c.1065); **second arch**—end of *Life of Noah*, and a strikingly vivid *Tower of Babel*; **second dome**—*Story of Abraham* and four tondi of *Prophets*; **third arch**—*SS. Alipio and Simon* and tondo of *Justice*; **third, fourth and fifth domes**—*Story of Joseph*; **sixth dome**—*Story of Moses*.

Three doges and one dogaressa have tombs in the Narthex. That of **Vitale Falier**, the doge who consecrated the Basilica in 1094, two years before his death, is the **oldest funerary monument in Venice**—it's at the base of the first arch. The others are of Felicita, wife of Doge Vitale Michiel (1101; second arch), Doge Bartolomeo Gradenigo (1342; under third dome) and Doge Marin Morosini (1253; under fourth dome). Two other doges besides these are buried in the narthex, but nobody has a clue where.

The Museo Marciano, the Loggia, and the Horses

On the right of the main door from the narthex into the body of the church (made in 1113–18 and based on the Basilica's main door) is a steep staircase up to the **Museo Marciano** and the **Loggia dei Cavalli** (L2000 entry). Apart from giving you an all-round view which it's difficult to tear yourself away from, the Loggia is also the best place from which to inspect the Gothic carvings of the facade—but the reason most people haul themselves up the steps is to see the **horses of San Marco**.

The original horses have been removed to a room attached to the Museo, allegedly to protect them from the risks of atmospheric pollution, although some cynics have insisted that the rescue mission had less to do with any danger to the horses than with the marketing strategies of the Olivetti corporation, who sponsored the operation. In fact, it's quite likely that the condensation produced by thousands of exhaling tourists make the air in this confined space more corrosive than any acids floating around outside. Thieved from the Hippodrome of Constantinople in 1204, the horses spent a few years in front of the Arsenale before being installed on the terrace of the Basilica, and so close did the association become between them and the people who had stolen them, that the Genoese in 1378 didn't boast that they would tame the lion of Saint Mark, but rather that they would "bridle those unbridled horses." The statues are almost certainly Roman works of the second century, and are the only *quadriga* (group of four horses harnessed to a chariot) to have survived from the classical world. Made from a bronze that contains an extraordinarily high percentage of copper, they were cast in two parts, the junction being masked by their collars; medallions used to hang round their necks, but they were missing when the horses returned to Venice in 1815 after an eighteen-year sojourn on the Champs Élysées. The marks on the horses' skins are not the result of mistreatment—it's now thought that the scratches and the partial gilding were added at the time of their creation in order to catch the sun.

The **Museo Marciano** is a miscellany of mosaic fragments, carvings, vestments and so forth from the church. The most interesting exhibits are the wooden cover for the Pala d'Oro, painted in 1345 by **Paolo Veneziano** and his sons, and the cycle of ten tapestries of *The Life of Christ* made c.1420 to designs by **Nicolò di Pietro**—but as likely as not they'll be under lock and key.

The Interior

With its undulating floor of patterned marble, its plates of eastern stone on the lower walls, and its 4000 square meters of mosaic covering every other inch of wall and vaulting, the golden **interior** of San Marco achieves a hypnotic effect.

Whether you look down or up, some decorative detail will catch your eye, drawing you into the narratives of its mosaics, or the geometric complexities of its sidewalks. One visit is not enough: there's too much to take in at one go, and the shifting light reveals some parts and hides others as the day progresses—at noon you might have to peer through the murk to see a patch of wall which two hours later could as bright as a projected picture. The only way to do it justice is to stop by for half an hour at the beginning and end of a couple of days.

The Mosaics

The majority of the **mosaics** were in position by the middle of the thirteenth century, but scenes were added right down to the eighteenth century, most of the later work being carried out to replace damaged early sections. An adequate guide to them would take volumes: this is only a key to the highlights. The mosaics in the nave, transepts and presbytery are dealt with first; the mosaics in the chapels come into the entries on those chapels. The complex shape of the Basilica makes it most convenient to locate the various features by points of the compass—the high altar marking the east.

On the **west wall, above the door**—*Christ between the Virgin and St Mark* (thirteenth century, restored). **West dome**—*Pentecost* (early twelfth century; the first of the domes to be decorated); the paired figures between the windows represent the diverse nations in whose languages the Apostles spread the Word after Pentecost. **Arch between west and central domes**—*Betrayal of Christ, Crucifixion, Marys at the Tomb, Descent into Limbo, Incredulity of Thomas* (all late twelfth century except *Marys*, which is a fifteenth-century copy); these are among the most inventive of all the ancient mosaics, both in terms of their richness of color and their presentation of the intense drama of the events. The **central dome**, a dynamic composition of concentric circles, depicts the *Ascension, Virgin with Angels and Apostles, Virtues and Beatitudes, Evangelists, Four Allegories of the Holy Rivers* (late twelfth century except St Mark and St Matthew, which are mid-nineteenth century); the four allegorical figures shown watering the earth are almost certainly a coded reference to the Christian destiny of the city built on water. **East dome**—*Religion of Christ Foretold by the Prophets* (early to mid-twelfth-century; tondo of Christ Emmanuel restored c.1500). A *Christ Pantocrator* (1506, based on twelfth-century figure) blesses the congregation from the position in the **east apse** traditionally occupied by such figures in Byzantine churches; between the windows below stand the *Four Patron Saints of Venice*, created around 1100 and thus among the earliest works in San Marco. **Arches above north and south singing galleries** (i.e. linking chancel to side chapels)—*Acts from the Lives of St Peter and St Mark* (early twelfth century, altered in nineteenth century); this sequence, mingled with *Scenes from the Life of St Clement*, is continued on the end walls, but is obscured by the organs.

North transept: dome—*Acts of St John the Evangelist* (early to mid-twelfth century); **arch to west of dome** (continued on upper part of adjacent wall)—*Life of the Virgin, Life of the Infant Christ* (late twelfth to early thirteenth century); **arch at north end of transept** (above Cappella di San Isidoro)—*Miracles of Christ* (late twelfth to early thirteenth century). On **wall of north aisle**—five mosaic tablets of *Christ with the Prophets Hosea, Joel, Micah and Jeremiah* (c.1210–30). This series is continued on the **wall of south aisle** with figures of *The Virgin, Isaiah, David, Solomon and Ezekiel*; above these five is the large and complex *Agony in the Garden* (early thirteenth century); Mark's Gospel tells us

THE MOSAICS OF SAN MARCO

1. Arrival of the Body of St. Mark
2. The Creation
3. Noah
4. Madonna, Apostles & Evangelists
5. Abraham
6. Joseph
7. Moses
8. Christ, the Virgin and St. Mark
9. Dome of Pentecost
10. From the Betrayal to the Resurrection
11. Dome of the Ascension
12. Dome of Emmanuel
13. Christ Pantocrator and Patron Saints
14. Lives of St. Mark and St. Peter
15. Dome of St. John
16. Life of the Virgin
17. Christ and Prophets
18. Virgin and Prophets & Agony in the Garden
19. Life of Christ
20. Dome of St. Leonard
21. Parables and Miracles
22. The 'Inventio'
23. The Lives of Christ & John the Baptist
24. Life of St. Mark

that Christ fell on the ground in the Garden of Gethsemane, Matthew describes him falling on his face, and Luke writes that he simply knelt down—the mosaic thus shows Christ in three different positions.

South transept: dome (the *Dome of St Leonard*)—*SS. Nicholas, Clement, Blaise and Leonard* (early thirteenth century), with *St Dorothea* (thirteenth century), *St Erasma* (fifteenth century), *St Euphamia* (fifteenth century) and *St Thecla* (1512) in the **spandrels**. The formality of the mosaics in the **arch between dome and nave**—*Scenes from the Life of Christ* (early twelfth century)—makes a striking contrast with the slightly later scenes on the church's central arch; the depiction of Christ's temptation is especially beautiful, showing the protagonists suspended in a field of pure gold. **Arch above Altar of the Sacrament**—*Parables and Miracles of Christ* (late twelfth century or early thirteenth, restored); **arch in front of Gothic window**—*SS. Anthony Abbot, Bernardino of Siena, Vincent Ferrer and Paul the Hermit* (1458); **west wall of transept**—*Rediscovery of the Body of St Mark* (second half of thirteenth century, restored).

This last picture refers to a miraculous incident known as the *Inventio* (or "Rediscovery"). In 1094 the body of Saint Mark, having been so well hidden during the rebuilding of the Basilica in 1063 that nobody could find it again, interrupted the service of consecration by breaking through the pillar in which it had been buried. The actual pillar is to your right as you enter the Sanctuary, and the very place at which the Evangelist's arm appeared is marked by a marble and mosaic panel.

The Sanctuary and the Pala d'Oro

Steps lead from the south transept up to the **Sanctuary** (L1000), via the **Cappella di San Clemente**, where most of the sculpture is by the **Dalle Masegne** family. On the fronts of the singing galleries next to the rood screen are eight **bronze panels** of *Scenes from the Life of St Mark* by **Sansovino** (1537), who also executed the figures of *The Evangelists* on the balustrade of the high altar. (The other four figures, *The Doctors of the Church*, are seventeenth-century pieces.)

Officially the remains of Saint Mark lie in the sarcophagus underneath the altar, but it's quite likely that the body was actually destroyed in the fire of 976. The altar **baldachin** is supported by four **alabaster columns** carved with mostly indecipherable scenes from the lives of Christ and His Mother; the date of the columns is a matter of intense argument—estimates fluctuate between the fifth and the thirteenth centuries.

Behind the altar, and usually enveloped by a scrim, is the most precious of San Marco's treasures, the **Pala d'Oro** (Golden Altar Screen). Commissioned in 976 in Constantinople, the Pala was enlarged, enriched and rearranged by Byzantine goldsmiths in 1105, then by Venetians in 1209 (to incorporate some less cumbersome loot from the Fourth Crusade) and again (finally) in 1345. The completed screen holds 83 enamel plaques, 74 enamelled roundels, 38 chiselled figures, 300 sapphires, 300 emeralds, 400 garnets, 15 rubies, 1300 pearls and a couple of hundred other stones. The subjects depicted on the screen are impossible to make out if you don't have 40/20 vision and an encyclopaedic knowledge of medieval iconography. Basically, at the top there's the Archangel Michael surrounded by medallions of saints, with *The Entry into Jerusalem, The Crucifixion, The Resurrection, Ascension, Pentecost* and *The Death of the Virgin* to the sides; below, a *Christ Pantocrator* is enclosed by a host of angels, prophets and saints, and on three sides of the border there are scenes from the lives of Christ and Saint Mark. Eighteen small panels representing profane subjects (set into lower part of frame, separated by tiny figures) survive from the first Pala.

Before leaving the Sanctuary, take a look at **Sanovino**'s door to the sacristy (invariably shut)—it incorporates portraits of Titian (top left) and Sansovino himself (under Titian's head).

The Treasury

Tucked into the corner of the south transept is the door of the **Treasury** (L2000), installed in a thick-walled chamber which is perhaps a vestige of the first Palazzo Ducale. A dazzling warehouse of chalices, icons, reliquaries, candelabra and other ecclesiastical appurtenances, it is an unsurpassed collection of Byzantine silver and gold work—a twelfth-century Byzantine incense burner in the shape of a domed church is particularly splendid. Much of the Treasury's stock owes its presence here to the great Constantinople robbery of 1204, and there'd be a lot more of the same on display if the French occupation force of 1797 hadn't given Venice a taste of its own medicine by helping itself to a few cartloads. To be fair to the Venetians, they at least gave the stuff a good home—the French melted down their haul, to produce a yield of 55 gold and silver ingots.

The sanctuary attached to the Treasury, in which are stored over 100 reliquaries, is hardly ever open to the public.

The Baptistery and the Cappella Zen

The **Baptistery** (next to the Treasury, but entered from the south aisle) was altered to its present form by **Doge Andrea Dandolo** (d.1354), whose tomb (facing the door) was Ruskin's favorite monumental sculpture in the city. It was Dandolo who ordered the creation of the Baptistery **mosaics** of *Scenes from the Lives of Christ and John the Baptist*, works in which the formality of Byzantine art is blended with the anecdotal observation of the Gothic. ("The most beautiful symbolic design of the Baptist's death that I know in Italy," wrote Ruskin.) The tomb of Dandolo's predecessor, Doge Giovanni Soranzo (d.1328) is on the right as you come in, and **Jacopo Sansovino**—who designed the enormous font—lies beneath a slab at the eastern end. The huge granite block at the altar is said to have been brought back from Tyre in 1126; more fancifully, it's also claimed as the stone from which Christ addressed the multitude.

In the **Cappella Zen**, adjoining the Baptistery, there's an object of similar mythical potency—a bas-relief of the Virgin that is supposed to have been carved from the rock out of which Moses struck water. As its rich decoration indicates, the portal from the chapel into the narthex used to be the entrance from the Piazzetta; this portico was enclosed in 1504–21 to house the tomb of Cardinal Giambattista Zen, whose estate was left to the city on condition that he was buried within San Marco. The two **mosaic angels** alongside the Virgin on top of the doorway are twelfth-century; the mosaics below are early fourteenth-century and the small statues between them date from the thirteenth. The mosaics on the **vault** show *Scenes from the Life of St Mark* (late thirteenth century, but restored). The Cappella Zen is sometimes known as the *Chapel of the Madonna of the Shoe*, taking its name from the *Virgin and Child* by **Antonio Lombardo** (1506) on the high altar.

Stonework, Carvings, and Icons

Back in the main body of the Basilica, make sure you give the **pavement** a good look—laid out in the twelfth and thirteenth centuries (but patched up frequently since), it's a constantly intriguing patchwork of abstract shapes and religious symbols. Of the church's other marvels, the next couple of paragraphs is but a partial list. The **rood screen** is surmounted by a silver and bronze **cross** (1394) and marble figures of *The Virgin, St Mark and the Apostles* (also 1394) by **Jacobello and Pietro Paolo Dalle Masegne**. The **pulpits** on each side of the screen were assembled in the early fourteenth century from assorted panels, some of them taken from Constantinople; the new doge was presented to the people of Venice from the right-hand pulpit.

Venice's most revered religious image is the **Icon of the Madonna of Nicopeia** (tenth century; in chapel on east side of north transept); until 1204 it was one of the most revered in Constantinople, where it used to be ceremonially carried at the head of the emperor's army. At the north end of this transept is the **Cappella di Sant'Isidoro**: the mosaics, which have scarcely been touched since their creation in the mid-fourteenth century, depict scenes from the life of the saint, whose remains were grabbed from Chios by Doge Domenico Michiel in 1125. A beautiful mid-fifteenth-century mosaic cycle of *Scenes from the Life of the Virgin*, one of the earliest Renaissance works in Venice, is to be seen in the adjacent **Cappella della Madonna dei Mascoli**, which takes its name from the male confraternity that took it over in the seventeenth century. (The Saint Isidore chapel is often closed; the Mascoli chapel is reserved for confessions but can be seen easily from outside.)

Against the west face of the end pillar on the north side of the nave stands **Il Capitello**, a tiny chapel fabricated from a variety of rare marbles to house the *Crucifix* on the altar; the painting arrived in Venice the year after the Nicopeia icon (and came from the same source), and in 1290 achieved its exalted status by spouting blood after an assault on it. Finally, the **galleries** merit a perusal from below (visitors are rarely allowed to walk round them): the parapets facing the aisle consist of reliefs dating from between the sixth and the eleventh century, some of them Venetian, some Byzantine. They weren't designed as catwalks, as they now appear. This is what was left when the original women's galleries (which covered the aisles) were demolished in the late twelfth century to let a bit more light into the building, after some windows had been bricked over to make more surfaces for mosaics. Apart from this, no major structural change has been made to the interior of San Marco since its consecration in 1094.

The Palazzo Ducale

Architecturally, the **Palazzo Ducale** is a unique mixture: the style of its exterior, with its geometrically patterned stonework and continuous tracery walls, can only be called Islamized Gothic, whereas the courtyards and much of the interior are based on Classical forms—a fusion that led Ruskin to declare it "the central building of the world." Certainly it's the finest secular building of its era in Europe, and the central building of Venice. The Palazzo Ducale was far more than the doge's residence—it was the home of all of Venice's governing councils, its law courts, a sizable number of its civil servants and even its prisons. All power in the Venetian Republic and its imperial domains was controlled within this one building.

The Government of Venice

Virtually from the beginning, the **government of Venice** was dominated by the merchant class, despite the existence, in the early years, of nominally democratic assemblies in which the general male populace was represented. The principal governing council evolved into a self-electing body, and in 1297 the exclusion of the public was institutionalized by an act known as the **Serrata del Maggior Consiglio** (Closure of the Great Council). From then onward, any man not belonging to one of the patrician families on the list compiled for the *Serrata* was ineligible to participate in the running of the city. After a while, this list was succeeded by a register of patrician births and marriages called the *Libro d'Oro*, upon which every patrician's claim to membership of the elite was based. By the second decade of the next century, the constitution of Venice had reached a form that was to endure until the coming of Napoleon; its civil and criminal code, defined in the early thirteenth century, was equally resistant to change.

The mythologists of the Republic always made out that its political tranquillity was due to the extraordinary selflessness of the patriciate and the highly developed civic pride of the masses. By the standards of its foreign and imperial exploits, Venice's domestic history seems placid to the point of tedium, but backstage politics were as sordid a business as anywhere else. Cabals of the *Case Grandi* (Great Houses) for centuries had a stranglehold on most influential positions, corruption in various guises was endemic, and voting conspiracies were constantly being hatched and thwarted. Even within the Case Grandi there were vicious struggles for influence, the battle lines being drawn between the *Longhi*, the families who claimed descent from the city's founders, and the *Curti*, whose genealogical tables ran a bit short. An outside observer, exposed to the machinations of Venice's rulers, observed—"They kill not with blood but with ballots."

But the very complexity of the system ensured its stability: power was exercised by a web of councils and committees which no individual could tyrannize. Furthermore, a political career in Venice was a protracted affair: most patricians entered the Maggior Consiglio at 25 (although a group of younger high-fliers was admitted annually) and could not expect a middle-ranking post before 45; from the middle ranks to the top was another long haul—the average age of the doge from 1400 to 1600 was 72. So, as promotion was dependent upon a network of supporters in the upper ranks, and admission to those ranks was barred to the youthful, it was guaranteed that the senior officials would be conservative. Marin Sanudo, in the sixteenth century, summed up the situation when he wrote—"Anyone who wishes to dissent must be mad."

The seeming compliance of the 98 percent of the population that was shut out from active politics is largely explained by the economic cohesion of the city: its governors were also its businessmen and its chief employers, so were unlikely to adopt policies damaging to the financial interests of themselves and their workforce. The paternalism of the Venetian system helped keep things quiet too—the public health measures and emergency plans for bad harvest years were admired throughout Europe. And when, on the odd occasion, the bosses did contemplate measures that would have been unpopular outside the council chambers, there is plenty of evidence that "the murmuring in the city" quickly put them right. In 1510, for example, a massive demonstration in the Piazza persuaded the government that they should imprison the defeated general whose arrest the people were demanding.

The Doge

Regarding the **doge**, it's often said that he was a mere figurehead, confined to his palace under a sort of luxurious house arrest. It's true that there were restrictions on his activities—his letters were read by censors, for example, and he couldn't receive foreign delegations alone—but these were steps taken to reduce the possibility that an ambitious leader might exploit his office, and they didn't always succeed. The dogeship was the monopoly of old men not solely because of the celebrated Venetian respect for the wisdom of the aged, but also because a man in his seventies will have fewer opportunities to abuse his position. So it was that in 1618 a certain Agostino Nani, at 63 the youngest candidate for the dogeship, feigned a life-threatening decrepitude to enhance his chances. Sitting on all the major councils of state and elected for life (whereas his colleagues were elected for terms as brief as a month), the doge was immensely influential in steering policy, and men campaigned for years to increase their chances of getting the job. A neat summary of the doge's powers was made by **Girolamo Priuli**, an exact contemporary of Sanudo—"It is true that if a doge does anything against the Republic, he won't be tolerated; but in everything else, even in minor matters, he does as he pleases."

The Exterior of the Palazzo

Like San Marco, the Palazzo Ducale has been rebuilt many times. The original fortress, founded at the start of the ninth century was razed by the fire of 976, and fire destroyed much of its replacement in 1106. The third palace was habitable within ten years, and was extended and altered frequently over the next couple of centuries. But it was with the construction of a new hall, parallel to the waterfront, for the Maggior Consiglio that the Palazzo began to take on its present shape. Work began in 1340, and the hall was inaugurated in 1419; then, three years later, it was decided to extend the new building along the Piazzetta, and to carry on in the same style. One feature of the exterior gives away the fact that its apparent unity is the product of two distinct phases of building: if you look at the Piazzetta side, you'll notice that the seventh column is fatter than the rest and has a tondo of *Justice* above it—that's where the two stages meet.

A huge restoration project in the 1880s entailed the replacement or repair of every external column of the palace, the opening up of the arcade on the waterfront side (partly blocked up since the 1574 fire—see below) and the repositioning of some of the columns there, and the substitution of copies for some of the thirty-six fourteenth- and fifteenth-century **capitals** of the portico. (It's fairly obvious which are the copies.) Ruskin is at his most fanciful when writing about these carvings, which for him exemplify the transition from the purity of the Gothic (see the heads of children on the fourth capital from the *Drunkenness of Noah*) to the vulgar decadence of the Renaissance (compare the fifteenth-century children, second from the *Porta della Carta*—"capable of becoming nothing but perfumed coxcombs"); if you've got a copy of *The Stones of Venice*, take it with you to the Palazzo Ducale—for all its dottiness, it's still the best guide to the sculpture.

The interventions of restorers are less obtrusive on the late fourteenth-century to early fifteenth-century **corner sculptures**: by the Ponte della Paglia— *Archangel Raphael* and *Drunkenness of Noah*; Piazzetta corner—*Archangel Michael* and *Adam and Eve*; Basilica corner—*Archangel Gabriel* and *Judgement of*

Solomon. Some see these pieces as a cogent sequence, illustrating justice (Solomon) and the counterbalancing qualities of severity (expulsion of Adam and Eve) and compassion (Noah's sons) needed for its administration; Ruskin, naturally, saw things slightly differently—whereas the humble Gothic mind dwells on the frailty of mankind (Noah's intemperance, Adam and Eve's disobedience), the vainglorious Renaissance man celebrates Solomon's God-like wisdom. The **balconied window** on the lagoon side is another contribution from the **Dalle Masegne** family (1404); the corresponding window on the Piazzetta facade is a mid-sixteenth-century imitation.

The principal entrance to the Palazzo—the **Porta della Carta** (its name derives perhaps from the archives kept nearby, or from the clerks' stalls around it)—was commissioned in 1438 by **Doge Francesco Fóscari** from **Bartolomeo and Giovanni Bon**, and is one of the most ornate Gothic works in the city. Many of its carvings used to be painted and gilded, and the lack of color isn't the only respect in which the Porta della Carta differs nowadays from its original state— the figures of Fóscari and his attendant lion are nineteenth-century replicas. The fifteenth-century pieces were smashed to bits in 1797 by the head of the stonemason's guild, who offered to do Napoleon a favor by removing from his sight all images of the lion of Saint Mark. Luckily, his iconoclastic career seems to have ended soon after it began.

The Arco Fóscari and the Courtyard

The passageway into the Palazzo ends under the **Arco Fóscari**, also commissioned from the Bons by Doge Fóscari but finished a few years after his death by **Antonio Rizzo** and **Antonio Bregno**. Rizzo's *Adam* and *Eve*, the best of the Arco Fóscari sculptures, have been replaced by copies—the originals, along with the original of Bandini's late sixteenth-century statue of *Francesco Maria I della Rovere*, (courtyard side) are on show inside. Yet another fire (in 1483) demolished most of the wing in front of you, and led to more work for Rizzo—he designed the enormous, over-ornamented **staircase** (*Scala dei Giganti*) and much of the new wing. Underneath the lion at the top of the staircase is the spot where the new doge was crowned; the ungainly figures of *Neptune* and *Mars* were sculpted in 1566 by **Sansovino**. Reconstruction of the east wing continued under **Pietro Lombardo**, **Spavento** and **Scarpagnino** (who created the *Senators' Courtyard* to the left of the staircase), and finally (c.1600) **Bartolomeo Monopola**, who finished the facade overlooking the Rio di Palazzo and completed the courtyard by extending the arcades along the other two sides.

The Interior

Several sections of the Palazzo Ducale can be dealt with fairly briskly. The building is clad with paintings by the hectare, but a lot of them are just wearying exercises in self-aggrandisement (no city in Italy can match Venice for the narcissism of its art), and if you take away the paintings, there's not much left to some of the rooms. But it seems wilful not to visit so integral a part of the city, and there are parts you will not want to rush. For this reason a visit needs to be timed carefully. In high season scores of tour groups are being propelled round the place by multilingual guides for much of the day. If you want any control over what you get to see, buy your ticket within half an hour of opening, or ninety minutes of closing.

The **opening hours** are as variable as the weather: at the time of writing they are 8:30am to 6:30pm daily from April 1 to mid-October, and 8:30am to 1pm for the rest of the year (L8000, reductions L4000; last admittance 30min before closing). The accessible sections vary too, as restoration work is always taking place somewhere in the building; there is never any indication before you go in as to how much of the building is under wraps, so prepare to be disappointed—you are almost certain to come across scaffolding and plywood barriers at some point.

Up the Scala d'Oro to the Sala delle Quattro Porte

Sansovino's **Scala d'Oro** (stuccoes by Vittoria, c.1558) takes you from the upper arcade to the **primo piano nobile** and the **doge's apartments**. Exhibitions are often held here, and the doors are likely to be locked if there isn't a show on. All the furniture and much of the decoration have been stripped from this floor, but some of the rooms have ornate ceilings and fireplaces, installed when the Lombardo family were in charge of rebuilding this part of the palace. The finest is in the first room, the **Sala degli Scarlatti** (probably named after the scarlet robes of the doge's attendants), which has a fireplace by **Antonio and Tullio Lombardo**, a bas-relief by **Pietro Lombardo** over the door and a gilded ceiling from 1505.

The Scala d'Oro continues up to the **secondo piano nobile**, ending in the **Atrio Quadrato** (ceiling painting of *Justice* by **Tintoretto**), a small anteroom to the first of the great public spaces, the **Sala delle Quattro Porte**. In 1574 a fire gutted this portion of the building, necessitating a major program of reorganization and decoration. (Three years later an even worse blaze destroyed the hall of the Maggior Consiglio and other rooms around it—this is why the Palazzo Ducale contains so few paintings that predate the 1570s.) Before 1574 this room was the meeting place of the Collegio (see below); after the repairs of 1575 it was where ambassadors awaited their summons to address the doge and his councillors. **Tintoretto's** ceiling frescoes, most of which are allegories of the Veneto cities subservient to the Republic, are in a generally woeful condition. The painting opposite the entrance is a reasonably accurate record of the show put on to welcome Henry III of France when he arrived in the city a few weeks before the fire of '74—by all accounts one week of Venetian hospitality put the young king into a lifelong daze. The easel painting at the far end of the room—*Venus Receiving the Homage of Neptune* by **G.B. Tiepolo**—can be seen at closer range when the itinerary doubles back through here.

The Anticollegio and Collegio

As regards the quality of its decorations, the next room—the **Anticollegio** (the inner waiting room)—is one of the richest in the Palazzo Ducale; it has looked like this only since the early eighteenth century, though—after the 1574 fire it was decked out with tapestries and gilded leather (the latter a Venetian specialty). Four pictures by **Tintoretto** hang on the door walls: *Vulcan's Forge, Mercury and the Graces, Bacchus and Ariadne*, and *Minerva Dismissing Mars* (all c.1578); it almost goes without saying that these pictures were open to a propagandist reading—e.g., Ariadne = Venice, Bacchus = Adriatic. Facing the window wall is **Veronese's** characteristically and incongruously benign *Rape of Europa*—"the brightest vision that ever descended upon the soul of a painter," sighed Henry James.

THE PALAZZO DUCALE

SECONDO PIANO NOBILE

1. Scala D'Oro
2. Doge's Apartments
3. Atrio Quadrato
4. Sala delle Quattro Porte
5. Anticollegio
6. Sala del Collegio
7. Sala del Senato
8. Anti-chapel
9. Chapel
10. Sala del Consiglio dei Dieci
11. Sala della Bussola
12. Armoury
13. Scala dei Censori
14. Andito del Maggior Consiglio
15. Sala della Quarantia Civil Vecchia
16. Sala del Guariento
17. Sala del Maggior Consiglio
18. Sala del Quarantia Civil Nuova
19. Sala dello Scrutinio

PRIMO PIANO NOBILE

Thoroughly humbled by now, the emissaries to Venice were ultimately admitted to the **Sala del Collegio**. Presiding over the Senate and deciding the agenda it would discuss, the Full Collegio was the cabinet of Venetian politics, and consisted of the doge, six ducal councillors, the three heads of the judiciary, and sixteen *Savi* (senators with special responsibility for maritime, military and governmental affairs). The *Signoria*, Venice's highest executive body, was the inner council of this inner council, comprising the Collegio minus the *Savi*. In Ruskin's opinion, in no other part of the palace could you "enter so deeply into the heart of Venice" as in the Sala del Collegio, but his observation referred not to the mechanics of Venetian power but to the luscious cycle of ceiling paintings by **Veronese**. (Outstanding is *Venice Triumphant*—central panel above throne.) Veronese also produced the picture on the wall over the throne—*Doge Sebastiano Venier Offering Thanks to Christ for the Victory of Lepanto*.

The Sala del Senato

The room next door—the **Sala del Senato**—was where most major policies, both domestic and foreign, were determined. It was also where the ambassadors of Venice delivered their reports on the countries in which they had served. These *relazioni* were essential to the formation of foreign policy, and a Venetian nobleman did his career prospects no harm by turning in a detailed document; few, however, equaled the conscientiousness of the sixteenth-century ambassador to France whose speech to the Senate kept them in their seats for two whole days. The Senate originally comprised sixty councillors invited to take the higher office by the doge (hence the alternative name *Sala dei Pregadi*, from *pregati*, "invited") but eventually grew to contain almost 300 officials under the doge's chairmanship. A motley collection of late sixteenth-century artists, Tintoretto and his pupils prominent among them, produced the mechanically bombastic decoration of the walls and ceiling. Tintoretto's personal touch is most evident in the picture above the throne: *Descent from the Cross, with Doges Pietro Lando and Marcantonio Trevisan*. (Sometimes the doors to the side of the the throne are open—they lead to the doge's chapel and its anteroom; only the marble *Virgin and Child* by **Sansovino**, in the former, is of interest.)

The Council of Ten

After recrossing the Sala delle Quattro Porte you enter the **Sala del Consiglio dei Dieci**, the room in which all matters relating to state security were discussed. The Council of Ten was established in 1310 in response to the revolt of disaffected nobles led by Bajamonte Tiepolo—and the secrecy and the speed of its deliberations, and the fact it allowed no defense counsel, soon made it the most feared of the Republic's institutions. Its members held office for one year and their number was supplemented by the doge and the ducal councillors—which meant, confusingly, that the Ten were never fewer than seventeen. In the sixteenth century the Ten became even stronger as a result of the War of the League of Cambrai, which saw places on the Senate taken by a bunch of social climbers as reward for the loans they'd made for the war effort. The men of the *Case Grandi* retaliated by increasing the power of the bodies they could still control—the Collegio and the Ten. Only in the seventeenth century, when the power of the old families was weakened by the sale of places on the Maggior Consiglio, did the Senate revert to being the nucleus of the Venetian state. Of the paintings here, the finest are a couple of **Veronese** panels on the ceiling, painted at the age of 25—*Juno Offering Gifts to Venice* and *Old Man in Oriental Costume with Young Woman*. The central panel is a copy of a Veronese original that was packed off to the Louvre by Napoleon and has never made it back.

The unfortunates who were summoned before the Ten had to await their grilling in the next room, the **Sala della Bussola**; in the wall is a *Bocca di Leone* (Lion's Mouth), one of the boxes into which citizens could drop denunciations for the attention of the Ten and other state bodies. Nobody could be convicted without corroborating evidence, and anonymous accusations were rejected, but nonetheless the legend spread throughout Europe that one word to the Ten was tantamount to a death sentence. The door in the corner leads to the office of the Three Heads of the Council of Ten, which in turn lead to the State Inquisitors' room, then on to the torture chamber and finally the prisons—a doleful route that can be followed on the *Itinerari Segreti* (see below). As for the decoration, the last sentence of the previous paragraph applies.

The Armoury and the Andito del Maggior Consiglio

From the landing, steps lead up to the four rooms of the **armory**, consisting in part of weapons assembled for the defense of the Palazzo Ducale, and in part of specially commissioned pieces and gifts from foreign rulers. You don't need an interest in militaria to be impressed by some of the items, such as the unique fourteenth-century beaked helmet in room 1, or the white armor given to Henry IV of France in 1603 (room 2). But if any section of the Palazzo is going to be shut because of staff shortages, this is it.

The **Scala dei Censori** takes you back to the second floor; here you go along the **Andito del Maggior Consiglio** (Lobby of the Great Council) past the **Sala della Quarantia Civil Vecchia**, the seat of the civil court, and the **Sala del Guariento**, the old ammunition store, containing the remnants of a fourteenth-century fresco by Guariento which used to be in Sala del Maggior Consiglio. The veranda at the end now houses the sculptures by **Rizzo** and Bandini from the Arco Fóscari; allegedly, the Duke of Mantua offered to buy Rizzo's *Eve* for her weight in gold, but for once the Venetians found the prospect of huge sums of money resistible.

The Sala del Maggior Consiglio

Now comes the stupendous **Sala del Maggior Consiglio**, the assembly hall of all the Venetian patricians eligible to participate in the running of the city. By the mid-sixteenth century 2500 men were entitled to sit here, but frequently as few as half that number were present. This was the forum of the so-called *giovani*, the younger men on the bottom rung, and it was here that the voice of the populace filtered into the system. Technically, the Maggior Consiglio had little direct impact on government—it voted directly only on administrative legislation—and for much of the time the *giovani* were eager to stay on the right side of the power-brokers and so kept fairly quiet. But if the bosses did something that alienated the majority of the underlings, the Maggior Consiglio was able to make things awkward, because the electoral process for nearly all state officials, including the doge, began here. Its last political act was the vote of May 12, 1797, when it put an end to Venice's independence by voting to accept Napoleon's constitution.

The disastrous fire of December 1577 destroyed the paintings by Bellini, Titian, Carpaccio, Veronese and others which had lined this room; most of the replacements have the sole merit of covering a lot of space. There are, of course, notable exceptions. The immense *Paradiso*, begun at the age of 77 by **Tintoretto** and completed by his son **Domenico**, is an amazing feat of pictorial organization and a perfect work for its setting; and two of the **ceiling panels** are well worth a crick in the neck—*The Apotheosis of Venice*, a late work by **Veronese** (large oval above tribune), and *Venice Welcoming the Conquered Nations* by **Palma il Giovane** (large oval at opposite end). Tintoretto was commissioned to replace the room's **frieze of portraits** of the first 76 doges (the series continues in the *Sala dello Scrutinio*), but in the event his son (with assistants) did the work. On the Piazzetta side the sequence is interrupted by a painted black veil, marking the place where **Marin Falier** would have been honored had he not conspired against the state in 1355 and (as the lettering on the veil says) been beheaded for his crime. After two years spent in the city, Byron wrote that Falier's black veil was for him the city's most memorable image. (For more on Falier's treason, see "Palazzo Falier" entry in Chapter Five.)

Falier remains the most celebrated of Venice's errant leaders, but he is far from being alone in the ranks of the disgraced—by the end of the twelfth century about half of the doges had been killed, exiled or simply run out of office. Nor is he the only eminent Venetian to be posthumously vilified in such a manner: for instance, under the arcade of the Palazzo Ducale you can find a plaque perpetuating the dishonor of Girolamo Loredan and Giovanni Contarini, exiled for abandoning their fort to the Turks. In the Venetian republic, where staunch service to the state was regarded as a duty, the backsliders were the ones singled out for special treatment—as nearly every writer on Venice has remarked, the city is almost devoid of public monuments to its great statesmen.

The Sala della Quarantia Civil Nuova and Sala dello Scrutinio

The door at the far end opens into the **Sala della Quarantia Civil Nuova**, where civil cases involving Venetian citizens outside the city were heard; it retains the only examples of Venetian gilt leatherwork left in the building, though nothing really grabs the attention. From here you pass into the **Sala dello Scrutinio**, the room in which votes by the Maggior Consiglio were counted and certain electoral committees met. The system for electing the doge was highly complex. In a nutshell: 30 men were selected by lot from the Maggior Consiglio; they reduced themselves by lot to 9 members; they elected 40, who reduced themselves to 12, who elected 25, who reduced themselves to 9, who elected 45, who reduced themselves to 11, who elected 41, who finally elected the doge by at least 25 votes. This rigmarole could last quite a while, you might think, and you'd be right—it took a minimum of five days, and in the record-breaking 1615 election the last stage alone went to 104 ballots, and lasted 24 days. And this intricately democratic machinery was in fact extremely undemocratic—everyone had an equal chance of getting through the first lottery, but only those with a lot of friends and hangers-on could expect to be nominated to the decisive committees. Perhaps to ensure that the electoral colleges kept their minds on the job, the decoration of the room is pretty dreary; among the celebrations of great moments in Venetian military history is one decent picture—*The Conquest of Zara*, a late **Tintoretto** painting (first on right). The frieze of the last 42 doges was begun by assistants of Tintoretto and continued by contemporaries of each of the doges.

The Prisons and the Loggia

Sometimes visits are directed down the staircase from the Sala dello Scrutinio, but more often you have to backtrack through the Sala del Maggior Consiglio to the Scala dei Censori, following it down to to the **Ponte dei Sospiri** (Bridge of Sighs) and the **Prigioni** (Prisons). The bridge was built in 1600 by Antonio Contino, and takes its popular name from the sighs of the prisoners who shuffled through its corridor. In reality, though, not a lot of sighing went on here. Before the construction of these cells in the early seventeenth century, prisoners were kept in the **Piombi** (the Leads), under the roof of the Palazzo Ducale, or in the **Pozzi** (the Wells) in the bottom two storeys. This new block was occupied mainly by petty criminals—political prisoners were still incarcerated in the Piombi, and a few hard cases went to the Pozzi.

After recrossing the bridge, you leave the building through the offices of the **Avogaria**, the officers who, from the sixteenth century onwards, prepared the documents for the courts. Before leaving the building altogether, take a turn round the upper **loggia** of the palace (staircase on Piazzetta side of courtyard)— it's a good place from which to look at the Porta della Carta, and a relatively peaceful vantage point for the Bacino di San Marco. In its middle section the loggia widens out, and on some of the columns you'll see painted coats of arms of the ducal families: this is where the guilds of Venice were invited to display their wares after the coronation of the dogaressa—if you look carefully you'll find the word *spaderi* on one of them, marking the sword-makers' pitch.

The Itinerari Segreti

If you want to see the rooms in which the day-to-day administration of Venice took place, take the **Itinerari Segreti del Palazzo Ducale**, a guided tour through the warren of offices and passageways that interlocks with the public rooms of the building. The myriad councils and committees of Venice required a vast civil service, which was staffed by men drawn from the social class immediately below the patriciate—the *cittadini originarii*. (To be accepted into this class of full citizens one had to have lived in Venice for 25 years and never engaged in manual labor.) Roaming through the shadow-palace in which these functionaries carried out their duties, you begin to understand why, for all the Palazzo Ducale's extravagant show of democratic rectitude, the Venetian republic aroused in many people the sort of dread a police state inspires.

The tour begins with the magnificently restored chambers of the Chancellery, the rooms in which all acts of state were drafted and tabulated. Then it's onward into the belly of the beast, through the judiciary's suites and into a high-ceilinged den where a rope hangs between two tiny wooden cells—the idea being that their two occupants, hearing the screams of the suspended victim, would need no farther encouragement to talk. Paintings by Veronese, Tintoretto and Hieronymus Bosch provide a civilizing gloss in the **Sala dei Tre Capi**—for the Heads of the Council of Ten—and the **Sala degli Inquisitori**—for the officers who investigated charges of treason.

After these, you're led up into the roof, to see the timber-lined **Piombi**. By the standards of the day they are not too grim, but there's a typically Venetian touch of refined malevolence—the doors have a superfluity of locks, just so that the noise of turning keys and slamming bolts would impress upon the inmate the finality of his incarceration. A few recalcitrant cases were not deterred—you're shown the cell from which Casanova escaped in 1775, by burrowing through the floor. Under the rafters there's a museum of Venetian history that deserves more time than is allotted for it, but you do have time to be stunned by the views from the portholes in the roof. And if you wondered, when you were in the Sala del Maggior Consiglio, how the hell the ceiling stayed up with no visible means of support, all is revealed near the end.

At L5000 the tour's not cheap, and the guide speaks only Italian, but if you can afford it and can understand even a little of the language, then go—few guided tours can be more enjoyable. Tours begin daily at 10am and noon (sometimes more frequently), and they last about an hour and a half; tickets must be booked at least a day in advance (three or four in summer), either by stopping by in person at the administration offices on the first floor of the Palazzo (on left just before the Scala d'Oro), or by phoning ☎5204287.

OUT FROM THE PIAZZA

From the Piazza the bulk of the pedestrian traffic flows **north to the Rialto** along the **Mercerie**, the most aggressive shopping mall in Venice and the part of the city which comes closest to being devoid of magic. Apart from the church of **San Giuliano**—one of Venice's lesser eccentricities—only the stately **San Salvatore** provides a diversion from the spotlights and price tags until you come to the **Campo San Bartolomeo**, the forecourt of the Rialto bridge and the locals' favored spot for an after-work drink and chat. Another lively square at the end of the day is the **Campo San Luca**, within a minute's stroll of *Al Volto*, the best-stocked *enoteca* (wine bar) in town. Secreted in the folds of the alleyways are the old Armenian quarter and the spiralling **Scala del Bovolo**—featured on a thousand postcards, but actually seen by a minority of visitors. And slotted away in a tiny square close to the Canal Grande you'll find the most delicate of Venice's museum buildings—the Palazzo Pésaro degli Orfei, home of the **Museo Fortuny**.

Leaving the Piazza **by the west side**, through the colonnade of the Ala Napoleonica, you enter another major shopping district, but one which presents a contrast to the frenetic and tawdry Mercerie: here the clientele are drawn almost exclusively from the city's well-heeled, or from the four-star tourists staying in the hotels that overlook the end of the Canal Grande. To a high proportion of visitors, this part of the city is just **the route to the Accademia**—many pass through with their noses buried in their maps, and hardly break step before they reach the bridge over the Canal Grande. It's true that none of the top-flight attractions are here and that much of the northern part of the area offers little but the pleasure of wandering through its alleyways, but there are things to see apart from the latest creations from Milan and Paris—the extraordinary Baroque facades of **Santa Maria Zobenigo** and **San Moisè**, for instance, or the graceful **Santo Stefano**, which rises at the end of one of the largest and most attractive squares in Venice. And two of the city's most stylish artistic venues lie within this district: **La Fenice**, an opera house so opulent as to be almost a parody of the genre; and the **Palazzo Grassi**, an exhibition center with just about the highest production values in Italy.

North from the Piazza

The **Mercerie**, a chain of streets that starts under the Torre dell'Orologio and finishes at the Campo San Bartolomeo, is the most direct route between the Rialto and San Marco and as the main land thoroughfare of the city has always been a prime site for its shopkeepers. (Each of the five links in the chain is a *merceria*: Merceria dell'Orologio, di San Zulian, del Capitello, di San Salvador and 2 Aprile.) A wide-eyed inventory of the Mercerie in the sixteenth century noted "tapestry, brocades and hangings of every design, carpets of all sorts, camlets of every color and texture, silks of every variety; and so many warehouses full of spices, groceries and drugs, and so much beautiful white wax!" Nowadays it's both slick and tacky: the empire of kitsch has a firm foothold here and in tributaries such as Calle Larga San Marco and Calle Canonica, sharing the territory with the likes of Benetton, Lacoste, Gucci and Cartier. The mixture ensnares more window-shoppers and buyers than any other part of Venice, and even in the off-season a stroll along the Mercerie is akin to a slalom run. In summer things get so bad that the police sometimes enforce a pedestrian one-way system.

For those immune to the charms of consumerism there are only a couple of things to stop for between the San Marco end of the Mercerie and the church of San Salvatore. Over the Sottoportego del Cappello (first left after the Torre) is a **relief** known as *La Vecia del Morter* (the Old Woman of the Mortar). The event it commemorates happened on the night of June 15, 1310, when the occupant of this house, an old woman named Giustina Rossi, looked out of her window and saw a contingent of Bajamante Tiepolo's rebel army passing below. Possibly by accident, she knocked from the sill a stone mortar which landed on the skull of the standard-bearer, killing him outright. Seeing the flag go down, Tiepolo's troops panicked and fled back towards the Rialto. (Scores of other rebels were killed in the Piazza—those ringleaders who survived the carnage were punished with execution or exile.) Asked what she would like as her reward for her patriotic intervention, Giustina requested permission to hang the Venetian flag from her window on feast-days, and a guarantee that her rent would never be raised; both requests were granted.

Further on is the church of **San Giuliano** (or San Zulian), rebuilt in the mid-sixteenth century with the generous aid of **Tommaso Rangone**, a physician whose munificence and intellectual brilliance are advertised by the inscriptions on the facade and by **Sansovino**'s portrait statue above the door. (Venice in Peril is now undertaking a major restoration of the exterior.) The central panel of the ceiling, *St Julian in Glory* by **Palma il Giovane** and assistants, is a cut above the man's general standard; over the first altar on the right is a late work by **Veronese**—*Pietà with SS. Roch, Jerome and Mark*; and in the chapel to the left of the chancel there are ceiling stuccoes by **Vittoria**, and three pieces by **Campagna**—terracotta figures of *The Virgin* and *The Magdalen*, and a marble altar panel (all from c.1583).

Obscure corners are to be discovered even in the vicinity of this main avenue. Very close to San Giuliano is the heart of the old Armenian quarter: take the bridge that comes into the Campo San Zulian opposite the church, into Calle Fiubera, and then take the first right—Calle degli Armeni. Under the *sottoportego* is the door to the best-hidden church in Venice, **Santa Croce degli Armeni**,

NORTH OF THE PIAZZA

which was founded as an oratory in 1496 and rebuilt as the community's church in 1688. Nowadays the congregation is small and the most visible Armenian community is the monastic one on the island of San Lazzaro degli Armeni— covered in Chapter Nine.

San Salvatore and its Campo

At the far end, the Mercerie veers right at the church of **San Salvatore**. The facade, applied in 1663, is less interesting than the interior, which was begun around 1508 by **Spavento** and continued by **Tullio Lombardo** and **Sansovino**. It's cleverly designed in the form of three domed Greek crosses placed end to end, thus creating the longitudinal layout required by the religious orders while paying homage to the centrally planned churches of Byzantium and, of course, to the Basilica di San Marco.

In the middle of the right-hand wall stands the **tomb of Doge Francesco Venier**, designed by **Sansovino**, who also sculpted the figure of *Faith* on the right (possibly his last sculpture). To the left hangs **Titian**'s *Annunciation* (1566), signed *"Fecit, fecit,"* supposedly to emphasize the wonder of his continued creativity; the ungainly angel is often held to be the fault of assistants. A scrap of paper on the rail in front of the picture records the death of the artist on August 25, 1576. The end of the right transept is filled by the **tomb of Caterina Cornaro**, one of the saddest figures in Venetian history. Born into one of Venice's preeminent families, she became Queen of Cyprus by marriage, and after her husband's death was forced to surrender the strategically crucial island to the doge. On her return to Venice she was led in triumph up the Canal Grande, as though her abdication had been entirely voluntary, and then was presented with possession of the town of Ásolo as a token of the city's gratitude. She died in 1510 and was given a heroine's funeral in the Apostoli church, her body being removed to San Salvatore, and this tomb erected, at the end of the century. (For her full story, see the "Ásolo" entry in the mainland section.)

The **altarpiece**, a *Transfiguration* by **Titian** (c.1560), covers a fourteenth-century silver reredos, and if you ask the sacristan nicely, he'll lower the picture to reveal it. Your L200 coin for the *Tranfiguration* also lights up an excellent painting from the workshop of Giovanni Bellini—*The Supper at Emmaus*. **Vittoria** designed the third altar of the left aisle (the altar of the sausagemakers' guild) and sculpted its figures of *St Roch and St Sebastian*. In front of the main altar, a glass disc set into the sidewalk allows you to see a recently unearthed merchant's tomb, with badly damaged decoration by Titian's brother Francesco.

Next door to the church is the former monastery, now the local headquarters of SIP (the phone company); the man at the desk might allow you a look at the beautiful **cloisters**, attributed to **Sansovino**. Overlooking the campo is the home of the last of the major scuole to be established, the **Scuola di San Teodoro**, which was founded 1530; the facade was designed in 1655 by Sardi, the architect responsible for the front of San Salvatore. After several years as a cinema, it's now a general purpose exhibition hall. The column in the center of the campo is a memorial to the revolt of 1848–49 and was placed here on the 50th anniversary of the insurrection.

Campo San Bartolomeo

The **Campo San Bartolomeo**, terminal of the Mercerie, is at its best in the evening, when it's as packed as any bar in town—the hum of voices can be picked up from a hundred meters away. To show off their new wardrobe the Venetians take themselves off to the Piazza, but Campo San Bartolomeo is the spot to head for if they just want to meet friends and talk. For a crash-course in the Venetian character, hang around the statue of the writer Goldoni at around 7pm. A handful of functional bars are scattered about, but it's really the atmosphere you come for.

The restoration of the **church of San Bartolomeo** has been going on for years, but has progressed far enough for the building to be opened for the occasional exhibition. For the foreseeable future, though, its notable paintings—organ panels by Sebastiano del Piombo—will remain in the Accademia; its most famous picture, the altarpiece painted by Dürer in 1505 at the request of the German merchant Christopher Fugger, long ago migrated to Prague. In the sixteenth century this area would have been swarming with men like Dürer's patron, as the base for the German traders was the **Fondaco dei Tedeschi**, now the main post office, at the far end of the campo. (For more on the Fondaco, see Chapter Seven.)

Campo San Luca and Around

If the crush of Bartolomeo is too much for you, you can retire to the **Campo San Luca** (past the front of San Salvatore and straight on), another open-air social center, but not as much of a pressure-cooker as San Bartolomeo. From Campo San Luca, Calle Goldoni is a direct route back to the Piazza, via the Bacino Orseolo—the city's major gondola depot, and one of the few places where you can admire the streamlining and balance of the boats without being hassled by their owners. Calle dei Fuseri leads down to the smart Frezzeria (its name derived from the arrow-makers who worked there), which takes you in one direction to La Fenice and in the other to the area just west of the Piazza.

Unusually, the church of **San Luca** is not on the campo named after it, but on a *campiello* some way off, down Salizzada San Luca, then right and then left. Somewhere in the church is buried a writer whose name would have been known to all Venetians in the mid-sixteenth century—**Pietro Aretino**. Nicknamed "The Scourge of Princes," Aretino milked a hefty income from the rulers of a dozen states, who coughed up either in response to his flattery or out of terror at the damage that his tongue could do. So adept was he at juggling his various sponsors that he managed simultaneously to be on the payroll of Emperor Charles V and his enemy King Francis I of France. With Sansovino and Titian (who painted his portrait many times and used him as a model for Pontius Pilate) he formed a clique that dominated artistic circles in the city and made life intolerable for anyone they didn't like—both Lorenzo Lotto and Pordenone suffered at their hands. Aretino's notoriety rested as much on his dubious morals as on his scurrilous poetry and brilliant letters (which were a Venetian bestseller); some idea of the man is given by the popular story that he died as a result of his uncontrollable laughter at a filthy story about his own sister. Today there's not even a tombstone left to mark his existence. The church itself is a drab nineteenth-century reconstruction, and its one picture of any importance—*The Virgin and St Luke* by **Veronese** (on high altar)—is in a ruinous state.

Campo Manin: the Aldine Press and Manin's Rebellion

Apart from Aretino and the altogether more proper Cardinal Bembo, Renaissance Venice produced virtually no writers—and yet it was the greatest printing center in Italy. By the second half of the sixteenth century there were over one hundred presses in Venice, and their output was more than three times greater than that of Rome, Florence and Milan added together. The doyen of Venetian printers was **Aldus Manutius**, publisher of the very first pocket editions of the classics, whose workshop stood on the site of the modern Cassa di Risparmio building on the edge of **Campo Manin**. Founded in 1490, the Aldine Press employed teams of printers, die-cutters, proofreaders and compositors, but was always on the lookout for casual labor, as the sign over the door made clear—"Whoever you are, Aldus earnestly begs you to state your business in the fewest words possible and begone, unless, like Hercules to weary Atlas, you would lend a helping hand. There will always be enough work for you and all who pass this way." Erasmus once begrudgingly did a stint here, when the Aldine workshop was producing an edition of his *Proverbs*.

The square was enlarged in 1871 to make room for the monument to **Daniele Manin**, the lawyer who led the revolt of 1848–49; his statue looks towards his house alongside the left-hand bridge. Under Manin's control the provisional government of Venice was run with exemplary efficiency—a legislative assembly was set up, a new currency printed, and even a newspaper was circulated. In the course of the Austrian blockade Venice became the first city ever to be bombarded from the air, when explosives attached to balloons were floated over the city. The damage caused by this ploy was not too substantial, but inevitably the resistance was short-lived, and on August 23, 1849, weakened by hunger and disease, the Venetians surrendered. Manin and the other leaders of the uprising died in exile.

The Scala del Bovolo, the Museo Fortuny, and San Benedetto

On the wall of the alley on the south side of Campo Manin, a sign directs you to the staircase known as the **Scala del Bovolo** (a *bovolo* is a snail shell in Venetian dialect). External staircases, developed originally as a way of saving space inside the building, were a common feature of Venetian houses into the sixteenth century, but this specimen, dating from around 1500, is the most flamboyant variation on the theme. The collection of wellheads in the garden (the oldest is eleventh-century) is one of the spots where cat-lovers are certain to be able to observe the scrawny Venetian species.

The fifteenth-century Palazzo Pésaro degli Orfei, now the **Museo Fortuny** (Tues–Sun 9am–7pm; L5000), is close at hand, hidden away in a campo you'd never accidentally pass—take either of the bridges out of the Campo Manin, turn at the first right, and keep going. In addition to making his famous pleated silk dresses (fine enough to be threaded through a wedding ring, it's claimed), **Mariano Fortuny** (1871–1949) was a painter, architect, engraver, photographer, theater designer and sculptor. The museum reflects his versatility, but you'll probably come out thinking that he's best known for what he was best at. The top floor houses a collection of paintings by Virgilio Guidi (1892–1983), about which the kindest comment would be that they are no worse than Fortuny's. Design and photography exhibitions are often held here, and as a rule are more interesting than the permanent displays—if the show's particularly good, you'll have to wait in line, as the palace is so fragile that only a few people at a time are allowed in.

The church of **San Benedetto**—founded in eleventh century, rebuilt 1685—gangs up with Fortuny's house to overwhelm the little square. It has a few good pictures: *St Sebastian* by **Strozzi** (second altar on right); two paintings of *St Benedict* by **Mazzoni** (over doors to side of high altar; 1649); and *St Francis of Paola* by **G.B. Tiepolo** (first altar on left; mid-eighteenth century). Finding this church open is a matter of chance—late afternoon is normally a good bet.

West of the Piazza

Heading west from the Piazza, on the road to the Accademia, you soon pass on the left the **Calle del Ridotto**, named after the most notorious of Venice's gambling dens, which operated from 1638 to 1774 in the Palazzo Dandolo (no. 1332). Gamblers of all social classes were welcome at the *Ridotto*—as long as they wore masks—but most of the clients came from the nobility. The consequent damage to the financial resources of the Venetian upper class became so great that the government was finally forced to close the joint. There was, though, no shortage of alternative houses in which to squander the legacy—in 1797 there were 136 gambling establishments in the city. The modern visitor to Venice can get the frisson of self-induced bankruptcy by nipping into *Harry's Bar*, right by the landing stage in the nearby Calle Vallaresso, and ordering a *Bellini* (Prosecco and fruit juice) and one of the fabled sandwiches. The eponymous Harry once borrowed some money from a barman named Giuseppe Cipriani, later repaying the loan threefold; Cipriani – later Venice's most famous hotelier – named his new bar after him in gratitude. Hemingway did some celebrated boozing here, but only the wealthiest inebriates should contemplate emulating him.

The first church you come across is **San Moisè** (daily 3:30–7pm), runaway winner of any poll for the ugliest church in Venice. (Its neighbor, the *Hotel Bauer-Grünwald*, would corner several votes for the Worst Building in All Categories.) The church's name means "Saint Moses," the Venetians here following the Byzantine custom of canonizing Old Testament figures. Its facade sculpture, featuring a species of camel unknown to zoology, was created in 1668 by **Heinrich** (or Enrico or Arrigo) **Meyring**; and if you think this display of bloated fauna and flora is in questionable taste, wait till you see the miniature mountain he carved as the main altarpiece, representing *Mount Sinai with Moses Receiving the Tablets*. In the sacristy you'll find a fine example of comparatively restrained proto-Baroque—a bronze altar panel of the *Deposition* by **Niccolò and Sebastiano Roccatagliata**.

If you're looking for an escritoire for your drawing room, an oriental carpet for the reception area, a humble Dutch landscape, a new Kenzo outfit, or simply an exquisite piece of leather, then you'll probably find what you're after on the broad **Calle Larga XXII Marzo**, which begins over the canal from San Moisè. Many of the streets off the western side of the Piazza are similarly dedicated to the beautification of the prosperous and their dwellings, with names such as Versace, Armani, Missoni and Gigli lurking round every corner.

Campo San Fantin and La Fenice

Halfway along the Calle Larga XXII Marzo, on the right, is the Calle del Sartor da Veste, which takes you over a canal and into the Campo San Fantin. The church of **San Fantin**, begun in 1507 by **Scarpagnino**, has a graceful domed apse, built in 1549–63 to plans by **Sansovino**. On the far side of the campo is the home of the **Ateneo Veneto**, a cultural institution which organizes some of Venice's more arcane exhibitions. The building was formerly occupied by a confraternity whose main service to the community was to comfort those sentenced to death—hence the name by which it was generally known: the Scuola della Buona Morte. Part of the scuola's collection of works of art has been dispersed, but pieces by Veronese and Alessandro Vittoria, among others, are still in the building; if you ask at the door in Calle della Verona you might be allowed a look, but the request could well be met with a reminder that the building is private property.

Inaugurated on December 26, 1792, the **Teatro la Fenice** (facing San Fantin) is Venice's oldest and largest theater. **Giannantonio Selva**'s gaunt Neoclassical design was not deemed a great success when it was unveiled, but nonetheless very little of the exterior was changed when the place had to be rebuilt after a fire in 1836. More extensive changes were made to the interior, a luxuriant late-Empire confection of gilt, plush and stucco; smile sweetly and the doorman might be persuaded to let you look in at the 1500-seat auditorium. La Fenice has seen some significant musical events this century—Stravinsky's *The Rake's Progress* and Britten's *The Turn of the Screw* were both premiered here—but the music scene was more exciting in the nineteenth century, when, in addition to being the first opera house to produce several operas by Rossini, Bellini and Verdi, it became the focal point for protests against the occupying Austrian army. Favorite forms of nationalist expression included bombarding the stage with bouquets in the colors of the Italian tricolor, and yelling "Viva Verdi!" at strategic points in the performance—the composer's name being the acronym for *Vittorio Emanuele, Re D'Italia* (Vittorio Emanuele, King of Italy).

Santa Maria Zobenigo and San Maurizio

Back on the main road to the Accademia, another extremely odd church awaits—**Santa Maria Zobenigo**. It was actually consecrated as Santa Maria del Giglio (. . . of the Lily), but its alternative title—derived from the name of the Jubanico family, who founded it in the ninth century—is more commonly used. You can stare at the front of this church all day and still you won't find a single unequivocally Christian image. The main statues are of the five Barbaro brothers, who financed the rebuilding of the church in 1678; Virtue, Honor, Fame and Wisdom hover at a respectable distance; and relief maps at eye level depict the towns distinguished with the brothers' presence in the course of their military and diplomatic careers. Antonio Barbaro—the central figure and chief benefactor of the church—was not rated quite so highly by his superiors as he was by himself: he was dismissed from Francesco Morosini's fleet for incompetence. The interior, full to bursting with devotional pictures and sculptures, overcompensates for the impiety of the exterior. A *Madonna and Child* in the sacristy is implausibly attributed to Rubens, but the eighteenth-century *Stations of the Cross* (by various artists) in the body of the church have a better claim on your attention, as do the

Evangelists by **Tintoretto** behind the altar. The detached one-story shop right by the church occupies the stump of the campanile, pruned to its current dimensions in 1774. The tilting campanile of Santo Stefano (see below) soon looms into view over the vapid church of **San Maurizio**, a collaboration between **Giannantonio Selva** and **Antonio Diedo**, secretary of the Accademia. The inside of the church has nothing to recommend it, and the exterior is overshadowed by the fifteenth-century Palazzo Zaguri, on the campo's east side. This district is the antiques center of Venice and from time to time the Campo San Maurizio is taken over by an antiques and bric-a-brac fair. One of the nostalgia industry's permanent representatives is *V. Trois*, where they sell the Fortuny-designed fabrics still manufactured over on La Giudecca.

If you wander off the campo down Calle del Dose you'll come to a short fondamenta on the Canal Grande, with fabulous views of its lower reach. Continuing along the Accademia route, at the beginning of Calle del Piovan stands a diminutive building that was once the **Scuola degli Albanesi**; it was established in 1497 and the reliefs on the facade date from shortly after that. In 1504 Carpaccio produced a cycle of *Scenes from the Life of the Virgin* for the Scuola, and the pictures remained here even after the declining Albanian community led to the disbanding of the confraternity in the late eighteenth century; it wasn't until 1808, when the baker's guild that had moved into the building was itself scrapped, that the series was broken up. The bits that remained in Venice are now in the Correr collection and the Ca' d'Oro.

Stop for a second on the bridge just after the Scuola, and look down the canal—you'll see that it runs right under the east end of Santo Stefano, the only church in Venice to have quite so intimate a relationship with the city's waterways.

Campo Francesco Morosini

The church of Santo Stefano closes one end of the next square—the **Campo Francesco Morosini** (or Santo Stefano). Large enough to hold several clusters of tourists, a few dozen café tables plus a kids' soccer match or two, the campo is always lively but never feels crowded; provided you're willing to do battle against the rapacious pigeons, a picnic can be spread around the wellhead or the base of the statue of Nicolò Tommaseo (an important Risorgimento idealogue)—and there's an additional inducement to sit down for a while in the form of *Paolin*, purveyors of the city's ultimate pistachio ice cream. One of the city's sunniest spots, this used to be one of its bloodiest—it was a popular bullfighting arena until 1802, when the collapse of a bank of seats killed a number of spectators and provoked an absolute ban on such events.

The campo takes its name from **Francesco Morosini**, who lived at the Canal Grande end of the square at no. 2802. The last doge to serve as military commander of the Republic (1688–94), Morosini became a Venetian hero with his victories in the Peloponnese (in southern Greece), as is attested by the triumphal arch built in his honor in the Palazzo Ducale's Sala dello Scrutinio, and the exhaustive documentation of his career in the Correr museum. But to those few non-Venetians to whom his name means anything at all, he's known as the goon who lobbed a missile through the roof of the Parthenon, detonating the Turkish gunpowder barrels that had been stored there. He then made matters even worse by trying to prise some of the decoration off the half-wrecked temple, shattering great chunks of statuary in the process. Morosini and Venice didn't come back from that campaign empty handed though—the Arsenale gate is guarded by two of his trophies (see Chapter Six).

San Vitale and the Palazzo Pisani

Right at the end of the campo, past the elongated **Palazzo Loredan** (originally fifteenth century but rebuilt c.1540; facade towards Santo Stefano added in 1618), stands the deconsecrated church of **San Vitale** (or Vidal). It's now a private art gallery, but has somehow hung onto a painting by **Carpaccio** of *San Vitale and Other Saints*, which you can just about see over the screens erected for the temporary exhibitions. If the facade of the church seems strangely familiar, that's because it's a slavish replica of San Giorgio Maggiore's.

Campiello Pisani, at the back of Morosini's house, is effectively a forecourt to the **Palazzo Pisani**, one of the biggest houses in the city, and now the Conservatory of Music. Work began on it in the early seventeenth century, continued for over a century, and at last was brought to a halt by the government, who decided that the Pisani, among the city's richest banking families, were getting ideas above their station. Had the Pisani got their way, they wouldn't have stopped building until they reached the Canal Grande. (See "The Brenta," on p.216.)

The Church of Santo Stefano

As a building, the church of **Santo Stefano**—founded in the thirteenth century, rebuilt in the fourteenth and altered again in the first half of the fifteenth—is notable for its Gothic **doorway** and beautiful **ship's keel roof**, both of which belong to the last phase of building. The airy and calm interior is one of the most pleasant places in Venice to just sit and think, but it also contains some major works of art. The **tomb of Giacomo Surian** (on the entrance wall) was designed and carved in the final decade of the fifteenth century by **Pietro Lombardo** and his sons. Less easily overlooked is the **tomb of Francesco Morosini**: it's the oversized bronze badge in the center of the nave. A more discreet funerary monument—**Canova**'s stele for Giovanni Falier (1808)—is in the baptistery (door off left aisle), but this part of the church is usually locked. The major paintings are in the sacristy: *The Agony in the Garden*, *The Last Supper* and *The Washing of the Disciples' Feet*, all late works by **Tintoretto**.

You can walk round the **cloister** (far door in left aisle), even though it's been appropriated by government offices, to see the **tomb of Doge Andrea Contarini**, head of state when the Venetians took on the Genoese at Chioggia. The weather long ago wiped out the frescoes by Pordenone that used to cover much of the walls—a few scraps are preserved in the Ca' d'Oro. Pordenone was for a while Titian's main rival in the city, and such was his fear of the great man and his cronies that he invariably turned up to work here with daggers and swords hanging from his belt. No assault actually occurred, but there has been plenty of bloodshed within the church precincts—so much, in fact, that the place has had to be reconsecrated half a dozen times.

Premature death on a terrible scale accounts for the peculiar raised sidewalk of **Campo Novo**, off Calle del Pestrin: formerly the churchyard of Santo Stefano, it was used as a burial pit during the catastrophic plague of 1630, and such was the volume of corpses interred here that for health reasons the site remained closed to the public from then until 1838.

Campo Sant'Angelo

A door leads from the cloister of Santo Stefano into the **Campo Sant'Angelo** (or Anzolo), a square almost as capacious as Campo Morosini, but which usually feels more like a crossroads than a meeting place. It's bounded by some fine buildings, however, including two magnificent fifteenth-century palaces: the **Palazzo Gritti** and, facing it, the **Palazzo Duodo**, home of the composer Cimerosa, who died there in 1801. The miniscule **Oratorio dell'Annunziata**—founded in the tenth century, rebuilt in the twelfth and once the home of the Scuola dei Sotti ("of the Lame")—contains a sixteenth-century crucifix and an *Annunciation* by the omni-present Palma il Giovane. No trace remains of Sant'Angelo church, but it's still remembered as a leading player in one of Venice's great architectural calamities. By 1445 the lean of the church's campanile had become so severe that urgent measures were deemed necessary to right it. It was discovered that there was a builder in Bologna who had made such problems his specialty, and so he was brought on to the case. The expert fixed it so the tower was as straight as a pine tree; the scaffolding was taken down; a banquet was held to honor the engineering genius; and the next morning the whole thing keeled over .

To the Palazzo Grassi and Ca' del Duca

Calle della Mandola, connecting Campo Sant'Angelo to Campo Manin, is a good place to buy food, as is Calle delle Botteghe–Crosera, in front of Santo Stefano. The latter goes up to Salizzada San Samuele; a left turn takes you past the house in which **Paolo Veronese** lived his final years, and on to **Campo San Samuele**. Built in the late twelfth century and not much altered since, the **campanile** of the church is one of the oldest in the city. The church itself was founded in the previous century but was largely reconstructed in the late seventeenth century; there are fifteenth-century frescoes by Paduan artists in the apse, but the building is generally more absorbing when there's a show on at the Palazzo Grassi, at which times it becomes an annex for showing videos and slides.

San Samuele is dwarfed by the glitzy **Palazzo Grassi**, which in 1984 was bought by Fiat and converted into a cultural center. No expense was spared in real-izing the plans drawn up by Gae Aulenti, the hyper-fashionable architect of Paris's Musée d'Orsay, and the refurbished palace now stages the flashiest exhibitions you'll ever see. For the 1988 blockbuster—*I Fenici* (The Phoenicians)—the glazed courtyard was filled with an artificial sand dune, every wall was painted with illus-trative maps and diagrams, and a full-color catalogue as heavy as a paving stone was produced. Reviewed by papers from all over Europe, *I Fenici* was visited by thousands of people who had come to Venice solely to see it, and the show has left a permanent mark on the city landscape—many of the designs in the windows of the jewellers and mask-makers were plundered from Phoenician images. As the numbers allowed inside the building at one time are strictly limited, a show at the Grassi can turn the campo into the city's most crowded spot.

From San Samuele a fairly straightforward chain of alleys leads back to Campo Morosini (follow the trail of "Palazzo Grassi" signs). On the corner of the first of these—Calle Malipiero—is a plaque marking the birthplace of one of the miniscule band of world-famous native Venetians: **Giovanni Giacomo Casanova**. Both his parents were actors, and the family lived within a stone's throw of one of Venice's main theaters, the San Samuele, which until its demoli-tion in the nineteenth century stood in the adjoining Calle del Teatro.

A right turn just before the Rio del Duca, into Corte del Duca, brings you to the **Ca' del Duca**, home of the **Raccolte d'Arte Orientale e di Porcellane**, Venice's most obscurely located museum (April–Oct Mon, Wed & Fri 9:30am–12:30pm, Sat 3–6pm; L2000). It combines two small collections of Oriental art and European porcelain, both of high quality, but neither of sufficient general interest to make a visit a top priority.

RESTAURANTS: *Al Bacareto*, Calle Crosera; *Latteria Zorzi*, Calle dei Fuseri; *Rosticceria San Bartolomeo*, Calle della Bissa .

SNACKS AND BARS: *Al Volto*, Calle Cavalli; *Harry's Bar*, Calle Vallaresso; *Osteria delle Botteghe*, Calle delle Botteghe; *VinoVino*, Ponte delle Veste.

CAFÉS AND PASTICCERIE: *Florian*, Piazza San Marco; *Marchini*, Ponte San Maurizio; *Paolin*, Campo Morosini; *Quadri*, Piazza San Marco; *Rosa Salva*, Campo San Luca, Calle Fiubera and Merceria San Salvador; around Calle della Bissa.

Reviews of all these places appear in Chapter 10.

DORSODURO

There were not many places among the lagoon's mudbanks where Venice's builders could be confident that their work wouldn't slide down into the water, but **Dorsoduro** was one of them; its name translates as "hard back," and it occupies just about the firmest land in the city. Some of the finest minor domestic architecture in Venice is concentrated here, and in recent years many of the area's best houses have been bought up by industrialists and financiers from elsewhere in northern Italy, investing in permanent or merely weekend havens from their places of work. The top-bracket colony is, however, pretty well confined to a triangle defined by the Accademia, the Punta della Dogana and the Gesuati. Stroll up to the area around Campo Santa Margherita and the atmosphere is quite different, in part because of the the population of students attending the nearby university.

Even if your stay's so short that you've only got time for the brightest highlights, you should give a day to Dorsoduro. The **Gallerie dell'Accademia**, replete with masterpieces from each phase in the history of Venetian painting, is the area's essential port of call, and figures on most itineraries as the place to make for when the Piazza's sights have been done. **Santa Maria della Salute**, the grandest gesture of Venetian Baroque and a prime landmark when looking across the water from the Molo, is architecturally the major religious building of the district—but in terms of artistic contents it takes second place to **San Sebastiano**, the parish church of **Paolo Veronese**, who decorated much of its interior. **Giambattista Tiepolo**, the master colorist of a later era, is well represented at the **Scuola Grande dei Carmini**, and for an overall view of Tiepolo's cultural milieu there's the **Ca' Rezzonico**, home of Venice's museum of eighteenth-century art and artifacts. Unusually for Venice, art of the twentieth century is also in evidence—at the **Guggenheim Collection**, which is at least the equal of the city's public collection in the Ca' Pésaro. And yet despite all these attractions the district as a whole is remarkably quiet—most tourists step across the Accademia bridge, whirl through the gallery, then cross back again over the Canal Grande.

As with San Polo, the area designated by the chapter title is slightly more extensive than the *sestiere* of the same name, because in order to simplify the scheme of the city it incorporates a portion of the Santa Croce *sestiere*—for the visitor, the most arbitrary and confusing of Venice's divisions. For our purposes Dorsoduro stretches from the Punta della Dogana and the Salute west to the docks of the Stazione Marittima, and north to the Piazzale Roma (technically in Santa Croce) .

The Accademia

The fame of Venice's school of art, the **Accademia di Belle Arti**, nowadays has nothing to do with the reputation of its staff or pupils—it's been going steadily downhill since the lively days of '68—and everything to do with the attached

DORSODURO

Gallerie dell'Accademia (Tues–Sat 9am–2pm, Sun 9am–1pm; L4000) one of the finest specialist collections of European art. A Napoleonic decree of 1807 moved the Accademia to its present site and instituted its galleries of Venetian paintings, a stock drawn largely from the city's suppressed churches and convents.

Parts of the premises were formerly religious buildings: the church of **Santa Maria della Carità** (rebuilt by **Bartolomeo Bon** 1441–1452) and the **Convento dei Canonici Lateranensi** (built by **Palladio** in 1561 but not completed) were both suppressed in 1807. The third component of the Accademia used to be the **Scuola della Carità**, founded in 1260 and the oldest of the six Scuole Grande; the Gothic building dates from 1343, but has an eighteenth-century facade. There is talk now of moving the school to another site, allowing the Gallerie to expand here. The Accademia is the third component—with San Marco and the Palazzo Ducale—of the triad of obligatory tourist sights in Venice, and the consequent crush sometimes gets so bad that admissions are restricted to batches of 180 people at a time. Accordingly, if you're going there in high summer and don't want to wait, get over the Accademia bridge before 9am.

The Early Renaissance

The first room of the Accademia's generally chronological arrangement is the fifteenth-century former chapter house of the Scuola (with its original gilded ceiling), now filled with pieces by the earliest known individual Venetian painters. The icon-like, Byzantine-influenced figures of **Paolo Veneziano** (first half of fourteenth century) are succeeded by the Gothic forms of his follower **Lorenzo Veneziano**—look at the swaying stances of his figures and the emphasis on the sinuous lines of the drapery. **Jacobello Alberegno**'s *Polyptych of the Apocalypse* (second half of fourteenth century) is a fine example too, with its wrathful God, seven-headed beast and many-eyed lamb.

Room 2 is given over to large altarpieces from the late fifteenth century and early sixteenth century, including works by **Giovanni Bellini**, **Cima da Conegliano** and **Vittore Carpaccio**. All of these paintings appear to have slightly warped perspectives: this is because they were intended to be placed above head height—a fact that the Accademia's picture-hangers have not taken into consideration. Carpaccio's strange *Crucifixion and Glorification of the Ten Thousand Martyrs of Mount Ararat* is the most gruesome painting in the room; the most charming is by him too: *The Presentation of Jesus in the Temple*, with its pretty, wingless, lute-playing angel.

The beginnings of the Venetian obsession with the way in which forms are defined by light (as differentiated from the Florentines' more geometrical notions of form), and the emergence of the characteristically soft and rich Venetian palette, are seen in **rooms 3, 4 and 5**. The last two are high points of the Accademia, and almost all of the small paintings here would alone be worth a detour. Outstanding are an exquisite *St George* by **Mantegna** (c.1466), a series of *Madonnas* and a *Pietà* by **Giovanni Bellini**, and two pieces by the most mysterious of Italian painters, **Giorgione**—his *Portrait of an Old Woman* and the so-called *Tempest* (c.1500). The first is an urgent and compassionate study of mortality (the inscription means "with time"), while the latter resists all attempts to deduce its meaning—the first known painting to have no historical, religious, mythological or factual basis, it seems to have been as perplexing to Giorgione's contemporaries as it is to us.

Tintoretto, Titian, and Veronese

Rooms 6 to 8 mark the entry of the heavyweights of the Venetian High Renaissance, the period in which the cult of the artist really took hold, with painters consciously cultivating their reputations and writers boosting their favorites while damning their rivals. These works would be the prize of many other collections, but here they are just appetizers for what's to come. Jacopo Robusti, alias **Tintoretto**, is represented by his sumptuous *Madonna dei Camerlenghi* (1566), showing the city's treasurers hobnobbing with the Mother of Our Savior—the facial types are still seen in Venice today. Tiziano Vecellio, alias **Titian**, comes in with an unenthralling *John the Baptist* (early 1540s), and Paolo Caliari, better known as **Paolo Veronese** (he came to Venice from Verona), is represented by a neck-cricking series of ceiling panels. One of the more compelling pictures is the *Young Man in his Study* by **Lorenzo Lotto** (c.1528), a portrait in which the subject's gaze manages to be simultaneously sharp and evasive. Lotto was eventually driven from Venice by the vindictiveness of Titian and his entourage; presumably a happier life was led by the unknown follower of Titian who produced the beguiling *Tobias and the Angel* nearby .

Room 6 is in effect the ante-room to **room 10**, one whole wall of which is needed for *Christ in the House of Levi* by **Paolo Veronese**, the third member of Venice's sixteenth-century artistic triumvirate. Originally called *The Last Supper*—it was to be a replacement for a Titian painting of the same subject which was destroyed by a fire in the refectory of San Zanipolo—this picture brought down on Veronese the wrath of the Inquisition, who objected to the inclusion of "buffoons, drunkards, Germans, dwarfs, and similar indecencies" in the sacred scene. (What really raised their hackles was the German contingent, who were perceived by the Holy Office as the Reformation menace incarnate.) Veronese's insouciant response was simply to change the title, an emendation that apparently satisfied his critics.

Among the works by **Tintoretto** is the painting that made his reputation: *The Miracle of the Slave* (1548), showing Saint Mark's intervention at the execution of a slave who had defied his master by traveling to the Evangelist's shrine. Comparison with Gentile Bellini and Carpaccio's unruffled depictions of miraculous events in rooms 20–21 (see below) makes it easy to understand the sensation caused by Tintoretto's whirling, brashly colored scene. The legend of Venice's patron saint is further elaborated by his dreamlike *The Translation of the Body of St Mark* (see entry on the Basilica for the story of the "translation"—ie theft), *St Mark Saving a Saracen* (both from the 1560s), and *The Dream of St Mark* (1570), which is largely by his son **Domenico**. Tintoretto's love of physical and psychological drama, the energy of his brush-strokes, and the sometimes uncomfortable originality of his colors and poses, are all displayed in this group. (And all over Venice you can see how his concentration on dramatic highlights and his use of gesture spawned a shoal of imitators whose clichéd contortions of pose and expression covered oceans of canvas.) Opposite is **Titian's** highly charged *Pietà* (1576), painted for his own tomb in the Frari; the immediacy of death is expressed in the handling of the paint, here scratched, scraped and dolloped onto the canvas not just with brushes but with the artist's bare hands. It was completed after Titian's death by Palma il Giovane, as the inscription explains.

The Eighteenth Century

A major shift occurs in **room 11**: at one end there's more from **Veronese** and **Tintoretto** (including a *Creation of the Animals* which features a few species that must have followed the unicorn into extinction, and an *Adam and Eve* in which Adam's back is a particularly fine piece of painting), while at the other hang pieces by **G.B. Tiepolo**, including the only two pieces to have survived the destruction of the Scalzi's ceiling in 1915. Although some of the side rooms contain a few decent sixteenth- and seventeenth-century pieces, the chief interest of the generally dull section that follows is provided by eighteenth-century painters. **G.B. Piazzetta**'s extraordinary *The Fortune-Teller* (1740), in **room 16a**, is also known as *The Enigma*, although the woman is offering the least enigmatic sexual invitation you'll ever see on canvas; some interpreters see it as a satirical allegory, showing how once-glorious Venice now behaved towards the rest of the world. In **room 17** there's the Accademia's only piece by **Canaletto**, accompanied by **Guardi**'s views of Venice, **Pietro Longhi**'s documentary interiors and a series of portraits by **Rosalba Carriera**, one of very few women shown in the collection. Carriera's work established the use of pastel as a medium in its own right, rather than as a preparation for oil paint, and her moving *Self-Portrait in Old Age*, done at a time when her sight was beginning to fail, is a high point of her work.

To The Miracles of the Relic of the Cross

The top part of the Carità church now forms **room 23**, which houses works mainly from the fifteenth and early sixteenth centuries, the era of two of Venice's most significant artistic dynasties, the **Vivarini** and **Bellini** families. Of the pieces by the Vivarini—**Antonio**, his brother **Bartolomeo** and his son **Alvise**—the most striking is Alvise's *Santa Chiara* (1485–90). **Giovanni Bellini** is represented by four workshop-assisted triptychs (painted for this church in the 1460s), and his brother **Gentile** by the intense portrait of *The Blessed Lorenzo Giustinian* (1445). One of the oldest surviving Venetian canvases and Gentile's earliest signed work, it was possibly used as a standard in processions, which would account for its tatty state.

There's more from Gentile over in **room 20**, which is entirely filled by the cycle of *The Miracles of the Relic of the Cross*. The work was produced by various artists between 1494 and 1501, and was commissioned by the Scuola Grande di San Giovanni Evangelista to extol the holy fragment it had held since 1369. Gentile's *Procession of the Relic in the Piazza* (1496), executed the year the Torre dell'Orologio was started (and with artistic licence shifting the campanile to the right), is perhaps the best-known image of the group; the devotional moment is easily missed—the bare-headed man in a red cloak kneeling as the relic passes him is one Jacopo de' Salis, praying for his son's recovery from a fractured skull. In *The Recovery of the Relic from the Canal of San Lorenzo* (1500) Gentile shows Andrea Vendramin, Grand Guardian of the Scuola, retrieving the relic from the spot where it had floated after being knocked into the water during a procession; the fourth figure from the left in the group of donors in the right foreground is alleged to be a self-portrait, and Caterina Cornaro is portrayed on the far left.

A wealth of anecdotal detail adds historical veracity to **Carpaccio**'s *Cure of a Possessed Man* (1494). Set by the Rialto (and showing one of the wooden precursors of the present bridge), its cast of characters includes turbanned Turks and Arabs, Armenian (or Greek) gentlemen in tall brimmed hats, an African gondolier, a woman beating carpets on an *altana* and a man repairing a roof; the miracle—the cure of a lunatic—is happening on the first floor of the building on the left. **Giovanni Mansueti**'s *Miracle of the Relic in Campo San Lio* (1494) shows what happened at the funeral of a dissolute and impious member of the confraternity: the relic refused to allow itself to be carried into the church for his service. Each window has a woman or child in it, witnessing the shame of the old reprobate. The reason for all these anecdotal details and the marginalizing of the miracles was not a lack of piety but quite the reverse: the miracle was authenticated by being depicted in the documentary context of teeming everyday life.

Carpaccio's St Ursula Paintings—and Titian's Presentation

Another remarkable cycle fills **room 21**—Carpaccio's *Story of Saint Ursula*, painted for the Scuola di Sant'Orsola at San Zanipolo in 1490–94. A superlative exercise in pictorial narrative, the paintings are especially fascinating to the modern viewer as a meticulous record of domestic architecture, costume, the decorative arts, and even ship design in Venice at the close of the fifteenth century—and a scrupulous recent renovation has further increased their luster. The legend is that a British prince named Hereus proposed marriage to Ursula, a Breton princess, who accepted on two conditions: that Hereus convert to Christianity, and that he should wait for three years, during which time he should accompany Ursula and her company of 11,000 virgins on a pilgrimage to Rome. The conditions were accepted, and the eventual consequence was that Ursula and her troop were massacred by the Huns near Cologne—as she had been forewarned by an angel in a dream.

After this room, you leave the Accademia through the former *albergo* of the Scuola; **Titian**'s *Presentation of the Virgin* (1539) occupies the wall over the door, the place for which it was painted—and the triptych by **Antonio Vivarini** and **Giovanni d'Alemagna** (1446) similarly hangs where it always has.

Eastern Dorsoduro

Along the east flank of the Accademia runs the wide Rio Terrà Foscarini, named after **Senator Antonio Foscarini**, victim of the Venetian judicial system's most notorious gaffe (see *The Canal Grande* for the story); he lived at no. 180–181, but the house was radically altered in the nineteenth century. The street cuts down almost as far as the Záttere, but for the direct route to the mouth of the Canal Grande you turn left along Calle Nuova a Sant'Agnese, one of the district's main shopping streets.

The Cini and Guggenheim Collections

Just before the Rio San Vio you pass the Palazzo Cini (no. 864), once the home of the industrialist Vittorio Cini (founder of the *Fondazione Cini* on San Giorgio Maggiore) and now occupied by the **Raccolta d'Arte Vittorio Cini** (summer Tues–Sun 2–7pm). Although Cini's private collection contains a miscellany of valuable manuscripts, porcelain and other artifacts, the substance of the museum is its gathering of Tuscan paintings, including pieces by Bernardo Daddi, Filippo Lippi, Piero di Cosimo and Pontormo.

A meatier aesthetic experience is provided by the **Peggy Guggenheim Collection**, installed in the peculiarly modernistic fragment of the quarter-built Palazzo Venier dei Leoni, a bit farther down the Canal Grande (April–Oct noon–6pm; closed Tues; L5000, reductions L3000, free Sat 6–9pm; open in winter for special exhibitions). Peggy Guggenheim was one of this century's most adventurous patrons of the arts, and she moved into the palace with her collection in 1949; since her death in 1979 the Guggenheim Foundation has looked after the administration of the place, and has turned the collection into one of the city's glossiest museums. It's a quirky and generally top-quality assembly of twentieth-century art, touching on most of the major modern movements. Prime pieces include **Brancusi**'s *Bird in Space* and *Maestra*, **De Chirico**'s *Red Tower* and *Nostalgia of the Poet*, **Max Ernst**'s *Robing of the Bride*; several of **Joseph Cornell**'s boxes, sculpture by **Laurens** and **Lipchitz**, and works by **Malevich** and **Schwitters**; other artists include Picasso, Braque, Chagall, Pollock, Duchamp, Giacometti, Picabia and Magritte. The water-gates are often closed to protect public decency from the erection flaunted by the rider of **Marino Marini**'s *Angel of the Citadel*, out on the terrace.

The Salute and Around

After the wrought iron and greenery of the tiny **Campo Barbaro** (from where you can see the Gothic back half of the Palazzo Dario—see Chapter Seven), a handful of glass workshops and furnaces lie in wait for the more monied Guggenheim clientele. From the next open space an underpassage burrows alongside the Gothic church of San Gregorio (now a restoration center) towards the Campo della Salute, where the dazzle off the water and the white stone of the Salute can give the eyeballs quite a jolt after the gloom of the tunnel.

In 1630–31 Venice was devastated by a plague which exterminated nearly 95,000 of the lagoon population—one person in three. In October 1630 the Senate decreed that a new church would be dedicated to Mary if the city were saved, and the result was the **Salute** (*salute* meaning "health"), or **Santa Maria della Salute**, to use its full title (8am–noon & 3–5pm). Resting on a platform of over 100,000 wooden piles, the Salute took half a century to build; its architect, **Baldessare Longhena**, only 26 years old when his proposal was accepted, lived just long enough to see it finished—he died in 1682, one year after completion.

Each year on November 21 (the feast of the Presentation of the Virgin) the Signoria processed from San Marco to the Salute for a service of thanksgiving, crossing the Canal Grande on a pontoon bridge laid from Santa Maria del Giglio. The *Festa della Madonna della Salute* is still a major event on the Venetian calendar, with thousands of people making their way over the water in the course of the day to pray for, or give thanks for, their health.

The form of the Salute owes much to the plan of Palladio's Redentore—the obvious model for a dramatically sited votive church (see Chapter Nine)—and to the repertoire of Marian symbolism. The octagonal plan and eight facades allude to the eight-pointed Marian star for example, while the huge dome represents Mary's crown and the centralized plan is a conventional symbol of the Virgin's womb. Its decorative details are saturated with coded references: the inscription in the center of the mosaic floor, "Unde Origo, Inde Salus" (From The Origins Came Salvation) refers to the coincidence of Mary's feast day and the legendary date of Venice's foundation—March 25, 421; encircling roses evoke the Marian rosary.

Less arcane symbolism is at work on the **high altar**, where the Virgin and Child rescue Venice (kneeling woman) from the plague (old woman); in attendance are Saint Mark and San Lorenzo Giustiniani, first Patriarch of Venice. The Byzantine painting, a little uneasy in this Baroque opulence, was brought to Venice in 1672 by Francesco Morosini, never a man to resist the opportunity for a bit of state-sanctioned theft (see "The Arsenale").

The most notable paintings in the Salute are the **sacristy**'s assembly of **Titian** pieces brought from the suppressed church of Santo Spirito in 1656: an early altarpiece of *St Mark Enthroned with SS. Cosmas, Damian, Sebastian and Roch* (the plague saints), three violent ceiling paintings of *David and Goliath, Abraham and Isaac* and *Cain and Abel* (1540s), and eight late *tondi* of the Doctors of the Church (Jerome, Augustine, Gregory and Ambrose) and the Evangelists. **Tintoretto** has included himself in the *dramatis personae* of his *Marriage at Cana* (1561)—he's the first Apostle on the left. Nearby is a fine *Madonna* by **Palma il Vecchio**, one of the sixteenth century's more placid souls.

The Manfrediana and the Dogana di Mare

Longhena was also the architect of the **Seminario Patriarcale**, within which lurks one of the city's more ramshackle museums. The collection of tombstones and sculptural pieces around the cloister, many of them trawled from suppressed religious foundations, was thrown together in the early years of the nineteenth century; it was augmented soon after by the **Pinacoteca Manfrediana**, a motley collection of artworks incorporating items as diverse as paintings by **Antonio Vivarini** and **Paolo Veronese**, and portrait busts by **Alessandro Vittoria**, **Gian'Lorenzo Bernini** and **Antonio Canova**. You have to phone to arrange a visit (☎5225558), but it's not a daunting experience—the usual reaction is delight that anyone knows of the collection's existence.

On the point where the Canal Grande and the Giudecca canal merge stands the **Dogana di Mare** (Customs House), another late seventeenth-century building. The figure which swivels in the wind on top of the Dogana's gold ball is said by most to represent Fortune, though others identify it as Justice. From the tip of Dorsoduro, the Punta della Dogana, is one of the city's great panoramas.

Along the Záttere

Known collectively as the **Záttere**, the sequence of waterfront sidewalks between the Punta della Dogana and the Stazione Marittima is now a popular place for a stroll or an *al fresco* pizza, but was formerly the place where most of the bulky goods coming into Venice were unloaded onto floating rafts (*záttere*). A fair quantity of cargo was carted into the state-run and highly lucrative **Magazzini del Sale** (Salt Warehouses), the vast low building near the Punta della Dogana, where some 44,000 tons of salt could be stored; it's now a boathouse.

The Gesuati and Santa Maria della Visitazione

Although there's an appealing mix of architectural exteriors around here—the fifteenth-century facade of Spirito Santo church, the pink Casa degli Incurabili (once one of Venice's four main hospitals, now a children's home), and the Veneto-

Byzantine church of Sant'Agnese (originally twelfth- and thirteenth- century but remodeled)—the first building to break stride for is the church of the **Gesuati** (or **Santa Maria del Rosario**; 8am–noon and 5–7pm). Built in 1726–43, this was the first church designed by **Giorgio Massari**, an architect whose work combines Rococo preciousness with a more robust classicism—note how the Gesuati forms a sort of counterpoint to the Redentore, over the water. He often worked with **Giambattista Tiepolo**, who painted the Gesuati's three ceiling panels of *Scenes from the Life of St Dominic* (1737–1739) and the first altarpiece on the right, *The Madonna and Child with SS. Catherine of Siena, Rose and Agnes* (c.1740).

Santa Maria della Visitazione, a couple of doors down, is entered through the gateway of the attached educational institute; the only part of the interior as attractive as its Lombardesque facade is the sixteenth-century **ceiling**, with panels painted by Umbrian artists. The lion's-mouth letter box to the right of the facade was for the use of residents with complaints relating to health and sanitation; a complaint sent to the authorities in 1498 resulted in punishment for tradesmen who had sold oil which was full of "immonditie e sporchezi" (filths and dirts)—syphilitic patients had been immersed in it as a cure.

San Trovaso and its Squero

Don't bother consulting your dictionary of saints for the dedicatee of **San Trovaso** church—the name's a baffling dialect version of Santi Gervasio e Protasio. Since its tenth-century foundation the church has had a checkered history, falling down once, and twice being destroyed by fire; this is the fourth incarnation, built in 1584–1657. There are two facades, one at the traditional "west" end, the other on the "south" side—legend says that this church was the only neutral ground between the Nicolotti and the Castellani factions (see "San Nicolò dei Mendicoli," below), who celebrated mutual weddings and other services here, but entered and departed by separate doors. It's a large dark church, best visited in the morning if you want a decent view of its pictures. **Tintoretto**'s last works, both of which were finished by his son Domenico and other assistants, hang on each side of the choir: *The Adoration of the Magi* and *The Expulsion from the Temple* (1594). In the chapel right of the altar is *St Crysogonus on Horseback* by **Michele Giambono** (c.1450), Venice's main practi-

---

GONDOLAS

Gondolas may be far less numerous than they used to be (a total of 10,000 operated on the canals of sixteenth-century Venice) but the tourist industry ensures steady employment for a few *squeri*, as the gondola yards are called. A display in the Museo Storico Navale (see Chapter Six) takes you through the construction of a gondola, but no abstract demonstration can equal the fascination of a working yard, and the most public one in Venice is the **squero di San Trovaso**, just on the Záttere side of San Trovaso church. (Another *squero* is tucked away on the Rio dell'Avogaria, a short distance west of here.)

The earliest mention of a gondola is in a decree of 1094, but the vessel of that period bore little resemblance to today's streamlined thoroughbred. As late as the thirteenth century the gondola was a twelve-oared beast with an iron beak—an adornment that evolved into the saw-toothed projection—the *ferro*—that fronts the modern gondola. (The precise significance of the *ferro*'s shape is unclear—traditon tioner of the International Gothic style; and next to the south door you'll find a marble altar-front carved with angels—dated around 1470, it's one of the first Renaissance low reliefs produced in Venice.

San Sebastiano and Beyond

At the end of the Záttere the barred gates of the Stazione Marittima deflect you away from the waterfront and towards the church of **San Sebastiano**. The parish church of **Paolo Veronese**, it contains a group of resplendent paintings by him that gives it a place in his career which is comparable to that of San Rocco in the career of Tintoretto. But in contrast to San Rocco, this is the most dejected of Venice's first-rank cultural monuments. A terse note on the door explains that the church can't afford a custodian (opening hours are thus a matter of guesswork), and although it was restored in the 1960s, the building's crying out for further repairs—to the nun's choir, for instance, which for years has been closed owing to its rickety state.

Veronese was still in his twenties when he was asked to paint the ceiling of the **sacristy** with a *Coronation of the Virgin* and the *Four Evangelists* (1555); once that commission had been carried out, he decorated the **nave ceiling** with *Scenes from the Life of St Esther*. His next project, the dome of the chancel, was later destroyed, but the sequence he and his brother Benedetto then painted on the walls of the church and the nun's choir at the end of 1550s has survived in pretty good shape. In the following decade he executed the last of the pictures—those around the **high altar** and on the **organ shutters**. Other riches include a late **Titian** of *St Nicholas* (1563; on the right as you enter), and the early sixteenth-century majolica pavement in the chapel to the left of the chancel—in front of which is Veronese's tomb slab.

Angelo Raffaele

Across the campo, the seventeenth-century church of **Angelo Raffaele**—so dilapidated it seems to be clamped upright by the two huge war memorials on the canal facade—has organ-shutters decorated by one or other of the **Guardi** brothers (nobody's sure which). In the campo behind the church is a **wellhead** built from the bequest of Marco Arian, who died in 1348 in an outbreak of plague

has it that the six main prongs symbolize the six *sestieri*, with the backward-facing prong representing La Giudecca.) Over the next two centuries the gondola shrank to something near its present dimensions, developed multicolored coverings and sprouted the little chair on carved legs that it still carries. By the sixteenth century it had become a mode of social ostentation, with gilded prows, fantastically uphol-stered *felzi* (cabins), cushions of satin and silk, and hulls decked out with a profu-sion of embroidery, carvings and flowers. Sumptuary laws were introduced to quash this aquatic one-upmanship, and though some of them had little effect, one of them changed the gondola's appearance for good—since an edict of 1562 gondolas have been uniformly black, a livery which prompted Shelley to compare them to "moths of which a coffin might have been the chrysalis." There's been little change in the gondola's shape since the end of the seventeenth century, the only changes being the adjustment of its assymetrical line to compensate for the weight of the gondolier—a characteristic that's particularly noticeable when you see the things out of water.

which he blamed on contaminated water. The **Palazzo Arian**, on the opposite bank of the canal, was built in the second half of that century and is adorned by one of the finest and earliest Gothic windows in Venice.

San Nicolò dei Mendicoli

Although it's located on the edge of the city, the church of **San Nicolò dei Mendicoli** ("of the beggars") is one of Venice's oldest churches, traditionally predated only by San Giacomo di Rialto. It gave its name to the *Nicolotti*, a working-class faction whose frequently violent rivalry with the equivalent faction from the other side of the city—the *Castellani*, from San Pietro di Castello—added a bit of spice to life from the fourteenth century right down to the nineteenth. The titular head of the *Nicolotti* was the so-called *Gastaldo* or the *Doge di Nicolotti*, whose election by the parishioners was followed by a ceremonial greeting from the Republic's doge.

Founded in the seventh century, the church has been rebuilt and altered at various times, and was last restored by *Venice in Peril* in 1977. The Veneto-Byzantine campanile dates from the end of the twelfth century, but more intriguing is the fifteenth-century porch, a type of construction once common in Venice and often used as makeshift accommodation for penurious nuns. The oldest parts of the interior are the twelfth-century apse and nave columns; the large wooden statue of *Saint Nicholas* is a mid-fifteenth-century piece possibly from Bartolomeo Bon's workshop. If you find the church locked, try asking at the door to the left of the side entrance.

The church of **Santa Teresa**, on the other side of the canal, is now permanently closed, and there's no reason to set foot on the island on which it stands—a grim zone of warehouses and docks.

Northern Dorsoduro—Campo Santa Margherita and Around

The vast, elongated **Campo Santa Margherita**, ringed by houses that date back as far as the fourteenth century, is the social heart of Dorsoduro, many of whose inhabitants come here daily to stock up at the market stalls. Students from the nearby university hang out in the campo's bars, and the place as a whole—with its herbalist, wholefood store and handpainted clothes shop—has an alternative feel to it. The church that gives the campo its name was closed in 1810, and for a while functioned as a cinema; the dragons that feature so prominently in the decorative stonework on and around the church relate to the legend of Saint Margaret, who emerged unscathed after the dragon that had swallowed her exploded. Isolated at the fishstall end of the campo stands the **Scuola dei Varotari** (tanners' guild), bearing an eroded relief of the Madonna with members of the Scuola.

The Carmini and Around

Just off the campo's southwest extremity is the **Scuola Grande dei Carmini**, built in the 1660s, probably to plans by Longhena, and effectively a showcase for the art of **Giambattista Tiepolo**, who in the 1740s painted the ceiling of the upstairs hall (Mon–Sat 9am–noon and 3–6pm; L2000). *St Simon Stock Receiving*

CAMPO DI S. MARGHERITA AND AROUND

the Scapular from the Madonna is the central panel; the four *Virtues* in the corners were such a hit with Tiepolo's clients that he was instantly granted membership of the Scuola.

The **Carmini** church (or Santa Maria del Carmelo) is a collage of architectural styles, with a sixteenth-century facade, a Gothic side doorway which preserves several Byzantine fragments, and a fourteenth-century basilican interior. A dull series of Baroque paintings illustrating the history of the Carmelite order covers a lot of space inside, but the second altar on the right has a *Nativity* by **Cima da Conegliano** (before 1510), and **Lorenzo Lotto**'s *St Nicholas of Bari* (1529) hangs on the opposite side of the nave.

The most imposing building on Fondamenta del Soccorso (leading from Campo dei Carmini towards Angelo Raffaele) is the **Palazzo Zenobio**, built in the late seventeenth century when the Zenobio family were among the richest in Venice. It's now an Armenian college, but visitors are sometimes allowed to see the ballroom, one of the richest eighteenth-century interiors in Venice. In the late sixteenth century a home for prostitutes who wanted to get off the game was set up at no. 2590 by **Veronica Franco**, a renowned ex-courtesan who was as famous for her poetry and her writers' and artists' salon as she was for her sexual allure; both Michel de Montaigne and King Henry III of France were grateful recipients of samples of her literary output.

(**Between here and Piazzale Roma** lies a predominantly residential area that constitutes the largest completely uninteresting sector of central Venice. Santa Maria Maggiore, the only church before you reach the bus station, is now part of the city **prison**. The fifteenth-century church of **Sant'Andrea della Zirada**, in the lee of the Piazzale's multistorey parking lot, is closed for restoration and only has its Baroque altar to recommend it anyway; and the diminutive Neoclassical **Nome di Gesù**, cringing underneath the overpass, has absolutely nothing going for it.)

San Barnaba

Cutting down the side of the Carmini church takes you over the Rio di San Barnaba, along which a fondamenta runs to San Barnaba. Just before the end of the fondamenta you pass the **Ponte dei Pugni**, the main connection between San Barnaba and Santa Margherita, and one of several bridges with this name. Originally built without parapets, they were the sites of mass fist-fights between the *Castellani* and *Nicolotti*; this one is inset with marble footprints marking the starting positions. By the early eighteenth century these punch-ups had become so violent that they were finally banned, and less bloody forms of competition, such as regattas, were encouraged instead. Pugilists have now been replaced by tourists taking shots of the photogenic San Barnaba grocery barge moored at the foot of the bridge.

San Barnaba church (open mornings only), built in 1749, has a small *Holy Family* attributed to Veronese and a trompe l'oeil ceiling painting of *St Barnabas in Glory* by Constantino Cedini, a follower of Tiepolo. At the time of the church's construction the parish was swarming with so-called *Barnabotti*, impoverished noble families who moved into the area's cheap lodgings to eke out their meager incomes. Forbidden as members of the aristocracy to practise a craft or run a shop, some of the *Barnabotti* supported themselves by selling their votes to the mightier families in the Maggior Consiglio, while others resigned themselves to subsistence on a paltry state dole. Visitors to the city often remarked on the incongruous sight of its silk-clad beggars—the nobility of Venice were obliged to wear silk, regardless of their ability to pay for such finery.

Ca' Rezzonico

The eighteenth century, the period of Venice's political senility and moral degeneration, was also the period of its last grand flourish in the visual and decorative arts, so it's not entirely surprising that the city's most opulent museum should be the **Museo del Settecento Veneziano** (Museum of the Venetian Eighteenth Century; Mon–Thurs & Sat 10am–4pm, Sun & hols 9am–12:30pm; L5000, reductions L3000). Culled from dozens of different buildings but arranged in such a way that you seem to be walking through the best-appointed palace in town, rather than through an array of exhibits, the collection spreads through most of the enormous **Ca' Rezzonico**, which the city authorities bought in 1934 specifically as a home for the museum.

Most of the decorations and furnishings in the Ca' Rezzonico are genuine items, and where originals weren't available (as with some of the fabrics) the eighteenth-century ambience has been preserved by using almost indistinguishable modern reproductions. Sumptuary laws in Venice restricted the quantities of silk, brocade and tapestry that could be draped around a house, so legions of painters, stuccoists, cabinetmakers and other such applied artists were employed to fanfare the wealth of their patrons to the world. The work they produced is certainly not to everyone's taste, but even if you find most of the the museum's contents frivolous or grotesque, the frescoes by the **Tiepolo** family and **Pietro Longhi**'s affectionate Venetian scenes should justify the entrance fee.

A man in constant demand in the early part of the century was the Belluno sculptor-cum-woodcarver **Andrea Brustolon**, much of whose output consisted of wildly elaborated pieces of furniture. A few of his pieces are displayed in the chandeliered ballroom at the top of the entrance staircase, and elsewhere on this floor there's an entire roomful of them, including the *Allegory of Strength* console (Hercules underneath, two river gods holding four vases and a fifth held up by three black slaves in chains), a creation that makes you marvel at the craftsmanship and wince at the ends to which it was used.

The less fervid imaginations of **Giambattista Tiepolo** and his son **Giandomenico** are introduced in room 2 with the ceiling fresco celebrating Ludovico Rezzonico's marriage into the hugely powerful Savorgnan family in 1758. This was quite a year for the Rezzonico clan, as it also brought the election of Carlo Rezzonico as Pope Clement XIII: the son of the man who bought the uncompleted palace and finished its construction, Carlo the pontiff was notorious both for his rampant nepotism and for his prudery—insisting that the Vatican's Classical nudes be made more modest by the judicious application of fig leaves. Two other Tiepolo ceilings enliven the rooms overlooking the Canal Grande on each side of the main *portego* (an *Allegory of Merit* by Giambattista and Giandomenico, and *Nobility and Virtue Triumphing over Perfidy*, a solo effort by the father), but you have to wait until the last suite of rooms (on the second floor) to see the museum's most engaging Tiepolo productions—Giandomenico's sequence of **frescoes from the Villa Zianigo** near Mestre, the Tiepolo family home. With the exception of the pieces from the villa's chapel, which date from 1749, the frescoes were painted towards the the end of the century, at a time when their satirical playfulness was going out of fashion. *The New World* shows a crowd turned out in its best attire to watch a Sunday peepshow; another room is devoted to the antics of *Pulchinello*, the ancestor of our Mr Punch; and typically good-humored centaurs and satyrs lark around on nearby walls.

Rosalba Carriera's pastels get a good area of wall space to themselves on the first floor and she crops up again in the more intimate rooms of the next floor, where the furnishings include a full suite of green and gold lacquer pieces—one of the finest surviving examples of Venetian chinoiserie. The only two canal views by **Canaletto** on show in public galleries in Venice are on this storey, as are **Francesco Guardi**'s scenes of high society in the parlor of San Zaccaria's convent and the gambling rooms of the *Ridotto*. Technically less adroit than Guardi's work, **Pietro Longhi**'s wide-ranging paintings of life in eighteenth-century Venice—including a version of the famous *Rhinoceros*—have more than enough curiosity value to make up for their shortcomings in execution. Visitors at *Carnevale* time will recognize several of the festival's components in the Longhi room: the beak-like *bauta* masks, for example, and the little doughnuts called *frittelle*, an essential part of the *Carnevale* scene.

The low-ceilinged rooms of the top floor contain yet more Longhi paintings, but the main point of clambering upstairs is to see the **pharmacy** and **puppet theater**. A sequence of wood-paneled rooms full of the appropriate furniture, ceramic jars and glass bottles, the pharmacy has to be viewed through windows, rather like peering into the set of a Longhi picture. The puppets are fairly unremarkable specimens, each about one foot high, but their very ordinariness makes their survival remarkable in itself.

From the Ca' Rezzonico, the quickest route up to the Rialto takes you across the herringbone-patterned sidewalk of the Campiello dei Squellini, past the entrance to the main university building and over the Rio Fóscari—whereupon you're in the *San Polo* section. (For background to the university building—the Ca' Fóscari—and the neighboring Palazzi Giustinian, see Chapter Seven.)

RESTAURANTS: *Frigittoria Da Bruno*, Calle Lunga San Barnaba; *Isola Misteriosa*, Rio Terrà Scozzera; *Locanda Montin*, Fondamenta di Borgo; *San Trovaso*, Fondamenta Priuli;

PIZZAS: *Alle Záttere*, Campo Sant'Agnese; *Antico Cappon*, Campo Santa Margherita.

BARS AND SNACKS: *Cantina del Vino gia Schiavi*, Fondamenta Maravegie; *Corner Pub*, Calle della Chiesa; *Da Codroma*, Fondamenta Briati; *Linea d'Ombra*, Záttere ai Saloni.

CAFÉS AND PASTICCERIE: *Nico*, Záttere ai Gesuati; *Vio*, Rio Terrà Toletta; around Campo Santa Margherita.

Reviews of all these places appear in Chapter 10

CHAPTER THREE

SAN POLO

B ounded on one side by the Rio Nuovo–Rio di Ca' Fóscari (the shortcut used by the *diretto* boat service from Piazzale Roma to the *Volta del Canal*) and on the others by the upper loop of the Canal Grande, the area covered by this chapter is composed of the entire **San Polo** *sestiere*, the greater part of the *sestiere* of Santa Croce and a couple of slivers of Dorsoduro. This jigsaw is not as baffling as it at first appears. There are two main routes through the district, each following approximately the curve of the Canal Grande—one runs between the Rialto and the Scalzi bridge, the other takes you in the opposite direction from the Rialto, down toward the Accademia. Virtually all the essential sights lie on, or just off, one of these two routes, and once you've become familiar with these the exploration of the streets and squares between them can be attempted with only a minimal risk of feeling that you'll never see friends and family again. Wherever you are in this area, you cannot be more than a couple of minutes' well-navigated walk from one of the two roads to the Rialto.

As far as the day-to-day life of Venice is concerned, the focal points of the district are the sociable open space of **Campo San Polo** and the **Rialto** area, once the commercial heart of the Republic and still the home of a **market** that's famous far beyond the boundaries of the city. The bustle of the stalls and the unspoiled bars used by the porters are a good antidote to cultural overload. Nobody, however, should miss the extraordinary pair of buildings in the southern part of San Polo: the colossal Gothic church of the **Frari**, embellished with three of Venice's finest altarpieces, and the **Scuola Grande di San Rocco**, decorated with an unforgettable cycle of paintings by Tintoretto.

In the northern part of the district, Venice's **modern art, oriental and natural history museums** are clustered together on the bank of the Canal Grande—the first two sharing one of the city's most magnificent palaces and the third installed in the former headquarters of the Turkish merchants. As ever, numerous treasures are also scattered among the minor churches—for example in **San Cassiano, San Simeone Grande** and **San Pantaleone**. Lastly, if you're in search of a spot in which to sit for an hour and watch the world go by, try the **Campo San Giacomo dell'Orio**, one of Venice's better-kept secrets.

From the Rialto to the Ponte degli Scalzi

Relatively stable building land and a good defensive position drew some of the earliest lagoon settlers to the high bank (*rivo alto*) that was to develop into the **Rialto** district. By 810, when the capital of the lagoon confederation was moved—in the wake of Pepin's invasion—from Malamocco to the more secure islands around here, the inhabited zone had grown well beyond the Rialto itself. While the political center of the new city was consolidated around San Marco, the Rialto became the commercial area. In the twelfth century Europe's first state

SAN POLO

S. Marcuola

Palazzo
Vendramin-Calergi

Traghetto

S. Marcuola
1

S. Stae
1

Fondaco
dei Turchi
(Museo Storia Nat.)

S. Stae

Palazzo
Mocenigo

Ca' Pésaro

Palazzo Corner
della Regina

Ca' d'Oro

Ca' d'Oro
1

S. Maria
Mater Domini

CAMPO S. MARIA
MATER DOMINI

S. Cassiano

Pescheria

Fabbriche
Nuove

Rialto Market

Fabbriche Vecchie

S. Giovanni
Elemosinario

Fondaco dei
Tedeschi

Palazzo
Soranzo

CPL. ALBRIZZI

S. Aponal

S. Giacomo di Rialto

Palazzo dei
Camerlenghi

PONTE DI
RIALTO

Palazzo Corner
Mocenigo

CAMPO DI
S. POLO

S. Polo

CPL. MELONI

S. Silvestro

CAMPO DI
S. SILVESTRO

Rialto
1, 2, 4

S. Bartolomeo

Palazzo
Dolfin-Manin

Palazzo
Donà

S. Silvestro
1

Palazzo Loredan

Palazzo
Cappello-
Layard

Palazzo Donà
della Madonnetta

S.
Salvatore

Museo
Goldoni

Palazzo Farsetti

Palazzo Grimani

S. Angelo
1

Traghetto

Tomà
4

Palazzo
Corner-Spinelli

Palazzi
Mocenigo

bank was opened here, and the financiers of this quarter were to be the heavy-weights of the international currency exchanges for the next three hundred years and more. The state departments that oversaw all maritime business were here as well, and in the early sixteenth century the offices of the exchequer were installed in the new **Palazzo dei Camerlenghi**, at the foot of the Rialto bridge.

The connection between wealth and moral turpitude was exemplified by the Rialto, which was almost as famous for its fleshpots as for its cashboxes. A sixteenth–century survey showed that there were about 3,000 patrician women in the city, but well over 11,000 prostitutes, the majority of them based in the banking quarter. One Rialto brothel, the *Casteletto*, was especially esteemed for the literary, musical and sexual talents of its staff, and a perennial Venetian bestseller was the *Catalogue of the Chief and Most Renowned Courtesans of Venice*, a directory that told you everything you needed to know, right down to addresses and prices. If Thomas Coryat's report of 1608 is anything to go by, they were seen in some quarters as the city's main attraction—"So infinite are the allurements of these amorous Calypsoes that the fame of them hath drawn many to Venice from some of the remotest parts of Christendome."

The Market

It was through the markets of the Rialto that Venice earned its reputation as the bazaar of Europe. Virtually anything could be bought or sold here: Italian fabrics, precious stones, silver plate and gold jewelry, spices and dyes from the Orient.

Trading had been going on here for over 400 years when, in the winter of 1514, a fire destroyed everything in the area except the church. (Most of the wells and canals were frozen solid, so the blaze burned virtually unchecked for a whole day.) The possibility of relocating the business center was discussed but found little favor, so reconstruction began almost straight away, the **Fabbriche Vecchie** (the arcaded buildings along the Ruga degli Orefici and around the Campo San Giacomo) being finished five years after the fire, and Sansovino's **Fabbriche Nuove** (running along the Canal Grande from Campo C. Battisti) following about thirty years later.

Today's **Rialto market** is tamer than that of Venice at its peak, but it's still one of the liveliest spots in the city, and one of the few places where it's possible to stand in a crowd and hear nothing but Italian spoken. There's a shoal of trinket sellers by the church, gathered to catch the tourists as they spill off the bridge, and a strong showing of glass junk, handbags and "Venezia" sweatshirts farther on, but swing to the right and you're in the true heart of the market—mainly fruit sellers around the **Campo San Giacomo**, vegetable stalls and butcher's shops as you go through to the **Campo Battisti**, then the **Pescheria** (fish market) beyond. (The Pescheria and most of the larger wholesalers close down for the day at around 1pm, but a lot of the smaller fruit and vegetable stalls keep normal shop hours.) Around the junction of **Ruga degli Orefici** and **Ruga Vecchia San Giovanni** you'll find wonderful cheese kiosks, and the Ruga Vecchia has a number of good *alimentari* among the kitsch merchants. If you're in need of liquid refreshment, the old-fashioned bars of Calle do Mori–Calle do Spade (by San Giovanni Elemosinario), which keep hours to match the working day of the

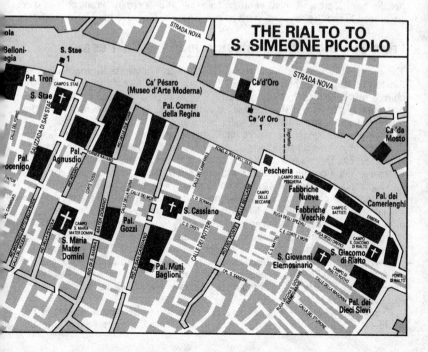

Rialto porters, are among the best in the city. In short, if you can't find something to excite your taste buds around the Rialto, they must be in a sorry state.

San Giacomo—and the Gobbo di Rialto

A popular Venetian legend asserts that the city was founded at noon on Friday March 25, 421 AD; from the same legend derives the claim that the church of **San Giacomo di Rialto** was consecrated in that year, and is thus **the oldest church in Venice**. It might actually be the oldest, though it was rebuilt in 1071, about the same time as San Marco's reconstruction. Parts of the present structure date from this period—the interior's six columns of ancient Greek marble have eleventh-century Veneto-Byzantine capitals—and it seems likely that the reconstruction of the church prompted the establishment of the market here. On the outside of the apse a twelfth-century inscription addresses the merchants of the Rialto—"Around this temple let the merchant's law be just, his weights true, and his promises faithful." Early Venetian churches often had lean-to porticoes like that of San Giacomo, but this is one of only two examples left in the city (the other being San Nicolò dei Mendicoli). The inaccuracy of the clock above—a fifteenth-century addition, like the portico—has been a standing joke in Venice since the day it was installed. The church is supposed to be open from 10am to noon, and sometimes is.

On the opposite side of the campo from the church crouches a stone figure known as the **Gobbo di Rialto** (the Rialto hunchback). It was carved in the sixteenth century and supports a granite platform from which state proclamations were read simultaneously with their announcement from the Pietra del Bando, beside San Marco; it had another role as well—certain wrongdoers were sentenced to run the gauntlet, stark naked, from the Piazza to the Gobbo.

From San Giovanni Elemosinario to the Ca' Pésaro

The fire of 1514 wrecked all of the church of **San Giovanni Elemosinario** (at the top of Ruga Vecchia) except for its early fifteenth-century campanile; the church was rebuilt in 1527–29, to designs by **Scarpagnino**, and decorated with paintings by **Titian** and **Pordenone**, among others. At the moment it's shut for restoration work, and will remain so for some time yet.

Once past the Pescheria, you're into a district which quickly becomes labyrinthine even by Venetian standards. A stroll between the Rio delle Beccarie and the Rio di San Zan Degolà will satisfy any addict of the picturesque—you cannot walk for more than a couple of minutes without coming across a workshop crammed into a ground-floor room or a garden spilling over a canalside wall.

The barnlike church of **San Cassiano** (9:45–11:30am and 4:30–7pm; no tourists allowed on Sun or hols) is a building you're bound to pass as you wander out of the Rialto. The thirteenth-century campanile is the only appealing aspect of the exterior, and the interest of the interior lies mainly with its three paintings by **Tintoretto**: *The Resurrection*, *The Descent into Limbo* and *The Crucifixion* (all 1565–68). The first two have been mauled by restorers, but the third is one of the most startling pictures in Venice—centered on the ladder on which the executioners stand, it's painted as though the observer were lying in the grass at the foot of the Cross.

Campo San Cassiano was the site of the **first public opera house** in the world—it opened in 1637, at the peak of Monteverdi's career. Long into the following century Venice's opera houses were among the most active in Europe; around 500 works received their first performances here in the first half of the eighteenth century.

A sign directs you from the campo over the right-hand bridge towards the Ca' Pésaro, home of the modern art and oriental collections, but before you reach it you'll pass the back of the **Palazzo Corner della Regina**, now the home of the Biennale archives. There's a small selection of works from past shows on display, which you can see after signing in at the desk; access to the Biennale libraries (books, magazines and videos) is at the discretion of the curators, but should be no problem for anyone with an interest.

A diversion down Corte Tiossi from Calle Tiossi brings you to **Santa Maria Mater Domini**, an early sixteenth-century church of disputed authorship— Mauro Coducci and Giovanni Buora are the leading candidates. Venice in Peril's comprehensive overhaul has now been completed, and funds have been found to pay a custodian—so you'll usually find it open. The crisp white and gray interior has blank spaces above its altars, where its paintings might return once they have been restored. One piece is certain to come back—the outstanding *Martyrdom of St Christina* by **Vincenzo Catena**, showing a flight of angels rescuing the saint from Lago di Bolsena, into whose waters she had been hurled with a millstone for an anchor. Few works by this elusive character have survived, and it is not even clear if he was primarily a businessman who painted as a recreation (he seems to have been a successful spice trader) or instead an artist who subsidized himself through commercial dealings (he is mentioned on the reverse of one of Giorgione's paintings as a "colleague").

The small **Campo Santa Maria Mater Domini** would have to be included in any anthology of the hidden delights of Venice; it's a typically Venetian miscellany—a thirteenth-century house (the Casa Zane), a few ramshackle Gothic houses, an assortment of stone reliefs of indeterminate age, a fourteenth-century wellhead in the center, a couple of bars, and an ironsmith's workshop tucked into one corner.

Back at the end of Calle Tiossi, in front of you on the other side of the bridge as you turn right for the Ca' Pésaro, is the late fourteenth-century **Palazzo Agnusdio**, which takes its name not from the family that lived there but from the *patera* of the mystic lamb over the water gate.

The **Ca' Pésaro** was bequeathed to the city at the end of the last century by the Duchessa Felicita Bevilacqua La Masa, who stipulated in her will that it should provide studio and exhibition space for impoverished young artists. Subsequent machinations did in the Duchess's enlightened plans, and in place of the intended living arts center the city acquired the **Galleria d'Arte Moderna** (Tues–Sat 10am–4pm, Sun 9:30am–12:30pm; L3000). Pieces bought from the Biennale formed the foundation of the collection, which consists predominantly of work by Italian artists, many of whom will be unfamiliar (and not surprisingly, you might think in some cases); the sculptures of the nineteenth-century Milanese artist **Medardo Rosso** are the main revelation. Of the major names you'd expect to come across, Klimt, Kandinsky, Matisse, and Klee get a look in— but it's not an outstanding selection. The **Museo Orientale**, on the palace's top floor (Tues–Sat 9am–1:30pm, Sun 9am–12:30pm; L2000), is built round the hoard of artifacts amassed by the Conte di Bardi in the last century during a long Far Eastern voyage. The jumble of lacquer work, armor, screens, weaponry and so forth is likely to perplex and tire all but the initiated.

From San Stae to the Museo di Storia Naturale

Continuing along the line of the Canal Grande from the Ca' Pésaro, Calle Pésaro takes you over the Rio della Rioda, and so to the seventeenth-century church of **San Stae** (a contraction of San Eustachio); its Baroque facade, enlivened by precarious statues, was added around 1710. Repairs to the *marmorino* (pulverized marble) surfaces of the interior have made San Stae as bright as an operating theater. In the chancel there's a series of paintings from the beginning of the eighteenth century, the pick of which are *The Martyrdom of St James the Great* by **Piazzetta** (low on the left), *The Liberation of St Peter* by **Sebastiano Ricci** (same row) and *The Martyrdom of St Bartholomew* by **G.B. Tiepolo** (opposite). In the first chapel on the left side there's a bust of **Antonio Fóscarini**, wrongly executed for treason, as the inscription explains; for the full story, see the entry on the Palazzi Mocenigo in the Canal Grande chapter. Normally the church is open from 10am to 1pm, but exhibitions are sometimes held here, and then the hours tend to change.

The building alongside San Stae, the early seventeenth-century **Scuola dei Battiloro e Tiraoro** (goldsmith's guild), is also used for exhibitions, not all of them quite in harmony with its decorous neighbor—a recent offering featured torture instruments through the ages.

Halfway down the salizzada flanking San Stae is the seventeenth-century **Palazzo Mocenigo**, the main rooms of which are decorated with late eighteenth-century frescoes by **Guarana** and others—the palace is open on Saturdays from 8:30am to 1:30pm (free entrance), but the paintings really are for cognoscenti only. Students of costume design and related subjects can use the facilities of the *Centro Studi di Storia del Tessuto e del Costume*, now housed in the palace (Tues & Wed 8:30am–1:30pm).

The signposted route to the train station passes the deconsecrated and almost permanently shut church of **San Giovanni Decollato** (or San Zan Degolà in dialect; it means "St John the Beheaded"). Established in the opening years of the eleventh century, it has retained its basilican layout through several alterations; the columns and capitals of the nave date from the first century of its existence, and parts of its fragmentary frescoes could be of the same age. Some of the paintings are certainly thirteenth-century, and no other church in Venice has frescoes that predate them. San Giacomo dell' Orio's sacristan might get you in; otherwise you just have to hope that the door is left unlocked during the preparations for the concerts that take place here. The **Museo di Storia Naturale** (Natural History Museum; Tues–Sat 9am–1:30pm, Sun 9am–1pm; L3000) is right by the church, in the **Fondaco dei Turchi**. Top-billing exhibits are the remains of a giant crocodile and an Ouranosaurus, both dug up in the Sahara in 1973; of stricter relevance to Venetian life is the display relating to the lagoon, and a pre-Roman boat dredged from the silt. (For an entry on the building itself, see Chapter Seven.)

From San Giacomo dell'Orio to San Simeone Piccolo

Unless you've got restless kids to keep quiet, in which case a twelve-meter crocodile could come in handy, your time would be better spent at **San Giacomo dell'Orio**, a couple of minutes from the Fondaco (7:30am–noon and 5–8:30pm). Standing in a shaded campo which, despite its size, you could easily miss if you weren't looking for it, the church has a fascinating interior, an agglomeration of materials and styles from the thirteenth century to the sixteenth. Founded in the ninth century and rebuilt in 1225—the approximate date of the campanile—San Giacomo was remodeled on numerous subsequent occasions. Its **ship's keel roof** dates from the fourteenth century; the massive columns, made stockier by frequent raisings of the sidewalk, are a couple of hundred years older. Two of the columns—behind the pulpit and in the right transept—were brought to Venice by the fleet returning from the Fourth Crusade; the latter, an extraordinary chunk of *verde antico*, was compared by the excitable Gabriele d'Annunzio to "the fossilized compression of an immense verdant forest." The shape of the main apse betrays its Byzantine origins, but the inlaid marbles were placed there in the sixteenth century. The altarpiece, *Madonna and Four Saints*, was painted by **Lorenzo Lotto** in 1546, shortly before he left the city complaining that the Venetians had not treated him fairly. The church's principal paintings are on the ceiling of the **new sacristy** (opened by sacristan): *Faith* and *The Doctors of the Church* by **Veronese**. Among the other pictures here is **Francesco Bassano's** *St John the Baptist Preaching*—the spectator on the far left, in the red hat, is Titian.

San Giacomo dell'Orio is plumb in the middle of an extensive residential district, much of which is as close to bland as you can get in Venice. Don't, though, leave out the church of **San Simeone Profeta** (or **Grande**)—remarkable for its reclining effigy of *St Simeon* (to left of chancel), a luxuriantly bearded, larger than lifesize figure whose half-open mouth disturbingly creates the impression of the moment of death. It was sculpted in 1317 by **Marco Romano**, and is the only example of his work in Venice. On the left immediately inside the door, there's a run-of-the-mill *Last Supper* by **Tintoretto**. Originating in the tenth century, the church has been often rebuilt—most extensively in the eighteenth century, when the city sanitation experts, anxious about the condition of the plague victims who had been buried under the flagstones in the 1630 epidemic, ordered the whole floor to be relaid. Close by the church, the Riva di Biasio allows a short walk on the bank of the Canal Grande, with a view across the water of San Geremia.

San Simeone Profeta is the last stop before the Scalzi bridge. Immediately after the bridge, the early eighteenth-century **San Simeone Piccolo** (with the conspicuous green dome), is closed; its main function nowadays is as a pigeon loft.

Campo San Polo and Around

The largest square in Venice after the Piazza, the **Campo San Polo** is the best place in the area to sit down and tuck into a bagful of supplies from the Rialto market. Most of the traffic passes down the church side, leaving a huge area of the campo free for those in no hurry to get a bit of sun, and for the budding Roberto Baggios of the parish to practice their ball skills. In earlier times it was the site of weekly markets and occasional fairs, and was also used as a bullfighting arena and parade ground.

Several palaces overlook the campo, the most impressive of which is the double **Palazzo Soranzo** (late fourteenth century to mid-fifteenth century), over the square from the church. This might seem an exception to the rule that the main palace facade should look onto the water, but in fact a canal used to run across the campo just in front of the Soranzo house. Casanova gained his introduction to the Venetian upper classes through a senator who lived in this palace; he was hired to work as a musician in the house and so impressed the old man that he was adopted as his son. On the same side as the church, but in the opposite corner, is the **Palazzo Corner Mocenigo**, designed c.1550 by **Sanmicheli**—the main facade is visible from the bridge beyond the church. In 1909 **Frederick Rolfe** (Baron Corvo) became a tenant here, an arrangement that came to an abrupt end the following year when his hosts discovered that the manuscript he was working on—*The Desire and Pursuit of the Whole*—was a vitriolic satire directed at them and many of their acquaintances. Rolfe was given the alternative of abandoning the libellous novel or moving out; he moved out, contracted pneumonia as a result of sleeping on the streets and became so ill he was given the last rites—but he managed to pull through, and lived for a further three disreputable years.

Restoration carried out in the early nineteenth century made a thorough mess of the fifteenth-century Gothic of **San Polo** church, which was established as far back as the ninth century (7:30am–noon and 4–7pm, Sun & hols 8am–12:15pm). The beautiful main doorway, possibly by **Bartolomeo Bon**, survives from the first church. The bleak interior is worth a visit for a superior *Last Supper* by **Tintoretto** (on the left as you enter) and a cycle of the *Stations of the Cross* by

Giandomenico Tiepolo (in the *Oratory of the Crucifix*—entrance under organ), a series painted when the artist was only twenty. The genuine piety of these pictures may persuade you to amend a few preconceptions about Giandomenico; nevertheless, you can't resist the suspicion that his interest was less in the central drama than in the society portraits which fill the edges of the stage. Paintings by **Giambattista Tiepolo** and **Veronese** are to be found on the second altar opposite the door and in the chapel on the left of the chancel—neither shows the artist at his best. The detached campanile, built in 1362, has a couple of twelfth-century lions at its base, one of which is playing with a snake, the other with a severed human head.

North from the Campo

Calle della Madonnetta, leading away from the campo in the direction of the Rialto, is the beginning of a sequence of shopping streets in which you'll find, at the San Polo end, a couple of the best *pasticcerie* in Venice and, farther on towards the Rialto, a cluster of tempting shoe and clothes shops. The really chic part of the route, with Gaultier outfits in the windows, runs past **Sant'Aponal** (in full, Sant'Apollinare), now used as an archive. Its most interesting feature is on the outside anyway—the *Crucifixion and Scenes from the Life of Christ* (1294), in the

THE RIALTO TO TOLENTINI

tabernacle over the door. Venetian legend has it that Pope Alexander III, on the run in 1177 from the troops of Emperor Frederick Barbarossa, found refuge close to Sant' Aponal; over the entrance to the Sottoportego della Madonna (to your left as you face the church), a plaque records his plight and promises a perpetual plenary indulgence to anyone saying a Pater Noster and Ave Maria on the spot.

Slip down Calle Sbianchesini from Sant'Aponal (towards the Canal Grande), and you come to the nondescript church of **San Silvestro**. It deserves a visit for Tintoretto's *Baptism of Christ*, one of his simplest paintings.

South from the Campo

Salizzada San Polo and Calle dei Saoneri, on the opposite side of the Campo San Polo from Calle Madonera, are effectively a continuation of the upmarket shopping strip—the chain of alleys from the Rialto's Ruga Vecchia San Giovanni down to this part of town being the right bank's nearest equivalent to the Mercerie of San Marco. And if you're in the market for high-class jewelry, here's the place to look, as the San Tomà parish is the base of many of Venice's silver and goldsmiths.

If you turn right halfway down Calle dei Saoneri, you're on your way to the Frari (see below); carry on to the end and then turn left, and you'll soon come to the fifteenth-century **Palazzo Centani**, in Calle dei Nomboli. This was the birthplace of the playwright **Carlo Goldoni** (1707–93), of whom it was said that he first adopted the indigenous theater of the Commedia dell' Arte, and then killed it off. Goldoni's plays are still the staple of theatrical life in Venice, and there's no risk of running out of material—allegedly, he once bet a friend that he could produce one play a week for a whole year, and won. The building now houses the *Istituto di Studi Teatrali* and the **Museo Goldoni**, a small collection of first editions, autograph papers and theatrical paraphernalia; the display is less diverting than the building itself, which has one of Venice's finest Gothic courtyards and a beautiful wellhead. (Mon–Sat 8:30am–1:30pm; free.)

The church of **San Tomà**, a few yards past Goldoni's house, is now a sad, broken-backed structure that looks as if it's been given up as a hopeless cause. In the days when the Venetians were known as the sharpest relic-hunters around, San Tomà was the city's bumper depository, claiming to possess some 10,000 sacred bits and pieces and a dozen intact holy corpses. At the other end of the campo, the facade of the **Scuola dei Caleghieri** (shoemaker's guild), has a relief by **Pietro Lombardo** (1478), showing Saint Mark healing the cobbler Ananias.

A **vaporetto and traghetto stage**—one of the transit system's most useful time-savers—is at the back of the church midway between the Rialto and Accademia bridges.

The Frari, the Scuola di San Rocco, and the Church of San Rocco

For a rapid survey of the summit of Venetian painting in its golden age, your first stop after the Accademia should be the constellation of buildings a few alleys west of San Polo—the **Frari**, the **Scuola Grande di San Rocco** and **San Rocco** church. The genesis of Ruskin's obsession with Venice was a visit to the Scuola, where a pictorial interpretation of the life of Christ by **Tintoretto** flows through the entire building; and if you can take yet more after the intensity of the Scuola's cycle, the church next door contains more works by him. A trio of magnificent altarpieces by **Bellini** and **Titian** are the principal treasures of the Frari, but even if these don't strike a chord there's bound to be something among the church's assembly of paintings, sculptures and monuments that'll get it onto your list of Venetian highlights.

The Frari

San Zanipolo and **Santa Maria Gloriosa dei Frari** (always abbreviated to the **Frari**) are the twin Gothic giants of Venice—from the Campanile of San Marco they can be seen jutting above the rooftops on opposite sides of the Canal Grande, like a pair of destroyers amid a flotilla of yachts.

The Franciscans were granted a plot of land here around 1250, not long after the death of their founder, but almost no sooner was the first church completed (in 1338) than work began on a vast replacement—a project which took well over a hundred years. The campanile, one of the city's landmarks and the tallest after San Marco's, was finished in 1396. Admirers of northern Gothic are unlikely to fall in love at first sight with this mountain of brick. Only a few pieces of sculpture relieve the monotony of the exterior: on the **west front**, there's a figure of *The Risen Christ* by **Vittoria**, and a *Virgin* and *St Francis* from the workshop of **Bartolomeo Bon**; an impressive early fifteenth-century Tuscan relief of the *Madonna and Child with Angels* is set into the side of the left transept. As is so often the case in Venice, though, the outside of the church is a misleadingly dull prelude to a remarkable interior. (Mon–Sat 9:30am–noon and 2:30–6pm, Sun & hols afternoon only; small entrance fee to cover cost of lighting, but free on Sun.)

Titian's Altarpieces

Paradoxically, Venice is under-endowed with paintings by **Titian**, its most illustrious artist: apart from the Accademia and the Salute, the Frari is the only building in Venice with more than a single significant work by him. One of these—the *Assumption*—you see almost immediately as you look towards the altar main through the monks' choir. A piece of compositional and coloristic bravura for which there was no precedent in Venetian art—for one thing, no previous altarpiece had been taller than it was wide—the *Assumption* nevertheless fits its surroundings perfectly. The spiralling motion of the Apostles and the Virgin complements the vertical movement of the surrounding architecture, an integration that is strengthened by the coincidence between the division of the painting's two major groupings and the division of the windows in the chancel. It seems to have disconcerted the friars for whom it was painted, but nonetheless was instantly recognized as a major work. **Marin Sanudo**, whose *Diaries* are an essential source for historians of the Republic, somehow wrote 58 volumes containing scarcely a mention of any Venetian artist—yet even he refers to the ceremony on May 19, 1518, at which the altarpiece was unveiled.

(The **monks' choir** itself shouldn't be ignored. Built in the late fifteenth century, with a marble screen by **Bartolomeo Bon** and **Pietro Lombardo**, it's now the only one left in Venice that occupies a site in the nave.)

The other Titian masterpiece here, the *Madonna di Ca' Pésaro* (to the left of the door), was completed eight years after the *Assumption* and was equally innovative, in its displacement of the figure of the Virgin from the center of the

THE FRARI

1. 'Madonna di Ca' Pésaro'
2. Cappella Emiliani
3. Monks' Choir
4. Cappella Corner
5. Vivarini and Basaiti's 'St. Ambrose'
6. Tomb of Doge Niccolo Tron
7. Titian's 'Assumption'
8. Tomb of Doge Francesco Fóscari
9. Donatello's 'St. John'
10. Bartolomeo Vivarini Altarpiece
11. Tombs of Paolo Savelli, Benedetto Pésaro and Beato Pacifico
12. The Bellini Altarpiece
13. Tomb of Jacopop Marcello
14. Vittoria's 'St. Jerome'
15. Titian's Monument
16. Tomb of Alvise Pasqualino
17. Tomb of Pietro Bernardo
18. Mausoleum of Canova
19. Tomb of Doge Giovanni Pésaro

picture. The altarpiece was commissioned by Bishop Jacopo Pésaro, who managed to combine his episcopal duties with a military career; in 1502 he had led a successful naval campaign against the Turks—hence the prisoners being dragged in, behind the kneeling figure of Pésaro himself, to meet the Redeemer and His Mother. Pésaro's tomb, with an effigy, is to the right (c.1547).

The Chapels, Chancel, and Sacristy

A doorway next to the the Pésaro monument leads into the **Cappella Emiliani**, which has a fifteenth-century marble altarpiece by followers of **Jacobello Dalle Masegne**. The **Cappella Corner** (end of left transept, often locked) contains a painting by **Bartolomeo Vivarini**, *St Mark Enthroned* (1474) and, on the font, a figure of *St John the Baptist* by **Sansovino** (1554).

St Ambrose and other Saints, the last painting by **Alvise Vivarini**, the nephew of Bartolomeo, is in the adjoining chapel. Overpopulated with meticulously drawn but lifeless figures, it was finished c.1503 by a pupil, Marco Basaiti. A plaque in the floor marks the grave of **Monteverdi**, for thirty years choirmaster of San Marco.

Two monuments illustrating the emergence in Venice of Renaissance sculptural style flank the Titian *Assumption*: on the left the proto-Renaissance **tomb of Doge Niccolò Tron**, by **Antonio Rizzo** and assistants (1476); on the right, the more archaic and chaotic **tomb of Doge Francesco Fóscari**, carved shortly after Fóscari's death in 1457 (after 34 years as doge) by **Antonio and Paolo Bregno**. The story of Fóscari's last days is one of the most poignant in Venice's history. Already in ill health and constantly harried by political enemies, Fóscari went into a rapid decline when his son, Jacopo, was found guilty of treason (on the flimsiest evidence) and exiled for life. Within half a year Jacopo was dead, and Doge Fóscari sank farther into a depression which his opponents lost no time in exploiting. After several months of pressure, they forced him into resignation; a week later he died. It was reported that when the senators and new doge were told of his death, as they were attending mass in San Marco, they looked guiltily at each other "knowing well that it was they who had shortened his life."

The wooden statue of *St John the Baptist*, in the next chapel, was commissioned from **Donatello** in 1438 by Florentine merchants in Padua; recent work has restored its luridly naturalistic appearance. In the last of the chapels stands a **Bartolomeo Vivarini** altarpiece—*Madonna and Child with Saints* (1482).

On the left of the **sacristy door** is the **tomb of Paolo Savelli** (c.1406), the first equestrian monument in Venice; next along is **Lorenzo Bregno**'s tomb of another Pésaro—Benedetto, head of the Venetian army, who died in Corfu in 1503; and the flamboyant Gothic work on the other side of the door is the terracotta **tomb of Beato Pacifico**, who is traditionally credited with beginning the present church and was placed here in 1437, nearly a century after his death.

On the altar of the **sacristy** (the site for which it was created), and in its original frame, is a picture which alone would justify an hour in the Frari—the *Madonna and Child with SS. Nicholas of Bari, Peter, Mark and Benedict*, painted in 1488 by **Giovanni Bellini**. There's little to add to the words of Henry James— "it is as solemn as it is gorgeous and as simple as it is deep." From the sacristy there's occasional access to the **chapter house**, with its **tomb of Doge Francesco Dandolo** (c.1340); the painting above it by **Paolo Veneziano** contains what is probably the first portrait of a doge ever painted from life.

The Rest of the Church

Back in the right transept, on the west wall, there's the very odd **tomb of Jacopo Marcello**, supported by small stooping figures (c.1485, probably by **Giovanni Buora**). High on the wall round the corner is something far less florid but equally strange—a plain black coffin which is said to have been meant for the body of the *condottiere* **Carmagnola**, who, having shown a suspicious reluctance to earn his money against the Milanese (his former employers), was executed after a dodgy treason trail in 1432. But Carmagnola is now in Milan, and another tenant occupies the coffin.

Facing the Pésaro altarpiece stands one of **Alessandro Vittoria**'s best marble figures—*St Jerome*, for which Titian was reputedly the model. The house-sized tomb farther along is the bombastic **monument to Titian**, built in the mid-nineteenth century on the supposed place of his burial. He died in 1576, in around his 90th year, a casualty of the plague; such was the esteem in which Titian was held, he was the only victim to be allowed a church burial in the course of the outbreak.

The delicate statuettes against the last columns, facing each other across the nave, are *St Anthony of Padua* and *St Agnes* by **Campagna** (1609). The **tomb of Procurator Alvise Pasqualino**, on the left of the door, is attributed to **Lorenzo Bregno**, whose death in 1523 preceded his client's by five years. Ordering your tomb in advance was not an unusual practice: **Pietro Bernardo** (died 1538), whose tomb (possibly by **Tullio Lombardo**, died 1532) is on the other side of the door, did the same thing—although the finished article was rather more humble than he had intended. In his will he specified, among other provisions, that his epitaph should be cut in letters legible from 25 paces, and should be accompanied by an epic poem of 800 stanzas, extolling the Bernardo family. His executors seem to have wriggled out of these and another clause as well, which ordered that a monastic choir should sing psalms in front of his tomb on the first Sunday of every month until Judgement Day.

The marble pyramid with the troop of mourners is the **Mausoleum of Canova**, erected in 1827 by pupils of the sculptor, following a design he himself had made for the tombs of Titian and Maria Christina of Austria. Only the artist's heart is actually entombed here—most of the body was interred at Possagno (see separate entry), but his right hand is somewhere in the Accademia.

On your way out you'll be stopped in your tracks by what is surely the most grotesque monument in the city; this is the tomb of yet another Pésaro—**Doge Giovanni Pésaro** (1669). The architecture is usually attributed to **Longhena**; for the gigantic ragged-trousered Moors and decomposing corpses, a German sculptor called **Melchiorre Barthel** must take the blame.

The Archives

At the fall of the Republic the Franciscan monastery alongside the church was taken over for use as the **Archivio di Stato** (State Archives). Its documents, cramming more than 300 rooms, relate to the Council of Ten, the courts, the embassies, the Arsenale, the *scuole*—to every aspect of Venetian public life—and go back as far as the ninth century. From time to time the archive puts on an exhibition of material dredged from the shelves; the shows habitually sound unenthralling (a theme in 1987 was Venice's management of the mainland forests), but if you're interested in the city's past you should get something from them.

The Scuola Grande di San Rocco—and the Church

Venice may not tell you much about Titian's work that you didn't already know, but in the case of **Tintoretto** the situation is reversed—until you've been to Venice, and in particular the **Scuola Grande di San Rocco** (summer daily 10am–1pm & 3:30–6:30pm; in winter 10am–2pm; L5000), you haven't really seen him. "As regards the pictures which it contains, it is one of the three most precious buildings in Italy," wrote Ruskin, and although the claim's open to argument, it's not difficult to understand why he resorted to such hyperbole. (His other votes were for the Sistine Chapel and the Campo Santo at Pisa—the latter was badly damaged in World War II.) The concentration and restlessness of Tintoretto's paintings won't inspire unqualified enthusiasm in everyone (Henry James, though an admirer, found the atmosphere of San Rocco "difficult to breathe"), but even those who prefer their art at a lower voltage will find the Scuola an overwhelming experience.

From its foundation in 1478 the special concern of this particular scuola was the relief of the sick—a continuation of the Christian mission of its patron saint, Saint Roch (Rocco) of Montpellier. The Scuola had been going for seven years when the body of the saint was brought to Venice from Germany, and the consequent boom in donations was so great that in 1489 it acquired the status of *Scuola Grande*. The intervention of Saint Roch was held to be especially efficacious in cases of bubonic plague, an illness from which he himself had been rescued by angelic assistance (which is why the churches of Venice are littered with paintings of the saint pointing to a sore on his thigh). When, in 1527, the city was hit by an outbreak of plague the Scuola's revenue rocketed to record levels as gifts poured in from people hoping to secure Saint Roch's protection against the disease. In 1515 the Scuola had commissioned a prestigious new headquarters from **Bartolomeo Bon the Younger**, but for various reasons the work had ground to a halt within a decade; the fattened coffers naturally prompted a second phase of building, and from 1527–49 the scheme was taken over by **Scarpagnino**.

When the scaffolding came down in 1560, the end product was incoherent and lopsided. Not that the members of the Scuola would have been bothered for long: within a few years the decoration of the interior was under way, and it was this decoration—**Tintoretto**'s cycle of more than fifty major paintings—that secured the confraternity's social standing. An opportunistic little trick won the first contract for Tintoretto. In 1564 the Scuola held a competition to decide who should paint the inaugural picture for the recently completed building. The subject was to be *The Glorification of St Roch*, and four artists were approached for proposals: Salviati, Zuccari, Veronese and Tintoretto. On the day for submissions the first three duly presented their sketches; Tintoretto, though, had painted a finished panel and persuaded a sidekick to rig it up, hidden by a veil, in the very place in which the winning picture was to be installed—the center of the ceiling in the Sala dell'Albergo. A rope was pulled, the picture revealed, and the commission, despite the opposition's fury, was given to Tintoretto. Further commissions ensued, which were to occupy much of his time until 1587.

The Sala dell'Albergo

The narrative sequence of the cycle begins with the first picture in the lower room—the *Annunciation*. But to appreciate Tintoretto's development you have to begin in the smaller room on the upper story—the **Sala dell'Albergo**. This is dominated by the stupendous *Crucifixion* (1565), the most compendious image of the event ever painted. Henry James made even greater claims for it: "Surely no single picture in the world contains more of human life; there is everything in it." Ruskin was reduced to a state of dumbfounded wonder—his loquacious commentary on the San Rocco cycle concludes with the entry: "I must leave this picture to work its will on the spectator; for it is beyond all analysis, and above all praise." The other works in the room inevitably suffer from such company, but several of them reward close attention. On the entrance wall are *The Way to Calvary*, *Christ Crowned with Thorns* and *Christ before Pilate*. The easel painting of *Christ Carrying the Cross* has been attributed to Giorgione but now is generally thought to be an early Titian; from c.1510 until 1955 it was displayed in the church of San Rocco, where it was revered as a miraculous image. The other easel painting is probably by a pupil of Giorgione.

The Chapter House and Lower Hall

Tintoretto finished work in the Sala dell'Albergo in 1567, and after a pause of eight years started on the main upper hall—the **Chapter House**. The Old Testament subjects depicted by the three large panels of the **ceiling** (the first part to be painted) are coded declarations of the Scuola's charitable program, with their references to the alleviation of physical suffering; they are—*Moses Striking Water from the Rock*, *The Miracle of the Brazen Serpent* and *The Miraculous Fall of Manna*. (If you want to know what's going on in the smaller panels, you can buy a detailed guide to the Scuola downstairs.)

The New Testament scenes around the **walls**, an amazing feat of sustained inventiveness, defy every convention of perspective, lighting, color and even anatomy. From this one room it's clear that Tintoretto was never content with inherited ideas; other treatments of the same themes by him elsewhere in Venice show that he was rarely content with his own—compare, for example, the *Fall of Manna* here with the depiction of it in San Giorgio Maggiore. On the **left wall** (as you face the altar)—*Nativity, Baptism, Resurrection, Agony in the Garden, Last Supper*; on the **right wall**—*Temptation of Christ* (underneath, a portrait by Tintoretto, often wrongly called a self-portrait), *Miracle at the Pool of Bethesda, Ascension, Raising of Lazarus, Miracle of the Loaves and Fishes*. On the **end wall**—*St Roch* and *St Sebastian*; on the **altar**—*The Vision of St Roch* (1588, with his son, Domenico); on **easels to side of altar**—*Annunciation* (**Titian**), *Visitation* (**Tintoretto**), *Hagar, Ishmael and an Angel* and *Abraham and an Angel* (early works by **G.B. Tiepolo**).

The trompe l'oeil bookcases and other virtuoso **carvings** were done in the late seventeenth century by **Francesco Pianta**—not far from the altar you'll find a caricature of the irascible Tintoretto (with a bouquet of paintbrushes). The painter's short temper was notorious—for instance, when a group of senators, seeing him at work on the *Paradiso* in the Palazzo Ducale, observed that some of his rivals painted more slowly and more carefully, he's said to have replied that this was possibly because they didn't have to contend with such stupid onlookers.

The paintings in the **Lower Hall** were created between 1583 and 1587, when Tintoretto was in his late sixties. The violent *Annunciation*, with the Archangel crashing through the wall pursued by a tornado of cherubim, is followed by *Adoration of the Magi, Flight into Egypt* (a magnificent landscape), *Massacre of the Innocents, St Mary Magdalen, St Mary of Egypt, Circumcision* (painted with workshop assistance) and *Assumption*.

The Church of San Rocco

Yet more Tintorettos are to be found in the **church of San Rocco**, built in 1489–1508 to designs by **Bartolomeo Bon the Younger**, but altered extensively in the eighteenth century. On the right wall of the nave you'll find *St Roch Taken to Prison*, and below it *The Pool of Bethesda*; only the latter is definitely by Tintoretto. Between the altars on the other side are a couple of good pictures by **Pordenone**—*St Christopher* and *St Martin*. Four large paintings by Tintoretto hang in the chancel, but they're usually either lost in the gloom or glazed with sunlight: the best (both painted in 1549) are *St Roch Curing the Plague Victims* (lower right) and *St Roch in Prison* (lower left). The two higher pictures are *St Roch in Solitude* and *St Roch Healing the Animals*—the second is a doubtful attribution.

For a quick dose of frivolity to leaven the day, pop round to the waterside sidewalk at the back of the Scuola; on the far side of the canal there's a house decked out with scores of toy windmills in all shapes and colors, evidently planted by someone for whom the Sixties never ended.

San Giovanni Evangelista, the Tolentini, and San Pantaleone

Another of the Scuole Grandi nestles in a line of drab buildings very near to the Frari—the **Scuola di San Giovanni Evangelista**, founded in 1261 by one of the many flagellant confraternities that sprang up at that time. This institution's finest hour came in 1369, when it was presented with a **relic of the True Cross**, an item that can be seen to this day in the first-floor **Oratorio della Croce**. The miracles effected by the relic were commemorated in the Oratory by a series of paintings by Carpaccio, Gentile Bellini and others, now transplanted to the Accademia.

Nowadays the delights of the Scuola are architectural. The **courtyards** are something of a composite: the mid-fifteenth-century facade of the Scuola incorporates two mid-fourteenth-century reliefs, and the **screen** of the outer courtyard was built in 1481 by **Pietro Lombardo**. The latter is one of Venice's pleasantest surprises—approached from the train station direction it just looks like any old brick wall, but round the other side it reveals itself to be as delicate a piece of marble carving as any church interior could show. Inside, a grand **double staircase** built by **Coducci** in 1498 rises to the main hall and the Oratorio; the climb is more enjoyable than its culmination, as the hall is clad with lifeless paintings, many showing scenes from the life of Saint John, most of them by Domenico Tintoretto. The Scuola is open Monday to Friday 9:30am to 12:30pm; ring for admission—they might balk at letting you into the Oratorio, but there shouldn't be any problem about getting a look at the Coducci bits, unless one of the Scuola's frequent conferences is in progress.

The church of San Giovanni Evangelista is one of the select band of religious buildings in Venice that are of no interest whatsoever.

The Tolentini

Calle della Lacca–Fondamenta Sacchere–Calle Amai is a dullish but uncomplicated route from San Giovanni Evangelista to San Nicolò da Tolentino, alias the **Tolentini** (daily 7:45am–noon & 4:30–7pm). A portentous church begun in 1590 by Palladio's follower **Scamozzi**, it was finished in 1714 by the addition of a free-standing portico—the first in Venice—designed by **Andrea Tirali**. Among the scores of seventeenth-century paintings, just two stand much chance of becoming lodged in the memory—*St Jerome* by **Johann Lys** (wall outside chancel on left) and *St Lawrence Giving Alms* by **Bernardo Strozzi** (round the corner from the Lys painting). Up the left wall of the chancel, though, swirls the best Baroque monument in Venice: the **monument to Francesco Morosini** (1678). That's Francesco Morosini, Patriarch of Venice, incidentally—on no account to be confused with Francesco Morosini, Doge of Venice 1688–94, buried in Santo Stefano. If fatigue is setting in and you need a pit-stop, the **Giardini Papadopoli**, once one of Venice's biggest private gardens but now owned by the city, is just over the Rio dei Tolentini. In winter you may have to make do with the sidewalk, because the park's often shut then.

San Pantaleone

To the south of the Frari runs the teeming Crosera San Pantalon, the atmosphere in whose shops, cafés and bars has a lot to do with the proximity of the university. Between this street and the Rio di Ca' Fóscari stands the church of **San Pantaleone** (or Pantalon; 8–11:30am & 4:30–7pm), which possesses a picture by **Antonio Vivarini and Giovanni d'Alemagna** (*Coronation of the Virgin*, in the Chapel of the Holy Nail, to left of chancel) and **Veronese**'s last painting, *San Pantaleone Healing a Boy* (second chapel on right). San Pantaleone was credited with medicinal capabilities only slightly less awesome than San Rocco's, and Veronese's scene emphasises the miraculous nature of his power (he spurns the offered box of potions) and the impotence of non-Christian treatment (symbolized by the limbless figure of Asclepius, the classical god of medicine). The church can also boast of having the most melodramatic **ceiling** in the city: *The Martyrdom and Apotheosis of San Pantaleone*. Painted on sixty panels, some of which actually jut out over the nave, it kept **Gian Antonio Fumiani** busy from 1680 to 1704. Sadly, he never got the chance to bask in the glory of his labors—he died in a fall from the scaffolding on which he'd been working.

RESTAURANTS: *Alla Madonna*, Calle della Madonna (near Rialto); *All'Anfora*, Lista Vecchia dei Bari; *Alla Rivetta*, Ponte San Provolo; *Da Silvio*, Calle San Pantalon; *Donna Onesta*, Calle della Madonna (near I Frari); *Trattoria Rialto Nuovo*, Campo Rialto Nuovo.

PIZZAS: *Alle Oche*, Calle del Tintor; *Da Sandro*, Campielo dei Meloni; *Giardinetto*, Fondamenta del Forner; *San Tomà*, Campo San Tomà.

SNACKS AND BARS: *Do Mori*, Calle Do Mori; *Do Spade*, Sottoportego delle Do Spade; Rialto district in general.

CAFÉS AND PASTICCERIE: Crosera San Pantalon and Campiello Meloni.

Reviews of all these places appear in Chapter 10.

CHAPTER FOUR

CANNAREGIO

Within the northernmost section of Venice, **Cannaregio**, you pass from one urban extreme to another in a matter of minutes, the time it takes to get away from the hubbub of the train station and the hustle of the execrable Lista di Spagna—the tawdriest street in Venice—and into the backwaters away from the Canal Grande. There may no longer be any signs of the bamboo clumps that were the source of the *sestiere*'s name (*canna* means "reed"), but in all of Venice you won't find as many village-like parishes as in Cannaregio, and exploring them at any time of year you'll be well away from the crowds.

Imprisoned in the very center of Cannaregio is the **Ghetto**, the first place in the world to bear that name, and one of Venice's most evocative areas. The pleasures of the rest of Cannaregio are generally more a matter of atmosphere than of specific sights, but there are a few special buildings to visit too: **Madonna dell'Orto**, with its astonishing Tintoretto paintings; **San Giobbe**, the Venetian debut of Pietro Lombardo; and **Sant'Alvise** and the **Palazzo Labia**, the first remarkable for canvases by Giambattista Tiepolo, the second for the same artist's frescoes.

From the Train Station to San Giobbe

The area around Venice's train station is one in which nearly every visitor sets foot but very few actually investigate. Nobody could pretend that it's one of the city's enticing spots, but it does repay a saunter. The station building itself is a functional 1950s effort, but the rail link to the mainland was opened in the 1840s; within a few years the expansion of traffic had made it necessary to demolish Palladio's church of Santa Lucia, the building from which the station's name is taken.

The Scalzi

Right by the station stands the **Scalzi** (formally Santa Maria di Nazareth), which was built in the 1670s for the barefoot ("scalzi") order of Carmelites, but is anything but barefoot itself. **Giuseppe Sardi**'s facade—fenced off for some time to protect mortals from falling angels—is fairly undemonstrative compared with **Baldessare Longhena**'s opulent interior, where the walls are plated with dark, multicolored marble and overgrown with Baroque statuary. Ruskin condemned it as "a perfect type of the vulgar abuse of marble in every possible way, by men who had no eye for color, and no understanding of any merit in a work of art but that which rises from costliness of material, and such powers of imitation as are devoted in England to the manufacture of peaches and eggs out of Derbyshire spar." Before an Austrian bomb plummeted through the roof in 1915 there was a splendid **G.B. Tiepolo** ceiling to introduce a bit of good taste into the proceed-

CANNAREGIO

SACCA DI
S. GIROLAMO

CAN. DI CANNAREGIO

Ponte d.
Tre Archi
5

Macello

PONTE DE
TRE ARCHI

F. DELLE CAPUCCINE

R. DI S. GIROLAMO

CAMPO
DI S. GIOBBE

San
Giobbe

F. DI CANNAREGIO
CAN. DI CANNAREGIO

Scola
Levantina

R. DELLA CREA

Pte. Guglie
5

PONTE
GUGLIE

Palazzo
Savorgnan

Palazzo
Labia

CAMPO.
S. GEREMIA

S. Geremia

R. T. LISTA DI SPAGNA

R. di

Canal Grande

Scalzi

Train
Station

Ponte
degli
Scalzi

Ferrovia
1

Traghetto

S. Simeone
Piccolo

ings; a couple of scraps are preserved in the Accademia, and some wan frescoes by him survive in the first chapel on the left and the second on the right.

As well as containing a pair of huge candlesticks that are about the most impressive examples of Murano glass you'll see, this last chapel is also the resting place of **Lodovico Manin** (d.1802), Venice's last doge. The bare inscription—"Manini Cineres" (The Ashes of Manin)—is a fair reflection of the low esteem in which he was held. His chief rival for the dogeship wailed "a Friulian as doge! The Republic is dead!" when Manin was elected, and although Lodovico can't take the blame for the death of independent Venice, he did on occasion display a certain lack of moral backbone. In response to French demands he meekly surrendered his insignia of office to be burned on a bonfire in the Piazza, and when later called upon to swear an oath of allegiance to Austria, he fell down in a dead faint .

Along the Lista di Spagna to San Geremia

Foreign embassies used to be corralled into this area to make life a little easier for the Republic's spies, and the **Lista di Spagna** takes its name from the Spanish embassy which used to be at no. 168. (*Lista* indicates a street leading to an embassy.) It's now completely given over to the tourist industry with shops and stalls, bars, restaurants and hotels all plying for the same desperate trade—people who are spending one day "doing Venice," or those who have arrived too late and too tired to look any farther. Whether you're hunting for a trinket, a meal or a bed, you'll find it cheaper and better elsewhere.

The church of **San Geremia**, at the end of the Lista, is where the travels of **Saint Lucy** eventually terminated—martyred in Syracuse in 304, her body was stolen from Constantinople by Venetian Crusaders in 1204, then ousted from her own church in Venice by the railroad authorities in the mid-nineteenth century. Lucy's response to an unwanted suitor who praised her beautiful eyes was to pluck out the offending organs, a display of otherworldliness that led to her adoption as the patron saint of eyesight (and, logically enough, of artists). Her dessicated body lies behind the altar, reclining above a donations box that bears the prayer "Saint Lucy, protect my eyes." Nothing else about the church is of interest, except the twelfth-century **campanile**, one of the oldest left in the city.

The Palazzo Labia

The **Palazzo Labia** (next door to San Geremia) was built in 1720–50 for a famously extravagant Spanish family by the name of Lasbias, who had bought their way into the *Libro d'Oro* (the register of the nobility) for the obligatory 100,000 ducats in the middle of the previous century. Their taste for conspicuous expenditure wasn't lessened by the cost of the house—a party here once finished with a member of the Labia family hurling the gold dinner service from the window into the canal and declaiming the worst-ever Venetian pun: "L'abia o non l'abia, sarò sempre Labia" ("Whether I have it or whether I have it not, I will always be a Labia). The impact of the gesture is somewhat lessened by the rumor that fishing nets had been placed in the canal so the service could be retrieved under cover of darkness. (The Labia spirit lived on into the twentieth century—in the 1950s the whole *belle monde* was set buzzing by the ball thrown here by the palace's Mexican proprietor, Carlos de Besteign.) No cost was spared on decoration either, and no sooner was the interior completed than **G.B. Tiepolo** was hired to cover the walls of the ballroom with **frescoes** depicting the story of Anthony and Cleopatra. (The architectural trompe l'oeil work is by another artist—Gerolamo Mengozzi Colonna.) Restored to something approaching their original freshness after years of neglect and some damage in the last war, this is the only sequence of Tiepolo paintings in Venice that are comparable to his narrative masterpieces in such mainland villas as the Villa Valmarana near Vicenza (see Chapter Twelve). RAI, the Italian radio and TV company, now owns the palace, but they allow visitors in for a few hours each week (currently Wed, Thurs & Fri 3–4pm; appointment essential; ☎781111); the public can also attend the concerts that are recorded here—for free tickets ask at the door or phone to reserve in advance.

San Giobbe

The Palazzo Labia's longest facade overlooks the Canale di Cannaregio, the main entrance to Venice before the rail and road links were constructed; if you turn left along its fondamenta rather than going with the flow over the the Ponte delle Guglie, you'll be virtually alone by the time you're past the late seventeenth-century Palazzo Savorgnan. (So great was the Savorgnans' social clout that the Rezzonico family marked their intermarriage by getting Tiepolo to paint a fresco celebrating the event in the Ca' Rezzonico.) Swing left at the Ponte dei Tre Archi (Venice's only multiple-span bridge) and you're at the church of **San Giobbe**, like San Moisè an example of Venice's habit of canonizing Old Testament figures.

"So went Satan forth from the presence of the Lord and smote Job with sore boils from the sole of his foot unto his crown" records the Bible. Job's physical sufferings—sanctioned by the Almighty in order to test his faith—greatly endeared him to the Venetians, who were regularly afflicted with malaria, plague and a plethora of damp-related diseases, and in the fourteenth century an oratory dedicated to him was founded here. Antonio Gambello began a Gothic replacement in the mid-fifteenth century, but the specially interesting parts of the building are its exquisitely carved doorway and chancel, early Renaissance works by **Pietro Lombardo**, whose first Venetian project this was.

Gambello's church was a commemoration of a recent visit by Fra Bernardino of Siena, an eminent member of the Observant Franciscans; their wide-ranging organization explains the presence of non-Venetian elements such as the roundels and tiles from the **Della Robbia** workshop in the Cappella Martini (2nd chapel on left). The tomb slab in the center of the chancel floor is that of **Doge Cristoforo Moro**, the donor of the new building; a satirical leaflet about Moro may have been a source for Shakespeare's *Othello*, even though—as the portrait in the sacristy shows—Moro bore no racial similarity to the Moor of Venice. San Giobbe's altarpieces by Bellini and Carpaccio have been removed to the damp-free environment of the Accademia; the parishioners might not weep if a crowbar were taken to the lions on the tomb of the magnificently named **Renato de Voyer de Palmy Signore d'Argeson**. James (Jan) Morris reckoned them the ugliest in Venice, and few would argue.

Around San Giobbe

At the top of the fondamenta, looking over the lagoon to the mainland, is the Macello Pubblico (municipal slaughterhouse), built by the hygiene-conscious Austrians in 1843 and adorned with ox-skulls. Now used by rowing clubs, its future is the subject of some discussion and has been for some time—Le Corbusier designed a hospital for the site in 1964, but the plan was shelved in the face of local opposition to the demolition of the building, opposition with which the architect himself sympathized.

On the opposite side of the Canale di Cannaregio, on the south side of the Ponte dei Tre Archi, stands the **Palazzo Surian**, once the French embassy. **Jean-Jacques Rousseau** lived here in 1743–44 as secretary to an indolent boss: "The French who lived in Venice would never have known that there was a French ambassador resident in the city, had it not been for me," he wrote. His *Confessions* record the political bickerings of his time here, and a number of discreditable sexual adventures.

The Ghetto

The name of the Venetian **Ghetto**—a name bequeathed to all other enclaves of deprivation—is derived from the Venetian dialect *getar*, to found, or *geto*, foundry, which is what this area was until 1390. It was in 1516 that the Ghetto Nuovo became Venice's Jewish quarter, when all the city's Jews were forced to move onto the island. At night the Ghetto was sealed by gates (marks left by their hinges can still be seen in the Sottoportego Ghetto Nuovo) and guarded by Christian watchmen, whose wages were paid by the Jews. In the daytime their movement wasn't restricted, but they were obliged to wear distinctively colored badges or caps. Regarded warily because of their mercantile and financial astuteness, yet exploited for those very qualities, the Jews were barred from certain professions but allowed to pursue others: they could trade in used cloth, lend money (you'll find the inscription *Banco Rosso* on no. 2911 in the campo) and also to practise medicine—Jewish doctors were the only people allowed out of the Ghetto at night, but only to visit sick Venetians. In addition, the Jews' property rights were limited and they were subjected to a range of financial penalties. Changing faith was not a way to escape the shackles, as converts were forbidden "to enter or to practise any activity under any pretext whatsoever in this city . . . on pain of hanging, imprisonment, whipping or pillory." (This statute is carved in stone a little way down Calle di Ghetto Vecchio.)

Yet the fact remains that Venice was one of the few states to tolerate the Jewish religion, and the Ghetto's population was often swelled by refugees from more oppressive societies. Jews expelled from Spain and Portugal in the 1490s came here, as did Jews later displaced from the Turkish-dominated eastern Mediterranean. Venice's burdensome protection was entirely pragmatic, however, as is shown by two conflicting responses to Church interference: when criticized by the Inquisition for not burning enough Jews as heretics, Venetian leaders replied that non-Christians logically could not commit heresy; yet when Pope Julius II ordered the destruction of the Talmud in 1553, the Signoria obligingly arranged a bonfire of Jewish books in the Piazza.

The Ghetto looks quite different from the rest of Venice, as a result of the overcrowding that remained a problem even after the Jewish population was allowed to spread into the **Ghetto Vecchio** (1541) and the **Ghetto Nuovissimo** (1633). As buildings in the Ghetto were not allowed to be more than one third higher than in the rest of Venice, storeys were made as low as possible in order to fit in the maximum number of floors; seven is the usual number—the first high-rises. The gates of the Ghetto were finally torn down by Napoleon in 1797, but it wasn't until the city's unification with the Kingdom of Italy in 1866 that the Jews achieved equal status with their fellow citizens.

The Scolas and the Campo

Each wave of Jewish immigrants, while enriching the overall cultural environment of the city (Venetians of all religions frequented the Ghetto's salons), also maintained their own synagogues with their distinctive rites: the **Scola Tedesca** (for German Jews) was founded in 1528, the **Scola al Canton** (probably Jews from Provence) in 1531–32, the **Scola Levantina** (eastern Mediterranean) in 1538, the **Scola Spagnola** (Spanish) at an uncertain date in the later sixteenth century, and the **Scola Italiana** in 1575. Since the Jews were disqualified from the profession of architect and forbidden to use marble in their buildings, the *scole* tend to have oddly Christian interiors, thickly adorned with gilt and stucco. Funded by particularly prosperous trading communities, the Scola Levantina and the Scola Spagnola are the most lavish of the synagogues (the latter, redesigned by **Longhena**, greatly influenced the look of the others), and these can be viewed with the Scola Tedesca in an informative and multilingual guided tour organized by the **Museo Israelitico** in Campo del Ghetto Nuovo. The museum's collection consists mainly of silverware, sacred objects, textiles and furniture (Nov–March 10am–12:30pm, April–June 10:30am–1pm & 2:30–5pm; July–Nov 10:30am–5pm; closed Sat, Sun afternoon & Jewish hols; L2000, with tour L6000; ☎715359).

In the northern corner of the campo is a reminder of the ultimate suffering of the Jewish people: a series of seven reliefs by **Arbit Blatas**, with a poem by **André Tranc**, commemorating the 202 Venetian Jews deported to the death-camps in 1943 and 1944.

Present-day Venice's Jewish population of around 600 (compared to the Ghetto's peak of around 5000) is dispersed all over the city, but the Ghetto is still the center of the community, with offices and a library in Calle Ghetto Vecchio (☎715012), a nursery, an old people's home, a small kosher restaurant (book in advance; ☎726002), and a baker of unleavened bread (in Calle del Forno).

Northern Cannaregio

Land reclamation and the consolidation of the lagoon's mudbanks has been a continuous process in Venice since the time of the first settlers, but the contours of the city have been modified with particular rapidity in the last hundred years or so. As its long straight canals and right-angled alleyways suggest, much of northern Cannaregio has come into existence comparatively recently: the Sacca di San Girolamo, for example, was reclaimed in the first half of this century to provide working-class housing of a higher standard than in much of the rest of the city.

In the area **northwest from the Ghetto**, inland from the Sacca, there's nothing to ferret out: the tiny seventeenth-century church of the Cappuccine (open for services) faces the equally dull but bigger and uglier (and closed) San Girolamo, a church once used by the Austrians as a steam-powered flour mill, with the campanile converted to a chimney. **Northeast of the Ghetto**, though, is one of the most attractive domestic quarters of Venice: its long fondamente dotted with food shops, bars and trattorias, and the colorful juxtapositions of walls, shutters, water and boats composing a scene like Henry James' evocation of the essence of Venice—"a narrow canal in the heart of the city—a patch of green water and a surface of pink wall . . . a great shabby facade of Gothic windows and balconies—balconies on which dirty clothes are hung and under which a cavernous-looking doorway opens from a low flight of slimy water-steps."

Sant'Alvise

For all the apparent rationality of the city's layout in this district, the church of **Sant'Alvise** is fairly tricky to get to, standing as it does on an island with no eastward land connection with the rest of the city. Dedicated to Saint Louis of Toulouse (Alvise being the Venetian version of Louis/Luigi), the church was commissioned in the 1380s by Antonia Venier, daughter of Doge Antonio Venier, after the saint appeared to her in a vision. It has recently undergone restoration work, as has the immense *Road to Calvary* by **Giambattista Tiepolo** (1743; in the chancel), which now looks as if it should reek of fresh paint. His *Crown of Thorns* and *Flagellation*, slightly earlier works, hang on the right-hand wall of the nave. Under the nun's choir are eight small tempera paintings, familiarly known as "The Baby Carpaccios" since Ruskin assigned them to the painter's precocious childhood; they're not actually by Carpaccio, but were produced around 1470, when he would indeed have been just an infant. The extraordinary seventeenth-century trompe l'oeil **ceiling** is by Antonio Torri (architectural work) and Paolo Ricchi (religious scenes).

To Madonna dell'Orto

To get from Sant'Alvise to Madonna dell'Orto you can either squander a few coins on a one-stop vaporetto hop, or cross over the canal to the Fondamenta della Sensa, the main street immediately to the south. One bridge after the early fifteenth-century **Palazzo Michiel** (the French embassy at the time of Henry III's visit), the fondamenta opens out at the **Campo dei Mori**, a square whose name possibly comes from the proximity of the now extinct *Fondaco degli Arabi* (Arabs' warehouse). There is another explanation: the four thirteenth-century **statues** around the campo are popularly associated with a family of twelfth-century merchants called the Mastelli brothers, who used to live in the palace into which two of the figures are embedded—they hailed from the Morea (the Peloponnese), and hence were known as *Mori*. Venice's more malicious citizens used to leave denunciations at the feet of *Sior Antonio Rioba* (the one with the rusty nose), and circulate vindictive verses signed with his name.

Just beyond the campo is the elegant fifteenth-century house where **Tintoretto** lived for the last two decades of his life (1574–94), accompanied by one of his daughters, **Marietta**. Supremely skilled as a painter, and a fine musician and singer too, Marietta was married off to a man who preferred his wife to produce portraits of his colleagues and his friends instead of painting more ambitious works. She died aged 34, four years before her father, her career having epitomized the confinement of women's talents to genres compatible with a life of domestic conformity. None of her paintings is on public show in Venice, though some scholars have detected her touch in some of her father's large-scale works.

Madonna dell'Orto

Marietta, her father, and her brother Domenico are all buried in **Madonna dell'Orto**, the family's parish church and arguably the superlative example of ecclesiastical Gothic in Venice (9am–noon & 3–5pm in winter, 7pm in summer). Ferrymen for the northern islands used to operate from the quays near here, and the church was founded in the name of Saint Christopher, their patron saint, some time around 1350. It was popularly renamed after a large stone *Madonna* by **Giovanni de'Santi**, found in a nearby vegetable garden (*orto*), began working miracles; brought into the church in 1377, the figure can still be seen (heavily restored), in the Capella di San Mauro. The main sculpture on the **facade** is a fifteenth-century *St Christopher* by the Florentine **Nicolò di Giovanni; Bartolomeo Bon**, formerly credited with the statue, designed the portal in 1460, shortly before his death. The **campanile**, finished in 1503, is one of the most notable landmarks when approaching Venice from the northern lagoon.

Restoration work in the 1860s made a mess of the **interior**, ripping up memorial stones from the floor, for instance, and destroying the organ, once described as the best in Europe. Partial reversal of the damage was achieved in the 1930s, when some over-painting was removed from the Greek marble columns, the fresco work and elsewhere, and in 1968–69 the building and its artworks were given a massive overhaul—the first major restoration project after the floods of 1966.

An amusing if implausible tale explains the large number of **Tintoretto** paintings here. Having added cuckold's horns to a portrait of a doge that had been rejected by its subject, Tintoretto allegedly took refuge from his furious ex-client in the church; the doge then offered to forget the insult if Tintoretto agreed to decorate the church, figuring it would keep him quiet for a few years. The painter was in fact out and about again within six months, most of which time must have been spent on the epic numbers on each side of the choir: *The Last Judgement*, described by Ruskin as the only painting ever to grasp the event "in its Verity . . . as they may see it who shall not sleep, but be changed," and *The Making of the Golden Calf*, in which the carriers of the calf have been speculatively identified as portraits of Giorgione, Titian, Veronese and the artist himself, and Aaron (pointing on the right) as Sansovino. There could hardly be a sharper shift of mood than that from the apocalyptic temper of *The Last Judgement* to the reverential tenderness of *The Presentation of the Virgin* (end of right aisle), which makes a fascinating comparison with Titian's Accademia version of the incident. It's by a long way the best of the other Tintorettos (many would say it's the best of the bunch), but most are interesting: *The Vision of the Cross to St Peter* and *The Beheading of St Paul* flank an *Annunciation* by Palma il Giovane in the chancel; four *Virtues* (the central one is anonymous) are installed in the vault above; and *Saint Agnes Reviving Licinius* stands in the fourth chapel on the left. Two major figures of the early Venetian Renaissance—**Cima da Conegliano** and **Giovanni Bellini**—are represented by a *Saint John the Baptist and Other Saints* (first altar on right) and a *Madonna and Child* (first chapel on the left) respectively.

To the Scuole della Misericordia

Diagonally south of the church, the **Palazzo Mastelli** (see the Campo dei Mori, above) looks across the canal, its facade a sort of architectural album featuring a Gothic top-floor balcony, thirteenth-century Byzantine fragments set into sixteenth-century work below, a bit of a Roman altar set into a column by the corner, and a quaint little relief of a man leading a laden camel (hence the alternative title Palazzo del Cammello). On the canal's north side stand the seventeenth-century **Palazzo Minelli Spada** and, one of the many palaces owned by the vast Contarini clan, the sixteenth-century **Palazzo Contarini dal Zaffo**. (The Casino degli Spiriti is in the latter's garden—see the next chapter.) Numerous though they once were, the last male of the Contarini line died in 1836, thus adding the family name to the many from the *Libro d'Oro* to vanish into oblivion in the nineteenth century. Lack of money almost certainly accounts for their extinction—already impoverished by loans made to the dying Republic and by the endless round of parties, the Venetian aristocracy were finally bankrupted by the Napoleonic and Austrian occupations, and so, no longer having money for dowries and other related expenses, simply chose not to marry.

Crossing the canal at the Sacca della Misericordia, you quickly come to the fondamenta leading to the defunct **Abbazia della Misericordia** and the **Scuola Vecchia della Misericordia**; neither is particularly lovely, and the latter's proudest adornment—**Bartolomeo Bon**'s relief of the *Madonna della Misericordia*—is exiled in London's Victoria and Albert Museum. The complex is now used as a restoration center. When the Misericordia became a Scuola Grande in the sixteenth century its members commissioned the huge **Scuola Nuova della Misericordia** (on the far side of the bridge), a move which benefitted Tintoretto, who set up his canvases in the upper room of the old building to work on the *Paradiso* for the Palazzo Ducale. Begun in 1532 by **Sansovino** but not opened until 1589, the new block was never finished; today a part of it serves as a gym, and strolling past at dusk you'll probably hear the thump of basketballs against the walls.

From San Marziale to San Leonardo

Cutting back westwards along the Fondamenta della Misericordia, past Longhena's **Palazzo Lezze**, the first bridge goes over to **San Marziale**. Admirers of **Sebastiano Ricci** won't want to miss his ceiling paintings, a set of works that made his reputation in the city; those who haven't acquired the taste will get more of a buzz from the dotty Baroque high altar, depicting St Jerome at lunch with a couple of associates—Faith and Charity.

In 1606 the **Palazzo Diedo** (on the far bank of the canal to the south of San Marziale) witnessed a peculiar incident, when an astrologer named Benedetto Altavilla rushed in to tell its owner that the stars had revealed to him that a quantity of gunpowder had been stacked feloniously under the Sala del Maggior Consiglio. The Council of Ten duly found the explosives, but suspected, not unreasonably, that Altavilla had put them there. Shaved and shorn, in case his hair gave him occult strength, the astrologer was tortured to unconsciousness and then hanged, protesting throughout his ordeal that the stars had told him everything.

The Servi and Fra Paolo Sarpi

Most of the island to the west of San Marziale is occupied by the remnants of the church and ex-convent of **Santa Maria dei Servi**. When the church was demolished in 1812, some of its monuments were thrown away and others were shuffled around Venice (such as Doge Andrea Vendramin's tomb, now in San Zanipolo); the ruins themselves were offered to Ruskin, who turned the deal down.

Unswerving moral rectitude and fierce intellectual rigor are not qualities that come first to mind when considering most of the public men of Venetian history, but both were exemplified by the Servite priest **Fra Paolo Sarpi**, one of Venice's titanic figures. Author of a magisterial history of the Council of Trent, discoverer of the mechanics of the iris of the eye and a partner in Galileo's optical researches, Sarpi is best known as the advisor to the Venetian state in its battle

with the Vatican at the start of the seventeenth century. Although Venice's tolera-
tion of non-Christians was a cause of recurrent friction, the area of greatest
discord was the Republic's insistence on separating the sovereignty of the
Church and that of the State—"The Church must obey the State in things temporal and the latter the former in things spiritual, each maintaining its proper
rights," to quote Sarpi himself.

Matters came to a head when Venice restricted the amount of money that
monasteries on the mainland could return to Rome from their rents and trading,
and then imprisoned two priests found guilty in secular courts of secular crimes.
Pope Paul V's demand for the return of the priests and the repeal of the monastic
legislation was firmly rebuffed, and the upshot was a Papal Interdict in April 1606
(forbidding all religious services in Venice) and excommunication for the entire
city. In retaliation, Venice booted out the Jesuits and threatened with exile or
death any priests who didn't ignore the Interdict—a priest in Padua who insisted
that the Holy Spirit had moved him to obey the pope was informed by the Council
of Ten that the Holy Spirit had already moved them to hang any who disagreed
with them. Sarpi and the dauntless Doge Leonardo Donà maintained their
closely-argued defiance of Rome until French mediation brought about a resolution which in fact required no compromises from the Venetians. The moral
authority of Rome was diminished forever. Six months later, Sarpi was walking
home past Santa Fosca when he was set upon by three men and left for dead with
a stiletto embedded in his cheek; the assassins failed, though, and Sarpi eventually died naturally on 15 January 1623. He's commemorated by a nineteenth-
century monument outside the unmemorable church of **Santa Fosca**.

San Felice and La Maddalena

Close to Santa Fosca, on the Strada Nova, is what is held to be the oldest pharmacy in Venice, the *Farmacia Ponci*, with seventeenth-century wood panelling
and furniture. Antiquarians might also investigate the early fifteenth-century
Palazzo Donà Giovanelli, just to the east of the church. Now owned by an
auctioneers, it's sometimes open for pre-sale viewings, an experience as interesting for the authentic decorations of the palace as for the collectables on show.
Continuing east, you're into the *Castello* section after the church of **San Felice**—
rebuilt in the 1530s, savagely renovated in the last century, and now very much a
local place of worship. One local curiosity: at the far end of the fondamenta going
up behind the church is the only bridge without parapets left in the main part of
Venice. It leads to a private house.

Going west from Santa Fosca, the little Neoclassical church of **La Maddalena**
(1760), a favorite church for weddings, is set back from the main street on its own
small campo. Its designer, the unprolific **Tomasso Temanza**, was more noted as
a theoretician than as an architect, and his *Lives of the Most Famous Venetian
Architects and Sculptors* (modeled on Vasari's *Lives of the Artists*) remains the classic text for those interested in the subject. A couple of twists and turns away from
La Maddalena is the land entrance of the **Palazzo Vendramin-Calergi,** where a
plaque records the death of Richard Wagner here in 1883; the surprisingly tatty
entrance is as far as you'll get unless your wallet's full and your attire impeccable,
because it's now the winter home of the Casino (Oct–March 3pm–2:30am;
L15,000 entrance; smallest bet L2000). It is one of just four licensed casinos in
Italy—but Venetian residents are forbidden to gamble here. (See Chapter Seven
for an entry on the building.)

San Marcuola

From the Canal Grande, the unfinished brick front of **Giorgio Massari**'s church of **San Marcuola** (1728–36) is as clear a landmark as the facade of the Palazzo Vendramin-Calergi, which stands a little to the east of it. (Its name is somehow arrived at from Santi Ermagora e Fortunato.) The tiered ledges and sockets of the exterior, intended for marble cladding but now crammed with pigeons, are a more diverting sight than the inside, where statues of the church's two patron saints by **Gian Maria Morleiter**, and an early *Last Supper* by **Tintoretto** (left wall of the chancel) are the only things to seek out. Those apart, the main interest in the church is a story about one of its priests. He was once foolish enough to announce from the pulpit that he didn't believe in ghosts, and that "where the dead are, there they stay"; that night all the corpses buried in the church rose from their graves, dragged him from his bed and beat him up.

Due north are the busy market stalls of the Campiello dell'Anconetta, from which the shopping street of Rio Terrà San Leonardo runs off to the station.

RESTAURANTS: *Ai Canottieri*, Ponte Tre Archi; *Al Ponte*, Rio Terrà Maddalena; *Antico Molo*, Fondamenta degli Ormesini; *Bruno*, Fondamenta delle Cappuccine; *Dalla Cea*, Calle del Fumo; *Paradiso Perduto*, Fondamenta della Misericordia.

SNACKS AND BARS: *Leon d'Oro: Bar Gobbi*, Rio Terrà della Maddalena; *Osteria alla Ghiacciaia*, Fondamenta di Cannaregio; train station buffet.

CAFÉS AND PASTICCERIE: between Rio Terrà San Leonardo and the Strada Nova.

Reviews of all these places appear in Chapter 10.

CHAPTER FIVE

CASTELLO

B ordering the *sestiere* of San Marco on one side and spreading across the city from Cannaregio in the west to the housing projects of Sant'Elena in the east, **Castello** is the most amorphous of the city's districts. An amalgamation of disparate units rather than an area with an overall identity, its points of interest are evenly distributed and extremely varied.

In terms of its importance and its geographical location, Castello's central building is the immense Gothic church of **Santi Giovanni e Paolo** (or **Zanipolo**), the pantheon of Venice's doges. A couple of minutes away stands the Renaissance **Santa Maria dei Miracoli**, the city's most refined architectural miniature and a startling contrast with both Zanipolo and the **Gesuiti**, a Baroque creation in the northern part of the district which boasts perhaps the weirdest of Venice's interiors. The main draw of the northwestern area is the **Ca' d'Oro**, a gorgeous Canal Grande palace now housing a fine collection of paintings and carvings. Castello's other museums lie in the southern zone—the **Querini-Stampalia** picture collection, and the **Museo Diocesano**, the city's chief assembly of sacred art. This latter area's dominant building is the majestic **San Zaccaria**, a church that has played a significant part in the history of the city—as has **Santa Maria Formosa**, around which spreads the liveliest and friendliest square in Castello. But busier still is the southern waterfront, the **Riva degli Schiavoni**, a stroll along whose promenade seems to be a statutory part of every Venetian's evening.

The boundaries of the *sestiere* from which this chapter takes its name are more likely to confuse than help the visitor, and therefore somewhat altered boundaries have been used in laying out the guide. In the west, the chapter starts off from the straight waterway that connects the Canal Grande to the inlet of the Sacca della Misericordia, rather than following the *sestiere*'s zigzagging border. In the east we've stopped a few blocks west of the Arsenale, in a line from the landmark **Pietà** church; the atmospherically distinct area beyond this boundary is covered in the next chapter.

The Gesuiti District

The Fondamente Nuove is the point at which the vaporetti leave the city for San Michele, Murano and the northern lagoon; on a clear day you can follow their course as far as the distant island of Burano, and you might even be treated to the startling sight of the white crags of the Dolomites, apparently hanging in the sky over the Veneto. Being relatively new, this waterfront isn't lined by buildings like its counterpart in the south of the city, the Záttere. The one house of interest is

CASTELLO

the **Palazzo Donà delle Rose** on the corner of the Rio dei Gesuiti—one of the very few Venetian residences still owned by the family for whom it was built. Architecturally the palace is an oddity, as the main axis of its interior runs parallel to the water instead of at ninety degrees; the cornerstone was laid in 1610 by **Doge Leonardo Donà** (Paolo Sarpi's boss), who died two years later from apoplexy after an argument with his brother about the house's layout.

From the northern tip of the Fondamente the sixteenth-century **Casino degli Spiriti** can be seen across the inlet known as the Sacca della Misericordia. A *casino* (little house)—a suite set aside for private entertainments—was a feature of many Venetian palaces, and a few were set up in separate pavilions in the grounds. This is one of only two surviving examples of the latter, but it's best known not for its architectural rarity but for the ghost story that's sometimes said to be the source of its name. A certain noblewoman took her husband's best friend as a lover, and this is where they would meet. At her paramour's sudden death she began to pine away, and shut herself in the *Casino* to die. No sooner had she exhaled her last breath than the ghost of her lover came in, raised her from the bed and, pushing the nursemaid to one side, made off with her. Whether they turned up in another city under assumed names is not recorded.

The Gesuiti, the Oratorio and Santa Caterina

The major monument of this area is **Santa Maria Assunta**, commonly known simply as the **Gesuiti** (10am–noon and 5–7pm—very approximately). Built for the Jesuits in 1714–29, six decades after the foundation on this site of their first monastery in Venice, the church was clearly planned to make an impression on a city that was habitually mistrustful of the order's close relationship with the papacy. Although the disproportionately huge facade clearly wasn't the work of a weekend, most of the effort went into the stupefying **interior**, where green and white marble covers every wall and stone is carved to resemble swags of damask—the result is jaw-dropping. The marble cladding is also so efficient a refrigeration unit that you can walk in here on a sunny day and instantly see your breath curling in front of you. Unless you're a devotee of Palma il Giovane (in which case make for the sacristy), the only painting to seek out is the *Martyrdom of St Lawrence* by **Titian** (1558; first altar on left), a night scene made doubly difficult to see by the lighting arrangements.

Almost opposite the church is the **Oratorio dei Crociferi** (April–June & Oct Fri, Sat & Sun 10am–noon; July–Sept Fri–Sun 4:30–6:30pm; free), reopened in 1984 after thorough restoration of **Palma il Giovane's** *Scenes from the History of the Order of the Crociferi* (1583–91). The paintings show Palma's technique at its subtlest, and the richness of the colors is a good advertisement for modern cleaning techniques. There's not much else to look at in the immediate vicinity. Titian use to live in Calle Larga dei Botteri (no. 5179–83), across the Rio dei Gesuiti—but the house has been virtually rebuilt and the building of the Fondamente Nuove did away with the waterside garden where he entertained such exalted clients as Henry III of France. A short distance to the west, past the huge sixteenth-century Palazzi Zen, the church of **Santa Caterina** comes into view. Another restoration scheme is in progress here: the fourteenth-century ship's keel ceiling, destroyed by fire in 1978, has now been rebuilt, but further work currently keeps the place shut.

Along the Strada Nova

Moving down from the Gesuiti area towards the Canal Grande, you'll hit the **Strada Nova**, a brisk and basic shopping street where you can buy anything from spaghetti to surgical supports. It was created in 1871 by plowing a line straight through the fabric of the district, as part of a scheme to rationalize movement round the north bend of the Canal Grande. The continuations of the route to the train station—streets such as Rio Terrà San Leonardo and Rio Terrà Lista di Spagna—were also created at this time, by filling in canals.

The Ca' d'Oro

Nearly halfway along the Strada an inconspicuous alleyway leads down to the **Ca' d'Oro** (House of Gold), the showpiece of domestic Gothic architecture in Venice and home of one of the city's most varied art collections, the **Galleria Giorgio Franchetti** (Tues–Fri 9am–2pm, Sun & hols 9am–1pm; L2000). Built for Marino Contarini (a procurator of San Marco) between 1425 and 1440, the palace takes its name from its Canal Grande **facade**. Incorporating parts of the thirteenth-century palace that used to stand on this site, the front of the house was lavishly highlighted in gold leaf, ultramarine and vermilion—materials which, as the three most expensive pigments of the day, spectacularly publicized the wealth of its owner.

The house's cosmetics have now worn off, but the facade at least has survived unaltered, whereas the rest of the Ca' d'Oro was badly abused by later owners. After the dancer Maria Taglioni had finished her home improvements, Ruskin lamented that it was "now destroyed by restorations," and today, despite the subsequent structural repairs, the interior of the Ca' d'Oro is no longer recognizable as that of a Gothic building. The staircase in the **courtyard** is an original feature, though—ripped out by Taglioni, it was reacquired and reconstructed by Franchetti, who likewise put back the well-head by Bartolomeo Bon (1427). There's a display on the restoration of the building in a room to the side of the first-floor loggia.

The gallery's main attraction is undoubtedly the *St Sebastian* painted by **Mantegna** shortly before his death in 1506, now installed in a chapel-like alcove on the first floor. Many of the big names of Venetian art are here too, but the canvasses by **Titian** and **Tintoretto** are not among their best, and **Pordenone**'s fragmentary frescoes from the cloister of Santo Stefano require a considerable feat of imaginative reconstruction, as do the remains of the frescoes by **Giorgione** and Titian from the Fondaco dei Tedeschi. You'll probably get more pleasure out of pieces from less elevated artists—**Tullio Lombardo**'s beautifully carved and tender *Young Couple* shows him at his peak, and **Biagio d'Antonio da Firenze**'s *The Story of Lucrezia* reminds us that for a long time suicide was one of the few "honorable" responses a woman could have to rape. **Andrea di Bartolo**'s fine *Coronation of the Virgin* shows one way in which the impossible female ideal was maintained.

Keep an eye out also for an anonymous *Madonna and Child* in the midst of the Flemish collection, a sixteenth-century English alabaster polyptych of *Scenes from the Life of St Catherine*, and a case of Renaissance medals containing fine specimens by **Gentile Bellini** and **Pisanello**, to name just two.

Santa Sofia and Santi Apostoli

A little farther down the Strada Nova, opposite a campo bordering the Canal Grande and camouflaged by house fronts, is the entrance to the small church of **Santa Sofia**, which has sculptures of four saints by followers of Antonio Rizzo. At the eastern end of the Strada you come to the Campo dei Santi Apostoli, an elbow on the road from the Rialto to the train station, and **Santi Apostoli**, a frequently renovated church last altered substantially in the eighteenth century. The **campanile** was finished in 1672—and soon afterwards, according to James (Jan) Morris, "an old and simple-minded sacristan" fell from it, "but was miraculously caught by the minute hand of the clock, which, slowly revolving to six o'clock, deposited him safely on a parapet." The **Cappella Corner**, off the right side, is the most interesting part of the interior—attributed to **Mauro Coducci**, its altarpiece is the *Communion of St Lucy* by **Giambattista Tiepolo** (1748). One of the inscriptions in the chapel is to Caterina Cornaro, who was buried here before being moved to San Salvatore; the tomb of her father Marco (on the right) is probably by **Tullio Lombardo**, who also carved the peculiar plaque of St Sebastian in the chapel to the right of the chancel, which makes him look as if he has a tree growing out of his head.

The Miracoli and San Giovanni Crisostomo

On the other side of the Rio dei Santi Apostoli from the campo stands the **Palazzo Falier**, parts of which date back to the second half of the thirteenth century. Traditionally this was the home of the ill-fated **Doge Marin Falier**, a branch of whose family was certainly in possession at the time of his dogeship (1354–55). A man noted for his probity, Falier was greatly offended by the licence allowed to the unruly nobles of Venice; when a lenient punishment was given to a young nobleman who had insulted Falier, his wife and her ladies, he finally went overboard and hatched a conspiracy to install himself as the city's benevolent despot—a plot into which he conscripted the overseer of the Arsenale and Filippo Calendario, one of the architects of the Palazzo Ducale. Their plan was discovered and Falier, admitting the conspiracy, was beheaded on the spot on which he had earlier been invested as doge. There's an unusual memorial to him in the Palazzo Ducale—see the entry on the "Sala del Maggior Consiglio."

Interlocking with the Falier house is the equally ancient **Ca' da Mosto**, reached through the passage on the right. This was the birthplace of **Alvise da Mosto** (1432–88), a Venetian merchant-explorer who joined forces with Portugal's Henry the Navigator and went on to discover the Cape Verde Islands. The popular *Albergo del Leon Bianco* occupied these premises for a long time—among its guests were J.M.W. Turner, who had himself rowed up and down the Canal Grande while he scribbled furiously in his notebook, and two German officers who in 1716 fought a duel in the courtyard and contrived to skewer each other to death.

Santa Maria dei Miracoli

Inland from these palaces, beyond the dull San Canziano, stands the church which Ruskin paired with the Scuola di San Marco as "the two most refined buildings in Venice"—**Santa Maria dei Miracoli**, always known simply by its last name. It was built in the 1480s to house a miracle-working image of the Madonna—it revived a man who'd spent half an hour at the bottom of the Giudecca canal and a woman left for dead after being stabbed. Financed by gifts left at the painting's nearby shrine, the church was most likely designed by **Pietro Lombardo;** certainly he and his two sons **Tullio** and **Antonio** oversaw the construction, and the three of them executed much of the carving. Richness of effect takes precedence over classical correctness on the **exterior:** pilasters are placed close together along the sides to create the illusion of longer walls, for example, and Corinthian pilasters are placed below Ionic (in defiance of classical rules) so that the viewer can better appreciate the former's more elaborate detailing. Venetian folklore has it that the materials for the multicolored marble cladding and inlays, typical of the Lombardi, were the surplus from the decoration of the Basilica di San Marco.

The marble-lined **interior** contains some of the most intricate decorative sculpture to be seen in Venice. The *Annunciation* and half-length figures of two saints on the balustrade at the altar end are thought to be by Tullio; the rest of the carvings at this end are arguable between the two brothers and their father. Ruskin was rather distressed by the children's heads carved to the side of the steps—"the man who could carve a child head so perfectly must have been wanting in all human feeling, to cut it off, and tie it by the hair to a vine leaf," he wrote; Ezra Pound, on the other hand, declared that the siren figures were so beautifully realized that "no one has been able to carve them" since. Extraordinary filigree carving covers the columns below the nun's choir—with very little prompting the sacristan will demonstrate its finesse by inserting a cocktail stick between the tiny birds and the face of the columns.

The patches of crystalline material on the marble both inside and out are due to overzealous repair work: the crumbling walls between the marble skins were stuffed with a sort of restorative foam cavity filling, but the holes were filled before proper drying-out had occurred. The result is that the marble is in places stuck fast to the new filling and is now disintegrating. Save Venice Inc. is embarking on a series of experiments to determine the best course of action.

Take Calle Castelli from the front end of the church and you'll come to the **Palazzo Soranzo-van Axel,** whose fine Gothic entrance, at the end of the fondamenta, retains its original wooden door—a unique feature in Venice.

San Giovanni Crisostomo and Around

Midway between the Apostoli and the post office stands **San Giovanni Crisostomo** (John the Golden-Mouthed), named after the eloquent Archbishop of Constantinople. An intimate church with a compact Greek Cross plan, it was built between 1497 and 1504, one of the last projects of **Mauro Coducci**. It possesses two outstanding paintings—**Giovanni Bellini**'s late altarpiece of *SS. Jerome, Christopher and Louis of Toulouse* (1513; on right), and **Sebastiano del Piombo**'s gracefully heavy *St John Chrysostom with SS. John the Baptist, Liberale, Mary Magdalen, Agnes and Catherine* (1509–11; on high altar). On the left side is a marble panel of the *Coronation of the Virgin* by **Tullio Lombardo**, a severe contrast with the more playful stuff in the Miracoli.

The calle virtually opposite the church leads to a secluded campiello flanked by the partly thirteenth-century **Palazzo Lion-Morosini,** whose external staircase is guarded by a little lion apparently suffering from indigestion; the campiello opens

CENTRAL CASTELLO

onto the Canal Grande, and if you're lucky you'll be able to enjoy the view on your own. Behind the church is the **Teatro Malibran**, opened in the seventeenth century, rebuilt in 1920 and now a venue for ballet, opera and concerts. The Byzantine arches on the facade of the theater are said to have once been part of the house of **Marco Polo**'s family. (They lived in the tatty place overlooking the canal at the back of the Malibran.) Polo's *Description of the World* (1298), detailing his experiences in seventeen years of service throughout the empire of Kublai Khan, was the first account of Asian life to appear in the West and for centuries was the most reliable description available; to many of his contemporaries, though, Polo's stories were bluffs and exaggerations, and he was accordingly given the title *Il Milione,* for his habit of talking in millions. The nickname is preserved by the Corte Prima and Corte Seconda del Milion—the latter is an interesting architectural mix of Veneto-Byzantine and Gothic elements, with a magnificently carved twelfth-century arch. From here the Ponte Marco Polo leads off to the Campo di Santa Marina; keep going straight for Santa Maria Formosa—pausing on the Ponte del Cristo for the seventeenth-century facade of the **Palazzo Marcello-Pindemonte-Papadopoli** (attributed to Longhena) and the Gothic **Palazzo Pisani** across the water.

Campo Santi Giovanni e Paolo

After the Piazza, the **Campo Santi Giovanni e Paolo** is the richest monumental public space in Venice. Dominated by the huge brick church from which it gets its name, the square is also overlooked by the most beautiful facade of any of the Scuole Grandi and one of the finest equestrian monuments in the world. A couple of bars and a perpetual gaggle of ball-playing kids keep the atmosphere lively, and there's a constant flow of traffic through the square, much of it heading for the civic hospital now installed in the Scuola.

The *condottiere* **Bartolomeo Colleoni** began his wayward career in Venice's army in 1429, after a spell in the pay of Naples, and for a while took orders from Gattamelata, who's commemorated in Padua by the other great Italian equestrian monument. In the succeeding years Colleoni defected to Milan, was imprisoned there, escaped, re-enlisted for Venice, fled once again, and finally joined the Republic's ranks for good in 1455—whereupon Venice suffered an outbreak of peace which resulted in his being called upon to fight on just one occasion during the last twenty years of his life. Resisting several lucrative offers from France and Rome, he settled into a life of prosperous leisure, and when he died in 1475 he left a legacy of over 100,000 ducats to the Venetian state. But there was a snag to this bequest: the Signoria could have the money only if an equestrian monument to him were erected in the square before San Marco—an unthinkable proposition to Venice's rulers, with their cult of anonymity. The problem was circumvented with a fine piece of disingenuousness, by which the Colleoni's will was taken to allow the state to claim his money if his statue were raised before the Scuola of San Marco, rather than the Basilica.

Andrea Verrocchio won the commission for the monument in 1481, and difficulties cropped up in this stage of the proceedings too. Verrocchio was preparing the figure of the horse for casting when he heard that another artist was being approached to sculpt the rider. Insulted, he smashed up his work and returned to Florence in a rage, to be followed by a decree forbidding him on pain of death to return to Venice. Eventually he was invited back, and was working again on the piece when he died in June 1488. The Signoria then hired **Alessandro Leopardi** to finish the work and produce the plinth for it, which he gladly did—even signing his own name on the horse's girth, and taking the self-bestowed title *del Cavallo*. According to Marin Sanudo, when the monument was finally unveiled in 1496 all of Venice came to marvel at it. Don't run away with the notion that Colleoni was a dead ringer for Klaus Kinski—this isn't a portrait (Verrocchio never met his subject), but rather an idealized image of steely masculinity. And talking of masculinity, Thomas Coryat noted that the name Colleoni "doth signify a testicle," but sadly did not speculate farther.

An entirely different spirit of that age is manifested by Colleoni's backdrop, the **Scuola Grande di San Marco,** which since its suppression in the early nineteenth century has provided a sumptuous facade and foyer for the *Ospedale Civile*. The **facade** was started by **Pietro Lombardo and Giovanni Buora** in 1487 and finished in 1495 by **Mauro Coducci**; taken as a whole, the perspectival panels by **Tullio and Antonio Lombardo** might not quite create the intended illusion, but they're some of the most charming sculptural pieces in Venice. The **interior** was radically altered by the Austrians in 1819 but partly reconstructed using some original bits; if you ask at the desk they might let you into the upstairs library, which still has its early sixteenth-century ceiling, and the church of **San Lazzaro dei Mendicanti** (mornings only), which contains a Veronese and an early Tintoretto.

Another hospital building is attached to Longhena's church of the **Ospedaletto** (or **Santa Maria dei Derelitti**; 1674), beyond the other end of the campo. The leering giants' heads and overripe decorations of its facade drew Ruskin's wrathful attention—"it is almost worth devoting an hour to the successive examination of five buildings as illustrative of the last degradation of the Renaissance. San Moisè is the most clumsy, Santa Maria Zobenigo the most impious, San Eustachio the most ridiculous, the Ospedaletto the most monstrous, and the head at Santa Maria Formosa the most foul." The interior, a much less extravagant business, has a series of eighteenth-century paintings high on the walls above the arches, one of which—*The Sacrifice of Isaac*—is an early **G.B. Tiepolo** (fourth on the right). The adjoining music room, frescoed in the eighteenth century, can sometimes be visited on request—or just pop your head round the door if you hear a rehearsal in progress.

The Church of Santi Giovanni e Paolo (San Zanipolo)

Once again, the Venetians constructed a completely new saint out of two old ones, as the twinned saints **Giovanni e Paolo** became slurred into **San Zanipolo**. Like the Frari, this massive Gothic brick edifice was built for one of the mendicant orders which sprang into existence mainly in the thirteenth–fourteenth century. Supporting themselves from the proceeds of begging, the mendicants were less inward-looking than the older orders, basing themselves in large urban settlements and working to relieve the sick and the poor. Reflecting this social mission, mendicant churches contain a vast area for the public congregation, and this requirement of space meant that the mendicants typically built on the edges of cities. In Venice the various mendicant orders are scattered all over the periphery of the city: the Dominicans here, the Franciscans at the Frari and San Francesco della Vigna, the Augustinians at Santo Stefano, the Carmelites at Santa Maria dei Carmelo and the Servites at Santa Maria dei Servi.

SANTI GIOVANNI E PAOLO
(SAN ZANIPOLO)

1. Tomb of Giovanni Mocenigo
2. Tomb of Pietro Mocenigo
3. Monument to Marcantonio Bragadin
4. Bellini's Altarpiece
5. Cappella della Madonna della Pace
6. Cappella di San Domenico
7. Shrine of Catherine of Siena
8. Paintings by Vivarini, Cima and Lotto
9. Tombs of Vettor Pisani and Marco Giustiniani
10. Tomb of Michele Morosini
11. Tomb of Andrea Vendramin
12. Tomb of Marco Corner
13. Tombs of Jacopo Cavalli & Giovanni Dolfin
14. Cappella del Rosario
15. Sacristy
16. Tomb of Pasquale Malipiero
17. Tomb of Tomasso Mocenigo
18. Tomb of Nicolò Marcello

The first church built on this site was begun in 1246 after **Doge Giacomo Tiepolo** was inspired by a dream to donate the land to the Dominicans; but that version was soon demolished to make way for this larger building, begun in 1333, though not consecrated until 1430. Tiepolo's simple sarcophagus is outside, on the left of the door, next to that of his son **Doge Lorenzo Tiepolo** (d.1275); both tombs were altered after the Bajamonte Tiepolo revolt of 1310, when the family were no longer allowed to display their old crest and had to devise a replacement. The **doorway**, flanked by Byzantine reliefs, is thought to be by **Bartolomeo Bon**, and is one of the major transitional Renaissance works in the city; apart from that, the most arresting architectural feature of the exterior is the complex brickwork of the **apse**. The **Cappella di Sant'Orsola** (closed), between the door to the right transept and the apse is where the two **Bellini** brothers are buried; it used to house the Scuola di Sant'Orsola, the confraternity which commissioned from Carpaccio the *Saint Ursula* cycle now installed in the Accademia.

The simplicity of the cavernous **interior**—290 feet long, 125 feet wide at the transepts, 108 feet high in the center—is offset by the profusion of tombs and monuments around the walls; twenty-five doges are buried here, but it can feel like all of them must be. (If you want a full inventory of Zanipolo, there's a guide on sale in the sacristy.)

The Mocenigo Tombs and Right Aisle

There's scarcely an inch of the entrance wall that isn't given over to the glorification of the Mocenigo family, one of Venice's top-notch dynasties. Above the niched pair of saints by **Pietro Lombardo**, the **tomb of Doge Alvise Mocenigo and his wife** (1577) wraps itself round the doorway; on its right is **Tullio Lombardo**'s **monument to Doge Giovanni Mocenigo** (d.1485); and on the left is the superb **monument to Doge Pietro Mocenigo** (d.1476), by **Pietro Lombardo**, with assistance from Tullio and Antonio. Pietro Mocenigo's sarcophagus, supported by warriors representing the three Ages of Man, is embellished with a Latin inscription (*Ex Hostim Manibus*) pointing out that his enemies paid for the tomb, and reliefs showing some of his valorous deeds, including the handing of the keys of Famagusta to the doomed Caterina Cornaro (see "Asolo" for her story).

Next to the first altar of the right aisle is the **monument to Marcantonio Bragadin**, the central figure in one of the grisliest episodes in Venice's history. The commander of the Venetian garrison at Famagusta during the Turkish siege of 1571, Bragadin marshalled a resistance which lasted eleven months until, with his force reduced from 7000 men to 700, he was forced to sue for peace. Given guarantees of safety, the Venetian officers entered the enemy camp, whereupon most were dragged away and cut to pieces, whilst Bragadin himself had his ears cut off in an assault that proved to be a foretaste of days of torture. His eventual execution was appalling—chained to a stake on the public scaffold, he was slowly flayed alive in front of the Pasha. His skin, stuffed with straw, was then mounted on a cow and paraded through the streets, prior to being hung from the bowsprit of the admiral's galley for the return voyage to Constantinople. Later the skin was brought back to Venice, and today it sits in that urn high up on the wall. **Giovanni Bellini**'s painting for the first altar went up in smoke some years ago (see below), but his marvelous polyptych of *SS. Vincent Ferrer, Christopher and Sebastian* has come through the centuries in magnificent shape, although it has lost the image of God the Father which used to accompany the upper-level *Annunciation* and *Pietà*. The oozing effigy reclining below is of the **Blessed Tommaso Caraffini**, confessor and biographer of Saint Catherine of Siena.

The next chapel but one, the **Cappella della Madonna della Pace**, is named after its Byzantine Madonna, brought to Venice in 1349 and attributed with amazing powers; above the chapel entrance the figures of **Doge Bertucci Valier** (d.1658), **Doge Silvestro Valier** (d.1700) and Silvestro's wife, **Dogaressa Elizabetta Querini** (d.1708), are poised like actors taking a bow. Elizabetta, incidentally, was the only dogaressa to be crowned with the doge's *beretto*. *St Dominic in Glory*, the only ceiling panel in Venice by **G.B. Piazzetta** (G.B. Tiepolo's immediate precursor), covers the vault of the neighboring **Cappella di San Domenico**, alongside which is a little shrine with the **foot of Saint**

Catherine of Siena. Born in 1347 as the youngest of 25 children, Catherine manifested early signs of uninhibited piety—wearing hair shirts, sleeping on bare boards, and crashing up and down stairs on her knees, saying a Hail Mary on each step. She died in 1380 and her body promptly entered the relic market—most of it is in Rome, but her head is in Siena, her foot here, and other lesser relics are scattered about Italy.

To the Chancel

San Zanipolo's best paintings are clustered in the **south transept: Alvise Vivarini**'s *Christ Carrying the Cross* (1474), a *Coronation of the Virgin* attributed to **Cima da Conegliano and Giovanni Martini da Udine**, and **Lorenzo Lotto**'s *St Antonine* (1542), recently restored. As payment for his work Lotto asked only for his expenses and permission to be buried in the church; presumably the first part of the deal went through all right, but Lotto soon afterwards quit the backbiting of Venice's artistic circles, and eventually died and was buried in Loreto.

Much of the right wall of the second apsidal chapel—the **Cappella della Maddalena**—is taken up with a twentieth-century reconstruction of the **monument to Admiral Vettor Pisani**. Pisani's role in the victory over the Genoese at Chioggia in 1380—a campaign in which he was mortally wounded—is neatly summed up by John Julius Norwich: "it would perhaps be an exaggeration to say that he saved Venice single-handed; the fact remains that she would not have survived without him" (for more see "Chioggia," in Chapter Nine). The tomb, supported by what look like the heads of giant elves, is of another sea captain, Marco Giustiniani (d.1346).

The **chancel** is one of the high points of funerary art in Venice. **Doge Michele Morosini**, who ruled for four months before dying of plague in 1382, is buried in the tomb on the right, a work which in Ruskin's eyes marked a fault-line in European civilization, showing as it does "not only the exactly intermediate condition in style between the pure Gothic and its final Renaissance corruption, but, at the same time, the exactly intermediate condition of feeling between the pure calmness of early Christianity, and the boastful pomp of the Renaissance faithlessness." The fallen Renaissance world is represented by the tomb of **Doge Andrea Vendramin** (d.1478), diagonally opposite from Morosini's, which was moved here in 1818 from the church of the Servi. The sculptor (probably **Tullio Lombardo**) carved only the half of the figure that could be seen from below, an act which Ruskin condemned as being of "such utter coldness of feeling as could only consist with an extreme of intellectual and moral degradation." Next to it is the Gothic tomb of **Doge Marco Corner** (d.1368), which was chopped up to make way for its neighbor.

Back to the Entrance

Of the **tomb of Jacopo Cavalli** (d.1384), on the right of the final chapel, Ruskin scornfully remarked: "I find no especial reason for the images of the Virtues, especially that of Charity, appearing at his tomb, unless it be this: that at the seige of Feltre, in the war against Leopold of Austria, he refused to assault the city because the senate would not grant his soldiers the pillage of the town." As if in response, the Virtues are no longer in place. On the left is the tomb of **Doge Giovanni Dolfin** (d.1361) who was beseiged by the Hungarians in Trieste when elected in 1356, and had to charge through enemy lines under cover of darkness in order to take up the post.

The **Cappella del Rosario**, at the end of the left transept, was built 1582 and dedicated to the victory over the Turkish fleet at Lepanto, which happened on the feast-day of the Madonna of the Rosary, 7 October 1571. In 1867 a fire destroyed its paintings by Tintoretto, Palma il Giovane and others, as well as Giovanni Bellini's *Madonna* and Titian's *Martyrdom of St Peter*, San Zanipolo's two most celebrated paintings, which were in here for restoration; arson by anti-Catholics was suspected, but nothing was ever proved. A lengthy twentieth-century restoration made use of surviving fragments and installed other pieces such as **Veronese**'s ceiling panels of *The Annunciation*, *The Assumption* and *The Adoration of the Shepherds*, and the other *Adoration* by him on the left of the door.

In the left aisle, **Bartolomeo Vivarini**'s *Three Saints* (1473), a portion of a dismantled polyptych, is the first thing to grab your eye. Busts of Titian, Palma il Vecchio and Palma il Giovane look down from over the sacristy door, forming the monument which the last of the three designed for himself. After the sacristy, the rest of the aisle is stacked with monuments, the first of which is that of **Doge Pasquale Malipiero** (d.1462)—created by **Pietro Lombardo**, it's one of the earliest in Renaissance style in Venice. After the **equestrian monument** of the *condottiere* **Pompeo Giustiniani** (aka *Braccio di Ferro*—Iron Arm) comes the **tomb of Doge Tommaso Mocenigo** (d.1423) by **Pietro di Nicolo Lamberti** and **Giovanni di Martino**, followed by another Pietro Lombardo monument, for **Doge Nicolò Marcello** (d.1474), just before the altar with the copy of Titian's *Martyrdom of St Peter*. Eminent Venetians of a more recent time—the Risorgimento heroes Attillo and Emilio Bandiera and Domenico Moro—are commemorated alongside; they're also honored by having a square named after them (see the next chapter). On the last altar is a somewhat over-dramatic figure of *St Jerome* by **Alessandro Vittoria** (1576).

Santa Maria Formosa and Around

The spacious **Campo di Santa Maria Formosa**, virtually equidistant from the Piazza, San Zanipolo and the Ponte di Rialto, is a major confluence of routes on the east side of the Canal Grande, and one of the most attractive and atmospheric squares in the city. Its fruit and vegetable stalls may be less numerous than those of the Rialto, but they're very nearly as fertile, and their owners are generally readier to pass the time of day with you. It's also a regular pitch for sellers of antiquarian bits and pieces, their tables laden with the harvest of a few attic clearances. A number of elegant buildings border the square, the most enigmatic of which is the sixteenth-century **Palazzo Priuli**, which has been closed up for some time, although someone collects the mail that is sometimes delivered there. The local PCI (communist party) offices occupy a suitably red building next door.

The Church of Santa Maria Formosa

Santa Maria Formosa was founded in the seventh century by San Magno, Bishop of Oderzo, who was guided by a dream in which the Madonna appeared to him as *formosa*—a word which closely translates as meaning both large-breasted and beautiful. In 944 it gained a place in the ceremonials of Venice when a group of its parishioners rescued some young women who had been abducted from San Pietro in Castello (see the entry on San Pietro); as a reward, the doge thereafter visited the church each year, when he would be presented with a straw hat to keep the rain off and wine to slake his thirst. The last hat given to the last doge can be seen in the Museo Correr.

Mauro Coducci, who rebuilt the church in 1492, followed quite closely the original Greek Cross plan, both as an evocation of Venice's Byzantine past and as a continuation of the tradition by which Marian churches were centrally organized to symbolize the womb. A dome was frequently employed as a reference to Mary's crown; this one was rebuilt in 1922 after an Austrian bomb destroyed its predecessor in World War I.

There are two **facades** to the church. The one facing the canal was built in 1542 in honor of the military leader Vincenzo Cappello (d.1541); Ruskin, decrying the lack of religious imagery on this facade, identified Santa Maria Formosa as the forerunner of those churches "built to the glory of man, instead of the glory of God." The decoration of the other facade, constructed in 1604, is a bit less presumptuous, as at least there's a figure of the Virgin to accompany the three portrait busts of other members of the Cappello clan. Ruskin reserved a special dose of vitriol for the **mask** at the base of the Baroque campanile: "huge, inhuman and monstrous—leering in bestial degradation, too foul to be either pictured or described ... in that head is embodied the type of the evil spirit to which Venice was abandoned." Pompeo Molmenti, the most assiduous chronicler of Venice's socio-cultural history, insists that the head is both a talisman against the Evil Eye and a piece of clinical realism, portraying a man with von Recklinghausen's disease, a rare congenital disorder whose most celebrated victim was the so-called Elephant Man.

The church contains two good paintings. Entering from the canal side, immediately on the right is **Palma il Vecchio's** *St Barbara* (1522–24), praised by George Eliot as "an almost unique presentation of a hero-woman, standing in calm preparation for martyrdom, without the slightest air of pietism, yet with the expression of a mind filled with serious conviction." Having added a third window to her two-windowed bathroom to symbolize the Trinity and having generally displayed an intolerable Christian recalcitrance, Saint Barbara was hauled up a mountain by her exasperated father and there executed. On his way down, the man was struck down by lightning, a fate which (with slightly obtuse logic) turned Barbara into the patron saint of soldiers, who are the terrestrial agents of sudden death. This is why Palma's painting stands in the former chapel of the *Scuola dei Bombardieri*, and shows her treading on a cannon. **Bartolomeo Vivarini's** *Triptych of the Madonna of the Misericordia* (1473), once the church's high altarpiece, is now in a nave chapel on the same side of the church as the *St Barbara*. It was paid for by the congregation of the church, and some of the figures under the Madonna's cloak are believed to be portraits of the parishioners. Such images of the merciful Madonna, one of the warmest in Catholic iconography, can be seen in various forms throughout the city—there's another example a few minutes' walk away (see below).

The Route to the Rialto

Either of the two bridges on the canal side of Santa Maria Formosa will take you onto the busy Salizzada di San Lio, a direct route to the Rialto that has one of the best *pasticcerie* in Venice (*Il Golosone*) and a handy supermarket. Calle del Paradiso, off to the right as you head towards the Rialto, is a pocket of Gothic Venice, overlooked at one end by an early fifteenth-century arch showing the

Madonna della Misericordia: unusually, she's sheltering a single person—the arch's donor. The coats of arms on the arch are those of the Fóscari and Mocenigo families, who owned the adjoining buildings.

San Lio church is notable for its ceiling panel of the *The Apotheosis of St Leo* by **Giandomenico Tiepolo**, and for the chapel to the right of the high altar, which was designed by the Lombardi and contains a *Pietà* possibly by **Tullio Lombardo**; there's also a low-grade Titian on the first altar on the left.

A diversion south from San Lio down Calle della Fava brings you to the church of **Santa Maria della Fava**, whose peculiar name derives from a sweet cake called a *fava* (bean), once an All Souls Day specialty of a local baker, and still a seasonal treat. Canova's tutor Giuseppe Bernardi (known as **Torretto**) carved the statues in niches along the nave; on the first altar on the right stands **Giambattista Tiepolo**'s early *Education of the Virgin* (1732), and on the other side of the church there's *The Madonna and St Philip Neri*, painted five years earlier by **G.B. Piazzetta**, the most influential painter in early eighteenth-century Venice.

To the Querini-Stampalia and the Museo Diocesano

Some of the most impressive palaces in the city stand on the island immediately to the south of Santa Maria Formosa; turn first left off Ruga Giuffa and you'll be confronted by the land entrance of the gargantuan sixteenth-century **Palazzo Grimani**, but for a decent view of the exterior you have to cross the Rio San Severo, which also runs past the Gothic **Palazzo Zorzi-Bon** and Coducci's neighboring **Palazzo Zorzi**.

If you take the alley that follows the south wall of Santa Maria Formosa, you pass into the Campiello Querini, forecourt of the Renaissance **Palazzo Querini-Stampalia**. From 1807 to 1850 this was the home of the Patriarch of Venice, and on 3 August 1849 was besieged by indignant Venetians when the patriarch refused to support resistance to Austrian rule. It now houses (on the second floor) one of the city's more recondite collections, the **Pinacoteca Querini-Stampalia** (Tues–Sun 10am–12:30pm; L5000, reductions L3000). Although there are a batch of Renaissance pieces—such as **Palma il Vecchio**'s marriage portraits of *Francesco Querini* and *Paola Priuli Querini* (for whom the palace was built), and **Giovanni Bellini**'s *Presentation in the Temple*—the general tone of the collection is set by the culture of eighteenth-century Venice, a period to which much of the palace's decor belongs. The winningly inept pieces by **Gabriel Bella** piled high in the first room form a comprehensive record of Venetian life in that century, and genre paintings by **Pietro and Alessandro Longhi**, a few rungs up the aesthetic ladder, feature prominently later on. All in all, unless you've a voracious appetite for the art of Venice's twilight decades, the Querini-Stampalia isn't going to thrill you.

Hurrying past the dangerously derelict church of **San Giovanni in Oleo** (or San Giovanni Nuovo), south of the Querini-Stampalia, you come down onto Campo Santi Filippo e Giacomo, which tapers towards the bridge over the Rio di Palazzo. The sixteenth-century **Palazzo Trevisan-Cappello** stands on one side of the foot of the bridge, facing the back of the Palazzo Patriarcale. This was once the home of Bianca Cappello, who was sentenced to death in her absence for eloping with her lower-class lover; all was forgiven when she later got hitched to Francesco de'Medici, and the couple lived here until their death by poisoning in 1587, a misfortune that rather embarrassed the Venetians, who couldn't publicly mourn their "daughter of the Republic" for fear of offending the couple's unknown but probably influential murderer.

On the other side a short fondamenta leads to the early fourteenth-century cloister of **Sant'Apollonia**, the only Romanesque cloister in the city. Fragments from the Basilica di San Marco dating back to the ninth century are displayed here, and a miscellany of sculptural pieces from other churches are on show in the adjoining **Museo Diocesano d'Arte Sacra** (daily 10:30am–12:30pm; free), where the permanent collection consists of a range of religious artifacts and paintings gathered from churches which have closed down or entrusted their possessions to the safety of the museum. In addition, works temporarily removed for restoration are often installed here for a while, which gives the museum an edge of unpredictability.

San Zaccaria, the Riva degli Schiavoni, and Around

The Salizzada di San Provolo, leading east out of Campo Santi Filippo e Giacomo runs straight to the elegant **Campo San Zaccaria**, a spot with a chequered past. The convent attached to the church was notorious for its libidinous goings-on—a state of affairs not so surprising if you bear in mind that many of the nuns were incarcerated here either because they were too strong-willed for their families or because their fathers couldn't afford a dowry. On one occasion officials sent to put a stop to the nuns' amorous liaisons were pelted with bricks by the residents, but behavior was customarily more discreet—Venice's upper classes supplied the convent with several of its novices, and the nuns' parlor became one of the city's most fashionable salons (as Guardi's painting of it in the Ca' Rezzonico shows).

There's a gory side to the area's history as well. In 864 **Doge Pietro Tradonico** was murdered in the campo as he returned from vespers, and in 1172 **Doge Vitale Michiel II**, having not only blundered in peace negotiations with the Byzantine empire but also brought the plague virus back with him, was murdered as he fled for the sanctuary of San Zaccaria. Michiel's assassins disappeared into Calle delle Rasse, between the Palazzo Ducale and San Zaccaria, and it was later decreed that only wooden buildings should be built there, to make it easier to flatten the hideout of any future doge-assassin; the decree wasn't contravened until 1948.

The Church of San Zaccaria

Founded as a shrine for the body of Zaccharias, father of John the Baptist, the church of **San Zaccaria** was rebuilt in 1444–1515, forming an unusually harmonious mix of Gothic and Renaissance styles. (Zaccharias is still here, under the second altar on the right.) Started by **Antonio Gambello**, the reconstruction was finished after Gambello's death (1481) by **Mauro Coducci**, who took over the facade from the first storey upwards—hence its resemblance to San Michele. The interior's notable architectural feature is its **ambulatory**: unique in Venice, it might have been built to accommodate the procession of the doges' Easter Sunday visit, a ritual that began after the convent had sold to the state the land that was to become the Piazza.

The church is stuffed with sevententh- and eighteenth-century paintings, all of them outshone by **Giovanni Bellini**'s large *Madonna and Four Saints* (1505; second altar on the left; you might think that the natural light is enough, but drop a coin into the lightbox and you'll see what you were missing). Further up the left aisle, by the sacristy door, is the tomb of **Alessandro Vittoria** (d.1608), including a self-portrait bust; he also carved the *St Zaccharias* and *St John the Baptist* for the two holy water stoups, and the now headless *St Zaccharias* on the facade above the door. The small fee payable to enter the **Cappella di Sant'Atanasio** and **Cappella di San Tarasio** is well worth it. The former—containing **Tintoretto's** early *The Birth of St John the Baptist* and some fifteenth-century stalls—was rebuilt at the end of the sixteenth century. Only in the latter does it become obvious that the chapels occupy much of the site of the old church; three wonderful *anconas* (composite altarpieces) by **Antonio Vivarini and Giovanni d'Alemagna** (1443) are the highlight here, and panels set into the floor reveal mosaics of the ninth and twelfth centuries. Downstairs is the spooky and perpetually waterlogged ninth-century crypt, the burial place of eight early doges.

The Riva degli Schiavoni

The broad **Riva degli Schiavoni**, stretching from the edge of the Palazzo Ducale to the canal just before the Arsenale entrance, is constantly thronged during the day, with an unceasing flow of promenading tourists and passengers hurrying to and from its vaporetto stops. It's at its best in the evening, when the crowds have dwindled and the sun goes down over the Salute. The name is a vestige of an ignominious side of the Venetian economy, as *schiavoni* denotes both slaves and the Slavs who in the early days of Venice provided most of the human merchandise. By the early eleventh century the Slavs were becoming extensively Christianized and so came to be regarded as too civilized for such treatment; in succeeding centuries the slave trade turned to Greece, Russia and Central Asia for its supplies, until the fall of Constantinople in 1453 forced a switch of attention to the black populations of Africa.

Now colonized by the aristocracy of the hotel trade, the Riva has long been one of Venice's smart addresses. **Petrarch** and his daughter lived at no. 4145 in 1362–67, and **Henry James** stayed at no. 4161, battling against the constant distractions outside to finish *The Portrait of a Lady*. George Sand, Charles Dickens, Proust, Wagner and the ever-present Ruskin all checked in at the **Hotel Danieli** (the former Palazzo Dandolo), which nowadays attracts the likes of Tina Turner and others with stratospheric income levels; and at the other end of the musical spectrum, Monteverdi's *Proserpina Rapita* was first performed here—one of the earliest opera productions. The *Danieli*'s nondescript extension, built in 1948, was the first transgression of the 1172 ban on stone buildings on this spot (see above).

The Pietà

Looking east from the Molo, the main eyecatcher—rising between the equestrian monument to King Vittorio Emanuele II and the tugboats berthed in the distance—is the white facade of **Santa Maria della Visitazione**, known less cumbersomely as **La Pietà**. **Vivaldi** wrote many of his finest pieces for the orphanage attached to the church, where he worked as violin-master (1704–18) and later as choirmaster (1735–38). During Vivaldi's second term **Giorgio Massari** won a competition to rebuild the church, and it's probable that the composer advised him on acoustic problems such as the positioning of the double choir on the entrance wall and two along the side walls. Building eventually began in 1745 (after Vivaldi's death), and when the interior was completed in 1760 (the facade didn't go on until 1906) it was regarded more as a concert hall than a church. You get some idea of the showiness of eighteenth-century Venice from the fact that whereas this section of the Riva was widened to give a grander approach to the building, Massari's plans for the orphanage were shelved owing to lack of funds.

The Pietà is still one of Venice's main music venues, and just about the only times you can get a peek inside is when the box office is open—and even then the entrance is usually barred by a rope. The newly restored white and gold interior, looking like a wedding cake turned outside in, is crowned by a ceiling painting of *The Glory of Paradise* by **Giambattista Tiepolo**, who also painted the ceiling above the high altar.

The Greek Quarter

A couple of minutes' walk north of La Pietà is **San Giorgio dei Greci**, with its alarmingly tilting campanile. The Greek presence here was strong from the eleventh century, and became stronger still after the Turkish seizure of Constantinople. This mid-fifteenth-century influx of Greek speakers provided a resource which was exploited by the city's numerous scholarly publishing houses, and greatly enriched the general culture of Renaissance Venice: the daughter of the condottiere Gianfrancesco Gonzaga, for example, is known to have written perfect Greek at the age of ten. At its peak, the Greek community numbered around 4000, some of whom were immensely rich: a Greek merchant murdered in Venice in 1756 left 4,000,000 ducats to his daughters, a legacy which was said to have made them the richest heiresses in Europe.

The church was built in 1539–1561 to a Sansovino-influenced design by **Sante Lombardo**; the cupola and campanile came later in the century. Inside, the Orthodox architectural elements include a *matroneo* (women's gallery) above the main entrance and an iconostasis (or rood screen) that completely cuts off the high altar. The icons on the screen are a mixture of works by a sixteenth-century Cretan artist called **Michael Danaskinàs**, and a few Byzantine pieces dating back as far as the twelfth century.

Permission to found an Orthodox church was given at the end of the fifteenth century, and a Greek college and scuola were approved at the same time. The college, redesigned in the 1670s by **Longhena**, is now home to the *Hellenic Center for Byzantine and Post-Byzantine Studies*, custodian of Venice's Greek archives. The **Scuola di San Nicolò dei Greci** houses the **Museo Dipinti Sacri Bizantini** (9am–12:30pm & 2:30–5pm, Sun & hols 9am–noon; closed Tues; L2000), a collection of predominantly fifteenth- to eighteenth-century icons, many of them by the *Madoneri*, a school of Greek and Cretan artists working in Venice in that period. Although many of the most beautiful of these works maintain the compositional and symbolic conventions of icon painting, it's fascinating to observe the impact of western influences—one or two of the artists achieve a synthesis, while others clearly struggle to harmonize the two worlds.

The area to the north of San Giorgio dei Greci is more interesting for its associations than its sights. The unfinished and hangar-like **San Lorenzo**—occasionally pressed into service as an exhibition space for the Biennale—was where Marco Polo was buried, but his sarcophagus went astray during sixteenth-century rebuilding. Gentile Bellini's *Miracle of the Relic of the Cross*, now in the Accademia, depicts an extraordinary incident that once occurred in the Rio di San Lorenzo—for the story, see the "Accademia" entry.

RESTAURANTS: *Aciugheta*, Campo Santi Filippo e Giacomo; *Ai Promessi Sposi*, Calle dell'Oca; *Alla Rivetta*, Ponte San Provolo; *Al Masceron*, Calle Lunga Santa Maria Formosa; *Al Milion*, Corte del Milion; *Da Paolo*, Campo dell'Arsenale.

PIZZAS: *Casa Mia*, Calle dell'Oca.

SNACKS AND BARS: *Trattoria Ca' d'Oro/Osteria della Vedova*, Calle del Pistor; along the Strada Nova.

CAFÉS AND PASTICCERIE: *Il Golosone*, Salizzada San Lio; along Salizzada San Giovanni Crisostomo and the Strada Nova.

Reviews of all these places appear in Chapter 10.

CHAPTER SIX

THE EASTERN DISTRICTS

For many visitors, Venice's eastern edge lies a few meters to the east of the Palazzo Ducale, and at first glance any map of the city would seem to justify this neglect of the eastern districts. Certainly the sights are thinly spread, and a huge bite is taken out of the area by the pools of the **Arsenale**, for a long time the largest manufacturing site in Europe, but now little more than a decoratively framed blank space.

Yet the section before you reach the Arsenale contains places that shouldn't be ignored—the Renaissance **San Francesco della Vigna**, for example, and the **Scuola di San Giorgio degli Schiavoni**, with its endearing cycle of paintings by **Carpaccio**. And although the mainly residential area beyond the Arsenale has little to offer in the way of cultural monuments other than the ex-cathedral of **San Pietro di Castello** and the church of **Sant'Elena**, it would be a mistake to leave the easternmost zone unexplored.

Except in the summer of even-numbered years, when the **Biennale** sets up shop in the specially built pavilions of the Giardini Pubblici and elsewhere in the neighborhood, few visitors stray into this latter area—and there lies one of its principal attractions. Stretching from Via Garibaldi to the Rio di Sant'Elena, the arc of green spaces formed by the **Giardini Garibaldi, Giardini Pubblici** (laid out originally by the French in 1810) and **Parco delle Rimembranze** can usually be relied on to provide a remedy for the claustrophobia that overtakes most visitors to Venice at some point. The whole length of the waterfront gives spectacular panoramas of the city, with the best coming last: from near the Sant'Elena landing stage you get a view that takes in the Palazzo Ducale, the back of San Giorgio Maggiore and La Giudecca, the tiny islands of La Grazia, San Clemente, Santo Spirito, San Servolo and San Lazzaro degli Armeni, and finally the Lido. A picnic here, having stocked up at the shops and markets stalls of Via Garibaldi, is guaranteed to recharge the batteries.

From San Francesco della Vigna to the Riva Ca' di Dio

If you continue **east from San Zanipolo**, you might soon begin to feel that you've roamed into one of Venice's drabber districts. The church of Santa Maria del Pianto, so prominent on the city's maps, turns out to be abandoned, and is barely visible over its surrounding wall. Cross the Rio di Santa Giustina and the shabby church of the same name confronts you; it's now part of a school. Follow the fondamenta down to the mouth of the canal, and to your right you'll get a view of the gasworks' rusting remains. But it's not all decay and dereliction—carry on east for a minute more, and a striking Renaissance church blocks your way.

San Francesco della Vigna

The ground occupied by **San Francesco della Vigna** has a hallowed place in the mythology of Venice, as according to tradition it was around here that the angel appeared to Saint Mark to tell him that the lagoon islands were to be his final resting place. (The angel's words—"Pax tibi" and so forth—remained unchanged on the book held by Venice's symbolic lion until Napoleon substituted the rubric "To the Rights of Men and Citizens" on official proclamations; "at last he's turned the page" remarked an anonymous wag.) Some time after the alleged annunciation the area was cultivated as a vineyard, and when the land was given to the Franciscans in 1253 as a site for a new church, the vines were immortalized in their church's name.

Begun in 1534, to a design by **Sansovino**, the present building was much modified in the course of its construction. **Palladio** was brought in to provide the **facade** (1568–72), a feature that looks like something of an afterthought from the side, but which must have been quite stunning at the time, when the only other all-white Istrian stone facade in Venice would have been that of San Michele. The **interior** (7–11:45am & 4:45–7pm) was altered by a humanist scholar monk, **Fra Francesco Zorzi** who rearranged the proportions along philosophically approved lines and generally amended its acoustic and decorative design. The calculated Renaissance improvements and cold coloring make the church less welcoming than the two great mendicant churches of San Zanipolo and the Frari, despite its less belittling dimensions; however, there are some fine works of art here, for whose light-boxes (essential) you should take a pocketful of coins.

Close to the door there's a trio of interesting pieces—a triptych attributed to **Antonio Vivarini** (on the entrance wall) and bronze figures of *St Francis* and *John the Baptist* by **Alessandro Vittoria**. Some of Venice's wealthiest families contributed to the cost of building San Francesco by paying for family chapels: the third on the right belonged to the **Contarini** (and contains memorials to a pair of seventeenth-century Contarini doges); the next is the **Badoer** chapel (with a *Resurrection* attributed to **Veronese**); and after that comes the chapel of the **Barbaro** family. The Barbaro ancestral device—a red circle on a white field—was granted in the twelfth century after a particularly revolting act by the Admiral Marco Barbaro: in the thick of battle he cut off a Moor's hand and used the bleeding stump to draw a circle on the man's turban, which he then flew as a pennant from the mast-head. Around the corner in the right transept is a large *Madonna and Child Enthroned* by **Antonio da Negroponte** (c.1450), a picture full of meticulously detailed and glowingly colorful birds and plants.

The church's foundation stone was laid by **Doge Andrea Gritti**, whose tomb is on the left wall of the chancel. Intellectually more versatile than many in his social stratum—he spoke six languages other than Italian and was a close friend of Sansovino—Gritti was also a formidable womanizer, of whom one rival remarked "we cannot make a doge of a man with three bastards in Turkey." After his election he carried on making bastards, including one with a nun named Celestina, but it was his equally Rabelaisian appetite for food that proved his undoing: he died after eating too many grilled eels on Christmas Eve. It's still a traditional Christmas dish in Venice.

Left of the chancel is the **Giustiniani** chapel, lined with marvelous sculpture by the **Lombardo** family and their helpers. Commissioned for the previous church by one of the Badoer clan and installed here after the rebuilding, they

EASTERN DISTRICTS

S. Giustina

S. Francesco della Vigna

CAMPO DELLA CELESTIA

R. DEL PONTEGO

R. DI S. FRANCESCO

S. Lorenzo

R. DELLA CELESTIA

CAMPO S. TERNITA

PIETA

CAMPO D GATTE

R. DEI SCUDI

Scuola di S. Giorgio

CPL. D. POZZI

R. DELLE GORNE

S. Antonio

SAL. D. GRECI

SAL. S. ANTONIN

R. DEL'ARCO

DARSENA ARSENALE VECCHIO

SAL. DEL PIGNATER

CAMPO DELL' ARSENALE

CAMPO BANDIERA e MORO

S. Giovanni in Bragora

S. Martino

La Pietà

R. DELL'ARSENALE

RIVA DEGLI SCHIAVONI

R. CA'DI DIO

S. Pietro di Castello

R. DI QUINTAVALLE

R. DEL GIARDINI

DARSENA DI S. ELENA

Campo Sportivo

CANALE DI

VLE S. ELENA

S. Elena

S. ELENA

Parco delle Rimembranze

VLE VITTORIO VENETO

Naval College

S. Elena
1,2,14,21

include a group of *Prophets* by **Pietro Lombardo and assistants** and reliefs of the *Evangelists* attributed to **Tullio and Antonio Lombardo**. Go out to the fifteenth-century cloisters for the Cappella Santa, which has a *Madonna and Child* by **Giovanni Bellini and assistants**. Back in the church, the first chapel after the cloister door (another Giustiniani chapel) contains a *Sacred Conversation*, painted by **Veronese** in 1562. Titian's Pésaro altarpiece in the Frari provided the model for Veronese's picture; Michelangelo, often characterized as Titian's antithesis, was the partial inspiration for **Alessandro Vittoria's** figures of *St Anthony Abbot*, *St Sebastian* and *St Roch*, in the penultimate chapel.

South and East of San Francesco

East of San Francesco is a remote corner which can be summarized as a vaporetto stop (*Celestia*), a scummy backwater of a canal, and a view of the sinister wall of the oldest part of the Arsenale. Immediately to the south lies an area which is destitute of monuments but could stand as the epitome of domestic Venice—densely textured, in places grotty and in others picturesque. The Salizzada and Campo delle Gatte ("Paved Street and Square of the Female Cats") are typical of the district; the peculiar name of this unexceptionally catty avenue is a corruption of "de legate," from the papal legates who used to stay here. An oddity to seek out is the sottoportego on the corner of Calle Zorzi and Corte Nuova: it's an open-air chapel, with a carved and painted ceiling, a couple of shrines (dedicated to the dead of various wars) and four paintings so flaked and grimy that they could depict anything.

San Giorgio degli Schiavoni

If there's one building in Venice that can be guaranteed to provide affectionate memories, it's the **Scuola di San Giorgio degli Schiavoni**, home of a brilliant cycle of pictures by the most seductive of Venetian artists, **Vittore Carpaccio**. (Tues–Sat 10am–12:30pm & 3:30–6pm, Sun & hols 10am–12:30pm; L3000, reductions L2000). Venice's relations with the Slavs ("Schiavoni") were not always untroubled—the city's slave markets were originally stocked with captured Slavs, and in later centuries the settlements of the Dalmatian coast were a harassment to Venetian shipping. By the mid-fifteenth century, though, Venice's Slavic inhabitants—many of them sailors and merchants—were sufficiently established for a scuola to be set up in order to protect their interests. After several years of meeting in the church of San Giovanni di Malta, the scuola built itself a new headquarters on the church's doorstep at the start of the sixteenth century, and summoned Carpaccio to brighten up the first-story hall. Painted from 1502–08 (after the Accademia's St Ursula cycle), Carpaccio's pictures were moved downstairs when the building was rearranged in 1551, and the interior has changed little since then.

The cycle illustrates mainly the lives of the Dalmatian patron saints (George, Tryphone and Jerome). The scenes depicted are: *Saint George and the Dragon*, *The Triumph of St George*, *St George Baptizing the Gentiles* (George had rescued the princess of of Selene, daughter of the royal couple being baptized); *The Miracle of St Tryphone* (the dainty little basilisk is a demon just exorcized from the daughter of the Roman Emporer Gordianus); *The Agony in the Garden*, *The Calling of Matthew*, *St Jerome Leading the Lion to the Monastery*, *The Funeral of St Jerome*, and *The Vision of St Augustine* (he was writing to Saint Jerome when a vision told him of Jerome's death). The *Madonna and Child* altarpiece (1541) is by **Benedetto Carpaccio**, Vittore's son; the paneled upstairs hall is decorated with early seventeenth-century paintings in honor of various brethren of the scuola, some of which are almost surreal in their composition.

From Sant'Antonino to the Waterfront

The frequently closed church of **Sant'Antonino**, the next stop south along the fondamenta, is an unenticing seventeenth-century effort, but has some good stories attached to it. It housed the body of a certain Saint Sabus from the mid-thirteenth century until 1965, when Pope Paul VI returned the relic to the the monastery in Constantinople whence it had been stolen by a future doge; for all that time the monks had been meeting disconsolately every night at their saint's empty sarcophagus. The emblems of Saint Anthony Abbot are a pig and a bell, and this church once kept a sty of notoriously unruly (and belled) pigs—though it's not clear whether the monks kept pigs because of the emblem, or if the emblem followed from the monastic pigs. The campanological swine were allowed to roam the parish unfettered, but eventually they so annoyed the locals that in 1409 their freedom was curtailed by a sumptuary edict. "Saint Anthony loved a pig" is still a Venetian saying, used to express a lack of surprise at an odd occurrence. James (Jan) Morris records that in 1819 an elephant escaped from a visiting menagerie and took refuge in Sant'Antonino; having cornered the hapless beast, its pursuers shot it.

San Giovanni in Bragora

The Salizzada Sant'Antonin curves down to the quiet **Campo Bandiera e Moro**. Its handsomest building, the fifteenth-century Palazzo Gritti Badoer, was a ruin in Ruskin's day (and "inhabited by the lowest orders," he added snootily) but has since been renovated as a hotel. Across the square stands **San Giovanni in Bragora**, probably best known to Venetians as the baptismal church of Antonio Vivaldi. Begun in 1475, about the same time that San Michele was finished and only six years before the Miracoli was started, this simple Gothic building shows no sign of the arrival of Renaissance architecture in Venice. But one can trace the inception of a more sophisticated Renaissance aesthetic in its best paintings: a triptych by **Bartolomeo Vivarini** (1478; chapel to left of chancel), a *Resurrection* by **Alvise Vivarini** (1498; to left of sacristy door) and a *Baptism* by **Cima da Conegliano** (1494; behind high altar). The body of Saint John the Almsgiver, stolen from Alexandria in 1247, lies in the second chapel on the right, though the Venetian church dedicated to him (San Giovanni Elemosinario) is way over in the Rialto.

San Martino—and the Riva

A group of Paduan refugees are said to have founded a church on the site of the nearby **San Martino** in 593, which would give it one of Venice's longest ecclesiological pedigrees; **Sansovino** designed the present Greek-cross building in around 1540 (11am–noon and 6–7pm, plus services). To get a decent perusal of **Domenico Bruni**'s distortedly perspectival ceiling painting (seventeenth-century) you have to lie on your back in the very middle of the church, more or less where most of **Doge Francesco Erizzo** (d.1646) is buried; his heart is in the Basilica. (For those in need, a public toilet is hidden between San Martino and San Giovanni in Bragora, on the corner of Calle Erizzo and Calle Morosina.)

The **Ca' di Dio**, which gives its name to the short stretch of waterfront with the *Arsenale* vaporetto stop, was founded in the thirteenth century as a hospice for pilgrims and Crusaders; the wing which Sansovino added in 1545 is visible from the bridge. To its right as you look north is the **Forni Pubblici** (1473), the bakery which supplied the ships leaving the Arsenale with ship's cookie.

The Arsenale

A corruption of the Arabic *darsin'a* (house of industry), the very name of the **Arsenale** is indicative of the strength of Venice's links with the eastern Mediterranean, and the workers of these dockyards and factories were the foundations upon which the city's maritime supremacy rested. Visiting dignitaries were often as astonished by the industriousness of the Arsenale as by the opulence of the Canal Grande. At the beginning of the fourteenth century Dante came to Venice twice (once as ambassador from Ravenna), and was so impressed by what he saw on his first mission that he evoked the sight in a famous passage of the *Inferno*, in which those guilty of selling public offices are tortured in a lake of boiling pitch like the caulkers' vats in the Arsenale.

The development of the Arsenale commenced in the early years of the twelfth century, and by the middle of that century a state monopoly in the construction of galleys was established here. By the third decade of the fifteenth century it had become the base for some 300 shipping companies, operating around 3000 vessels of 200 tons or more; at its peak, the wet and dry docks, the rope and sail factories, the ordnance depots and gunpowder mills employed a total of 16,000 men—the size of population you'd have found in a major town of the period.

In *The City in History*, Lewis Mumford credits the Venetians with the invention of "a new type of city, based on the differentiation and zoning of urban functions, separated by traffic ways and open spaces," and cites the island of Murano and the Arsenale as Europe's first examples of industrial planning. Of these two, the Arsenale most closely resembled a modern factory complex. Construction techniques in the Arsenale were the most sophisticated of their time; one awestruck visitor in the fifteenth century recorded the Venetians' production-line process for equipping their warships, in which the vessels were towed past a succession of windows, to collect ropes, sails, armaments, oars and all their other supplies (ending with the barrels of hard cookies), so that by the time they reached the lagoon the vessels were fully prepared for battle. The productivity of the wharves was legendary: at the height of the conflict with the Turks in the sixteenth century, one ship a day was being added to the Venetian fleet. On the occasion of the visit of Henry III of France in 1574, the lads from the Arsenale put on a bravura performance—in the time it took the king and his hosts to work their way through a state banquet in the Palazzo Ducale, the *Arsenalotti* assembled and made seaworthy a ship sturdy enough to bear a crew plus a cannon weighing 16,000 pounds.

To an extent, the governors of the city acknowledged their debt to the workers of the Arsenale. They were a privileged group within the Venetian proletariat, acting as watchmen at the Palazzo Ducale whenever the Maggior Consiglio was in session, carrying the doge in triumph round the Piazza after his inauguration, and serving as pallbearers at ducal funerals. By the standards of other manual workers they were not badly paid either, although the 50 ducats which was the typical wage of a master shipwright in the early sixteenth century should be set against the 40,000 ducats spent by Alvise Pisani, one of the most powerful politicians of the period, on the weddings of his five daughters. The *Arsenalotti* were also less docile than most of their fellow artisans, and were responsible for a number of strikes and disturbances. A dramatic protest took place in 1569, when a gang of 300 *Arsenalotti* armed with axes smashed their way into the hall of the Collegio to present their grievances to the doge in person.

Expansion of the Arsenale was particularly rapid in the fourteenth century and continued into the sixteenth—**Sanmicheli**'s covered dock for the state barge (the *Bucintoro*) was built in 1544–47, for example, and **da Ponte**'s gigantic ropefactory – the *Corderia* or *Tana* – in 1579. (The greater part of the *Tana* runs along the Rio della Tana; at 316m long – not far off twice the length of the Piazza – it makes a magnificent exhibition space for the *Aperto* section of the Biennale.) By then, though, the maritime strength of Venice was past its peak: Vasco da Gama had rounded the Cape of Good Hope in 1497, thus opening a direct sea route to the east; the New World routes were growing; and there was the perpetual threat of the ever stronger Turkish empire. The shrinkage of the Venetian mercantile fleet was drastic—between 1560 and 1600 the volume of shipping registered at the Arsenale was halved. Militarily as well, despite the conspicuous success at Lepanto (1571), Venice was on the wane, and the reconquest of the Morea (Peloponnese) at the end of the seventeenth century was little more than a glorious interlude in a long story of decline. When **Napoleon** took over the city in 1797 he burned down the docks, sank the last *Bucintoro* (it had lasted seventy years) and confiscated the remnant of the Venetian navy, sailing off with it to attempt the invasion of Ireland. After the failure of that expedition the fleet was taken back to the Mediterranean, only to be destroyed by Nelson at the battle of Aboukir.

Under Austrian occupation the Arsenale was reconstructed, and it stayed in continuous operation until the end of 1917 when, having produced a number of ships for the Italian navy in World War I, the dockyards were dismantled to prevent them being of use to the enemy forces which seemed likely to invade the lagoon. Since then it has been used by the navy for storage and repairs, but plans exist to extend the Museo Storico Navale into the Arsenale buildings and to convert other parts into sports halls.

The Arsenale Buildings

There is no public access to the Arsenale. You can get a look at part of it, however, from the bridge connecting the Campo Arsenale and the Fondamenta dell'Arsenale; a better view can be had by taking the vaporetto #5, which cuts through the oldest part of the complex, taking you past Sanmicheli's *Bucintoro* building, alongside which is the mouth of the *Darsena Grande*.

The main **gateway** to the Arsenale was the first structure in Venice to employ the classical vocabulary of Renaissance architecture. Built by **Antonio Gambello** in 1460 (but incorporating, at ground level, Veneto-Byzantine capitals of the twelfth century), it consists of a triumphal arch topped by a less precisely classical story—a design that was possibly intended to create the illusion that the entrance to the Arsenale was an amalgam of a genuine Roman edifice and more modern Venetian building. You'll notice that the Lion of Saint Mark is holding a closed book, perhaps because the book's traditional inscription—"Pax tibi . . ."— was thought to be too pacific for this context; the statue above his head, *Santa Justina* by **Campagna**, was put there in 1578.

The **four lions** to the side of the gateway feature in coffee-table books on Venice almost as frequently as the San Marco horses, and, like the horses, they are stolen goods. Exactly when the two on the right were grabbed isn't known, but they probably came from the Lion Terrace at Delos, and date from around the sixth century BC; the left-hand one of the pair (with the prosthetic head) was positioned here to mark the recapture of Corfu in 1716—the other was in place slightly earlier. The larger pair aren't as enigmatic: they were swiped from Piraeus in 1687 by Francesco Morosini, after the reconquest of the Morea. (See "West of the Piazza" for more on Morosini.) The blurred and incomprehensible inscription on the shoulder and side of the lion on the far left (which started life as an ancient Greek fountain) is a piece of runic graffiti, the handiwork of a Norse mercenary serving with the army hired by the Byzantine Emperor in the eleventh century to suppress a rebellion of his Greek subjects.

The Museo Storico Navale and San Biagio

Nearby, on the other side of the Rio dell'Arsenale, is the **Museo Storico Navale**, most of which is housed in a former granary (Mon–Fri 9am–1pm, Sat 9am–noon; closed Sun; L1000; last ticket 30min before closing). Documenting every conceivable facet of Venice's naval history, the museum is another loose baggy monster like the Correr, but a selective tour is an essential supplement to a walk round the Arsenale district—and it's laid out far better than the Correr, with bilingual captions on many of the exhibits. Improbable though it sounds, the models of Venetian craft—from the gondola to the 224-oar fighting galley and the last *Bucintoro*—will justify the entrance fee for most people. It was common practice in the Venetian shipyards to build their boats not from scale drawings but from models, and the most meticulous pieces in the collection (on the first floor) are the functional models retrieved from the yards after Napoleon's arsonists had done their work. At ground level there's a miscellany of armaments and a room dedicated to Angelo Emo, the last admiral of the Republic (with a monument by **Canova**; 1795). Models of more recent ships take up much of the second floor; the third has a large display on the evolution of the gondola and a roomful of models of Far Eastern vessels. The top storey's installation, illustrating the part played by Sweden in the maritime history of Venice, is not as eccentric as you might think, but is nonetheless strictly for specialists. About 250 meters along the fondamenta is the second section of the museum, the **Padiglioni delle Navi**—a vast shed full of craft with Venetian connections.

The church of **San Biagio**, alongside the main museum block, was the Greek community's church before San Giorgio dei Greci, and took on its present municipal office appearance after an eighteenth-century rehaul. It's now the naval chapel and is rarely open—no great loss, as apart from **Giovanni Ferrari's** reclining statue of Admiral Angelo Emo (1792), there's nothing much in it. Tucked behind the church is the concrete bunker known as Palasport (or Palazzetto dello Sport), the city's main indoor sports hall, used for handball and basketball matches.

To San Pietro di Castello and Sant'Elena

In 1808 the greater part of the canal connecting the Bacino di San Marco to the broad inlet of the Canale di San Pietro was filled in to form what is now **Via Garibaldi**, the widest street in the city and the busiest commercial area in the eastern district. (The pattern of the sidewalk shows clearly the course of the former canal.) The bars, *pasticcerie* and *alimentari* of Via Garibaldi are as good as most of those in the more comfortable areas of the city, are generally quite a bit cheaper, and are far less likely to treat you as a tedious occupational hazard. Roaming through the alleyways and squares of the vicinity, it's almost possible to forget that you're in the most commercialized city in the country.

There's little of cultural or historical significance along Via Garibaldi: the first house on the right was for a time the home of the navigators **John and Sebastian Cabot**, explorers respectively of Newfoundland and Brazil in the late fifteenth century and early sixteenth; the church of **San Francesco di Paola**, opposite the entrance to the Giardini Garibaldi, has a painting by **Giandomenico Tiepolo**—*Liberation of a Possessed* (on the cornice). Beyond the market stalls, the right-hand side of the street becomes the Fondamenta di Sant'Anna: this takes you onto the Ponte di Quintavalle, and so to the island of San Pietro.

San Pietro di Castello—Venice's former Cathedral

Originally named **Castello**, after a castle that used to stand here (built by either the Romans or the first "Venetian" settlers), the island of **San Pietro** was one of the very first of parts of central Venice to be occupied. Nowadays this is a run down district where the repairing of boats is the main occupation, yet it was once the ecclesiastical center of Venice. By 775 the settlement here had grown sufficiently to be granted the foundation of a bishopric under the authority of the Patriarch of Grado. Within the next half-century Castello joined the immediately surrounding islands to form Rivoalto, the embryonic city of Venice. From the beginning, the political and economic power was concentrated in the Rialto and San Marco districts, and the relationship between the church and the geographically remote rulers of the city was never to be close. In 1451 the first **Patriarch of Venice** was invested, but still his seat remained at Castello, and succeeding generations of councillors and senators showed no inclination to draw the father of the Venetian church into the center of power. San Pietro di Castello remained the cathedral of Venice, emblematically marooned on the periphery of the city, until 1807 (ten years after the Republic had ceased to exist), when the Patriarch was at last permitted to install himself in San Marco.

One of the major Venetian festivals—the Festival of the Marys—had its origin in an incident that occurred here in the tenth century. A multiple marriage in the church was interrupted by a posse of Slav pirates, who carried away the brides and their substantial dowries. Men from the parish of Santa Maria Formosa led the pursuit, which succeeded in retrieving the women. To celebrate their safe return, every year two girls were chosen from each *sestiere* to be married in a single ceremony at San Pietro, the weddings being followed by an eight-day junket that culminated at Santa Maria Formosa on the Day of the Purification of Mary—the day on which the brides had been kidnapped.

As with the Arsenale, the history of San Pietro is more interesting than what you can see. A church was raised here as early as the seventh century, but the present **San Pietro di Castello** was built nearly a millenium later (winter 8am–noon & 3–6pm; summer 8am–noon & 4:30–7pm). A new facade was designed in the mid-sixteenth century by **Palladio**, but the work was not carried out until the end of the century, and the executed project was a feeble version of the original scheme. Similarly, the interior is an early seventeenth-century derivation from a plan by Palladio, and is unlikely to convince any Ruskinite that classicism has something to it after all. Nor will the paintings put a skip in your stride: best of the bunch are *SS. John the Evangelist, Peter and Paul*, a late work by **Veronese** (left aisle), and the altarpiece by **Luca Giordano** in the Cappella Vendramin (left transept). The Vendramin chapel and the high altar were both designed by **Longhena**; take a look as well at the Cappella Lando (left aisle), which has a fifth-century mosaic fragment and a bust of San Lorenzo Giustiniani, the first Patriarch of Venice, by a follower of Antonio Rizzo. The most unusual feature of the church is the so-called **Throne of Saint Peter** (right aisle), a marble seat made in the thirteenth century from an Arabic funeral stone cut with texts from the Koran.

The **campanile**, one of the most precarious in the city, was rebuilt by Mauro Coducci in the 1480s, and was the first tower in Venice to be clad in Istrian stone. Its original cupola was replaced with the present one in 1670.

Sant'Elena

The island of **Sant'Elena**, the city's eastern limit, was greatly enlarged during the Austrian administration, partly to furnish accommodation and exercise grounds for the troops. Much of the island used to be covered by the meadow of Sant'Elena, a favorite recreation area in the last century, but the strip of park along the waterfront is all that's left of it, houses having been built on the rest. Still, the walk out here is the nearest you'll get to country pleasures in central Venice, and the **church of Sant'Elena**, approached between the concrete walls of the naval college and sports stadium, is worth a visit.

A church was erected here in the thirteenth century, following the acquisition of the body of Saint Helena (Constantine's mother), and rebuilt in 1435. From 1807 to 1928 it was abandoned (except for a spell as an iron foundry) but the spartan Gothic interior has recently been restored, as have the cloister and campanile—the latter so zealously that it now looks like a power-station chimney. The main attraction is the **doorway** to the church, an ensemble created in the 1470s by **Antonio Rizzo** and incorporating the *Monument to Comandante Vittore Cappello*, showing the admiral kneeling before Saint Helena.

Rizzo's group is the one work of art in this easternmost area that shouldn't be missed, but if you want to squeeze every last drop from it, call in at the church of **San Giuseppe di Castello** (between the Biennale pavilions and Rio di San Giuseppe). It houses **Alessandro Vittoria**'s *Monument to Procurator G. Grimani* (in the chancel), and a vast *Monument to Doge Marino Grimani*, designed in the late sixteenth century by **Vincenzo Scamozzi**, with reliefs and figures by **Campagna** (left side).

RESTAURANTS: *Al Marca* and *Toscana*, both Via Garibaldi. (See Chapter 10 for reviews.)

BARS, CAFÉS AND PASTICCERIE: concentrated along the Via Garibaldi.

CHAPTER SEVEN

THE CANAL GRANDE

K nown to the locals as the *Canalazzo*, the Canal Grande is Venice's main street, and divides the city in half, with three *sestieri* to the west and three to the east. Only three bridges cross it—at the station, Rialto and Accademia—but traversing the city is not quite the complex procedure it might seem, as a number of *traghetti* operate along the canal, ferrying people from one bank to the other. The Canal Grande is almost four kilometers long and varies in width between thirty and seventy meters; it is, however, surprisingly shallow, at no point much exceeding five meters. (In the fourteenth century an earthquake pulled the plug out and the entire contents drained away: for the best part of a fortnight Venice's finest waterway was an avenue of slime.)

The Palaces

The majority of the most important palaces in Venice stand on the Canal Grande— and all have their main facades on the canalside. It's not the case, however, that the Canal Grande was Venice's sole smart address; each parish had its important families, and the palaces of those families were the pivots of each parish. The Canal Grande has a lot of palaces because it cuts through a lot of parishes.

Virtually all the surviving Canal Grande palaces were built within a span of about 500 years, and in the course of that period the **basic plan** varied very little. The typical Venetian palace has an entrance hall (the *andron*) on the ground floor, and this runs right through the building; it is flanked by storage rooms. Above comes the mezzanine floor—the small rooms on this level were used as offices or, from the sixteenth century onwards, as libraries or living rooms. On the next floor—often the most extravagantly decorated—you find the *piano nobile*, the main living area, arranged as suites of rooms on each side of a central hall (*portego*), which runs, like the *andron*, from front to back. The plan of these houses can be read from the outside of the palace, where you'll usually see a cluster of large windows in the center of the facade, between symmetrically placed side windows. Frequently there is a second *piano nobile* above the first—this generally would have been accommodation for relatives or children (though sometimes it was the main living quarters); the attic would have been for servants' rooms or storage.

The Venetian taste for surface **decoration** was as durable as this general palace plan. Just as the facades of the older palaces were adorned with carved panels and slabs of colored marble, so the later ones were studded with reliefs and heraldic devices, and sometimes were frescoed. Underneath their decorative skins, nearly all the palaces are made of **brick**, which is cheaper, lighter and easier to obtain in the Veneto than building stone. Obviously mudbanks are not the stablest of bases, so the builders' usual procedure was to drive oak piling into the mud as a foundation, and then consolidate this with a superstructure of planks and cement. Between this "raft" and the brickwork, they often placed a damp-proof course of water-resistant Istrian stone.

CANAL GRANDE

PIAZZA SAN MARCO

Pal. Giustinian

San Marco Vallaresso 1, 2, 4, 34

La Fenice

Pal. Contarini-Fasan

S. Maria d. Salute

Pal. Pisani

Salute #1

Traghetto

S. Stefano

S. M. del Giglio

Pal. Dario

Pal. Corner d. Ca' Grande

a. Mocenigo

Pal. Barbaro

Pal. Venier d. Leoni

Pal. Contarini d. Figure

Pal. Grassi

Pal. Franchetti

Ca' del Duca

Accademia 1, 2, 4

Pal. Contarini dal Zaffo

S. Samuele

Ca' Rezzonico 1

Accademia

Ca' Foscari

Pal. Giustinian

Pal. Contarini Corfu

Ca' Rezzonico

Pal. Loredan

Canal Grande

A couple of features of the Venetian skyline call for explanation. The bizarre **chimneys** were designed to function as spark traps—fire being a constant hazard in a city where the scarcity of land inevitably resulted in a high density of housing. (The development of Venice has been punctuated by terrible fires—notably at the Rialto, San Marco and, at least four times, the Palazzo Ducale.) The **roof-level platforms** (*altane*) you'll see here and there had a variety of uses: drying laundry and bleaching hair being two of the most common. For the latter operation, the women of Renaissance Venice wore wide-brimmed crownless straw hats, which allowed them to get the sun on their hair while keeping it off their complexions.

The frequency with which the same **family names** recur can be confusing. More than ten palaces bear the Contarini name, for example, and at one time there were around thirty. Intermarriage between families is one reason for this—dynastic marriages were often marked by grafting the new relatives' surname onto the house's original name. The other main explanation is the fact that under Venetian law the eldest son was not the sole heir—the sons of wealthy patricians would often, upon receiving their shares of the father's estate, set up their own branches of the family in houses in other parts of the city. This did not always involve commissioning a new building; palaces were regularly bought and sold within the patriciate, and the transaction often resulted in another double-barrelled palace name.

The section that follows is principally a guide to the Canal Grande palaces—the churches and other public buildings that you can see from the vaporetto are covered in the appropriate geographical sections. You'd need an amazing reading speed and a rubber neck to do justice to the Canal Grande in one run, though; even these edited highlights cover around fifty buildings (less than a third of the total). Try to allow for several trips, and don't miss the experience of a nocturnal boat ride—the romance of Venice at night survives even the din of a vaporetto.

The Left Bank

If you come into Venice by train, your first sight of the Canal Grande will be from the upper stretch of its left bank, with the vaporetto landing-stages directly in front. To the left is the **Ponte degli Scalzi**, successor of an iron structure put up by the Austrians in 1858–60; like the one at the Accademia, it was replaced in the early 1930s, to give the new steamboats enough clearance. The boat passes two churches, the **Scalzi** and **San Geremia**, before the first of the major palaces comes into view—the **Palazzo Labia** (completed c.1750). The main facade of the building stretches along the Canareggio canal, but from the Canal Grande you can see how the side wing wraps itself round the campanile of the neighboring church—such interlocking is common in Venice, where maximum use has to be made of available space. The ballroom of the Palazzo Labia contains fabulous frescoes by Tiepolo, which can be seen by appointment.

Not far beyond the unfinished church of **San Marcuola** stands the **Palazzo Vendramin-Calergi**, begun by Mauro Coducci at the very end of the fifteenth century and finished in the first decade of the sixteenth, probably by Tullio Lombardo. This is the first Venetian palace to be influenced by the classically-based architectural principles of Leon Battista Alberti, and is frequently singled out as the Canal Grande's masterpiece. The round-arched windows enclosing two similar arches are identifying characteristics of Coducci's designs. In the seventeenth century a new wing was added to the palace, but soon after its completion two sons of the house conspired to murder a member of the Querini-Stampalia family; as the brothers hadn't physically committed the crime themselves, the court had to limit its sentence to exile, but it ordered the demolition of the new building for good measure. The most famous subsequent resident was Richard Wagner, who died here in February 1883; the size of the palace can be gauged from the fact that his rented suite of fifteen rooms occupied just a part of the mezzanine level.

The **Palazzo Soranzo**, a bit farther along, dates from the same period as the Vendramin-Calergi; appealing in itself, it gives you an idea of the originality of Coducci's design. The **Palazzo Gussoni-Grimani della Vida**, on the near side of the Rio di Noale, was rebuilt to Sanmicheli's designs in the middle of the sixteenth century. From 1614–1618 it was occupied by the English consul Sir Henry Wotton, at the time of whose residence the facade of the palace was covered with frescoes by Tintoretto—they have long since faded. Wotton spent much of his time running a sort of import-export business: when he wasn't buying paintings to ship back to England he was arranging for Protestant texts to be brought into Venice, a city he thought ripe for conversion. The Venetians, however, remained content with their idiosyncratic version of Catholicism, as exemplified by Wotton's friend, Paolo Sarpi (see *Cannaregio*). In Britain, Wotton is best remembered for his rueful definition of an ambassador—"an honest man sent to lie abroad for the good of his country."

The next palace of interest is the most beguiling on the canal—the **Ca' d'Oro**. (*Ca'* is an abbreviation of *Casa*—house. It was only after the fall of the Republic that the title *Casa* was dropped in favor of *Palazzo*.) Incorporating fragments of a thirteenth-century palace that once stood on the site, the Ca' d'Oro was built in the 1420s and 30s, and acquired its nickname—"The Golden House"—from the gilding that used to accentuate much of its carving. It now houses a large art collection, details of which are given in the *Cannaregio* chapter.

To the Rialto

The facade of the **Palazzo Sagredo**, on the near side of the Campo Santa Sofia, is an overlay of different periods, and a good demonstration of the Venetian custom of adapting old buildings to current needs and principles. The tracery of the *piano nobile* is fourteenth-century, and clearly later than the storeys below; the right wing of the palace, however, seems to belong to the fifteenth century.

On the near corner of the Rio dei Santi Apostoli stands the **Palazzo Mangilli-Valmarana**, built in the eighteenth century for the English consul, Joseph Smith, who was one of the chief patrons of Canaletto. Architecturally more interesting is the **Ca' da Mosto**, close to the Rio's opposite bank. The arches of the second floor and the carved panels above them are remnants of a thirteenth-century Veneto-Byzantine building, and thus are among the oldest structures to be seen on the Canal Grande. Alvise da Mosto, discoverer of the Cape Verde Islands, was born here in 1432; by the end of that century it had become the *Albergo del Lion Bianco*, and from then until the last century the palace was one of Venice's most popular hotels.

As the canal turns, the **Ponte di Rialto** comes into view. The huge building before it, with five arches at water level, is the **Fondaco dei Tedeschi**, once headquarters of the city's German merchants. On the ground floor their cargoes were weighed, packaged and stored (under Venetian supervision); the upper storeys contained a refectory and around sixty bedrooms, many of which were rented on an annual basis by the biggest firms. The German traders were economically the most powerful foreign grouping in the city, and as early as 1228 they were leased a building on this central site. In 1505 the original Fondaco burned down, and was rebuilt by Spavento and Scarpagnino; Giorgione and Titian, who had helped the firefighters on the night of the blaze, were then commissioned to paint the exterior walls. The remains of their contribution are now in the Ca' d'Oro. The Fondaco has been renovated several times since the sixteenth century, and is now the main post office.

The famous **bridge** superseded a succession of wooden and sometimes unreliable structures—in 1444 a forerunner collapsed under the weight of the crowd gathered on the bridge to watch the wedding procession of the Marquis of Ferrara; and one of Carpaccio's *Miracles of the True Cross*, in the Accademia, shows you what the subsequent drawbridge looked like. The decision to construct a stone bridge was taken in 1524, and over the following sixty years proposals by such architects as Michelangelo, Vignola, Sansovino and Palladio were considered and rejected. Eventually the job was awarded to the aptly named Antonio da Ponte, the topheaviness of whose design prompted Edward Gibbon to describe it as "a fine bridge, spoiled by two rows of houses upon it." Until 1854, when the first Accademia bridge was built, the Rialto was the only point at which the Canal Grande could be crossed on foot.

From the Rialto to the Volta del Canal

Immediately before the next *rio* is Sansovino's first palace in Venice, the **Palazzo Dolfin-Manin**. It dates from the late 1530s, a period when other projects by Sansovino—the Libreria, the Zecca and the Loggetta—were transforming the center of the city. The public passageway (*sottoportego*) running under the facade is a feature common to many Venetian houses. Lodovico Manin, the last Doge of Venice, lived there—he had the interior rebuilt, so the facade is the only bit entirely by Sansovino.

The **Palazzo Loredan** and the **Palazzo Farsetti**, standing side by side at the end of the Fondamenta del Carbon, are heavily restored Veneto-Byzantine palaces of the thirteenth century. The former was the home of **Elena Corner Piscopia**, who in 1678 graduated from Padua University, so becoming the first woman ever to hold a university degree. The two buildings are now occupied by the town hall.

Work began on the **Palazzo Grimani** (near side of the Rio di San Luca) in 1559, to designs by Sanmicheli, but was not completed until 1575, sixteen years after his death. Ruskin, normally no fan of Renaissance architecture, made an exception for this colossal palace, calling it "simple, delicate, and sublime." A Venetian folktale attributes the scale of the palace to a thwarted passion: it's said that the young man who built it was in love with a woman from the Coccina-Tiepolo palace over the way, but was turned away by her father, who wanted someone wealthier for his girl. The suitor's revenge was to humiliate the father by building a palace which had windows bigger than the main doorway at the Coccina-Tiepolo.

The **Palazzo Corner Contarini dei Cavalli**, on the other side of the *rio*, was built c.1445; the *cavalli* part of the name comes from the horses on the crest of the facade's coat of arms. The pink **Palazzo Benzon**, just before the next canal, was where the most fashionable salon of early nineteenth-century Venice used to meet—regular guests included Byron, Thomas Moore, Ugo Foscolo and Canova. Their hostess, the Contessa Querini-Benzon, was celebrated in a song that still occupies a place in the gondoliers' repertoire—*"La biondina in gondoleta"* (The Blonde in a Gondola). The **Palazzo Corner-Spinelli**, on the far side of the Rio di Ca' Santi, is another work by Coducci; it dates from 1490–1510, so preceding his more monumental Palazzo Vendramin-Calergi.

Four houses that once all belonged to the Mocenigo family stand side by side on the *Volta del Canal*, as the Canal Grande's sharpest turn is known: the **Palazzo Mocenigo-Nero**, a late sixteenth-century building; the double **Palazzo Mocenigo**, built in the eighteenth century as an extension to the Nero house; and the **Palazzo Mocenigo Vecchio**, a Gothic palace remodeled in the seventeenth century.

One of the great Venetian scandals centers on the first of the four. In 1621 Lady Arundel, wife of one of King James' most powerful courtiers, became its tenant; before long it was rumored that the house was being visited by **Antonio Foscarini**, a former ambassador from Venice to England, whose term in London had ended with an abrupt recall home and a three-year stay in prison under suspicion of treason. On that occasion Foscarini had finally been cleared, but now there were renewed allegations of treacherous behavior, and the Council of Ten quickly shifted into top gear. Foscarini was arrested, interrogated, and, twelve days later, executed. Lady Arundel instantly demanded an audience with the doge, the result of which was a public declaration that she had not been involved in any plot; and within a few months the Council of Ten had conclusive evidence that Foscarini had been framed. The men who had accused him were put to death, and Foscarini's body was exhumed and given a state funeral. (See "San Stae" p.000)

Byron and his menagerie—a dog, a fox, a wolf and a monkey—lived in the Mocenigo-Nero palace for a couple of years. Much of his time was taken up with a local baker's wife called Margarita Cogni, the most tempestuous of his mistresses—her reaction to being rejected by him was to attack him with a table knife and then, having been shown the door, hurl herself into the Canal Grande. The Palazzo Mocenigo Vecchio is supposed to be haunted by the ghost of the philosopher-alchemist Giordano Bruno, whose betrayal by Giovanni Mocenigo in 1592 led ultimately to his torture and execution.

The neighboring building is the early-sixteenth-century **Palazzo Contarini delle Figure** (the *figure* are the almost invisible figures above the water entrance). It was begun by Spavento and completed by Scarpagnino, a combination already employed on the Fondaco dei Tedeschi and the Palazzo Ducale.

From the Volta to the Palazzo Giustinian

The vast and pristine palace round the *Volta* is the **Palazzo Grassi**. Built in 1748–72 by Massari, under whose supervision Longhena's Ca' Rezzonico (opposite) was completed, its first owners were accepted into the ranks of the nobility in return for a hefty contribution to the war effort against the Turks in 1718. Nowadays it's owned by Fiat—hence the sparkling renovation—and is used as an exhibition and conference center (see "West of the Piazza," in Chapter One).

On the edge of the first canal after the campo of San Samuele stands the **Ca' del Duca**; commissioned in the mid-fifteenth century from Bartolomeo Bon, it was left unfinished in 1461 when the Corner family sold it to Francesco Sforza, Duke of Milan (from whom it takes its name). Had it been completed to plan, the main hall would have been even larger than that of the Maggior Consiglio in the Palazzo Ducale; the wedge of rusticated masonry on the corner gives some idea of the sort of fortified house the Corners had in mind. In 1514 Titian had a studio here, while he was working on paintings for the Palazzo Ducale.

Across the *rio* there's the tiny **Palazzetto Falier**, a reworked Gothic house of the fifteenth century, chiefly remarkable for its two roofed terraces. Although they used to be quite common, very few examples of this feature (called a *liagò*) have survived. Next door is one of Longhena's earliest projects, the **Palazzo Giustinian-Lolin** (1623).

As the larger vaporetti couldn't get under the iron **Ponte dell' Accademia** built by the Austrians in 1854, it was replaced in 1932 by a wooden one. The measure was meant to be temporary but has become permanent. At the foot of the bridge, on the far side, is the huge fifteenth-century **Palazzo Franchetti**; repaired and enlarged at the end of the nineteenth century, it's often cited as one of the city's most heavy-handed pieces of restoration work.

On the opposite side of the Rio dell'Orso are the twinned **Palazzi Barbaro**; the house on the left is early fifteenth-century, the other late seventeenth-century. Henry James, Monet, Whistler, Browning and John Singer Sargent were among the luminaries who stayed in the older Barbaro house as guests of the Curtis family in the late nineteenth century. James wrote *The Aspern Papers* here, and used it as a setting for *The Wings of a Dove*; so attached was he to the place that when given the opportunity of buying a home in Venice at a very reasonable price, he decided he would rather go on living here as a lodger.

Soon after the short fondamenta comes the tiny **Casetta delle Rose**, where Canova once had his studio and D'Annunzio lived during World War I. The *Casetta* lies in the shadow of one of the Canal Grande's most imposing buildings—Sansovino's **Palazzo Corner della Ca' Grande**. The palace that used to stand here was destroyed when a fire lit to dry out a stock of sugar in the attic burned out of control, an incident that illustrates the dual commercial-residential function of many palaces in Renaissance Venice. Sansovino's replacement, commissioned by the nephew of Caterina Cornaro, was built from 1545 onwards. The rustication of the lower storey—a distinctive aspect of many Roman and Tuscan buildings of the High Renaissance—makes it a prototype for Longhena's Ca' Pesaro and Ca' Rezzonico. Nowadays it's the home of the Prefecture, the representative of the central government in Venice.

The heavily restored fifteenth-century **Palazzo Pisani**, now the *Gritti Hotel*, looms over the *Santa Maria del Giglio* landing stage—John and Effie Ruskin stayed here in 1851, the year *The Stones of Venice* began to appear in print. Squeezed into the line of buildings that follows is the narrow **Palazzo Contarini-Fasan**, a mid-fifteenth-century palace with unique wheel tracery on the balconies. It's popularly known as "the house of Desdemona," but although the model for Shakespeare's heroine did live in Venice, her association with this house is purely sentimental. The last major building before the Giardinetti Reali is the fifteenth-century **Palazzo Giustinian**; now the HQ of the Biennale offices and the tourist board, in the last century it was one of the plushest hotels in town, its registers being signed by the likes of Verdi, Ruskin, Gautier and Proust.

The Right Bank

Arriving in Venice by road, you come in on the right bank of the Canal Grande at Piazzale Roma, opposite the train station. Orientation is initially difficult, with canals heading off in various directions and no immediate landmark; it's not until the vaporetto swings round by the train station that it becomes obvious that this is the city's main waterway.

Having passed the green-domed church of **San Simeone Piccolo**, the end of the elongated campo of **San Simeone Grande** and a procession of nondescript buildings you come to the **Fondaco dei Turchi** (opposite **San Marcuola**). A private house from the early thirteenth century until 1621 (including spells when it was used as a guesthouse for VIPs), the building was then turned over to the Turkish traders in the city, who stayed here until 1838. By the 1850s it was in such a terrible state that a campaign for its restoration was started, with Ruskin at the helm; the city undertook the repair, but the result was judged nearly as bad an eyesore as the ruin had been, and has had few admirers since. There's hardly an original brick left in the building, but whatever the shortcomings of the work, the building's towers and long water-level arcade give a reasonably precise, if schematic, picture of what a Veneto-Byzantine palace would have looked like. One of the sarcophagi underneath the portico belongs to the family of the disgraced Marin Falier (see "The Palazzo Ducale"). The Fondaco housed the Correr collection from 1880 to 1922, and now contains the Museo di Storia Naturale.

The crenellated structure next along from the Fondaco is the fifteenth-century **Depositi del Megio** (public granary); its neighbor is another palace by Longhena—the **Palazzo Belloni-Battagia** (1647–63). Longhena's client experienced severe cash-flow problems not long after the house was finished, a consequence of simultaneously building the house and buying his way into the pages of the *Libro d' Oro* (the register of the nobility), and so was obliged to rent the place out rather than live in it himself.

A short distance down the canal, after the church of **San Stae**, stands a far more impressive Longhena building—the thickly ornamented **Ca' Pésaro**, bristling with diamond-shaped spikes and grotesque heads. Three houses had to be demolished to make room for this palace and its construction lasted half a century—work started in 1652 and finished in 1703, long after Longhena's death. Unusually, the Ca' Pésaro has a stone-clad side facade: most houses in Venice have plain brick sides, either because of the cost of stone, or because of the possibility that a later building might be attached. The palace now contains the Galleria d' Arte Moderna and the Museo Orientale.

The next large building is the **Palazzo Corner della Regina**, built in 1724 on the site of the home of Caterina Cornaro, Queen of Cyprus, from whom the palace takes its name. (See "Ásolo," in the Veneto section.) The base of the Biennale archives, it was formerly the *Monte di Pietà* (municipal pawnshop).

Beyond, there's nothing especially engrossing until you reach the **Rialto markets**, which begin with the neo-Gothic fish market, the **Pescheria**, built in 1907; there's been a fish market here since the fourteenth century. The older buildings which follow it, the **Fabbriche Nuove di Rialto** and (set back from the water) the **Fabbriche Vecchie di Rialto** are by Sansovino (c.1550) and Scarpagnino (c.1520) respectively. The large building at the base of the Rialto bridge is the **Palazzo dei Camerlenghi** (c.1525), the former chambers of the

Venetian exchequer. Debtors could find themselves in the cells of the building's bottom storey—hence the name *Fondamenta delle Prigioni* for this part of the canalside. At the foot of the Rialto Bridge, on the other side, the offices of the state finance ministers occupied Scarpagnino's **Palazzo dei Dieci Savi**.

From the Rialto to the Palazzi Giustinian

From the Rialto down to the *Volta del Canal* the right bank is of more sporadic interest. The **Palazzo Papadopoli** (aka **Palazzo Coccina-Tiepolo**), on the far side of Rio dei Meloni, was built in the 1560s; the Venetian mercantile class rarely wanted adventurous designs for their houses, and the conservative Papadopoli palace, with its emphasis on blank wall spaces broken up with applied decoration, was to prove extremely influential. (Contrast it with the contemporaneous Grimani palace, on the opposite side of the Canal Grande.) The adjacent **Palazzo Donà** and **Palazzo Donà della Madonnetta** (named after the fifteenth-century relief on the facade) date from the twelfth and thirteenth centuries; they have been frequently altered, but some original features survive—notably the main windows.

The tracery of the mid-fifteenth-century **Palazzo Bernardo** (across the Rio della Madonnetta), among the most beautiful on the Canal Grande, is copied from the loggia of the Palazzo Ducale—you'll find echoes of the pattern all over the city. The sixteenth-century **Palazzo Cappello-Layard**, on the edge of the wide Rio San Polo, was the home of the English ambassador Sir Henry Layard, whose astuteness assured that the British public profited from the destitution of Venice in the last century. His collection of nineteen major Venetian paintings, picked up for a song, were left to the National Gallery in London. Another of the National's masterpieces—Veronese's *The Clemency of Alexander*—was bought in 1857 from the **Palazzo Pisani della Moretta** (mid-fifteenth-century), second along on the other side of the rio.

The cluster of palaces at the *Volta* constitutes one of the city's architectural glories. The **Palazzo Balbi**, on the near side of the Rio di Ca' Fóscari, is the youngest of the group, a proto-Baroque design executed in the 1580s to plans by Alessandro Vittoria (whose sculpture is to be found in many Venetian churches). Nicolo Balbi is reputed to have been so keen to see his palace finished that he moored a boat alongside the building site so that he could watch the work progressing—and died of a chill caught by sleeping in it. Had Frank Lloyd Wright got his way, the Palazzo Balbi would have acquired a new neighbor in the 1950s, but local opposition, orchestrated from the Balbi palace, scuppered the scheme.

On the opposite bank stands the **Ca' Fóscari** (c.1435), which Ruskin thought "the noblest example in Venice" of late Gothic architecture. The largest private house in Venice at the time of its construction, it was the home of one of the more colorful figures of Venetian history, Doge Francesco Fóscari, whose extraordinarily long term of office (thirty-four years) came to an end with his forced resignation (see "The Frari," in Chapter Three). When Henry III of France passed through Venice on his way to his coronation in 1574, it was at the Ca' Fóscari that he stayed. After a banquet for which all sumptuary laws had been suspended and at which the tables had been set with utensils and decorative figures made from sugar to Sansovino's designs, Henry reeled back here to find his rooms decked out with silks and cloth of gold, and lined with paintings by Bellini, Titian, Veronese and Tintoretto. Venice's university now owns the building.

Adjoining it are the **Palazzi Giustinian**, a pair of palaces built in the mid-fifteenth century for two brothers who wanted attached but self-contained houses. In the twelfth century the Giustinian family was in danger of dying out, and such was the panic induced in Venice by the thought of losing one of its most illustrious dynasties (it traced its descent from the Emperor Justinian), that papal permission was sought for the young monk who was the one surviving male of the clan to be released from his vows in order to start a family. The pope gave his consent, a bride was found, and twelve Giustinians were propagated; his duty done, the father returned to his monastery, and his wife went off to found a convent on one of the remoter islands of the lagoon. For a while the Palazzo Giustinian was Wagner's home: finding the rooms inimical to the creative process he made a few improvements such as hanging the walls with red cloth and importing his own bed and grand piano from Zurich. Having made the place comfortable, he settled down, flirted with the idea of suicide, and wrote the second act of *Tristan und Isolde*.

From the Ca' Rezzonico to the Dogana di Mare

A little farther along is Longhena's **Ca' Rezzonico**, as gargantuan as his Ca' Pésaro, but less aggressive. It was begun in 1667 as a commission from the Bon family, but their ambition exceeded their financial resources, and not long after hiring Giorgio Massari to complete the upper part they were obliged to sell the still unfinished palace to the Rezzonico, a family of Genoese bankers. Despite having lashed out 100,000 ducats to buy their way into the *Libro d'Oro* (at a time when 1000 per annum was a comfortable income for a noble), the new owners could afford not only to keep Massari on to finish the top floor but even to tack a ballroom and staircase onto the back. Among its subsequent owners was Pen Browning, whose father Robert died here in 1889; and both Whistler and Cole Porter stayed here briefly. Much of the interior of the Ca' Rezzonico is open to the public, as it now houses the Museo del Settecento Veneziano.

After a couple of canals you pass the **Palazzo Loredan dell' Ambasciatore**, opposite the Ca' del Duca. Taking its name from the Austrian embassy that used to be here, it was built in the fifteenth century, and is notable mainly for the figures in niches on the facade, which possibly came from the workshop of Antonio Rizzo. On the far side of the next canal, the Rio di San Trovaso, stand the **Palazzo Contarini-Corfu** and the **Palazzo Contarini degli Scrigni**. The "Corfu" bit of the first name derives either from the fact that a Contarini was once a military commander on that island, or from the name of a family that lived in the parish before the Contarini crew. The two palaces form a single unit: the Scrigni was built in 1609 as an extension to the Corfu, a fifteenth-century Gothic house. A similar operation was carried out at the Palazzi Barbaro (opposite, just after the Accademia bridge), with less jarring results.

Yet another Contarini palace stands a few yards past the Accademia bridge—the **Palazzo Contarini-Polignac**. This branch of the Contarini family made itself rich through landholdings around Jaffa, and the dialect version of that place-name is the source of the alternative name for the palace: **Contarini dal Zaffo**. The facade, which was applied to the Gothic building in the late fifteenth century, represents a transitional phase between the highly decorative style associated with the Lombardi and their imitators (see the Palazzo Dario, below) and the classicizing work of Coducci.

The unfinished **Palazzo dei Leoni** (soon after the Campo San Vio), would have been the largest palace on the canal, but its construction, begun in 1759, never progressed farther than the first storey—it's sometimes known as the *Palazzo Nonfinito*. Its abandonment was almost certainly due to the ruinous cost, but there's a tradition which says the project was stopped by the objections of the Corner family across the water, who didn't want their sunlight blocked by a house that was bigger than theirs. The stump of the building and the platform on which it is raised (itself an extravagant and novel feature) are occupied by the Guggenheim collection of modern art.

The one domestic building of interest between here and the end of the canal is the miniature **Palazzo Dario**, the next building but one after the Palazzo dei Leoni. Compared by Henry James to "a house of cards that hold together by a tenure it would be fatal to touch," the palace was built in the late 1480s not for a patrician family but for a member of the middle ("citizen") class—a chancery secretary named Giovanni Dario; it was later owned by the Rolling Stones' manager. The multicolored marbles of the facade are characteristic of the work of the Lombardo family, and the design may actually be by the founder of the dynasty, Pietro Lombardo. Two doors down, the technicolor **Palazzo Salviati** was built in 1924 by the glassmakers of the same name; the nastiest building on the canal, it's a foretaste of what awaits you in the glass showrooms of Murano.

The focal point of this last stretch of the canal is Longhena's masterpiece, **Santa Maria della Salute**—it's dealt with in the Dorsoduro chapter, as is the **Dogana di Mare** (Customs House), the Canal Grande's final stop.

CHAPTER EIGHT

THE NORTHERN ISLANDS

T he islands lying to the north of Venice—**San Michele**, **Murano**, **Burano**, Torcello and **San Francesco del Deserto**—are the places to visit when the throng of tourists in the main part of Venice becomes too oppressive, or when the stone sidewalks and ravines of brick become wearying and you want to enjoy the smell of plants growing again. An excursion through this part of the lagoon will reveal the origins of the glass and lace work touted in so many of the city's shops, and give you a glimpse of the origins of Venice itself.

To get to the islands, the main **vaporetto stop** is the **Fondamente Nuove**. The **vaporetto #5** (*circolare destra* or *circolare sinistra*—right or left circular) runs about every fifteen minutes from here to **San Michele** and **Murano**. If you're hopping onto the *circolare* elsewhere in the city, be careful: take the *destra* if you are at the station or on the Canale di Cannaregio, and the *sinistra* if you are on Guidecca or just down from San Marco at San Zaccaria—the round trip from the station to the Fondamenta Nuove the wrong way can take a good hour. For **Torcello** and **Burano** there is the **vaporetto or steamer #12** (every 60–90min, depending on time of day; the journey takes 45min to Burano, then it's a short hop to Torcello); this can also be caught from Murano, but only from the *Faro* landing stage. If you take this journey at low tide the reason for the route markers (*bricole*) will be apparent: over half the lagoon is *laguna morta*, and only covered at high tide. Nowadays it's virtually impossible to rent a boat to explore the lagoon independently, as so many enthusiastic visitors became stranded on the mud flats that the novelty of rescuing them wore off years ago.

San Michele

A church was founded on the innermost of the northern islands in the tenth century, and a monastery established in the thirteenth. Its best-known resident was Fra Mauro (d.1459), whose map of the world—the most accurate of its time—is now one of the most precious possessions of the Libreria Sansoviniana. The monastery was suppressed in the early nineteenth century, but in 1829, after a spell as an Austrian prison for political offenders, it was handed back to the Franciscans, who look after the church and the cemetery to this day.

The high brick wall around the island gives way by the landing stage for the elegant white facade of **San Michele in Isola**, designed by **Mauro Coducci** in 1469. With this building Coducci quietly revolutionized the architecture of Venice, advancing the principles of Renaissance design in the city and introducing the use of Istrian stone as a material for facades. Easy to carve yet resistant to water, Istrian stone had long been used for damp courses, but never before had anyone clad the entire front of a building in it; after the construction of San Michele, most major buildings in Venice were given an Istrian veneer.

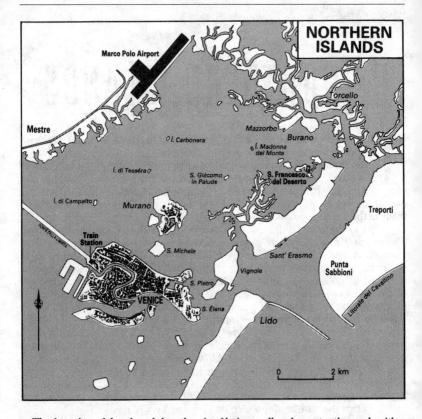

The **interior** of the church has the air of being well and constantly used, with a scent which is a mixture of fresh flowers, incense and a little hint of the cypress trees. Attached on the left is the dainty hexagonal **Cappella Emiliana**, built c.1530 by **Guglielmo dei Grigi**, and completely marble-lined. Ruskin was impervious to its charm: "It is more like a German summer-house, or angle-turret, than a chapel, and may be briefly described as a bee-hive set on a low hexagonal tower, with dashes of stonework about its windows like the flourishes of an idle penman." In front of the main entrance a floor plaque marks the final resting place of **Fra Paolo Sarpi** (d.1623), Venice's principal ideologist during the protracted tussle with the papacy at the beginning of the seventeenth century (see Chapter Four for a full account); buried first in his Servite monastery, Sarpi's remains were removed here when that order was suppressed in 1828.

The Cemetery

The main part of the island, through the cloisters, is covered by the **cemetery** of Venice (open 8:15am–4pm), established here by a Napoleonic decree which forbade further burials in the center of the city. Space is at a premium, and the majority of Venetians lie here in cramped conditions for just ten years or so, when their bones are dug up and removed to an ossuary, and the land recycled. Thus the boats to the cemetery release a steady procession of people coming to tend the graves of their recently dead relatives, and the main part is always ablaze with flowers. Only those who can afford to lease a plot stay longer; a still empty mausoleum is engraved *La Famiglia Antony Quinn*, but most here are Venetians.

At the entrance to the cemetery you can pick up a small plan of the various sections. Most dilapidated is the **protestant** section (no. XV), where admirers can find **Ezra Pound's grave**—a crude slab with his name on it, but missing the epitaph he wrote for himself:

> *Ezra Pound*
> *Got around*
> *He was born in Hailey*
> *But he was buried in San Michele*
> *not the terzo cielo*
> *but socially meglio*

(not the third heaven, but socially the best). Adjoining is the **Greek and Russian Orthodox** area (no. XIV), including the simple gravestones of **Igor and Vera Stravinsky**—Stravinsky was given a funeral service in San Zanipolo, the highest funeral honor the city can bestow—and the more elaborate tomb for **Serge Diaghilev**, which is permanently flower-laden. (There is a separate Jewish cemetery over on the Lido.) Fans of **Frederick Rolfe** (Baron Corvo) can reach his disconsolate memorial by going through the gap in the wall-graves to the right of sections M and N, then doubling back behind section M: he's up on the top row of block 13. The most poignant section is C, for **infants**, behind which are piled the discarded crosses of dug-up graves, many still hung with dead flowers.

Murano

In 1276 the island of **Murano** became a self-governed enclave within the Republic, with its own judiciary, its own administration and a *Libro d'Oro* to register its nobility. By the early sixteenth century Murano had 30,000 inhabitants, and was a favorite summer retreat for Venice's upper classes, who could lay out gardens here which were far more extensive than those in the cramped center of the city. The Mocenigo family had a house here, and Caterina Cornaro often stayed at her family's palace. The intellectual life of the island was especially healthy in the seventeenth century, when literature, philosophy, the occult and the sciences were discussed in the numerous small *accademie* that flourished here. In the same century the mint on Murano was granted the privilege of forging the tribute medals known as *oselle*. But Murano nowadays owes its fame entirely to its **glass-blowing industry**, and its main fondamente are crowded with shops selling the fruit of the furnaces, most of it repulsive and some of it laughably pretentious. Don't despair, though: Murano does have other things to offer and is definitely worth a visit.

If you're setting off for a day in the northern islands, and intend spending lunchtime on Murano, take a picnic. Although Thomas Coryat declared in 1611 "here did I eate the best oysters that ever I did in all my life," food on Murano today is nothing to write home about and there's no cheap but perfect trattoria waiting to be discovered. The bars on the main fondamente are almost exclusively male out of season and tourist-dominated in season. Best stock up with your own supplies and settle outside Santi Maria e Donato or somewhere on the shore.

Venetian Glass

The glass furnaces were moved to Murano from Venice as a safety measure in 1291, and thenceforth all possible steps were taken to keep the secrets of the trade locked up on the island. Although Muranese workers had by the seventeenth century gained some freedom of movement, for centuries prior to then any glass-maker who left Murano was hunted down as a traitor. Various privileges reduced the temptation to rove—unlike other artisans, the glass-blowers were allowed to wear swords, and from 1376 the offspring of a marriage between a Venetian nobleman and the daughter of a glass-worker were allowed to be entered into the *Libro d'Oro*, unlike the children of other cross-class matches. Normal principles of justice were sometimes waived for the glass-blowers—on one occasion a man who had committed a murder and then fled Murano was accepted back without punishment once his father had hinted to the city's governors that his son might set up a furnace in Mantua.

A fifteenth-century visitor judged that "in the whole world there are no such craftsmen of glass as here," and the Muranese were masters of every aspect of their craft. They were producing spectacles by the start of the fourteenth century, monopolized the European manufacture of mirrors for a long time (and continued making larger mirrors than anyone else even after the monopoly had gone), and in the early seventeenth century became so proficient at making colored crystal that a decree was issued forbidding the manufacture of false gems out of glass, as many were being passed off as authentic. Understatement has never been a characteristic of Murano produce: in 1756 Lady Mary Wortley Montague was wonderstruck by a set of furniture made entirely in glass, and earlier this century the less favorably impressed H.V. Morton longed "to see something simple and beautiful," adding that sixteenth-century customers felt the same way "when, looking around for something to take home, they were repelled by drinking-glasses in the shape of ships, whales, lions and birds." Murano kitsch extends to all price categories, from the mass-produced nicknacks sold for a couple of thousand lire, through to monstrosities such as the Peggy Guggenheim's pieces based on figures from the works of Picasso—specially commissioned by her, they are on show in that bastion of modernist art, the Guggenheim Collection. Plenty of Murano's furnaces are open to the public; entry is free, on the assumption that you will then want to buy something, though you won't be pressed too hard to do so.

Around the Island

From the vaporetto you step onto the Fondamenta dei Vetrai, traditionally the core of the glass industry (as the name suggests) and now the principal tourist trap. Towards the far end is the Dominican church of **San Pietro Martire**, one of only two churches still in service on the island (compared with seventeen when the Republic fell in 1797). Begun in 1363 but largely rebuilt after a fire in 1474, its main interest lies with its paintings, which are lit by an annoying system that entails a lot of running about with a lot of L100 coins. Save most of your change for the large and elegant *Madonna and Child with St Mark, St Augustine and Doge Barbarigo* (1488) by **Giovanni Bellini**, hanging on the right wall; a second Bellini (an *Assumption*) is at present being restored. On the opposite side of the church are two pieces by **Veronese**—*St Agatha in Prison* and *St Jerome in the Desert*. The *Cappella del Sacramento*, to the left of the main altar, was originally dedicated to the angels and contains four paintings of personable representatives of the heavenly host. Also worth a look is the sacristy, where characters such as Nero, Caasar, Socrates, Pythagoras, Castor and Pollux, Herod and Pontius Pilate are depicted in seventeenth-century carved panels, along with scenes from the life of John the Baptist.

Just round the corner is the main bridge, the **Ponte Vivarini**, a few yards beyond which is the **Palazzo da Mula**, a Gothic palace altered in the sixteenth century, one of the few surviving examples of a Venetian summer residence on Murano. Many of the other palaces were demolished in the nineteenth century.

The Museo Vetrario

A left turn on the far side of the bridge comes to a dead end at the most recently closed of Murano's churches, **Santa Maria degli Angeli**, in whose convent Casanova had an amorous experience involving many changes of costume.

Turn right along Fondamenta Cavour and you'll soon come to the seventeenth-century Palazzo Giustinian, facing the sixteenth-century Palazzo Trevisan across the canal. Home of the Bishop of Torcello until his diocese was joined to Venice in 1805, the Palazzo Giustinian now houses the **Museo Vetrario** (Glass Museum; 10am–4pm, Sun & hols 9am–12:30pm; closed Wed; last entry 30min before closing; L3000, reductions L1500). Featuring pieces dating back to Roman times and examples of Murano glass from the fifteenth century onwards, the museum exerts a fascination even if you can't read the Italian of the perfunctory labels—how *did* the aristocracy manage to drink in the seventeenth century? A separate display, with captions in English this time, covers the history of Murano glass techniques—look out for the extraordinary *Murine in Canna*, the method of placing different colored rods together to form an image in cross-section.

Hang on to your ticket as it will also get you into the recently opened **Modern and Contemporary Glass Museum** on Fondamenta Manin (opposite Fondamenta Vetrai; same opening hours), where you'll see pieces of functional glassware that try to look like modernist sculptures, and one or two modernist sculptures (ersatz Hepworths and Moores) that look like giant pieces of functional ware. But there are some interesting works: the baby by Alfredo Borbini which looks as though it's carved from lava, for instance, or the mirror with gold leaf by Piero Fornasetti.

Santi Maria e Donato

The other Murano church, and the main reason for visiting the island today, is **Santi Maria e Donato**. It was founded in the seventh century but rebuilt in the twelfth, and is one of the lagoon's best examples of Veneto-Byzantine architecture—the ornate **rear apse** being particularly fine. Originally dedicated to the Virgin, the church was re-dedicated in 1125 when the relics of Saint Donatus were brought here from Cephalonia by **Doge Domenico Michiel**, who also picked up the remains of Saint Isidore and the stone on which Jesus stood to preach to the men of Tyre—both of which are now in the Basilica di San Marco. Saint Donatus once slew a dragon simply by spitting at it, and four splendid bones from the unfortunate beast now hang behind the altar.

The glory of the interior (8am–noon & 4–7pm) is its **mosaic floor** (dated 1141 in the nave), a beautiful weave of abstract patterns and figures—an eagle carries off a deer; two roosters carry off a fox, slung from a pole. The floor was extensively restored in 1977, a process illustrated in a photographic display; proceeds from the sale of the guide to the church help finance further work. Apart from the **twelfth-century mosaic of the Madonna** in the apse, the features that invite perusal are the fifteenth-century ship's-keel roof, the sixthcentury pulpit and the Veneto-Byzantine capitals.

Burano—and San Francesco del Deserto

After Murano, the next stop for the #12 boat is at the small island of **Mazzorbo**, a place that doesn't amount to much more than a few scattered villas, a lot of grassy space, and the church of Santa Caterina (thirteenth century, rebuilt in fifteenth century). You can either get off the boat here, and walk round Mazzorbo to the bridge to Burano, or continue on the boat to the main Burano stop.

After the peeling plaster and eroded stonework of the other lagoon settlements, the brightly painted houses of **Burano** come as something of a surprise; once symbolic, the colors are now used in whatever fashion takes the occupants' fancy. A resident called Bepe is the most fearless exterior decorator on the island—his house, covered in a constantly changing arrangement of painted diamonds, triangles, and bars, is in a courtyard off the alley opposite the *Galuppi* restaurant in Via Baldessare Galuppi, the main street. (Galuppi was an eighteenth-century Buranese composer, often known to his admirers as *Il Buranello*.)

Burano is still largely a fishing community, and you can't walk far along the shores of the island without seeing a fishing boat beached for repair, or nets laid out to dry or be mended, or a jumble of crab boxes. It's a solitary way of life under any circumstances, but a couple of fishermen have scavenged wood and other materials to build vulnerable-looking houses out on the higher mud flats, and now lead an existence not too dissimilar from that of their earliest Venetian ancestors—perpetually tending to the fabric of the house and boat, fishing among the water-birds, and selling the catch at the Burano or Rialto *pescherie*. *Vongole* (small clams) are a local delicacy, cooked not by immersion in boiling water, but by tipping the tightly-closed shells into a large frying pan of hot olive oil and garlic; add lemon juice, then cover and cook a few minutes until the shells open. Take the fish out of their shells, mix them with the oil and lemon liquor, and serve with spaghettini cooked *al dente*, preferably garnished with fresh parsley. The dish can be sampled in the island's restaurants, where a meal will generally be of a better quality than one for the same price in Venice.

If the men of Burano depend on the lagoon, the women's lives are given over to the production and sale of **lace**, and the shops lining the narrow street leading into the village from the vaporetto stop are full of the stuff. Lacemaking used to be a skill that crossed all social boundaries: for noblewomen it was an expression of feminine creativity; for nuns it was an exercise in humility and contemplation; and for the poorest it was simply a source of income. (It's interesting that, unlike all other crafts in Venice, the lacemakers had no scuola or guild to represent them—perhaps because its workforce was exclusively female.) Its production was once geographically diverse too—**Dogaressa Morosina Morosini** set up a large and successful workshop near Santa Fosca in the late sixteenth century, for instance—but nowadays Burano is the exclusive center. Much sentimental nonsense has been written about how "young women with beautiful hands bend over their cushion, patient and intent on their fine lace work" (Lorenzetti) and how "every Burano cottage doorway has its demure lace-maker, stitching away in the sunshine, eyes screwed up and fingers flickering" (Morris). In fact, making Burano point and Venetian point lace is extremely exacting work, both highly skilled and mind-bendingly repetitive, taking an enormous toll on the eyesight. Each woman specializes in one particular stitch, and as there are seven stiches in all, each piece is passed from woman to woman during its construction. An average-size table center requires about a month of work.

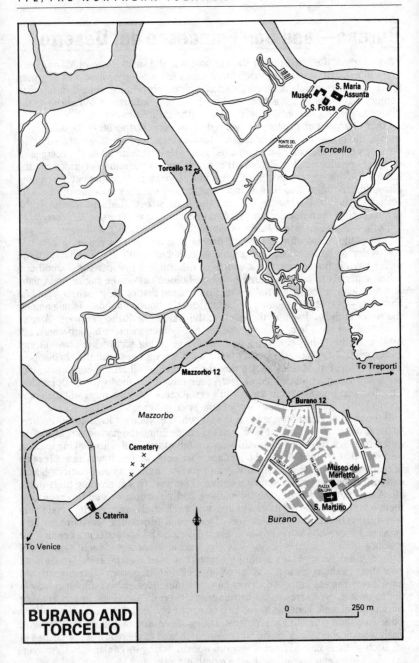

Museo

S. Maria Assunta

S. Fosca

PONTE DEL DIAVOLO

Torcello

Torcello 12

To Treporti

Mazzorbo 12

Burano 12

Mazzorbo

Cemetery

Museo del Merletto

CALLE S. MAURO

VIA GALUPPI

PIAZZA GALUPPI

S. Caterina

S. Martino

To Venice

Burano

0   250 m

BURANO AND TORCELLO

Lacemaking is still taught at Burano's **Scuola dei Merletti**, in the island's main square, Piazza Baldessare Galuppi (Mon–Sat 9am–6pm, Sun 10am–4pm; L2000, reductions L1000). The school was opened in 1872, when the indigenous crafting of lace had declined so far that it was left to one woman, Cencia Scarpariola, to transmit the necessary skills to a younger generation of women. Pieces produced here are displayed in the attached museum, along with specimens dating back to the sixteenth century; after even a quick tour you'll easily distinguish the real thing from the machine-made and imported lace that fills the Burano shops.

The church of **San Martino** (hypothetically open 7am–noon & 3–7pm), with its drunken **campanile**, contains a *Crucifixion* by **G.B. Tiepolo**.

San Francesco del Deserto

While on Burano, try to get to across to the island of **San Francesco del Deserto**. This will mean negotiating either for a taxi (prohibitively expensive unless a group of you can share the cost), or for someone to row you across in a *sándolo*, when the charge will vary with the time of year and the disposition of the person you ask. An added complication is the Buranese dialect, which has even fewer consonants than the Venetian.

Saint Francis ran aground here in 1220 and decided to build a chapel and cell on the island. The owner, Jacopo Michiel, gave it to the Franciscans soon after the saint's death, and apart from deserting it for a while in the fifteenth century because of malaria, and being pushed out in the nineteenth century by the military, they've been here ever since. The present chapel was built over the original one in the fifteenth century, and was lovingly and simply restored in 1962, uncovering some of the original floor and foundations. Nine friars live here, some in retreat, and a few young men stay for a year before becoming Franciscan novices. With its birdsong, its variety of plants, and its cypress-scented air, the monastery is the most tranquil place in the lagoon. You can be shown round the island from 9 to 11am and 3 to 5.30pm; a couple of thousand lire should be left as a donation.

Torcello

Some of John Ruskin's purplest prose was prompted by the sight of **Torcello**: "Mother and daughter, you behold them both in their widowhood—Torcello and Venice," his elegy for the island begins. The place has certainly come full circle. Settled by the very first refugees from the mainland in the fifth century, it became the seat of the Bishop of Altinum in 638 and in the following year its cathedral was founded. By the fourteenth century its population had peaked at around 20,000, but Torcello's canals were silting up and the ascendancy of Venice was imminent. By the end of the fifteenth century Torcello was largely deserted—even the bishop lived in Murano—and today only about one hundred people remain. There is little visible evidence of the island's prime: just the two churches, a couple of buildings round a dusty square, and pottery shards that come to light in the fields.

Santa Maria dell'Assunta

The main reason for a visit is to see Venice's first cathedral and the serenest building in the lagoon—**Santa Maria dell'Assunta** (daily 10am–12:30pm & 2–5:30pm; L1000). A Veneto-Byzantine building dating substantially from 1008, the cathedral has evolved from a church founded in the seventh century, of which the waterlogged **crypt** and the circular foundations in front of the **Baptistery**'s main doors have survived. The first major transformation of the original church occurred in the 860s, the period to which the **facade and portico** belong (though they were altered in later centuries). For the most unusual features of the exterior, go down the right side of the cathedral, where the windows have eleventh-century **stone shutters**. Ruskin described the view from the ancient **campanile** as "one of the most notable scenes in this wide world of ours"—you'll have to take his word for it, as the tower's now too shaky to keep open.

The dominant tones of the **interior** come from the watery green-gray marble of its columns and panelling, which cast a cool light on the richly patterned eleventh-century **mosaic floor**. (Look for the two wooden panels which lift to reveal portions of the church's first floor.) On the semi-dome of the apse a stunning twelfth-century **mosaic of the Madonna and Child**, the figures isolated in a vast field of gold, looks down from above a **frieze of the Apostles** of the previous century. Below the window at the Madonna's feet is an image of **Saint Heliodorus**, the first Bishop of Altinum, whose remains were brought here by the first settlers. It makes an interesting comparison with the gold-plated face mask on his Roman sarcophagus in front of the high altar (another seventh-century vestige). Mosaic work from the ninth and twelfth centuries adorns the chapel to the right of the high altar, while the other end of the cathedral is dominated by a tumultuous **mosaic of the Last Judgement**—created in the twelfth century, but renovated in the nineteenth. Have a good look too at the **rood screen**, where paintings of *The Virgin and Apostles* are supported by eleventh-century columns and finely carved translucent marble panels.

Santa Fosca and the Museo dell'Estuario

Torcello's other church, **Santa Fosca** (same hours as Santa Maria), was built in the eleventh and twelfth centuries for the body of the saint, brought to Torcello from Libya some time before 1011 and now resting under the altar. Much restored, the church retains the Greek Cross form and a fine exterior apse; the bare interior, with beautiful marble columns and elegant brick arches, exudes a calmness which no number of visitors can quite destroy.

In the square outside sits the curious **chair of Attila**, perhaps once the throne of Torcello's judges in its earliest days. Local folklore has it that if you sit in it, you will be wed within a year—you have been warned. Behind it, the well laid-out **Museo dell'Estuario** (Tues–Sun 10am–12:30pm & 2–5:30pm; L2000) includes thirteenth-century beaten gold figures, jewelry, mosaic fragments (including pieces from the cathedral's *Last Judgement*, in which the hands of several artists can be differentiated) and a mish-mash of pieces relating to the history of the area. A major archaeological survey was carried out by a Polish team in 1961–2, but it's possible still to find pot shards as you wander off looking for a picnic spot. And anything more ambitious than a picnic is really not on—there are a couple of **bars** near the parapetless Ponte del Diavolo, but the restaurants (one owned by the *Cipriani*) are for the distinctly well-monied.

RESTAURANTS: the only pleasant and affordable places in the northern islands are on Burano's Via Baldessare Galuppi.

BARS: on Murano, along the main waterfronts; on Burano, Via Baldessare Galuppi.

CHAPTER NINE

THE SOUTHERN ISLANDS

T he section of the lagoon to the south of the city, enclosed by the long islands of the **Lido** and **Pellestrina**, has far fewer outcrops of solid land than the northern half. Once past San Giorgio Maggiore and La Giudecca, and clear of the smaller islands beyond, you could look in the direction of the mainland and think you were out in the open sea—an illusion strengthened by the sight of tankers making their way across the lagoon to the port of Marghera. On the other hand, the shallowness of most of the lagoon is brought home to you with a jolt when you happen upon a fisherman standing on a barely submerged sandbank a long way from the shore—a spectacle that initially prompts thoughts of the Second Coming.

The nearer islands are the more interesting: the Palladian churches of **San Giorgio** and **La Giudecca** are among Venice's most significant Renaissance monuments, while the alleyways of the latter are full of reminders of the city's manufacturing past. The Venetian tourist industry began with the development of the **Lido**, which has now been eclipsed by the city as a vacation resort, yet still

SOUTHERN ISLANDS

draws thousands of people to its beaches each year, many of them Italians. A visit to the Armenian island, **San Lazzaro degli Armeni**, makes an absorbing afternoon's round trip, and if you've a bit more time to spare you could undertake an expedition to the fishing town of **Chioggia**, at the southern extremity of the lagoon. The farther-flung settlements along the route to Chioggia may have seen more glorious days, but the voyage out from the city is a pleasure in itself.

San Giorgio Maggiore

Palladio's church of **San Giorgio Maggiore** (open daily 9am–noon & 2:30–6pm), facing the Palazzo Ducale across the Bacino di San Marco, is one of the most prominent and familiar of all Venetian landmarks. It is a startling building, whose isolation almost forces you to have an opinion as to its architectural merits. Ruskin didn't much care for it: "It is impossible to conceive a design more gross, more barbarous, more childish in conception, more servile in plagiarism, more insipid in result, more contemptible under every point of rational regard." Goethe, on the other hand, sick of the Gothic art that was to Ruskin the index of spiritual health, gave thanks to Palladio for purging his mind of medieval clutter.

Designed in 1565, but only completed in 1610, San Giorgio Maggiore was a greatly influential solution to the chief problem of Renaissance church design: how to use Classical forms in a structure that, with its high central nave and lower aisles, had no precedent in Classical culture. Palladio's answer was to superimpose two temple fronts: the nave being defined by an upper pediment supported by gigantic Composite columns, and the aisles by lower half-pediments resting on Corinthian pilasters. Inside, the relationship between the major Composite order and the minor Corinthian is maintained, so unifying the facade of the church and its interior. The scale of Palladio's forms and his use of shadow-casting surfaces ensures that the design of the facade retains its clarity across the water.

The Interior

The Venetians were the first to cover church interiors with white stucco, and the technique is used to dazzling effect in San Giorgio Maggiore—"Of all the colors, none is more proper for churches than white; since the purity of color, as of the life, is particularly gratifying to God," wrote Palladio. It's hard to imagine how anyone could remain totally unmoved by the interior's finely calculated proportions and Counter-Reformation austerity, but in Ruskin's opinion, only the paintings inside justified the effort of opening the door.

The first altar on the right has an *Adoration of the Shepherds* by **Jacopo Bassano**, which is followed by an alarming late fifteenth-century Crucifix—not, as the label says, by Brunelleschi, but by an anonymous Venetian artist. Most of the other pictures are from the workshop of **Tintoretto**, with two outstanding pictures by the master in the chancel: *The Last Supper*, perhaps the most famous of all Tintoretto's works, and *The Fall of Manna*, one of the few depictions of the event to dwell on the fact that the shower was not a single miraculous deluge but rather a supply that continued for forty years. They were painted as a pair in 1592–94—the last two years of the artist's life—to illustrate the significance of the Eucharist to the communicants at the altar rail. A *Deposition* of the same date, in the Cappella dei Morti (through the door on the right of the choir), may well be Tintoretto's last completed painting. The picture alongside is a photograph of

Carpaccio's *St George and the Dragon*, painted several years after the equally gruesome version in the Scuola di San Giorgio degli Schiavoni. (The original is in a private room elsewhere in the building.)

There are few pieces of woodwork in Venice more impressive than the **choir-stalls** of San Giorgio Maggiore. Decorated with scenes from the life of St Benedict, they were carved in the late 1590s, as the church was being completed; the bronze figures of *St George* and *St Stephen* on the balustrade are by **Niccolò Roccatagliata** (1593), who also made the florid candlesticks at the entrance to the chancel. Apart from Roccatagliata's pieces, the best sculptures in the church are the *Evangelists* by **Vittoria**, incorporated into the **tomb of Doge Leonardo Donà**, on the west wall. A close friend of Paolo Sarpi and Galileo, the scholarly Donà was the redoubtable leader of Venice at the time of the Interdict of 1602. The Papal Nuncio was sent packing by him with the lofty dismissal—"We ignore your excommunication: it is nothing to us. Now think where our resolution would lead, were our example to be followed by others."

The door on the left of the choir leads to the **campanile**; rebuilt in 1791 after the collapse of its predecessor, it rivals that of San Marco as the best vantage point in the city.

The Monastery—and the Harbor

Since the ninth century there's been a church on this island, and at the end of the tenth century the lagoon's most important Benedictine monastery was established here. Both church and monastery were destroyed by an earthquake in 1223, but were rebuilt straight away, and subsequently renovated and altered several times. Cosimo de' Medici stayed at the monastery in 1433, during his exile from Florence, and it was with his assistance that the monastic library was set up; by the end of the century the Benedictines of San Giorgio Maggiore had become renowned for their erudition. With the upheavals of the early nineteenth century things changed rapidly. When the conclave that elected Pope Pius VII met here in 1800, having been turfed out of Rome by Napoleon, the confiscation of the monastery's property had already begun, and six years later the order was suppressed. By the mid-nineteenth century the monastery had been converted into workshops and offices for the Austrian artillery, and the decline of the complex continued for another hundred years until, in 1951, it was acquired by Count Vittorio Cini and converted into the home of the **Fondazione Giorgio Cini** (named after Cini's son), an organization that now runs an arts research institute, a naval college, and a craft school on the island.

The restored monastery is one of the architectural wonders of the city. Two adjoining **cloisters** form the heart of the complex: the Cloister of the Bay Trees, planned by Giovanni Buora and built by his son Andrea in c.1516–40; and the Cloister of the Cypresses, designed in 1579 by Palladio. Inside, there's a 128-meter-long **dormitory** by Giovanni Buora (c.1494), a **double staircase** (1641–43) and **library** (1641–53) by Longhena and, approached by an ascent through two ante-rooms, a magnificent **refectory** by Palladio (1560–62)—for which Veronese's *Marriage at Cana*, now in the Louvre, was painted. Exhibitions are regularly held at the Fondazione (often solemn and bookish affairs), and the *Teatro Verde* is occasionally used for plays and concerts. It's always possible to visit the monastery at other times by ringing for an appointment (☎5289900); if you just turn up unannounced, a word with the custodian could do the trick if he's not feeling harassed, or you can convince him of an unquenchable interest in Palladian architecture.

The little **harbor** on the other side of the church was expanded during the second French occupation of 1806–15, when Napoleon decided to accord the island the status of a free port, in emulation of the tariff-free port of Trieste. A professor of architecture at the Accademia designed the two diminutive lighthouses in 1813.

La Giudecca

In the earliest records of Venice the chain of islets now called **La Giudecca** was known as Spina Longa, a name clearly derived from its shape; the modern name might refer to the Jews (*Giudei*) who were based here from the late thirteenth century until their removal to the Ghetto, or to the disruptive noble families who, from the ninth century, were shoved into this district to keep them out of mischief (*giudicati* means "judged"). Before the Brenta river became the prestigious site for summer abodes, La Giudecca was where the wealthiest aristocrats of early Renaissance Venice built their villas. Michelangelo, exiled from Florence in 1529, consoled himself in the gardens of the island, and here and there on the south side traces of them remain. The most extensive of La Giudecca's surviving private gardens, the so-called *Garden of Eden* (at the end of the Rio della Croce), is bigger than any other in Venice—larger even than the public Giardini Papadopoli (at the head of the Canal Grande). Its name refers not to its idyllic properties but to Mr. Eden, the English gardener who planted it.

The present-day suburb is a strange mixture of decrepitude and vitality—the busy boatyards and the fishing quays on the south side interspersed with half-abandoned factories, roofless sheds, and a miscellany of other ruins. Venice's

**LA GIUDECCA &
SAN GIORGIO MAGGIORE**

public transit boats used to be made on La Giudecca; an asphalt factory and a distillery were neighbors on the western end; and the matting industry, originating in the nineteenth century, kept going until 1950. The clock and watch firm Junghans is still one of La Giudecca's major employers, but it nowadays occupies only part of its 1940s factory, which stands like a Fritz Lang film-set between Rio del Ponte Lungo and Rio del Ponte Piccolo. Even the public face of La Giudecca, the side facing the rest of the city, presents a remarkable economic contrast: at the western edge is the derelict neo-Gothic fortress of the Mulino Stucky flour mill, the largest industrial wreck in Venice (see below), and at the other stands the *Cipriani*, the city's most expensive hotel.

Swathes of La Giudecca are now purely residential areas, but one result of the partial decline is that artists, theater cooperatives and other groups have moved into a number of the redundant buildings. Their presence isn't especially visible, though, and in the bars along the main fondamenta you're still more likely to overhear complaints about the day's lousy catch.

Le Zitelle and the Redentore

The first vaporetto stop after San Giorgio Maggiore is in front of the tiny church of **Le Zitelle**, built in 1582–86 from plans worked out some years earlier by Palladio, albeit for a different site. In the eighteenth century the convent attached to the church was renowned for the delicacy of the lace produced by the young girls who lived in its hostel. (Open only Sunday morning for mass.) The *Casa de Maria*, to the right of Le Zitelle, is a clever reworking of Venetian Gothic. Built as a studio by the painter Mario de Maria in 1910–13, its diaper-pattern brickwork, derived from that of the Palazzo Ducale, is the only example of its kind in Venetian domestic building.

La Giudecca's main monument, beyond the tugboats' mooring and the youth hostel (once a granary), is the Franciscan church of the **Redentore**, designed by **Palladio** in 1577 (daily 7:30am–noon & 3:30–7pm). In 1575–76 Venice suffered an outbreak of plague which killed nearly 50,000 people—virtually a third of the city's population. The Redentore was built by the Senate in thanks for Venice's deliverance, and every year until the downfall of the Republic the doge and his senators attended a mass here to renew their declaration of gratitude, walking to the church over a pontoon bridge from the Zattere. The *Festa del Redentore* has remained a major event on the Venetian calendar—celebrated on the third Sunday of July, it's marked by a general procession over the temporary bridge and a huge fireworks display on the previous evening. A large number of people spend the night out on the water, partying with friends on board their boats.

Palladio's commission called for a church to which there would be three distinct components: a choir for the monks to whom the church was entrusted, a tribune around the altar for the dignitaries of the city, and a nave with side-chapels for the humbler worshipers. The architect's scheme, in which the tribune forms a circular chapel which opens into the nave and blends into the choir through a curved screen of columns, is the most sophisticated of his church projects, as well as the one most directly evolved from the architecture of ancient Rome (the Imperial baths in particular). Unfortunately, the present state of the Redentore makes an appreciation of its subtleties a bit of an effort—the plaster-work is dowdy, statues with fairy-light halos clutter the place and a rope prevents visitors going beyond the nave. The best paintings in the church, including a *Madonna with Child and Angels* by **Alvise Vivarini**, are in the sacristy (ask the sacristan), alongside a gallery of eighteenth-century wax heads of illustrious Franciscans, arranged in glass cases all round the room, in various attitudes of agony and ecstasy.

Sant'Eufamia and the Factories of La Giudecca

Sant'Eufamia (Mon–Sat 9am–noon & 6–7pm, Sun & hols 7am–12:30pm) stands between the Fortuny factory (where they still make fabrics designed by the founder) and the Mulino Stucky. Founded in the ninth century and often rebuilt, it's one of Venice's most engaging stylistic discords: late sixteenth-century portico, nave, and aisles still laid out as in the original basilica (with some eleventh-century columns and capitals), stuccowork and painted decoration in eighteenth-century boudoir mode. It has one good painting, immediately on your right as you go in: *San Rocco and Angel* (with lunette of *Madonna and Child*), the central panel of a triptych painted in 1480 by **Bartolomeo Vivarini**.

The **Mulino Stucky** got to look the way it does in 1895–96, after Giovanni Stucky had brought in a German architect, Ernst Wullekopf, to convert and expand the premises of his flour mill. Planning permission for the brick bastion which Wullekopf came up with was obtained by the simple expedient of threatening to fire all the workers if the okay were withheld. By the beginning of this century Stucky had become one of the richest men in the city and in 1908 he bought one of the Canal Grande's less discreet houses, the Palazzo Grassi. He didn't enjoy his occupancy for long, though—in 1910 one of his employees murdered him at the entrance to the railroad station. With the development of the industrial sector at Marghera after World War I, the Mulino Stucky went into a nosedive, and in 1954 it closed. Since then its future has been a perenially contentious issue—plans are afoot to convert it into housing but there doesn't seem to be any likelihood of action in the short term.

There's not much point in going past the Stucky building: Sacca Fisola, the next island along, is all modern apartments, and is bordered on one side by boatyards and on the other by the site at which waste is mixed with silt to form the basic material of land reclamation in the lagoon. For a taste of the economic past and present of La Giudecca, double back along the waterfront and then turn down the Fondamenta del Rio di Sant' Eufamia; a circuitous stroll from the run down Campo di San Cosmo to the Rio Ponte Lungo will take you through the core of Guidecca's manufacturing district. The interior of the island on the other side of the Rio Ponte Lungo is not so densely built up, with a fair amount of open space (even vegetable gardens) around the Redentore and the husk of Santa Croce church (built in 1508–11 and long ago deconsecrated). Frustratingly, hardly any of La Giudecca's alleyways lead down to the lagoon on the south side; if you want a view across the water in that direction it's best to take Calle Michelangelo, which comes onto the main fondamenta between the Zitelle and the youth hostel.

The Lido

The shores of the Lido have seen some action in their time: in 1202 a huge French army, assembled for the Fourth Crusade, cooled its heels on the beaches while its leaders bargained with the Venetians over the terms for transport to the East; Henry III of France was welcomed here in 1574 with fanfares and triumphal monuments made in his honor; and every year, for about eight centuries, there was the hullaballoo of Venice's **Marriage to the Sea**.

This ritual, the most operatic of Venice's state ceremonials, began as a way of commemorating the exploits of Doge Pietro Orseolo II, who on Ascension Day of the year 1000 set sail to subjugate the pirates of the Dalmatian coast. (Orseolo's standard, by the way, possibly featured the first representation of what was to become the emblem of Venice—the Lion of Saint Mark with its paw on an open book.) According to legend, the ritual reached its definitive form after the Venetians had brought about the reconciliation of Pope Alexander III and Frederick Barbarossa in 1177; the grateful Alexander is supposed to have given the doge the first of the gold rings with which Venice was married to the Adriatic. It's more likely that the essential components of the ritual—the voyage out to the Porto di Lido in the *Bucintoro* with an escort of garlanded vessels, the dropping of the ring into the brine, "In sign of our true and perpetual dominion," and the disembarkation for a solemn mass at the church of San Nicolò al Lido—were all fixed by the middle of the twelfth century. Unless you steadfastly shun all the public collections in Venice, you're bound to see at least one painting of the ceremony during your stay. Nowadays the mayor, patriarch, and a gaggle of other VIPs annually enact a sad facsimile of the grand occasion. And in case you're thinking of launching a salvage operation for all those gold rings, a fifteenth-century traveler recorded that—"After the ceremony, many strip and dive to the bottom to seek the ring. He who finds it keeps it for his own, and, what's more, lives for that year free from all the burdens to which dwellers in that republic are subject."

In the twelfth century the Lido was an unspoiled strip of land, and it remained so until relatively recently. Byron used to gallop his horses across the fields of the Lido every day, and as late as 1869 Henry James could describe the island as "a very natural place." Before the nineteenth century was out, however, it had become the smartest **bathing resort** in Italy, and although it's no longer as chic as it was when Thomas Mann installed von Aschenbach, the central figure of *Death in Venice*, as a guest at the Lido's rambling *Grand Hotel des Bains*, there's usually less room on its beaches now than ever before. (The great algae scare of the last two years has reduced bookings all along the east coast.) But unless you're staying at one of the flashy hotels standing shoulder to shoulder along the seafront, or are prepared to pay a ludicrous fee to rent one of their beach huts for the day, you won't be allowed to get the choicest Lido sand between your toes.

If you're the sort of person who regards access to the sea as a God-given right, then you'll have to content yourself with the ungroomed **public beaches** at the northern and southern ends of the island—though why anyone should want to jeopardize his or her health in the filthy waters of this stretch of the Adriatic is one of the great imponderables. (The traffic is the other health hazard of the Lido. Just as the Venetians were once regarded as the worst riders in Italy, they are now ranked as its most inept drivers.) The northern beach is fifteen minutes' walk from the vaporetto stop at Piazzale Santa Maria Elisabetta; the southern one, right by the municipal golf course, necessitates a bus journey from the Piazzale, and is consequently less of a crush.

In the vicinity of the Piazzale, one building alone—the **Fortezza di Sant'Andrea**—is of interest, and you have to admire that from a distance, across the Porto di Lido. The principal defense of the main entrance to the lagoon, it was designed by **Sanmicheli**; work began on it in 1543, in the face of some skepticism as to whether the structure would be strong enough to support the Venetian artillery. The doubters were silenced when practically all the cannons to hand in the Arsenale were brought out to the Fortezza and fired simultaneously from its terraces, with no harmful effects except to the eardrums. The church and Benedictine monastery of **San Nicolò**, from where you get a good view of the Fortezza, were founded in 1044, when there wasn't so much as a brick wall in the area. The doge and his entourage used to visit this church twice a year: on Ascension Day, after the acquatic wedding service, and on the feast day of Saint Nicholas of Myra (a.k.a. Santa Claus), whose body, so the Venetians claimed, had rested here since it was stolen from the Norman port of Bari in 1099. In fact the theft never happened—the Venetian raid on Bari was a classic piece of disinformation, devised to score points off the Normans, and the grand display on the saint's day was a propagandist sham. The present church is notable only for its seventeenth-century choir stalls. A stroll along the nearby Via Cipro (facing the San Nicolò vaporetto stop) will bring you to Venice's **Jewish cemetery** (founded in 1386). Adjoining is a Catholic burial ground, in a corner of which have been stacked the stones from the old Protestant cemetery, ploughed over in the 1930s to make more room for the Lido's airstrip.

Towards the southern end of the seafront road are two 1930s buildings which (with the fire station on the Rio di Ca' Fóscari) constitute Venice's main examples of Fascist architecture. In late August and early September the **Venice Film Festival** occupies the **Palazzo del Cinema**. Across the way, the summer **Casino** might appeal to inveterate gamblers in possession of a snappy wardrobe.

From the Lido to Chioggia

The trip across to **Chioggia** is a protracted business, but will give you a curative dose of salt air and a good knowledge of the lagoon. In July and August a boat goes there from Riva degli Schiavoni (taking about 2hr), but throughout the year you can take the #11 bus from Gran Viale Santa Maria Elisabetta (the main street from the Lido landing stage to the sea front). Leaving more or less hourly (but check the timetable—they don't all go to Chioggia), the #11 goes down to **Alberoni**, where it drives onto a ferry for the five-minute hop to Pellestrina; the 10km to the southern tip of Pellestrina are covered by road, and then you switch from the bus to a steamer for the 25-minute crossing to Chioggia. The entire journey takes about eighty minutes, and costs L3500.

Malamocco and Pellestrina

The fishing village of **Malamocco**, about 5km into the expedition, is the successor of the ancient settlement called Metamauco, which in the eighth century was the capital of the lagoon confederation. In 810 the town was taken by **Pepin**, son of Charlemagne, and there followed one of the crucial battles in Venice's history, when Pepin's fleet, endeavoring to reach the islands of Rivoalto (forerunner of Venice), became jammed in the mudbanks and was swiftly pounced upon. After the battle the capital was promptly transferred to the safer islands of Rivoalto, and in 1107 the old town was destroyed by a tidal wave. The new town has a place in the bloodier footnotes of later Venetian history—the **Canal Orfano**, close to the Malamocco shore, was the spot where some of those condemned by the Council of Ten were bound, gagged, weighted and thrown overboard by the executioner. Malamocco's most appealing building—the church's scaled-down replica of the Campanile of San Marco—can be seen without getting off the bus.

The most ferocious defenders of the lagoon in the war against Pepin came from the small island of **Poveglia**, just off Malamocco. Once populous enough to have a practically independent administration, it suffered greatly in the war against Genoa (see below) and went into a steep decline immediately after, becoming little more than a fort. For much of this century it was a hospital island, but since the closure of the hospital in the late 1960s it has been abandoned.

Fishing and the production of fine pillow-lace are the mainstays of life in the village of **Pellestrina**, which is strung out along nearly a third of the ten kilometers of the next island. There's one remarkable structure here, but you get the best view of it as the boat crosses to Chioggia. This is the **Murazzi**, the colossal walls of Istrian boulders, 4km long and 14m thick at the base, which were constructed at the sides of the Porto di Chioggia to protect Venice from the battering of the sea. The maintenance of the water level in the lagoon has always been a preoccupation of Venetian life: very early in the city's development, for example, the five gaps in the *lidi* (the Lido–Chioggia sand bars) were reduced to the present three to strengthen the barrier against the Adriatic and to increase the dredging action of the tides through the three remaining *porti*. In time a special state official, the *Magistrato alle Acque*, was appointed to supervise the management of the lagoon, and the Murazzi were the last major project undertaken by the *Magistrato*'s department. Devised as a response to the increased flooding of the early eighteenth century, the Murazzi took 38 years to build, and remained unbreached from 1782, the year of their completion, until the flood of November 1966.

Chioggia

Chioggia was the scene, in 1379, of the most serious threat to Venice since Pepin's invasion, when the Genoese, after copious shedding of blood on both sides, took possession of the town. Venice at this time had two outstanding admirals: the first, Vettor Pisani, was in prison on a charge of military negligence; the second, Carlo Zeno, was somewhere off in the East. So serious was the threat to the city that Pisani was promptly released, and then put in command of the fleet that set out in December—with the doge himself on board—to blockade the enemy. Zeno and his contingent sailed over the horizon on the first day of the new year and there followed months of siege warfare, in the course of which the Venetian navy employed shipboard cannons for the first time. (Casualties from cannonballs were as high on the Venetian as on the Genoese side, and some crews refused to operate these suicidal weapons more than once a day.) In June 1380, with medieval Chioggia in ruins, the enemy surrendered, and from then until the arrival of Napoleon's ships the Venetian lagoon remained impregnable.

Modern Chioggia is the second largest settlement in the lagoon after Venice, and one of Italy's busiest fishing ports. Lorenzetti describes the *Chioggiotti* as "extremely individual types and among the most expert and intrepid sailors of the Adriatic," but those with insufficient time to plumb the depths of the local character will probably find Chioggia one of the less charming towns of the region. With the exception of a single church, you can see everything worth seeing in a hour's walk along the **Corso del Popolo**, the principal street in Chioggia's gridiron layout. The exception is the church of **San Domenico**, which houses **Carpaccio's** *St Paul*, his last known painting, plus a couple of pictures by **Leandro Bassano**; you get to it by taking the bridge to the left of the Chioggia landing stage and going straight on until you can't go any farther.

The boat puts you down at the **Piazzetta Vigo**, at the head of the Corso. The locals are reputedly touchy about the excuse for a lion that sits on top of the column here, a beast known to the condescending Venetians as the *Cat of St Mark*. Only the thirteenth century campanile of the church of **San Andrea** (rebuilt in 1743) is likely to catch your eye before the street widens at the **Granaio**, a grain warehouse built in 1322 but got at by nineteenth-century restorers; the facade relief of the *Madonna and Child* is by Sansovino. Behind the Granaio is the **fish market**; open for business every morning except Monday, it's a treat for gourmet and marine biologist alike—make sure you don't arrive too late to see it.

In the Piazzetta Venti Settembre, immediately after the town hall, there's the church of the **Santissima Trinità**, radically altered in 1703 by Andrea Tirali and almost perpetually shut—the Oratory, behind the main altar, has an impressive ceiling set with paintings by followers of Tintoretto. **San Giacomo Apostolo**, a bit farther on, has a sub-Tiepolo ceiling by local boy Il Chiozzotto, and a much venerated fifteenth-century Venetian painting known as the *Madonna della Navicella*. Soon you pass a house once occupied by the family of **Rosalba Carriera** and later by **Goldoni** (in Chioggia this counts as an important historical item), and then, on the opposite side of the road, just before the Duomo, the **Tempio di San Martino**, built immediately after the war of 1380. It's rarely open except for temporary exhibitions.

The **Duomo** was the first major commission for **Longhena**, who was called in to design a new church after the previous cathedral was burned down in 1623; the detached fourteenth-century campanile survived the blaze. The chapel to the left of the chancel contains half a dozen good eighteenth-century paintings, including one attributed to Tiepolo; except in freakish weather conditions they're all but invisible, a drawback which the oversensitive might regard as a blessing in view of the subjects depicted—*The Torture of Boiling Oil*, *The Torture of the Razors*, *The Beheading of Two Martyrs*, and so on.

Buses run from the Duomo to **Sottomarina**, Chioggia's lower-rent answer to Venice's Lido. On the beaches of Sottomarina you're a fraction closer to nature than you would be on the Lido, and the resort does have one big plus—after your dip you can go back to the Corso and have a fresh seafood meal that's cheaper than any you'd find in Venice's restaurants and better than most.

The quickest way **back to Venice** is by bus from the Duomo or Sottomarina to Piazzale Roma, but it's a dispiriting drive, slightly dearer than the island-hop route, and only about twenty minutes quicker.

San Lazzaro degli Armeni and the Other Minor Islands

No foreign community has a longer pedigree in Venice than the Armenians. Their position in the economy of the city, primarily as tradesmen and money-lenders, was secure by the end of the thirteenth century, and for around five hundred years they have had their own church within a few yards of the Piazza, in the narrow Calle degli Armeni (see "North of the Piazza," in Chapter One). The Armenians are far less numerous now than formerly, and the most conspicuous sign of their presence is the Armenian island by the Lido, **San Lazzaro degli Armeni**, identifiable from the city by the onion-shaped summit of its campanile.

From the late twelfth century to the beginning of the seventeenth the island was a leper colony—hence *Lazzaro*, Lazarus being the patron saint of lepers—but the land was disused when in 1717 a Roman Catholic Armenian monastery was founded here by one Manug di Pietro. Known as **Mechitar** ("The Consoler") he had been driven by the Turks from the religious foundation he had established with Venetian aid in the Morea. Within a few years the monks of San Lazzaro earned a wide reputation as scholars and linguists, a reputation that has persisted to the present. Today, Vienna has the only community outside the Soviet Union that can compare to Venice's as a center of Armenian culture. (If you're wondering how the Armenians escaped suppression by the French, it's allegedly got something to do with the presence of an indispensible Armenian official in Napoleon's secretariat.)

The monastery's collection of precious manuscripts and books—the former going back to the fifth century—is a highlight of a visit to the island, and you can expect the father who shows you round to be trilingual, at the very least. Reflecting the encyclopaedic interests of its occupants, the monastery is in places like a whimsically arranged museum, nowhere more so than in the old **library**, where a mummified Egyptian body is laid out near Canova's figure of Napoleon's infant son and a miscellany of letters and printed paraphernalia. Elsewhere you'll be shown antique writing instruments, pieces of pottery, firearms, a gallery of paintings by Armenian painters, and a ceiling panel by the young GB. Tiepolo. The tour lingers in two smaller rooms: the cell occupied by Mechitar (including the scourging chain found on the body after his death), and the room in which Byron stayed while lending a hand with the preparation of an Armenian-English dictionary. Finally you're led into a **printing and typesetting hall**, the nerve center of the polyglot press which has been operating here continuously since 1789; it's all up-to-date machinery (in a side office you can look over the shoulder of a monk setting Armenian texts on a computer screen) and the range of material produced here is enormous—everything from books to wine labels. You're expected to leave a donation as you leave, or buy something from the press—the old maps and prints of Venice are a bargain. (Visitors are received Thurs & Sun 3–5pm; take the #10 vaporetto from Riva degli Schiavone—you have to catch the one just before 3pm to have any time on the island.)

The "Hospital Islands"

San Lazzaro is the only minor island of the southern lagoon that's of interest to the tourist. The boat out to San Lazzaro calls at **La Grazia**, successively a pilgrims' hostel and a monastery, now a hospital, and **San Servolo**, once one of the most important Benedictine monasteries in the region (founded in the ninth century), then a hospital for the insane (the main setting in Jeanette Winterson's *The Passion*), and now used by the Council of Europe's School of Craftsmanship. **San Clemente**, to the south of La Grazia, is another hospital island but is due to be closed down, a fate which overtook **Sacca Sessola**, the large hospital island to the southwest of San Clemente, in 1980. A sports complex has been planned for the ex-ammunition factory on **Santo Spirito**, southeast of Sacca Sessola; until the mid-seventeenth century there was a monastery here, with a church redesigned by Sansovino, but when the order was suppressed most of its treasures, including paintings by Titian, were sent to the then unfinished Salute church on the Canal Grande, where they can now be seen. **Lazzaretto Vecchio** (south of San Lazzaro), at present a dogs' home, is also due to have a sports complex built on it; from the twelfth century the site of a pilgrim's hostel, the island took a place in medical history when, in 1423, it became the site of Europe's first permanent isolation hospital for plague victims.

RESTAURANTS: *Altanella*, Calle dell'Erbe (La Giudecca); *Do Mori*, Fondamenta Sant'Eufamia (La Giudecca); in Chioggia—along the Corso del Popolo.

BARS: on La Giudecca the bars are strung along the main waterfront; in Chioggia, the Corso del Popolo is again the best area.

CHAPTER TEN

EATING, DRINKING, AND SPENDING

A lthough there's an element of truth to Venice's reputation as a place where only the wealthy eat well, the picture is not all bleak for those on a tighter budget. A scattering of good-value **restaurants** does exist— it's just that they tend to be hidden away in the city's quieter places. And if the options for an evening's low-cost gastronomic indulgence are more limited here than in many other Italian cities, there's ample opportunity for less formal arrangements.

Stocking up for an *al fresco* lunch, you'll be spoiled for choice at the stalls of the Rialto and the smaller **markets** pitched in a number of Venice's campi, whilst there's a host of tempting *alimentari* to supplement supplies. For a quick **snack**, pop into a bar and sample a couple of plump *tramezzini* (sandwiches), chasing them down with an *ombra*, the quick shot of wine that punctuates many a Venetian's working day. As enticing as many of the city's bars are its **cafés** and *pasticcerie*, where a variety of waistline-threatening delicacies are on offer, some of them originating from the period of Austrian rule. Finally, Venetian **ice cream** might not be quite in the same class as the Neapolitan equivalent, but there aren't too many nicer things you can do to your taste buds than hit them with a coneful from *Paolin* or *Nico*.

Night owls have a fairly tough time of it. The locals seem to be a homey crowd, for whom a sociable end to the day usually means having a few friends round for a meal, perhaps after a brief call at the local bar. By 9:30pm most of the shutters are down for the night; all the places that stay open later are included in the restaurant/bars/cafés listings, but it's a pretty scrawny roll-call.

The torpor of the city after dark is inversely proportional to the hustle of its shopping streets in the daytime, where vast sums are trawled daily from the tourists' pockets. Contrary to first appearances, Venice's **shops** are not all stocked with junk or with stuff priced way beyond the average pocket, and this chapter ends with entries on where you can buy Venetian souvenirs you'll not be embarrassed by later.

Venetian Food and Drink

Venetian cuisine bears little trace of the city's past as Europe's trading cross-roads, when spices from the East were among the most lucrative commodities sold in Venice's markets. Nowadays Venetian food is known for its simplicity, with plain pepper and salt as the principal means of gingering up a meal. **Fish and seafood** dominate the restaurant menus, the former being netted in the Adriatic and the rivers and lakes of the mainland, the latter coming from the lagoon and open sea. Prawns, squid and octopus are typical Venetian *antipasti* (usually served with a plain dressing of olive oil and lemon), as are Murano crabs and *sarde in saor* (marinated sardines). Dishes like eel cooked in Marsala wine, *baccalà* (salt cod) and *seppioline nere* (baby cuttlefish cooked in its own ink) are other Venetian staples, but the quintessential dish is the **risotto**, made with rice grown along the Po valley. Apart from the seafood variety (*risotto bianco, risotto di mare* or *risotto dei pescatori*), you'll come across risottos that incorporate some of the great range of vegetables grown in the Veneto, and others that draw on such diverse ingredients as snails, tripe, quails and sausages.

Venetian **soups** are as versatile as their risottos, with *brodetto* (mixed fish) and *pasta e fasioi* (pasta and beans) being the most popular kinds. **Polenta** is another recurrent feature of Venetian meals; made by slowly stiring corn flour into boiling salted water, it's served as an accompaniment to a number of dishes, in particular liver (*fegato*), a special favorite in Venice.

Pastries and sweets are also an area of Venetian expertise. Look out for the thin oval cookies called *baicoli*, the ring-shaped cinnamon-flavored *bussolai* (a specialty of Burano), and *mandolato*—a cross between nougat and toffee, made with almonds. The Austrian occupation has left its mark in the form of the ubiquitous *strudel* and the cream- or jam-filled *krapfen* (doughnuts).

Particular foods are traditional to certain **feast days**. During Carnevale you can buy small doughnuts known as *frittelle*, which come plain, *con frutta* (with fruit), *con crema* (confectioner's cream) or *con zabaglione* (which is made out of egg yolks and Marsala). During Lent there's an even greater emphasis on fish, and also on omelettes (*frittata*), often made with shrimps and wild asparagus; lamb is popular at Easter. On Ascension Day it's customary to have pig's trotter, either plain or stuffed, while for the feast of the Redentore (third Sunday in July) *sarde in saor* or roast duck are in order. Tiny cookies called *fave* ("beans") fill the *pasticcerie* around All Saints' Day and All Souls' Day (November 1st and 2nd); on the feast of San Martino (November 11th) you get cookies or heavy quince jello cut into the shape of Saint Martin on his horse; and on the feast of the Madonna della Salute (November 21st), it's traditional to have *castradina* (salted smoked mutton). On Christmas Eve everyone eats eel, usually grilled, though with variations from island to island; Christmas Day brings roast turkey, veal, duck or capon.

Many of the **wines** of the Veneto will already be familiar, especially *Valpolicella* and *Bardolino* (red) and *Soave* (white); far more rarely exported are *Cartizze* and *Prosecco*, light, champagne-like wines from the area around Conegliano—don't miss a chance to sample the delicious *Prosecco Rosé*. Wines from neighboring Friuli are well worth exploring too: *Pinot Nero, Refosco, Merlot* and *Cabernet* (red) and *Tocai, Pinot Bianco,* and *Sauvignon* (white) are the most common. *Grappa* is the local fire-water—originally from Bassano del Grappa, it's made from grapes, juniper berries or plums, and will take your head off if you don't exercise a degree of caution.

Non-alcoholic drinks include *frullati*, a milk shake made with fruit; a freshly squeezed fruit juice is a *spremuta* and is usually *d'arancia* (orange), *pompelmo* (grapefruit), *limone* (lemon) or *mele* (apple).

VENETIAN FOOD AND DRINK

Basics and Snacks

Aceto	Vinegar	Pane	Bread
Aglio	Garlic	Pane integrale	Wholemeal bread
Biscotti	Cookies	Panino	Bread roll
Burro	Butter	Patatine	/sandwich
Caramelle	Sweets	Patatine fritte	Crisps
Cioccolato	Chocolate	Pepe	Chips
Focaccia	Oven-baked snack	Pizzetta	Pepper
Formaggio	Cheese		Small cheese and
Frittata	Omelette		tomato pizza
Gelato	Ice-cream	Riso	Rice
Grissini	Bread sticks	Sale	Salt
Maionese	Mayonnaise	Uove	Eggs
Mermellata	Jam	Yogurt	Yoghurt
Olio	Oil	Zúcchero	Sugar
Olive	Olives	Zuppa	Soup

Pizzas

Calzone	Folded pizza with ham, cheese, and tomato	Frutta di mare	Sea food; usually mussels, prawns, squid and clams
Capricciosa	Literally "capricious"; topped with whatever they've got in the kitchen, usually including baby artichoke, ham and egg	Margherita	
		Marinara	
		Napoli/Napolitana	Cheese and tomato Tomato
		Quattro formaggi	Tomato, anchovy and olive oil "Four cheeses", usually including mozzarella, fontina and gruyère
Disco Volante	("Flying Saucer") A Capricciosa with a pastry "lid"	Quattro stagioni	
Funghi	Mushroom; tinned, sliced button mushrooms unless it specifies fresh mushrooms, funghi freschi		"Four seasons"; the toppings split into four sections, usually including ham, green pepper, onion, egg, etc

Antipasti and Starters

Antipasto misto	Mixed cold meats and cheese	Melanzane in parmigiana	Eggplant in tomato and parmesan cheese
Caponata	Mixed eggplant, olives, tomatoes	Peperonata	Green and red peppers stewed in olive oil
Caprese	Tomato and mozzarella cheese salad		
Insalata di mare	Seafood salad	Pomodori ripieni	Stuffed tomatoes
Insalata di riso	Rice salad	Prosciutto	Ham
		Salame	Salami

The first course (il primo): soups, pasta ...

Brodo	Clear broth	*Penne*	Smaller version of rigatoni
Cannelloni	Large tubes of pasta, stuffed		
Farfalle	Literally "butterfly"-shaped pasta	*Ravioli*	Ravioli
		Rigatoni	Large, grooved tubular pasta
Fettucine	Narrow pasta ribbons		
Gnocchi	Small potato and dough dumplings	*Risotto*	Cooked rice dish, with sauce
Lasagne	Lasagne	*Spaghetti*	Spaghetti
Maccheroni	Tubular spaghetti	*Spaghettini*	Thin spaghetti
Minestrina	Any light soup	*Stracciatella*	Broth with egg
Minestrone	Thick vegetable soup	*Tagliatelle*	Pasta ribbons, another word for fettucine
Pasta al forno	Pasta baked with minced meat, eggs, tomato, and cheese	*Tortellini*	Small rings of pasta, stuffed with meat or cheese
Pasta fagioli	Pasta soup with beans		
Pastina in brodo	Pasta pieces in clear broth.	*Vermicelli*	Very thin spaghetti (literally "little worms")

... and the sauce (salsa)

Arrabiata	Spicy tomato sauce, with chillies	*Peperoncino*	Olive oil, garlic, and fresh chillies
Bolognese	Meat sauce	*Pesto*	Green basil and garlic sauce
Burro	Butter		
Carbonara	Cream, ham and beaten egg	*Pomodoro*	Tomato sauce
Funghi	Mushroom	*Ragù*	Meat sauce
Panna	Cream	*Vóngole*	Clam and tomato sauce
Parmigiano	Parmesan cheese		

The second course (Il secondo): meat (carne) ...

Agnello	Lamb	*Involtini*	Meat slices, rolled and stuffed	*Pancetta*	Bacon
Bistecca	Steak			*Pollo*	Chicken
Cervello	Brain	*Lingua*	Tongue	*Polpette*	Meatballs
Coniglio	Rabbit	*Maiale*	Pork	*Rognoni*	Kidneys
Costolette	Chops	*Manzo*	Beef	*Salsiccia*	Sausage
Cotolette	Cutlets	*Mortadella*	Salami-type cured meat	*Saltimbocca*	Veal with ham
Fegatini	Chicken livers			*Spezzatino*	Stew
Fegato	Liver	*Ossobuco*	Shin of veal	*Tacchino*	Turkey
				Trippa	Tripe

... and fish (pesce) and shellfish (crostacei)

Acciughe	Anchovies	*Gamberetti*	Shrimps	*Sarde*	Sardines
Anguilla	Eel	*Gámberi*	Prawns	*Sgombro*	Mackerel
Aragosta	Lobster	*Granchio*	Crab	*Sógliola*	Sole
Baccalà	Dried salted cod	*Merluzzo*	Cod	*Tonno*	Tuna
Calamari	Squid	*Ostriche*	Oysters	*Triglie*	Red mullet
Céfalo	Mullet	*Pescespada*	Swordfish	*Trota*	Trout
Cozze	Mussels	*Pólipo*	Octopus	*Vóngole*	Clams

Vegetables (contorni) and salad (insalata)

Asparagi	Asparagus	Finocchio	Fennel
Basílico	Basil	Funghi	Mushrooms
Bróccoli	Broccoli	Insalata verde/	Green salad/mixed
Cápperi	Capers	mista	salad
Carciofi	Artichokes	Melanzane	Eggplant
Carciofini	Artichoke hearts	Orígano	Oregano
Carotte	Carrots	Patate	Potatoes
Cavolfiori	Cauliflower	Peperoni	Peppers
Cávolo	Cabbage	Piselli	Peas
Cetriolo	Cucumber	Pomodori	Tomatoes
Cipolla	Onion	Radicchio	Chicory
Fagioli	Beans	Spinaci	Spinach
Fagiolini	Green beans	Zucchini	Zucchini

Sweets (dolci), fruit (frutta), cheeses (formaggi), and nuts (noce)

Amaretti	Macaroons	Mozzarella	Bland soft white cheese used on pizzas
Ananas	Pineapple		
Anguria/Coccómero	Water melon	Parmigiano	Parmesan cheese
Arance	Oranges	Pecorino	Strong tasting hard sheep's cheese
Banane	Bananas		
Ciliegie	Cherries	Pere	Pears
Fichi	Figs	Pesche	Peaches
Fichi d'India	Prickly pears	Pignoli	Pine nuts
Fontina	Northern Italian cheese used in cooking	Pistacchio	Pistachio nut
		Provolone	Hard strong cheese
Frágole	Strawberries	Ricotta	Soft white cheese made from ewe's milk
Gelato	Ice cream		
Gorgonzola	Soft blue-veined cheese	Torta	Cake, tart
Limone	Lemon	Uve	Grapes
Macedonia	Fruit salad	Zabaglione	Dessert made with eggs, sugar and marsala wine
Mándorle	Almonds		
Mele	Apples	Zuppa Inglese	Trifle
Melone	Melon		

Some terms and useful words

Affumicato	Smoked	Grattuggiato	Grated
Arrosto	Roast	Alla griglia	Grilled
Ben cotto	Well done	Al Marsala	Cooked with Marsala wine
Bollito/lesso	Boiled	Milanese	Fried in egg and breadcrumbs
Brasato	Cooked in wine	Pizzaiola	Cooked with tomato sauce
Cotto	Cooked (not raw)	Ripieno	Stuffed
Crudo	Raw	Sangue	Rare
Al dente	Firm, not overcooked	Allo spiedo	On the spit
Ferri	Grilled without oil	Surgelato	Frozen
Fritto	Fried	Úmido	Steamed/stewed

Specialties: a few dishes

Primi

Bigoi in salsa	Spaghetti in sauce of oil, butter, onion and sardines
Brodetto	Fish soup with oil, garlic and tomatoes
Pasta e fasioi	Pasta and bean soup
Risotto alla sbirraglia	Risotto with chicken, ham and vegetables
... con le cape	... with shellfish
... di mare	... with seafood
... in nero	... with cuttlefish cooked in its own ink
Risi e bisi	... with peas, ham and parmesan

Secondi

Baccalà mantecato	Mashed salt cod
Bisato in umido	Baked eel
Cape sante	Scallops
Fegato alla Veneziana	Sliced liver in olive oil
Scampi alla griglia	Grilled scampi
Seppie ...	Grilled cuttlefish
... alla Veneziana	Cuttlefish in oil, parsley and tomatoes
... in nero	... cooked in its own ink

Dolci

Frittole alla Veneziana	Anise and rum flavored fritters stuffed with pine nuts and dried fruit
Tiramisù (lit. "pick-me-up")	Sponge layered with coffee and mascarpone cheese, dosed with kirsch or Marsala—allegedly invented in Treviso

Antipasti

Misto di mare	Fried seafood mixture
Prosciutto crudo	Raw Parma ham ("San Daniele" is the best)
Sarde in saor	Marinated and sautéd sardines

Contorni

Polenta	A cornmeal porridge, allowed to set and then often grilled

Drinks

Acqua minerale	Mineral water	*Latte*	Milk	*Vino*	Wine
Aranciata	Orangeade	*Limonat*	Lemonade	*Rosso*	Red
Bicchiere	Glass	*Selz*	Soda water	*Bianco*	White
Birra	Beer	*Spremuta*	Fresh fruit juice	*Rosato*	Rosé
Bottiglia	Bottle	*Spumante*	Sparkling wine	*Secco*	Dry
Caffè	Coffee	*Succo*	Concentrated fruit juice with sugar	*Dolce*	Sweet
Cioccolata calda	Hot chocolate			*Litro*	Litre
Ghiaccio	Ice	*Tè*	Tea	*Mezzo*	Half
Granita	Iced coffee /fruit-drink	*Tónico*	Tonic water	*Quarto*	Quarter
				Salute!	Cheers!

Restaurants

Virtually every restaurant in Venice advertises a set-price **Menu Turistico**, which at its best will offer a choice of three or four dishes (*piati*) for each course. This can be a cheap way of sampling Venetian specialties, but the quality and certainly the quantity won't be up to the mark of an **à la carte** meal. Cover charge (*coperto*) and service should be included in the *menu turistico* price; if you're going *à la carte*, don't forget that the *coperto* plus a service charge will be added to your bill—together they'll put a few thousand lire onto the cost of the meal.

As a general rule, **value for money** tends to increase with the distance from San Marco; plenty of restaurants within a short radius of the Piazza offer menus that seem to be reasonable, but you'll probably find the food unappetizing, the portions tiny and the service abrupt.

(In all the listings in this and subsequent sections, the address is followed by the name of the chapter in which the street or campo lies. The price categories used below are for a full meal with a quarter-liter of wine.)

Under L20,000

Aciugheta, Campo Santi Filippo e Giacomo; Castello. A bar with a pizzeria and restaurant next door. The closest spot to San Marco to eat without paying through the nose. The bar is the kind of place that if you befriend the bar staff, make it a regular haunt and leave the occasional tip, the prices fall; and if you look set for a couple more rounds, the glasses get bigger. Good bar-food to nibble or have as a meal. The name translates as "the little anchovy" and there are portraits of anchovies on the wall. *Menu turistico* from L14,000, pizzas from L4000. 11:30am–3pm and 6:30–10pm; closed Wed.

Ai Canottieri, Ponte Tre Archi; Cannaregio. *Primo* around L5000, *secondo* L9000. Has live music occasionally, but as usual bar prices go up to pay the band. Bar and restaurant open 7pm–midnight. Closed Sun.

Ai Promessi Sposi, Calle dell'Oca; Castello. Specializes in *baccalà* and other traditional fish recipes; very friendly bar too. Closed Tues.

All'Anfora, Lista Vecchia dei Bari; San Polo. An unpretentious local restaurant that's open for breakfast coffee and still going late at night, and where a woman eating alone is welcomed and not patronized. Has a pizza list, but the trattoria list is not too expensive and features dishes you might find in a Venetian home. The seafood risotto is good, as is the *spaghetti del doge*. Closed Fri.

Alla Rivetta, Ponte San Provolo (near Campo SS. Filippo e Giacomo); Castello. Excellent *sepie in nero*, best eaten *con polenta*. Getting under L20,000 might require a bit of self-restraint. Closed Mon.

Alla Rivetta, Campiello dei Meloni; San Polo. Pleasant canalside site between San Polo and Sant'Aponal. Fair *menu turistico* at L12,000. Closed Mon.

Al Marca, Via Garibaldi (top end); Eastern Districts. Has a filling *menu turistico*, which is more than can be said for some places on this street, but overall not as good as the nearby *Toscana* (see below). Closed Sun.

Al Ponte, Rio Terrà Maddalena; Cannaregio. Worth mentioning if only because they have the cheapest *menu turistico* on a main street at L9500; food is okay but not wonderful.

Bruno, Fondamenta delle Cappuccine; Cannaregio. Very pleasant little canalside trattoria in deepest Cannaregio; tasty seafood at good prices. Closed Sun.

Dalla Cea, Calle del Fumo (down from Fdm. Nuove); Cannaregio. A basic trattoria, catering to workers of the area; has a few outside tables under the trellis in the summer. Try the *seppie alla griglia*; *menu turistico* at L12,000.

Da Paolo, Campo dell'Arsenale; Castello. Tables outside in the summer, facing the Arsenale entrance. Good *sarde in saor*; house wine not too hot. Closed Mon.

Donna Onesta, Calle della Madonna (near the Frari); San Polo. Popular and very friendly— ask about the day's special dish; substantial meal and fair quantities of wine for a couple of thousand under L20,000. Noon–3:30pm and 6–11pm; closed Sun.

Frigittoria da Bruno, Calle Lunga San Barnaba; Dorsoduro. Similar to *Donna Onesta*, but a bit cheaper, rougher and more homey; go for the *à la carte* meals. 1–2:30pm and 6:15–10:30pm; closed Thurs lunchtime and all Sun.

Isola Misteriosa, Rio Terrà Scozzera (just off Campo S. Margherita); Dorsoduro. Nice food (with some vegetarian options) but small portions, and a touch overpriced. It's possible to sit and drink here when it's not full of people eating, and there's a stand-up bar. Newly opened in 1988, it appeals to those who wear sunglasses at midnight and never smile. Open 11am–3pm and 6–11:30pm.

Latteria Zorzi, Calle dei Fuseri; San Marco. Billed as Venice's solitary vegetarian restaurant, the Zorzi serves very small portions of the sort of food a carnivore rustles up when a cranky relative is due, and watery wine too. With a full meal costing around L15,000, you could be better off with a pasta followed by a selection of vegetables at a regular restaurant.

Paradiso Perduto, Fondamenta della Misericordia; Cannaregio. Opens around noon, closes midnight or later, depending on how things are going. Fronted by a popular bar, it has a lively relaxed atmosphere, attracting architecture students, arty types (it shows stuff by local artists) and some of the gay community. Makes its own pasta daily and has nice fish sometimes. Bar prices higher when live music is playing—usually Sunday. Full meals start at around L15,000, but go up to L30,000. Closed Wed.

Rosticceria San Bartolomeo, Calle della Bissa; San Marco. Downstairs it's a sort of glorified snack bar, the meals starting from under L10,000—the trick is to first grab a place at the long tables along the windows, then order from the counter. Good if you need to refuel quickly and cheaply, but can't face another pizza. There's a less rudimentary (and less good value) restaurant upstairs. Noon–2:30pm and 4:30–9pm; closed Mon.

San Trovaso, Fondamenta Priuli; Dorsoduro. A restaurant-pizzeria which serves a menu of basic Venetian dishes at prices just a little higher than *La Donna Onesta*. Closed Mon afternoon and Tues.

Toscana, Via Garibaldi (bottom end); Eastern Districts. Plain, with a tiny menu, but all of it's dishes are good and inexpensive. The best bet on the street. Noon–2pm and 6–8pm; closed Wed.

L20,000–30,000

Al Bacareto, Calle Crosera; San Marco. Handy for the Palazzo Grassi. Best to eat standing here: excellent *risotto alla pescatore* (fisherman's risotto) and a glass of wine for around L5000; good *baccalà mantecato*. Sitting, a full meal can go up to L25,000. Closed Sun.

Alla Madonna, Calle della Madonna (near the Rialto); San Polo. Often chock-full; traditionally brusque service but genuinely Venetian food. Closed Wed.

Al Masceron, Calle Lunga Santa Maria Formosa; Castello. Arty feel and interesting bar food, but definitely two types of clientele—Italians and non-Italians—with service and prices to match. Has a good reputation among the locals though, and worth a try if you're confident with the language and they're not too busy. *Primo* L4000–L6000; *secondo* L8000–L12,000. 11am–3pm and 6–11pm; closed Sun.

Al Milion, Corte del Milion (behind San Giovanni Crisostomo); Castello. Trattoria with bar where you can get snacks. Wide selection of Veneto wines. 10:30am–2:30pm and 5:30–10:30pm; closed Wed.

Antico Molo, Fondamenta degli Ormesini (near the Ghetto); Cannaregio. Originally a family-run, local place, but becoming trendier by the year. Good food, good value. Closed Wed.

Da Silvio, Calle San Pantalon; San Polo. The best of the clutch of trattorias in this alley, with a reputation for its *tortellini*; a full meal for L20,000 or a jot more is feasible. Closed Sun.

Do Mori, by Sant'Eufamia landing-stage (Giudecca); Southern Islands. Run by the former chef at the snazzy *Harry's Dolce*, on the other side of the bridge; a blow-out will take you into the upper reaches of this price bracket, but it's worth every lira. Closed Sun.

Trattoria Rialto Nuovo, Campo Rialto Nuovo (just off Ruga Orefici); San Polo. Extensive, intriguing menu; it's possible to dip under the L20,000 mark, but most of the meals will take you somewhere over it. Closed Sun.

● Restaurants
★ Snacks & Bars
■ Cafés, Pasticcerie
   & Ice Creams

RESTAURANTS
Under L20,000
1. Achiughetta
2. Ai Canottieri
3. Ai Promiessi Sposi
4. All' Anfora
5. Alla Rivetta
6. Alla Rivetta
7. Al Marca
8. Al Ponte
9. Da Bruno
10. Dalla Cea
11. Da Paola
12. Donna Onesta
13. Frigittoria da Bruno
14. Isola Misteriosa
15. Latteria Zorzi
16. Paradiso Perduto
17. Rosticceria San Bartolomeo
18. San Trovaso
19. Toscana

L20-30,000
20. Al Bacareto
21. Alla Madonna
22. Al Masceron
23. Al Milion
24. Antico Molo
25. Da Silvo
26. Do Mori
27. Rialto Nuovo

L30,000+
28. Altanella
29. Locanda Montin

PIZZAS
30. Alle Oche
31. Alle Zattere
32. Antico Cappon
33. Casa Mia
34. Da Sandro
35. Giardinetto
36. San Toma

SNACKS & BARS
37. Al Volto
38. Cantina del Vino gia Schiavi
39. Corner Pub
40. Da Codroma
41. Do Mori
42. Do Spade
43. Leon d'Oro: Bar Gobbi
44. Harry's Bar
45. Linea d'Ombra
46. Osteria elle Botteghe
47. Osteria alle Ghiacciaia
48. Train Station Buffet
49. Trattoria Ca'd'Oro/Osteria della Vedova
50. Vino Vino

CAFES, PASTICCERIE & ICE CREAM
51. Florian
52. Il Golosone
53. Latteria Zorzi
54. Marchini
55. Nico
56. Paolin
57. Quadri
58. Rosa Salva
59. Vio

VENICE: RESTAURANTS AND BARS

Over L30,000

Altanella, Calle dell'Erbe (Giudecca); Southern Islands. Recommended for a treat; beautiful fish dishes, plus a terrace overlooking the island's central canal. Definitely best to reserve—☎5227780. Closed Mon, Tues, and all winter.

Locanda Montin, Fondamenta di Borgo; Dorsoduro. Very highly rated, but the quality's more erratic than you'd expect for the money; you'll pay in the region of L30,000 here for what would cost L20,000 in some places. It's always been a place for the literary/artistic set— Pound, Hemingway, Peggy Guggenheim and Visconti, for example—and the restaurant doubles as a commercial art gallery. Often essential to ring for a table—☎5227151. Closed Tues and Wed, and for two weeks in both Jan and Aug.

Pizzas

Pizza is a generally reliable stand-by here as elsewhere in Italy, but as a principle steer clear of the places in the immediate vicinity of the Piazza and Mercerie, where the offerings might well remind you of home. The batch listed below are as good as any in the city.

Alle Oche, Calle del Tintor (south side of Campo S. Giacomo dell'Orio); San Polo. Has about fifty varieties to choose from, so if this doesn't satisfy you, nothing will; in the evenings if you're not there by 8pm you may have to line up on the sidewalk. Closed Mon.

Alle Záttere, Campo Sant'Agnese; Dorsoduro. *Primavera*, with vegetables, can be recommended.

Antico Cappon, Campo Santa Margherita; Dorsoduro. Wide range of pizzas including such novelties as gorgonzola and walnut; good prosciutto to start. Closed 3–6pm each day and all Wed.

Casa Mia, Calle dell'Oca (off Campo SS Apostoli); Castello. Invariably heaving with locals, who always go for the pizza list rather than the menu. The *disco volante* (flying saucer) is a cheap way to a full stomach. Closed Tues.

Da Sandro, Campiello dei Meloni; San Polo. Split-site pizzeria, with rooms on both sides of the campiello and tables on the sidewalk. Often frenetic, though not aggressively so. Closed Mon.

Giardinetto, Fondamenta del Forner; San Polo. Big but not impersonal, with wide shaded courtyard. Popular with students. Closed Mon.

San Tomà, Campo San Tomà; San Polo. Outdoor tables on the campo and under a pergola out the back; pizzas are succulent, but the L2000 *coperto* and 12 percent service bump the price up. Also serves delicious home-made pasta. Closed Mon.

Snacks and Bars

One of the most appealing aspects of Venetian social life is ecapsulated in the phrase "andemo a ombra," which translates literally as an invitation to go into the shade, but is in fact an invitation for a drink—more specifically, a small glass of wine, customarily downed in one. (The phrase is a vestige of the time when wines were unloaded on the Riva degli Schiavoni and then sold at a shaded kiosk at the base of the Campanile; the kiosk was shifted as the sun moved round, so as to stay in the shade.) Stand at a bar any time of the day and you won't have to wait long before a customer drops by for a reviving mouthful. Occasionally you'll come across a group doing a *giro de ombra*, the highly refined Venetian version of the bar-crawl; on a serious *giro* it's almost obligatory to stop at an *enoteca*— a bar where priority is given to the range and quality of the wines (for example, *Al Volto*).

Most bars serve some kind of **food**, their counters usually bearing trays of the fat little sandwiches called *tramezzini*. Devoid of natural fiber (even the crusts are removed) but stuffed with delicious fillings—eggs and mushrooms, eggs and anchovies, Parma ham and artichokes—they can cost anything from L500 up to about L1500; three or four of them make a good lunch on the run. At the older-style *osterie* there's often a choice of little snacks called *cicheti*, which you can either nibble at or heap up on a plate; the array will typically include *polpette* (small beef and garlic meatballs), *carciofini* (artichoke hearts), hard-boiled eggs, anchovies, *polipi* (baby octopus or squid), sun-dried tomatoes, peppers and zucchini cooked in oil. Some *osterie* also produce one or two more substantial dishes each day—particularly tasty is *baccalà,* dried salt cod mashed up with mayonnaise, eaten with bread and a dry white wine.

Don't refuse the receipt that's handed over with everything; bars and restaurants are now legally required to give you one, following years of irate tourists complaining about being ripped off.

In addition to the specific places given below, general areas worth scouring for bars are the **Rialto** district, the **Strada Nova** and **Via Garibaldi**, and along **La Giudecca**'s main waterfront.

Al Volto, Calle Cavalli (near Campo S. Luca); San Marco. An *enoteca*, or wine bar in the true sense of the word—1300 wines from Italy and elsewhere, some cheap, many not; good snacks too. Always full, with a hefty contingent of AmEx types. Shows small-scale works by Venetian artists. 9am–1pm & 4:30–9pm; closed Sun and all Aug.

Cantina del Vino gia Schiavi, Fondamenta Maravegie (opposite S. Trovaso); Dorsoduro. Great wine shop and bar—do some sampling before you buy. Wines at all prices. Daily 9am–1:30pm & 3:15–8:30pm.

Corner Pub, Calle della Chiesa; Dorsoduro. Looks a bit like a pub, and (like *Vino Vino*) usually has a few expatriate art history students, but is authentically Venetian nonetheless. Ask for whisky and you're likely to get half a tumbler on a good night. 7am–3pm & 6pm–2am; closed Tues.

Da Codroma, Fondamenta Briati; Dorsoduro. The kind of place you could sit for an hour or two with a beer and a book and feel comfortable. Interesting toasted sandwiches—brie with different sauces, for example. Shows work by local artists, and is a venue for poetry readings and live music. Good place to go for refreshment after visiting the Accademia. Clientele mainly in the 30s–40s, with a smattering of students. Closed Thurs.

Do Mori, Calle Do Mori (just off Ruga Vecchia S. Giovanni); San Polo. A narrow, standing-only bar, catering mainly for the Rialto porters and traders, and thus frustratingly shut at lunchtime when they all nip home. Delicious snacks and terrific atmosphere. One of the best of a number of authentic bars in the market area. 9am–1pm & 5–8pm; closed Wed afternoon and all Sun.

Do Spade, Sottoportego delle Do Spade; San Polo. Imposible to locate from a map—walk past the *Do Mori* and keep going as straight as possible. Larger than *Do Mori* (it has tables), but a very similar place. 9am–1pm & 5–8pm; closed Sun.

Leon d'Oro: Bar Gobbi, Rio Terrà della Maddalena; Cannaregio. A pleasant family-run place on a main street, a couple of doors down from the flashier *Alla Maddalena*. Excellent thick hot chocolate; good range of sandwiches, including *porchetta*—a salty roast sucking pig. *Osteria* food at the back—its possible to get a meal for L5000. Open from 7:30am to 12:30am.

Harry's Bar, Calle Vallaresso; San Marco. Trendiest bar in town since time immemorial; famed in equal measure for its cocktails, its sandwiches and its (celebrity league) prices. 3pm–1am; closed Mon.

Linea d'Ombra, Záttere ai Saloni; Dorsoduro. A late-night piano bar—up-market clientele with up-market prices.

Osteria alle Botteghe, Calle delle Botteghe (near S. Stefano); San Marco. Sumptuous sand-wiches, but most lunchtimes you need a shoehorn to get in the place. Closed Sun.

Osteria alla Ghiacciaia, Fondamenta di Cannaregio; Cannaregio. Small local bar with an impressive kitchen. One main dish which changes daily—a generous meal for two, with wine, shouldn't top the L15,000 mark. Tends to shut early; closed Sun.

Train Station Buffet; Cannaregio. A good place to fill up cheaply. Open 6am–10pm daily, with self-service buffet meals 11:30am–3pm & 6:30–9:30pm, and restaurant service 11:30am–3pm.

Trattoria Ca' d'Oro/Osteria della Vedova, Calle del Pistor (parallel to the Strada Nova); Castello. Run by the same family for over a century. Mouthwatering selection of *cicheti*, wide selection of wines.

VinoVino, Ponte delle Veste (near La Fenice); San Marco. A wine bar like *Da Codroma*; though more formal and slightly posey. However, the atmosphere improves as the evening passes, and it does stock over 100 wines. 10am–2pm & 5pm–1am; closed Tues.

LATE NIGHT

As noted earlier, there aren't too many places in Venice for a late-night drink; the possibilities are:

Ai Canottieri, All'Anfora, Al Masceron, Al Milion, Corner Pub, Da Codroma, Harry's Bar, Isola Misteriosa, Leon d'Oro, Linea d'Ombra, Paradiso Perduto, Vino Vino.

Cafés, Pasticcerie, and Ice Cream

When **coffee** first appeared in Venice in 1640, imported by the Republic from the Levant, it was treated as a medicine; today it's a drug of which all Venetians need a fix several times a day. (Tea-drinkers will be horrified by the Venetian notion of their favored beverage—in some instances a jug of hot water with a tea-bag lying on the saucer.)

As with bars, if you **sit in a café** you will be charged more, and if you **sit outside** the bill will be even higher. Many **pasticcerie** also serve coffee, but will have at most a few bar-stools; they're all right for a swift caffeination before the next round of church-visiting, but not for a session of postcard writing or a longer recuperative stop. Elbow-room in the city's *pasticcerie* is especially restricted first thing in the morning, as the citizens pile in for a coffee and *cornetto* (croissant). If the women outnumber the men on the breakfast shift, it's because the latter have headed off to a bar to get a bite and the first *ombra* of the day (though you can get pastries or little *pizzette* in many *pasticcerie*).

Strict budgeting is farther jeopardized by Venice's **gelaterie**, where the ice cream comes in forms that you won't have experienced before, unless you're a seasoned traveler in Italy.

General areas to find good cafés include:

Campo Santa Margherita, with *Causin*, an old, slightly pricy *pasticceria* and *gelateria*; *Il Doge*, with home-made ice cream and a large assortment of *granite* (crushed ice flavored with syrups), and *Il Caffè*, which specializes in *spritz*, a mixture of wine, water and a spirit.

Crosera San Pantalon, running just south of San Rocco, which has a number of good cafés.

Campiello Meloni (between S. Polo and S. Aponal), which has a couple of excel-lent *pasticcerie* whose doors remain open on Sundays.

Other streets to investigate are **Calle della Bissa** (behind Campo S. Bartolomeo), **Salizzada San Giovanni Crisostomo**, the **Strada Nova** and its continuations towards the train station, and **Via Garibaldi**. In one way or another, the following specific places stand out from the rest:

Florian, Piazza San Marco. Opened in 1720 by Florian Francesconi, and frescoed and mirrored in a passable pastiche of that period, this has long been the café to be seen in. A simple *cappuccino* will set you back L10,000 if the band's performing and you'll have to take out a mortgage for a cocktail. One room has recently been handed to some contemporary artists to decorate. Closed Wed.

Il Golosone, Salizzada San Lio; Castello. *Pasticceria* and bar with a glorious spread of cakes; does a delicious apple *spremute*. Closed Mon.

Latteria Zorzi (see "Restaurants"). Recommended for its *cioccolata con panna* (hot chocolate with cream) and its selection of *frullati* (milkshakes with fresh fruit juice).

Marchini, Ponte San Maurizio; San Marco. The most delicious and most expensive of Venetian *pasticciere*, where people come on Sunday morning to buy family treats. Indulge at least once.

Nico, Záttere ai Gesuati; Dorsoduro. A high-point of a wander in the area, celebrated for an artery-clogging creation called a *gianduiotto*—ask for one *da passeggio* (to take out) and you'll be given a paper cup with a block of praline ice cream drowned in whipped cream. Closed Thurs.

Paolin, Campo Morosini; San Marco. Thought by many to be the makers of the best ice cream in Venice; certainly their pistachio is amazing, and the outside tables have one of the finest settings in the city. Closed Fri.

Quadri, Piazza San Marco. In the same league as *Florian* price-wise, but not as pretty. Austrian officers patronized it during the occupation, while the natives stuck with *Florian* over the way, and it still has something of the air of being a runner-up in the society stakes. Closed Mon.

Rosa Salva, Campo San Luca, Calle Fiubera and Merceria San Salvador; all San Marco. Venice's premier catering chain, rated for their coffee, but slightly surgical in decor.

Vio, Rio Terrà Toletta; Dorsoduro. More great cakes—one to make for after the Accademia.

Do-it-yourself: Takeouts, Markets, and Shops

The campi, parks and canalside steps make picnicking a particularly pleasant alternative in Venice, and if you're venturing off to the outer islands it's often the only way of fuelling yourself. Supplies are always sold by weight (even bread): order by the *chilo*, *mezzo chilo* (kilo, half kilo) or the *etto* (100g; plural, *etti*). Bear in mind that food shops are generally open 8:30am–1pm and 4–7pm or thereabouts and that the great majority are closed all day Sunday and on Wednesday afternoon. And don't try to picnic in the Piazza—the by-laws against it are strictly enforced.

Takeout pizza is all over the place, though most of it is pretty miserable fare. For the best and widest range of pizzas and pies go to *Cip Ciap* in Calle Mondo Nuovo (near S. Maria Formosa; Castello; closed Thurs). Their spinach and *ricotta* pie is especially tasty and filling, at about L3800 for a large slice; say if you want your food *caldo* (hot) or *fredo* (cold). *Il Golosone* (see "Cafés," above) also sells good pizza slices.

Open-air **markets** for fruit and vegetables are held in various squares every day except Sunday; check out **Santa Maria Formosa**, **Santa Margherita**, **Campiello dell'Anconetta**, **Rio Terrà San Leonardo** and the barge moored by **Campo San Barnaba**. The market of markets however is the one at the **Rialto**, where you can buy everything you need for an impromptu feast—wine, cheese (the two best stalls in the city are here), fruit, salami, vegetables, and bread from nearby bakers or delis. The stalls of the Rialto *Erberia* (fruit & veg), arranged with wonderful color sense, are laden at different times of the year with peaches, peppers, apples, artichokes, fresh herbs and salad leaves nameless in English—look out for the produce labeled *Sant'Erasmo*, which is grown on that island and held by many locals to be the best quality. The Rialto market is open Monday to Saturday 8am–1pm, with a few stalls opening again in the late afternoon; the *Pescheria* (fish market)—of no practical interest to picnickers but a sight not to be missed—is closed on Monday as well.

Virtually every parish has its **alimentari** (delicatessens) and most of them are good; one to single out, though, is *Aliani Gastronomia* (Ruga Vecchia S. Giovanni; San Polo)—scores of cheeses, meats and salads that'll have you drooling as soon as you're through the door.

Best value **local booze** to buy is the series with a brownish imitation-handwritten label and a small twig tied to the bottle's neck—reds, whites, and grappa. A bar that sells **draught Veneto wine to take out** is to be found in deepest Dorsoduro, a few minutes' walk from San Nicolò dei Mendocoli at the northern end of Fondamenta dell'Arziere: *Tocai, Merlot* or *Robosso* for L1400–L1500 a liter (bring your own bottle). *Al Volto* and the *Cantina del Vino* (see "Snacks and Bars") boast comprehensive cellars, and many *alimentari* have an impressive choice of Italian wines—there's a marvelous selection in the one in Salizzada San Rocco .

Alternatively, you could get everything from one of Venice's well-hidden **supermarkets**. Most central is *Su.Ve.*, on the corner of Salizzada San Lio and Calle Mondo Nuovo (Castello); others are on Campo Santa Margherita (Dorsoduro; it's tucked behind the telephone booths as you head for San Barnaba), Rio Terrà Frari (San Polo) and Záttere Ponte Lungo (Dorsoduro). The last is the largest and cheapest. They have similar hours—approximately 8:30am–12:30pm and 3–7:30pm (closed Wed afternoon). Finally, Campo Santa Margherita has a **wholefood** shop, should you crave something fibrous.

Nightlife

Even a generation ago Venice was a night city, with people in the residential areas setting out tables on the street at the flimsiest excuse. Nowadays, with the streets overrun by outsiders, the social life of the Venetians is more of an indoor business—a restaurant meal or a drink with friends might feature in most people's diary for the week, and a conversational stroll is certainly a favorite Venetian pastime, but home entertainment takes up most time and energy. That said, Venice's calendar of special events is pretty impressive. To find out what's on in the way of concerts and films, check *Un Ospite di Venezia*, a free bilingual (Italian/English) magazine available from the tourist office and some hotels—it's produced weekly in peak season, monthly in winter. For news of events outside the mainstream, check the posters.

Music and Theater

Music in Venice, to all intents and purposes, means classical music—rock bands rarely come nearer than Padua. The top-bracket **music venues** are **La Fenice** (Campo S. Fantin; San Marco; ☎5210161; closed Aug) and the **Teatro Goldoni**

(Calle Goldoni; San Marco; ☎5205422; both box offices open 9:30am–12:30pm & 4–6pm). The third-ranking Italian opera house after Milan's *La Scala* and Naples' *San Carlo, La Fenice* isn't quite as expensive as some other such establishments, but it isn't in the international first division any more either. Tickets start at about L15,000, though for the exciting stuff, such as a visit by the Kirov, you've about as much chance of a seat as you have of a private audience with the pope. In addition to the main auditorium, *La Fenice* contains the *Sale Apollinee*, a hall used for concerts of more limited appeal—a recent recital of Messiaen's music, for instance. Music performances at the *Goldoni* are somewhat less frequent than at *La Fenice*; the repertoire here isn't as straitlaced, with a jazz series cropping up on the schedule every now and then.

Classical concerts are also performed at the **Palazzo Prigione Vecchie**, the **Scuola Grande di San Giovanni Evangelista** and the churches of **Santo Stefano**, the **Frari** and the **Pietà**. The last has excellent acoustics and is the most regularly used of the group, but the cheapest seats are in the same range as *La Fenice*'s, which the quality of the concerts doesn't often justify. The state radio service records concerts at the **Palazzo Labia**, to which the public are admitted free of charge, as long as seats are reserved in advance (☎716666).

For most of the year the *Goldoni* specializes in the works of the eponymous writer. Other **theaters** are: the **Malibran** (behind S. Giovanni Crisostomo; Castello; ☎5225339)—mainly dance and concerts; **Del Ridotto** (Calle Vallaresso; San Marco, ☎5222939)—predominantly twentieth-century plays; and **L'Avogaria** (Calle de L'Avogaria; Dorsoduro; ☎5206130l).

Up-beat and down-market from the theater and classical concerts, some **bars** have live music: the main ones are *Paradiso Perduto* (usually jazz), *Ai Canottieri* (hot and sweaty dancing) and *Da Codroma*. They don't charge for entrance, but a mark-up on the drinks pays for the bands.

Cinemas

English-language films are the basic fare for Venice's moviegoers, but virtually every screening is dubbed rather than subtitled. If you fancy brushing up your Italian on a rainy night, the movie theaters are as follows:

Accademia, Calle Corfu (by the Accademia; Dorsoduro; ☎5287706). Mixture of general release and art-house films.

Centrale, Piscina da Frezzeria (east of S. Fantin; San Marco; ☎5228201). *The Venice Experience*, a 45-minute historical travelogue on the city, runs from 9am to 5pm (10pm in Aug); in the evenings it's often a program of blood and guts.

Olimpia, Campo San Gallo (just north of the Piazza; San Marco; ☎5205439). Similar repertoire to the *Accademia*.

Ritz, Calle dei Segretaria (by S. Giuliano; San Marco; ☎5204429). General releases.

Rossini, Calle delle Muneghe (facing church of San Luca; San Marco; ☎5230322). General releases.

The **Venice Film Festival** takes place on the Lido every year in late August–early September. The tourist office will have the festival program a few weeks in advance, as will the two movie theaters where the films are shown—the main **Palazzo del Cinema** (Lungomare G. Marconi; ☎5260188) and the **Astra** (Via Corfu; ☎5260289). Tickets are available for the general public, but you have to go along and line up for them on the day of performance. Outside the festival season, the *Palazzo* and *Astra* are run as ordinary commercial movie theaters.

Other Options

Disco-dancers have only one place to go in central Venice—**El Souk**, in Calle Corfu, two minutes' walk from the Accademia. It's a "Pub American Bar" from 9am to 8pm (closed Sat afternoon and Sun), and a disco from 10pm to 4am (closed Sun). Only those deemed by the doorman to be fit for admission get to pay the entrance charge of L14,000, a fee that includes the price of your first drink. If purple carpets and smoked glass mirrors don't appeal, you'll have to hop over the causeway into Mestre. **Martini** (Campo S. Fantin; San Marco) is more of a nightclub, aimed at the well-heeled (10pm–3:30am; closed Tues & Nov–Jan). There are a couple of discos over on the Lido, both packed with the people who have spent the day on the Lido beaches: **Club 22**, at Lungomare Marconi 22, and **Parco delle Rose**, Gran Viale Santa Maria Elisabetta 56.

If you're feeling wealthy and lucky, and can sport a neatly pressed Armani number, then you could roll along to the **Casino** (3pm–2:30am, sometimes later; entrance L15,000, minimum bet L2000). From October to March it's at the Palazzo Vendramin-Calergi (Cannaregio) on the Canal Grande; in summer it migrates to the Lido, served by a vaporetto that leaves from near the San Marco landing-stage every half hour.

Shopping

Venice's shops are not immediately inviting. It's easy to get the impression that they're polarized at two extremes—geared either to the trinket trade or to expense-account fashion and accessories. The middle ground does exist, however, and it doesn't take too much ferreting around to find it: small work-shops all over the city produce a range of reasonably priced items such as bags and purses, masks, jewelry and decorative papers; unusual prints and books are on sale in a number of shops; and there's even the odd bargain to be picked up amid the antique stalls.

Lace

It's cheaper to buy lace on **Burano** than in the center of Venice, but be warned that the cheapest stuff is machine-made and not from Burano either. The hand-made work is expensive, though not in a way that's disproportionate to the hours and labor that goes into making it (see the "Burano" entry). If you want an inex-pensive example of the work, a little butterfly goes for about L5000. In **Venice** itself, the most impressive shop is *Jesurum* (Ponte Canonica), installed in a converted church at the rear of the Basilica di San Marco.

Glass

As with lace, you're better off going to the main source of production, in this case **Murano**. And as with Burano, finding the outlets is no problem—step off the boat at the Colonna stop and there they are, the most expensive and most pretentious shops to the fore, the rest stretched out beyond. Pseudo-artistic ornaments, extor-tionately expensive tableware and ranks of eye-bruising kitsch make up the bulk of the stock. The farther you wander from the landing-stage, the more likely you are to find nicer pieces (a pair of earrings, for instance, or a millefiore paper-weight), but the Murano showrooms are generally all the same.

Of the central **Venice** showrooms, the more adventurous are: *L'Isola* (Salizzada San Moisè and the Mercerie; both San Marco) and *Venini* (Piazzetta dei Leoncini; San Marco).

Masks

Many of the Venetian masks on sale today are derived from the Carnevale of old: the ones representing characters from the *Commedia dell'Arte* (Pierrot, Harlequin, Columbine) for example, and the classic white half-mask, with a kind of beak over the mouth so the wearer could eat and drink.

Although masks are worn only during the ten days of Carnevale, they are on sale all year round; all are hand-made, though most designs are conveyor-belt stuff which you'll soon recognize. For genuinely crafted examples, go to *Paulo Vasques* (Corte Lucatello, near San Giuliano; San Marco) or *Emile Massaro* (Calle Vitturi, near Campo Morosini; San Marco); the former paints his masks using painstaking traditional techniques, while the latter sells his stuff to retailers all over the city—buy them at his workshop and you'll save the mark-up. For something more funky, go to *Mondonovo* (Rio Terrà Canal, south of Campo S. Margherita; Dorsoduro), a workshop that doubles as a theatrical costumier. Another authentic mask-maker is *Laboratorio Artigiano Maschere* (Barbaria delle Tole, near San Zanipolo; Castello).

Books

Cluvo, next to the university's architecture department (Campo dei Tolentini; San Polo), is unsurprisingly the most comprehensive stockist of books on **architecture.** For the glossiest, weightiest and most expensive **art** books, *Fantoni Libri* (Salizzada S. Luca; San Marco) leads the way, with *Sangiorgio* (Calle Larga XXII Marzo; San Marco) and *Sansovino* (Bacino Orseolo; San Marco) close behind.

For **books about Venice in Italian**, *Filippi Editore Venezia* (Calle della Bissa; San Marco—and Calle del Paradiso; Castello) is a must; the shop also produces a vast range of facsimile editions, including Francesco Sansovino's sixteenth-century guide to the city—the first city guide ever published. *Libreria Serenissima* (Merceria dell'Orologio; San Marco) has an impressive selection of **books on Venice in English** and a good choice of maps. *Libraio a San Barnaba* (Fondamenta Gherardini; Dorsoduro) keeps a good stock of **books in English and French**, though their English titles are obviously a fair bit more expensive than they would be at home.

The best **general bookshop** is *Goldoni* (Calle dei Fabbri; San Marco), which also keeps an array of maps and posters. *Libreria della Toletta* (Sacca della Toletta; Dorsoduro) sells **reduced price books**, mainly in Italian, but some dual language and translations—the place to buy an album of Fulvio Roiter photos or your copy of Lorenzetti's *Venice*. Finally, for **remaindered and second-hand books**, including a number of art-book bargains, check out *Alberto Bertoni* (Rio Terrà degli Assassini; San Marco).

Prints/Posters/Postcards/Paper

The best range of **posters and inexpensive prints** is at *Antonio Porto* (Rio Terrà dei Nomboli; San Polo); *Goldoni* (see "Books") also carries a selection of posters. *Segno Grafico* (Campo S. Fantin; San Marco) is a print workshop and gallery that sells **hand-printed booklets and pamphlets**, many of them related to the history of the city. For reprints of 16–19C topographical engravings of

Venice at very moderate prices, visit the Armenian island of **San Lazzaro** (see *Southern Islands* chapter). Almost next door to *Pietro Gradenigo* (see "Leather," below) is a shop selling scale replicas of gondolas and other Venetian vessels, plus some beautifully drawn boat-builders' plans, good enough to frame.

Postcards are on sale everywhere, though the fund of images isn't as imaginative as it could be. Just inside the Basilica di San Marco there's a stall selling a vast spread of good quality cards of the church and its mosaics, but Venice's museums are a letdown, usually offering a choice of a bare half dozen. For something a little more unusual try *Filippi Editore Venezia* (specializing in old photos of Venice; see "Books"), *Graffiti* (next to the Frari) or *ZWF* (Campiello Meloni; San Polo).

Most of the decorative **paper** on sale comes from Florence or is affiliated to or inspired by Florentine producers, but is none the worse for that. Shops selling these marbled papers, notebooks and so forth are all over the city; larger retailers are to be found in Campo dei Frari (San Polo), Calle della Mandola (San Marco) and Calle del Piovan (San Marco). Purely Venetian work is turned out by *Legatoria Piazzesi* (Campiello della Feltrina, near Santa Maria Zobenigo; San Marco), which uses old wooden blocks to produce some stunning hand-printed papers and cards; they do a nice line in pocket diaries too. *Alberto Valese* (Salizzada S. Samuele and Calle del Teatro; both San Marco) not only produces the most luscious marbled papers in Venice, but also transfers the designs onto silk scarves and a variety of ornaments; *Serigrafia Grafco* (just off the west side of Campo S. Pantalon; San Polo) is worth visiting as well.

Clothes

As you'd expect, many of the top-flight Italian designers—Versace, Missoni, Valentino, Krizia, Zelda—are represented in Venice, most of their outlets being clustered within a street or two of the Piazza. For those with wallets as deep as oil wells, the **Mercerie, Frezzeria**, and the area around **Calle Larga XXII Marzo** are the most fruitful zones. (A favorite shop with the Venetians is *Elizabetta alla Fenice* on Campo San Fantin—a place so pretentious they write their astronomical prices not in figures but in longhand.) If you are hell-bent on getting a classy *firmato* (designer label), the least ruinous way to do it is to call at *Emporio Armani* in Rio Terrà delle Colonne (San Marco), where the clothes are essentially soft-contoured versions of classic Anglo-American casuals; prices are several notches cheaper than the Armani collection proper, and a degree lower than you'll find in Emporio outside Italy, but you could still be looking at half a million lire for a jacket.

For good quality, moderately priced clothes, there's the inevitable *Benetton* and *Stefanel* (both in the Mercerie), and *Coin*, a national department store based in Venice. *Coin*'s Venetian branch specializes in clothing, and is located between the Rialto and San Giovanni Crisostomo. The area **between Campo San Bartolomeo and Santi Apostoli** is well supplied with shops aimed at a young clientele, as is the line of streets running from **Ruga Vecchia San Giovanni to San Polo**, on the other side of the Canal Grande.

More idiosyncratic stuff is sold at *Lespritznuvo* (Campo S. Margherita; Dorsoduro), where they design, make up and decorate their own clothes. *Aldo Strasse* (Campo S. Giustina; Castello) is good for **trendy second-hand clothes** and some new pieces too. You can buy mock gondolier's hats everywhere, but for the real McCoy, as well as the shirts, jackets and pants, go to *Emilio Ceccato* (Sottoportego di Rialto; San Polo).

Shoes and Leather

As far as chic shoes, bags and wallets go, the shops around the **Mercerie** are not as expensive as they might first appear, and sales are a regular occurrence. *Zecchi*, right beside the Torre dell'Orologio, has some of the cheapest high-class leather footwear, and it's worth checking the windows at the other end of the Mercerie and round Sant'Aponal (San Polo). **Velour slippers** in a variety of colors are sold in a number of shoe shops and gift shops; perhaps derived from Commedia dell'Arte costume, they're made at *La Pantofola* (Calle della Mandola; San Marco) and cost around L14,000–L16,000—a bit more than espadrilles, but longer lasting .

If money is no object, go browsing between the Calle dell'Ascensione and the far end of Calle Larga XXII Marzo, where names such as *Vogini*, *Bottega Veneta* and *Delmo* uphold the city's reputation for immaculately produced leather goods. More rugged purses, bags and cases are sold by Pietro Gradenigo, whose one-man workshop is in Calle Seconda Saoneri, between San Polo and the Frari.

Art Materials

Should you want to add your own contribution to the stockpile of visual images of Venice, all the necessary materials can be bought in the city. *Testolino* is the best-known supplier (Fondamenta Orseolo, north of the Piazza), though *Seguso* (Calle dei Fabbri, in the same area) is almost as good. Two other general suppliers are in Campiello di Ca' Zen (north side of the Rio dei Frari; San Polo) and right next to the Accademia. *Pontini* (off Campo Anconetta; Cannaregio) sells stretched and primed canvases, while *Renato Burelli* (Calle Lunga San Barnaba; Dorsoduro) is the place to go for special pigments, media with which to mix them and a range of varnishes. Pigment is also sold on Burano, in a shop on Via Galuppi that has two numbers, 194 and 310; it's recognizable by the old copper pots it sells.

Antiques

Although the antiques shops around **San Maurizio** and **Santa Maria Zobenigo** cater to the wealthier collectors, bargain hunters should be able to pick something up at the **antiques fairs** that crop up throughout the year in Campo San Maurizio, where the stalls groan under the weight of old books, prints, silverware and general bric-a-brac. (The tourist office will be able to tell you if one is due.) The traders in the **San Barnaba** district are also slightly down-market, running the kind of places where you could find a faded wooden cherub or an old picture frame. The **auction house** in the Palazzo Giovanelli, near Santa Fosca (Cannaregio) is good for a browse on their viewing days, too, even if you can't afford to join in the bidding.

Miscellaneous

If you can't be bothered to chase out to the islands to look for glass and lace, or traipse round Venice looking for out-of-the-way shops, try *Venziartigiana* (Calle Larga San Marco), which sets itself up as the showcase for Venice's **craft-workers**. It's by no means fully representative, though, and even those it does represent are better stocked at their own bases.

All manner of small **hand-made gifts** in wood, tapestry and various other materials can be found at *Toti Campizi* (Calle Marcello, off campo S. Marina; Castello). Jigsaw-like wooden objects—musical instruments, palace facades—are sold by *Signor Blum* from their workshop in Calle Lunga San Barnaba (Dorsoduro) and a second shop in Calle della Mandola (San Marco).

Next to the Accademia, on the left as you come down the bridge, is a gallery which sells **jewelry** made out of old Venetian glass, African beads etc; earrings from L9000. Ceramic jewelry can be found at *Al Canale* (Ruga Rialto; San Polo); farther on, in Ruga Ravano, you will find a couple more jewellers selling Indian, African and Middle Eastern work.

Campo Santa Margherita's **herbalist** shop (Dorsoduro) concocts some interesting cosmetics, including an extraordinary vanilla perfume.

Lastly, aficionados of souvenir **kitsch** can have a field day around the main tourist traps, especially the Lista di Spagna (Cannaregio): plastic gondolas set against blurred photos and fixed in illuminated plastic frames; gondolas that play *O Sole Mio*, gondola cigarette-lighters . . . the list is endless.

PART THREE

THE

VENETO

THE VENETO: AN INTRODUCTION

aking its name—as does Venice itself—from the pre-Roman people known as the Veneti, the present-day region of the **Veneto** essentially covers the area that became the core of the Republic's mainland empire. Everywhere in the Veneto you'll find the imprint of Venetian rule. In **Belluno**, right under the crags of the Dolomites, the style of the buildings declares the town's former allegiance. A few kilometers away, the lion of Saint Mark looks over the central square of the hill town of **Feltre**, as it does over the market square of **Verona**, on the Veneto's western edge. On the flatlands of the Po basin (the southern border of the region) and on farming estates all over the Veneto, the elegant **villas** of the Venetian nobility are still standing.

Yet the Veneto is as diverse culturally as it is geographically. The aspects of Verona's urban landscape that make the city so attractive were created long before the expansion of Venice's *terra firma* empire, and in **Padua** (a university seat since the thirteenth century) the civilization of the Renaissance displays a character quite distinct from that which evolved in Venice. Even in **Vicenza**, which reached its present form mainly during its long period of subservience, the very appearance of the streets is proof of a fundamental independence.

Nowadays this is one of Italy's wealthiest regions. Verona, Padua, Vicenza and **Treviso** are all major industrial and commercial centers, while intensive dairies, orchards and vineyards (around Conegliano, for example) have made the Veneto a leading agricultural producer as well.

Much of the Veneto's income is earned by the industrial complex of **Mestre** and **Marghera** (see *Contexts*), the grim conurbation through which all road and rail lines from Venice pass before spreading out over the mainland. It's less a city than an economic life-support system for Venice, and the negative impression you get on your way though is entirely justified. Some people trim their vacation expenses by staying in Mestre's cheaper hotels (Venice's tourist offices will supply addresses), but venturing farther inland is a far more pleasurable cost-cutting exercise.

The administrative region of the Veneto extends right to the Austrian border, taking in the portion of the Dolomites known as the Cadore, the main town of which is **Pieve di Cadore**—Titian's birthplace. Further north still is **Cortina d'Ampezzo**, the swishest ski resort of the eastern Dolomites since it hosted the Winter Olympics in 1956. This whole area offers some of Italy's most sublime landscapes, but the mountains are quite distinct from Venice's immediate hinterland, and cannot really be visited on an excursion from the city. As the purpose of this section of the guide is to reveal the mainland sights and towns that can be seen on a day's excursion from Venice, its northern limit is Belluno.

GETTING AROUND THE VENETO

The Veneto's public transit system will easily get you to almost all the places covered in the following chapters, at generally low cost. In nearly all cases a day-trip from Venice is feasible, though obviously the larger towns need more than a day to do them justice. Only the generalities are given below—fuller details appear at the end of each town entry.

BY TRAIN

For longer distances, **trains** are the cheapest form of public transit in the Veneto. Prices on the Italian State Railroads (*Ferrovie dello Stato* or *FS*) are calculated by the kilometer—for instance, the return journey from Venice to Bassano, a round trip of 122km, costs around L6,000. All the major towns are interconnected: one main line runs from Venice through Treviso and northwards, another through Castelfranco up to Bassano, and a third through Padua, Vicenza and Verona.

There are four types of train: a major inter-city service is known as either a *Rápido* (the fastest) or an *Espresso*; *Diretto* trains stop at most stations, while a *Locale* stops everywhere—slow, but handy for getting to some of the rural villas and other more secluded spots. Supplements are payable on *Rápido* trains; timetables make it clear which services this applies to—if you intend taking a *Rápido*, pay your supplement when you buy your ticket, otherwise you'll have to cough up a far bigger surcharge to the conductor.

As for **rail passes**, *Eurail* gives free travel on the whole *FS* network (though you'll be liable for supplements on the fast trains), and there are two specific Italian passes available: a *Biglietto turistico libera circolazione* (travel-at-will ticket: 8 days, $90; 15 days, $107; 21 days, $125; 30 days $155), valid for free travel on all *FS* trains, including a *Rápido*; and a *Chilométrico* ticket, valid for up to five people at once, giving 3000km worth of free travel on a maximum of twenty separate journeys—cost $95. You can get both these tickets before you leave from *FS* agents in the US. Other **reductions** on normal fares are for families (minimum four people traveling, adults 30 percent discount, kids 65 percent discount), kids (50 percent discount for 4–12 year olds) and for

---

MAIN VENETO TRAIN SERVICES

From Venice to Milan (every 30min; 3hr 30min) via Padua (30min), Vicenza (55min) and Verona (1hr 30min); Treviso (every 30min; 30min); Conegliano (hourly; 50min); Vittório Véneto (3 daily direct, 6 changing at Conegliano; 1–2hr); Feltre (1 daily; 1hr 30min); Castelfranco Véneto (2hr; 50min); Bassano (10 daily; 1hr); Belluno (1 daily, otherwise change at Conegliano; 2hr); Udine (hourly; 2hr); Monsélice (10 daily; 50min); Rovigo (10 daily; 1hr 30min); Florence (hourly; 4hr 30min) via Bologna (2hr); Trieste (hourly; 2hr 10min).

From Padua to Venice (every 30min; 30min); Vicenza (hourly; 25min); Verona (hourly; 50min); Rovigo (10 daily; 30min); Monsélice (hourly; 20min); Bologna (10 daily; 1hr 25min); Bassano (10 daily; 1hr 5min); Belluno (10 daily; 2–3hr) via Feltre (1hr 20min–2hr); Milan (hourly; 2hr 25min).

From Rovigo to Venice (10 daily; 90min) via Monsélice and Padua.

From Monsélice to Venice (10 daily; 50min) via Padua (20min); Montagnana (6 daily; 25min) via Este (10min).

From Vicenza to Venice (every 30min; 55min) via Padua (20min); Milan (every 30min; 2hr) via Verona (30min); Treviso (hourly; 1hr) via Cittadella (30min) and Castelfranco (40min).

From Verona to Venice (every 30min; 1hr 30min) via Vicenza (30min) and Padua (50min); Milan (30min; 1hr 30min); Rome (6 daily; 6hr).

From Treviso to Venice (every 30min; 30min); Vicenza (hourly; 1hr) via Castelfranco and Cittadella; Udine (hourly; 90min).

From Conegliano to Venice (hourly; 50min); Udine (hourly; 1hr 10min); Vittório Véneto (9 daily; 15min), with onward service to Belluno (60–90min from Conegliano).

From Belluno to Calalzo (6 daily; 1hr); Conegliano (8 daily; 60–90min) via Vittório Véneto (45–75min).

Senior Citizens (reductions on production of a Senior Citizen's Rail Card); more information from the Italian State Tourist Office.

The main routes (*Rápido* and *Espresso* trains only) are covered by *FS*'s little national timetable, *Principali Treni*, issued twice yearly and free from most railroad stations, but if you're traveling extensively by train you should pick up the free *FS* leaflets detailing individual lines (readily available from the larger stations) or invest L2600 in a copy of the bi-annual *Tutta Italia* booklet, which gives all the information you'll need. Pay attention to the timetable notes, which may specify the dates between which some services run (*Si effetua dal . . . al . . .*), or whether a service is seasonal (*periódico*).

BY BUS AND COACH

On the whole, **buses and coaches** offer little competition to the trains, being invariably more expensive and generally less frequent. Traveling out from Venice, the only excursion you're likely to do by bus is the trip along the River Brenta. Moving around the mainland, though, there is sometimes no alternative—Ásolo, for instance, has no train connection. Usually the bus station

(*Autostazione*) is close to the train station, and even when the terminal is elsewhere, many services stop at the train station along their route. Tickets have to be bought before getting on board, either from the bus company's office at the station, or from the nearest agent—their name and address is always shown on the timetable at the bus stop. If you're setting off for a remote place, it's always a good idea to buy your ticket for the return leg at the point of departure, as some villages have just a single outlet which might well be closed when you need it. Services are drastically reduced, or non-existent, on Sunday, and note that lots of departures are linked to school requirements—which sometimes means no services during school vacations.

In contrast, **city buses** are always cheap, usually a L500–700 flat fare, and can be a great help to the weary, or if you're staying in accommodation out of town. Again, tickets should be bought before getting on—either from offices at bus terminals and stops, or from *tabacchi* and other shops displaying the company's logo and ticket emblem. Stamp your ticket in the machine on board—inspectors get on board quite regularly.

MAIN VENETO BUS SERVICES

From Venice regular services to Malcontenta, Strà, Padua, Chioggia, Treviso, Marco Polo airport.

From Padua regular services to Venice, Vicenza, Bassano, Ábano Terme and Montegrotto Terme.

From Vicenza to Bassano (hourly; 1hr), via Maróstica (45min), and regular services all over the Veneto.

From Treviso to Padua (every 30min); Ásolo (hourly); Bassano (every 2hr); and very regular services to Venice.

From Belluno frequent *Dolomiti-Bus* services to Cortina d'Ampezzo and rest of eastern Dolomites.

From Bassano to Masèr (every 3hr), Possagno (every 1–2hr), Maróstica (2–3hr) and Ásolo (1–2hr).

BY CAR

Although public transit is adequate for most occasions, there are instances when a **car** is a great convenience. **Car rental** is not cheap, however: in Venice the most reasonable deal on offer from the companies on Piazzale Roma is *Europcar*'s weekend package for L108,000 (unlimited mileage). In larger places such as Verona, Padua, Vicenza and Treviso the car-rental offices congregate around the train station—if you see anything for under L60,000 a day, you've

found a bargain. You'll save money by arranging car rent in conjunction with your flight or holiday—most travel agents or tour operators can provide details. **Gas** is currently around L1500/litre, so take your own car and you're entitled to **gas coupons** (worth 15 percent off) and concessions on the highway tolls; information from the Italian State Tourist Office.

For **documentation** you need a valid driving licence plus an Italian translation (available from the Italian State Tourist Office), and an international green card of insurance. It's compulsory to carry your car documents and passport while you're driving, and you'll be required to present them if you're stopped by the police. **Rules of the road** are straightforward: drive on the right; at junctions, where there's any ambiguity, give precedence to vehicles coming from the right; observe the speed limits (50kph in built-up areas, 110kph on country roads and on motorways during the week, 130kph on highways at weekends); and *don't* drink and drive. If you **break down**, dial ☎116 at the nearest phone and tell the operator where you are, the type of car and your registration number: the nearest office of the *Automobile Club d'Italia (ACI)*, an *AAA* equivalent, will be informed and they'll send someone to help, though it's not a free service. If you need towing anywhere you can count on it costing a fairly substantial amount, and it might be worth joining *ACI* to qualify for their discounted repairs scheme; write to *ACI*, Via Marsala 8, 00185 Rome.

ACCOMMODATION AND INFORMATION

Hitchhiking (*autostop*) can be a thankless way of passing a day. It's only between the major centers that there's much likelihood of a lift, and even then you can be waiting for a long time. Best bet is to stand at an *autostrada* on-ramp; venturing onto the highway itself risks a spot-fine. Needless to say, hitching is not something that women should do on their own.

Although rock-bottom hotel prices are almost unheard of in the affluent Veneto, the cost of accommodation on the mainland is appreciably lower than in Venice itself, and it might be worth your while becoming a vacation commuter in order to keep costs down. Treviso, Padua and Vicenza are the places to concentrate on, and our entries on those cities include advice on staying there. To get the most out of the less accessible sights of the Veneto it makes sense to base yourself for a day or two somewhere other than Venice anyway—perhaps in the northern town of Bassano or in the more central Castelfranco. With these smaller towns as with the cities, accommodation details appear at the end of the entry.

Virtually every town has an **EPT** or **APT** office; where there isn't a branch of either, tourist information is handled by a **Pro Loco**, usually situated close to the center. Their usefulness is variable: some will hand out maps, hotel lists and additional leaflets on special events, whereas others will reply to whatever questions you have but offer next to nothing in the way of printed material. As a general rule, the bigger the town, the better the service, though some smaller places clearly feel they have to try harder. Opening hours tend to follow business hours—if no details are given in the text, assume that the office will be closed from around 12:30pm to around 3pm.

CHAPTER ELEVEN

PADUA AND THE SOUTHERN VENETO

Summer in Venice used to be the season for people to leave the city in great numbers, rather than pour into it as they do today. When the temperature rose, the gentry would make for their country retreats along the **Brenta**, which flows into the lagoon at the nearest point on the mainland to the city. Many of these houses still stand, and the finest of them can be visited easily by taking one of the buses that run along the Brenta from Venice to Padua.

Situated a little under forty kilometers west of Venice, **Padua** is the obvious place to seek a room if the hotels of Venice are reaching capacity. It's only half an hour's train journey away, accommodation is comparatively cheap, and the city's university guarantees a lively social scene. Moreover, Padua itself has plenty of sights to fill a protracted stay. The **Cappella degli Scrovegni**, for instance, with its astonishing fresco cycle by Giotto, or the **Basilica di Sant'Antonio**, a pilgrimage church which contains some of the finest Renaissance sculpture in the Veneto.

Of the small towns to the **south of Padua** the most enticing are **Monsélice**, which has a superbly restored castle, and **Montagnana**, whose medieval town walls have survived in almost pristine form. And if you need a rest from urban pursuits, the green **Colli Euganei** (Euganean Hills) offer a pleasant excursion, while the **Po Delta**'s nature reserves and beaches are the quietest stretches of coastline in the area.

The Brenta

The southernmost of the three main rivers that empty into the Venetian lagoon (the other two are the Sile and Piave), the **Brenta** caused no end of trouble to the earliest settlers on both the mainland and the islands: on the one hand, its frequent flooding made agriculture difficult, and on the other, the silt it dumped into the lagoon played havoc with Venice's water channels. Land reclamation schemes were carried out from the eleventh century, but it was in the fourteenth century that Venice began the large-scale canalization of the Brenta, an intervention which both reinforced the banks of the river and controlled the deposition of its contents in the lagoon. The largest of the artificial channels, *La Cunetta*, which runs from Stra to Chioggia, was finished as recently as 1896, but by the sixteenth century the management of the Brenta was sufficiently advanced for the land along its lower course, from Padua to the river-mouth at Fusina, to become a favored building site for the Venetian aristocracy.

Some of these Venetian **villas** were built as a combination of summer residence and farmhouse—most, however, were intended solely for the former function. From the sixteenth century to the eighteenth the period from mid-June to mid-November was the season of the *villeggiatura*, when the patrician families of Venice would load their best furniture onto barges and set off for the relative coolness of the Brenta. Around one hundred villas are left standing: some are derelict, a large number are still inhabited and a handful are open to the public. Of this last category, two are outstanding—the Villa Fóscari and the Villa Pisani.

The Villa Fóscari

The **Villa Fóscari** at **MALCONTENTA** (sometimes known as the Villa Malcontenta) was designed in 1559 for the brothers Alvise and Niccolò Fóscari by **Palladio**, and is the nearest of his villas to Venice. (Open May–Oct Tues, Sat and first Sun of each month 9am–noon; L8000.) None of Palladio's villas more powerfully evokes the architecture of ancient Rome: the heavily rusticated exterior suggests the masonry of Roman public buildings; the massive Ionic portico alludes to classical temple fronts (which Palladio believed to be derived from domestic architecture); and the two-storey main hall was inspired by the bath complexes of Imperial Rome, as was the three-sectioned arched window (a feature known as a thermal window, from the Roman *thermae*). Palladio was practical as well as erudite: to keep the living quarters well clear of the swampy land, he raised them on a high podium, and to keep building costs down he used the cheapest materials that would do the job—look closely at the columns and you'll see that they're made out of hundreds of bricks in the shape of cake slices. (For more on Palladio's villa designs, see the "Castelfranco" entry.)

The main hall and the rooms leading off it (only some of which are open to the public) were frescoed as soon as the walls were up, by **Battista Franco** and **Giovanni Battista Zelotti**, a colleague of Veronese; their work includes what is said to be a portrait of a women of the Fóscari family who was exiled to the house as punishment for an amorous escapade, and whose consequent misery, according to legend, was the source of the name *Malcontenta*. The reality is more prosaic—the area was known by that name long before the Fóscari arrived, either because of some local discontent over the development of the land, or because of the political *malcontenti* who used to hide out in the nearby salt marshes.

Only two things detract from the pleasure of a trip to the Villa Fóscari—the proximity of the chimneys of Marghera, and the entry fee, which is exorbitant in view of the very limited section of the house that's open.

The Villa Pisani—and the Villa Widmann Fóscari

At **STRA**, virtually on the outskirts of Padua, stands the **Villa Pisani** (or **Nazionale**), an immense country palace that looks more like a product of the *ancien régime* than a house for the Venetian gentry (villa and grounds open Tues–Sun 9am–1:30pm; L3000). The branch of the Pisani family for whom this place was built was an astronomically wealthy dynasty of bankers, based in Venice in the similarly excessive Palazzo Pisani at Santo Stefano (see "West of the Piazza," in Chapter One). When Alvise Pisani was elected doge of Venice in 1735, the family celebrated by commissioning the villa from the Paduan architect **Girolamo Frigimelica**; later on the work was taken over by **F.M. Preti** (see "Castelfranco" for more specimens of his work). By 1760 it was finished—the biggest such residence to be built in Venetian territory during the century. It has appealed to megalomaniacs ever since: Napoleon bought it off the Pisani in 1807 and handed it over to Eugène Beauharnais, his stepson and Viceroy of Italy; and in 1934 it was the place chosen for the first meeting of Mussolini and Hitler.

Entry to the suite of rooms on the main floor of the villa is carefully controlled—you're shepherded round in groups of thirty—and most of what you see is unexciting. The house has been stripped of nearly all its original furnishings, and it's as hard to thrill to the eighteenth-century frescoes of smiling nymphs and smirking satyrs that decorate some of the rooms as to the almost blank walls elsewhere. But then there's the **ballroom**, its ceiling covered with a fresco of *The Apotheosis of the Pisani Family*, the last major piece painted by **G.B. Tiepolo** before his departure for Spain in 1762, at the age of 66. It's a dazzling performance, full of space without being diffuse; if you're trying to figure out what's going on—the Pisani family, accompanied by Venice, are being courted by the Arts, Sciences and Spirits of Peace, while Fame plays a fanfare in praise of the Pisani and the Madonna looks on with appropriate pride. The monochrome frescoes on Roman themes around the musicians' gallery are by Giambattista's son, Giandomenico.

In the **grounds**, the long fish pond ends in front of a stable-block which might be mistaken from a distance for another grand house. Off to the right (as you look away from the villa) is a peculiar belvedere, resembling a chapel with its dome lopped off; and close by there's an impressive maze—unless a blizzard is blowing, it'll be packed with half a dozen busloads of Italian schoolkids.

MAJOR VILLAS OF THE VENETO

0   15 km

1. Villa Fóscari at Malcontenta
2. Villa Pisani at Stra
3. Villa Cornaro at Piombino Dese
4. Villa Emo at Fanzolo
5. Villa Barbaro at Masèr
6. Villa Godi Malinverni & Villa Piovene at Lugo di Vicenza
7. Villa Porto-Colleoni at Thiene
8. Villa Rotonda & Villa Valmarana, outside Vicenza
9. Villa Thiene at Quinto Vicentino
10. Villa Cordellina-Lombardi at Montecchio Maggiore
11. Villa Pisani at Bagnolo
12. Villa Pojana at Pojana Maggiore
13. Villa Badoer at Fratta Polesine

A third villa often features on suggested itineraries of the Brenta: the **Villa Widmann Fóscari** at MIRA PORTE, just after Oriago (April–Sept Tues–Sun 9am–noon & 2–6pm; rest of year 9:30am–noon & 2:30–5pm; closed Mon; L5000). Built in the early eighteenth century and redecorated fifty years or so later, it's probably a delight for admirers of French Rococo style, but for most people it will only demonstrate by contrast how inventive Tiepolo was.

Getting There

During the eighteenth century, the mode of transportation the gentry used for the *villeggiatura* was a capacious and well-padded vessel known as the *Burchiello*. The modern *Burchiello*—as advertised in a dozen tourist ofices—is a tub that looks like a river-going shoebox. It shuttles tourists along the river at L98,000 a shot, making a few pit-stops at selected villas, pausing rather longer for lunch, and finally unloading them at Padua or Venice to catch the bus back to where they started. Lunch and bus ticket are inclusive, you'll be glad to know.

Others can get to **Malcontenta** for L600 by **bus** from Piazzale Roma—they leave every hour, and the trip takes fifteen minutes. On your way back, if the first bus that comes along isn't going to Venice, take it as far as Corso del Popolo in Mestre, then cross the road for a #4 to Piazzale Roma—you can do it on one ticket, as it's valid for an hour.

For **Stra**, the Padua bus (which leaves every half hour, takes 45min and costs L2000), goes right past the door and gives you a good view of dozens of villas on the way. They're particularly thick on the ground from **ORIAGO** onwards (16km out of Venice), the most attractive stretch being centered on the elongated town of **MIRA**, shortly after Oriago. The Villa dei Contarini in Mira was one of Henry III of France's ports of call on his visit of 1574, and Byron wrote part of *Childe Harold* in the Palazzo Fóscarini (now the post office), where he lived from 1817–19.

The *Azienda di Promozione Turistica Riviera del Brenta* produces various leaflets on the villas and hotels of the Brenta, most of them aimed at the sort of tourist who finds the *Burchiello* irresistible; their HQ is at Mira Porte (Via Don Minzoni), but the information office a few yards from the Villa Pisani has most of their stuff, and the tourist office in Venice should supply it too.

Padua

Extensively reconstructed after the damage caused by World War II bombing, and hemmed in by the sprawl which has accompanied its development as the most important economic center of the Veneto, **PADUA** (PADOVA) is not immediately the most alluring city in northern Italy. It is, however, one of the most ancient and culturally one of the richest, with plentiful evidence remaining of its impressive lineage.

Legend has it that Padua was founded in 1185 BC by Antenor of Troy—a story propagated first by the Roman historian Livy (d.18 AD), who was born in a nearby village and spent much of his life here. A Roman municipium from 45 BC, the city thrived until the barbarian onslaughts and the subsequent Longobard invasion at the start of the seventh century. Recovery was slow, but by the middle of the twelfth century, when it became a free commune, Padua was prosperous once again. The university was founded in 1221, and a decade later the city became a place of pilgrimage when **Saint Anthony**, who had arrived in Padua in 1230, died and was buried here.

The appalling **Ezzelino da Romano** occupied Padua for two decades from 1237 (see "Cittadella," in Chapter Thirteen), and then struggles against the **Scaligeri** of Verona lasted until the **Carraresi** (or da Carrara family) established their hold in 1337. Under their domination, Padua's cultural eminence was secured—Giotto, Dante and Petrarch were among those attracted here—but Carraresi territorial ambitions led to conflict with Venice, and in 1405 the city's independence ended with its conquest by the neighboring republic. Though politically nullified, Padua remained an artistic and intellectual center: Donatello and Mantegna both worked

PADUA

here, and in the seventeenth century Galileo researched at the university, where the medical faculty was one of the most ambitious in Europe. With the fall of the Venetian Republic the city passed to Napoleon, who handed it over to the **Austrians**, after whose regime Padua was annexed to Italy 1866.

The City

From the train station, the Corso del Popolo and Corso Garibaldi lead south through a gap in the Renaissance city walls towards the center of the city, passing after a short distance the **Cappella degli Scrovegni** and Museo Civico (summer Tues–Sun 9am–7pm; winter Tues–Sun 9am–5:30pm; joint ticket L5000, groups L2500, students L1000). For many people the **Giotto frescoes** in the Scrovegni are *the* reason for coming to Padua, and the building is frequently full, though the crush is alleviated at crisis periods by a strict time control on large groups.

The chapel was commissioned in 1303 by Enrico Scrovegni in atonement for his father's usury, which was so vicious that Dante allotted him a place in the *Inferno*. (He died screaming "give me the keys to my strong box so no one can get my money" and was denied a Christian burial.) As soon as the walls were built, Giotto was commissioned to cover them with illustrations of the life of Mary, the life of Jesus and the story of the Passion; the finished cycle, arranged in three tightly-knit tiers and painted against a backdrop of saturated blue, is one of the high points in the development of European art.

Although Duccio and Cimabue, the two earliest major figures of Italian painting, had done much to relax the stylized, icon-like conventions of painting, it was in the work of Giotto that the first traces of humanism appeared. The Scrovegni series is a marvelous demonstration of this new attention to the inner nature of the figures depicted—the exchange of looks between the two shepherds in the *Arrival of Joachim* is particularly powerful, as are the *Embrace of Joachim and Anna at the Golden Gate* and the *Visit of Mary to Elizabeth*. On occasion even the buildings and landscape have been manipulated to add to the drama for example in the *Deposition*, where a strong diagonal leads the eye straight to the faces of Jesus and Mary.

Beneath the main pictures are shown the vices and virtues in human (usually female) form, while on the wall above the door is the *Last Judgement*, with rivers of fire leading from God to Hell, and an angel rolling back the painting to remind us that this is an imaginative scene and not an authoritative vision of eternity. Directly above the door is a portrait of Scrovegni presenting the chapel; his tomb is at the far end, behind the altar with its statues by **Giovanni Pisano**.

The **Museo Civico**, formerly the monastery of the Eremitani, is a recently opened home for the civic collection, all of which will soon have completed its transfer from its previous home near the Basilica. There are some marvelous early paintings, the highpoints being a Crucifixion by Giotto that was once in the Scrovegni chapel and a sequence of devils overcoming angels by Guariento. After these, it's a trudge through Etruscan pot-shards, dull Egyptian and Roman works, generally dire nineteenth-century paintings and sculpture, and an assortment of coins, medals and other metalwork. There's also a helpful information desk here, which gives out information on Padua's cultural events.

The Eremitani

The nearby church of the **Eremitani**, built at the turn of the fourteenth century, was almost completely wrecked by an Allied bombing raid in 1944 and has been fastidiously rebuilt (summer 8:15am–noon & 3:30–6:30pm; winter 8:15am–noon & 3:30–5:30pm; Sun & hols generally opens at 9am and closes 30min earlier than weekdays). Photographs to the left of the apse show the extent of the damage, the worst aspect of which was the near total destruction of **Mantegna**'s frescoes of the lives of Saint James and Saint Christopher—the war's severest blow to Italy's artistic heritage.

Produced between 1454 and 1457, when Mantegna was in his mid-twenties, the frescoes were unprecedented in the thoroughness with which they exploited fixed-point perspective—a concept central to Renaissance humanism, with its emphasis on the primacy of individual perception. Furthermore, Mantegna's compositions had to take into account the low viewpoint of the person in the chapel. The extent to which he overcame these complex technical problems can now be assessed only from the fuzzy photographs and the sad fragments preserved in the chapel to the right of the high altar. On the left wall is the *Martyrdom of St James*, put together from fragments found in the rubble; and on the right is the *Martyrdom of St Christopher* which had been removed from the wall before the war.

Towards the Basilica del Santo

The **Porta Altinate**, one of the medieval gates of the city, bears a plaque recording its violent recapture from Ezzelino da Romano on 20 June 1256. More recent military history is recorded in the former residence of Cardinal Pietro Bembo (Via Altinate 59); once the HQ of the Italian Third Army (NE Division) and now the HQ of the army's artillery division, the palace houses the **Museo della Terza Armata** (9am–noon & 3–4:30pm; Sun & hols 10am–noon), a collection of militaria primarily related to World War I.

Continuing past the dull sixteenth-century church of **San Gaetano** and a scattering of fine houses, you come to the church of **Santa Sofia** (9am–noon & 4–6:30pm). It's the oldest church in Padua, going back to the sixth century; most of today's beautiful brick-built structure dates from the twelfth and thirteenth centuries. The apse in particular shows Veneto-Byzantine influence, and is reminiscent of the cathedral at Torcello or Santi Maria e Donato on Murano.

To the south, the church of **San Francesco** (8am–noon & 3–8pm), in the road of the same name, has an unengaging painting by Paolo Veronese; the street leads back into the center of town past the **Tomba di Antenore**, resting place of the city's legendary founder.

Piazza del Santo

A little before Antenor's tomb, Via del Santo leads left to the **Piazza del Santo**, where stalls aim to catch the tourists and the pilgrims in one swoop by selling garishly decorated candles and outsize souvenir rosaries.

The main sight of the piazza is **Donatello**'s monument to the *condottiere* Erasmo da Narni—more generally known as **Gattamelata** (The Honeyed Cat), by virtue of his feline adroitness in battle. He died in 1443 and this monument was raised ten years later, the earliest large bronze sculpture of the Renaissance. It's a direct precursor to Verrocchio's monument to Colleoni in Venice (and Colleoni was under Gattamelata's command for a time), but could hardly be more different: Gattamelata was known for his honesty and dignity, and Donatello has given us an image of comparative sensitivity and restraint, quite unlike Verrocchio's image of power through force. The modelling of the horse makes a double allusion: to the equestrian statue of Marcus Aurelius in Rome, and to the horses of San Marco.

The Basilica di Sant' Antonio (Il Santo)

Within eighteen months of his death in 1231, Saint Anthony had been canonized and his tomb was attracting enough pilgrims to warrant the building of the **Basilica di Sant'Antonio**, or **Il Santo** (summer daily 6:30am–7:45pm; winter 6:30am–7pm). It was not until the start of the fourteenth century that the church reached a state that enabled the saint's body to be placed in the chapel designated for it. The **exterior** is an outlandish mixture, with *campanili* like minarets, Byzantine domes, and Romanesque and Gothic features on the facade and apse.

The **interior** is similarly heterogeneous: the plan up to the transepts being much like that of Italian mendicant churches, whereas the complex ambulatory with radiating chapels is more like the layout of French churches of the period. Saint Anthony's chapel—the **Cappella del Santo**—is in the left transept, plastered with votive photographs of healed limbs, car crashes survived thanks to the saint's intervention, and other offerings irresistible to the voyeur. The chapel's more formal decoration includes a sequence of nine **panels** showing scenes from Saint Anthony's life; carved between 1505 and 1577, they are the most important series of relief sculpture created in sixteenth-century Italy. Reading from the left: Saint Anthony receives his Franciscan habit; a jealous husband stabs his wife, whom the saint later revived; Saint Anthony raises a man from the dead to prove the innocence of his father; he revives a drowned woman (panel by **Sansovino**); he revives a drowned baby (**Sansovino & Minello**); he directs mourners to find the heart of a miser in his coffer (**Tullio Lombardo**); he restores the severed foot of a boy (**Tullio Lombardo**); a heretic throws a glass which miraculously does not break; and a newborn baby tells of the innocence of its mother (**Antonio Lombardo**).

Adjoining the chapel is the **Cappella della Madonna Moro** (named after its fourteenth-century French altar statue), which in turn lets onto the **Cappella del Beato Luca**, where Saint Anthony's body was first placed: its late fourteenth-century frescoes show scenes from the lives of the Apostles Philip and James the Lesser, including a lovely image of Saint James lifting a prison tower to free a prisoner. Back in the aisle, just outside the Cappella del Santo, is Padua's finest work by **Pietro Lombardo**, the monument to Antonio Roselli (1467). More impressive still are the high altar's bronze sculptures and reliefs by **Donatello** (1444–45), the works which introduced Renaissance classicism to Padua. Aggravatingly, they are often inaccessible, though a word with one of the sacristans may get you a closer view. The stylized neo-Gothic frescoes of the apse, choir and presbytery were begun by **Achille Casanova** in 1903, and took about forty years. Trying to imitate Giotto's use of blue, he ended up turning this end of the Basilica into a cavern.

Built onto the farthest point of the ambulatory, the **Cappella del Tesoro** (8am–noon & 2:30–7pm) was designed in the 1690s by **Filippo Parodi** (a pupil of Bernini); its most important relics are from Il Santo himself—his tongue and chin, kept in a head-shaped container.

Most of the back wall of the **Cappella di San Felice** (occupying the right transept) is taken up by a glorious *Crucifixion*, frescoed in the 1370s by **Altichiero da Zevio**. Other things to seek out are the **monuments to Cardinal Pietro Bembo and Alessandro Contarini**, both designed by **Sanmicheli** with a bust by **Danese Cattaneo** (1550s; on the nave's second pair of columns), and the **tomb of Gattamelata** (in the first chapel on the right).

The **cloisters** house the bookshop, toilets and tombs—one of them containing the *interiora* of Thomas Howard, Earl of Surrey and Arundel (1586–1646).

The South Side of the Piazza

To the left as you leave the Basilica are the **Oratorio di San Giorgio** and **Scuola di Santo** (Dec–Jan daily 9am–12:30pm; Feb–March & Oct–Nov 9am–12:30pm & 2:30–4:30pm; April–Sept 8:30am–12:30pm & 2:30–6:30pm; L1000). The **Oratorio** was founded in 1377 as a mortuary chapel, its frescoes by **Altichiero di Zevio** and **Jacopo Avanzi** being completed soon after. The *Crucifixion* on the altar wall shows the souls of the two thieves being received, one by a devil and one by an angel; the scenes from the life of Saint George on the left wall show not just the customary dragon-slaying, but also the saint being released by angels from a wheel of torture; and the opposite wall is adorned with the wonderfully titled *St Lucy Remains Immoveable at an Attempt to Drag Her with the Help of Oxen to a House of Ill Repute.*

The **Scuola di San Antonio**, a confraternity run on the same lines as the scuole of Venice, was founded soon after Anthony's canonization, though this building dates only goes back as far as the early fifteenth century. The ground floor is still used for religious purposes, while upstairs is maintained pretty much as it would have looked in the sixteenth century, with its fine ceiling and paintings dating mainly from 1509–1515. Four of the pictues are said to be by **Titian**— *The Jealous Husband Stabbing his Wife*, with an almost insignificant intervention by Il Santo in the background; *St Anthony Reattaching the Severed Foot of a Young Man*; *The Distribution of Blessed Bread*; and the *Newborn Infant Defends the Honor of its Mother*. If any of these are genuine, they would be the earliest known extant works by him. The *Miser's Heart Found in his Treasure Chest* is attributed to Titian's brother, **Francesco Vecellio**. Some of the other paintings are charming oddities, such as the *Mule Worshipping the Sacrament* and *St Anthony Confronting Ezzelino da Romano*—a perilous diplomatic exercise which may or may not have happened.

Next door to the Scuola, the **Pinacotecca Civica** (Tues–Sat 9am–1pm, Sun 9:30am–1pm; L2000, free Sun) is a wide-ranging assembly of art from the Veneto, with works by Bellini, Titian, Tintoretto, Palma il Giovane and Canova. These are in the process of being transplanted to a new home next to the Scrovegni chapel, a move projected for completion in late 1990.

A good way to relax from all this art is to stroll round the corner to the **Orto Botanico**, the oldest botanic gardens in Europe (Nov–Feb 9am–1pm, closed Sun & hols; March–April & Sept 16–Oct 31 9am–1pm, Sun & hols 9:30am–1pm; May 1–Sept 15 Mon–Fri 9am–1pm & 3–6pm, Sat & Sun 9am–1pm; L3000, reductions L1500). Planted in 1545 by the university's medical faculty as a collection of medicinal herbs, the gardens are laid out much as they were originally, and the specimens on show haven't changed too much either. Goethe came here in 1786 to see a palm tree that had been planted in 1585; the selfsame tree still stands.

The Prato della Valle and Santa Giustina.

A little to the south sprawls the **Prato della Valle**, claimed to be the largest town square in Italy; it's a cheerless area, ringed by over-wide roads, and even the summer funfair does little to make it jollier. The greenery in the center follows the oval plan of the extinct Roman amphitheater; the two rings of statues commemorate 78 worthy Paduans, both native and honorary.

One side is fronted by the sixteenth-century **Basilica di Santa Giustina**—at 120m long, one of the world's largest churches (Mon–Sat 7:30am–noon & 3:30–7:30pm, Sun & hols 7am–1pm & 3:30–7:30pm). A pair of fifteenth-century griffins, one holding a knight and the other a lion, are the only notable adornments to the plain brick facade; the freezing interior (scarves are worn by the Benedictine monks even when it's warm outside) is offputtingly clinical, with little of interest except a huge *Martyrdom of St Justina* by **Paolo Veronese** (in the apse), some highly proficient carving on the choir stalls, and the sarcophagus which once contained the relics of Luke the Evangelist (apse of left transept).

Far more appealing are the vestiges of the church's earlier incarnations. In the right transept a stone arch opens onto the **Martyrs' Corridor**, named after a well containing martyrs' bones, now part of the catacombs below the corridor (ask sacristan for access). This part of the building is a composite of fifth- to twelfth-century architectural fragments, and leads to the **Sacellum di Santa Maria e San Prosdocimo**, burial place of Saint Prosdocimus. He was the first bishop of Padua back in the fourth century, when the church was founded and is depicted here on a fifth-century panel. The fifteenth-century **old choir** is reached by a chain of corridors from the left-hand chapel of the right transept; the choir stalls are inset with splendid marquetry panels, and the **sacristy** beyond has an amusing painting of *St Marus Rescuing St Placid from a Lake* by someone called Toeput.

To the University

Via Umberto leads towards the **university**: a left turn at the canal takes you to the leafy Piazza del Castello (where Ezzelino da Romano's fortress now serves as a prison), while the continuation northwards passes the Gothic church of Santa Maria dei Servi before reaching the university's main building, the **Palazzo del Bò** (tours Mon–Fri 9:30am, 11:30am, 3:30pm & 5:30pm, Sat 9:30am & 11:30am; closed afternoons in Aug). The name translates as "of the Ox," after an inn that used to stand here.

Established in September 1221, the University of Padua is older than any other in Italy except that of Bologna, and the coats of arms that encrust the courtyard and Great Hall attest to the social and intellectual rank of its alumni. The first permanent **anatomy theater** was built here in 1594, a facility that doubtless greatly helped William Harvey, who went on to develop the theory of blood circulation after taking his degree here in 1602. Galileo taught physics here from 1592 to 1610, declaiming from a lectern that is still on show. And in 1678 Elena Lucrezia Corner Piscopia became the first woman to collect a university degree when she was awarded her doctorate in philosophy here—there's a statue of her in the courtyard.

The Central Squares

The area north and west of the university forms the hub of the city. A little way up from the university, on the left, is the Neoclassical **Caffè Pedrocchi**, which used to be the city's main intellectual salon; it's no longer that, but it does have a multiplicity of functions—chic café, concert hall and conference center.

The **Piazza delle Frutta** and **Piazza delle Erbe**, the sites of Padua's daily markets, are lined by bars, restaurants and shops. Separating them is the extraordinary **Palazzo della Ragione**, or **Salone** as it is more commonly known (Tues–Sun 9:30am–12:30pm & 3:30–7:30pm; L2000; entrance by right-hand staircase, towards the Municipio). At the time of its construction in the 1210s this vast hall was the largest room to have been built on top of another storey. Its decoration would once have been as astounding as its size, but the original frescoes by

Giotto and his assistants were destroyed by fire in 1420, though some by **Giustio de'Menabuoi** have survived; most of the extant frescoes are by **Nicola Miretto** (1425–1440). Mainly used as the city council's assembly hall, it was also a place where Padua's citizens could plead for justice—hence the appellation *della Ragione*, meaning "of reason." The black stone to the right inside the door, called the *pietra del vituperio* (stone of insults), also played a part in the judicial system: Thomas Coryat recorded that a bankrupt person could dissolve his debts (within certain limits) by sitting on it "with his naked buttocks three times in some public assembly." The gigantic wooden horse with disproportionately gigantic gonads is modeled on Donatello's *Gattamelata*, and was made for a joust in 1466.

Both the Piazza delle Frutta and the Piazza delle Erbe have some attractive buildings around them, as does the **Piazza dei Signori**, which lies a little to the west. At one end of the piazza, beyond the Lombard **Loggia della Gran Guardia** (c:1500) is the **Palazzo del Capitano**, the sixteenth-century headquarters of the city's Venetian military commander, which incorporates the early fifteenth-century **Torre dell'Orologio**, a structure that predates even Venice's clock-tower. At the end of the Corte Capitaniato, beyond the Torre, is the university's arts faculty, the **Liviano**; the frescoes in its fourteenth-century **Sala dei Giganti** (upstairs) include a portrait of Petrarch (Sept–July Sat 3–6pm).

North to the Carmine

The road north of the Piazza del Capitaniato runs straight up to the *Teatro Dante* (box office open 8:30am–1:15pm; ☎049/42891), to the east of which stands the church of **San Nicolò** (8am–noon & 4–7pm)—basically an altered thirteenth-century building, though it retains an eleventh-century chapel. The nearby **Scuola di San Rocco** is now principally a venue for art exhibitions.

The **Ponte Molino**, at the northern end of Via Dante, carries a plaque record-ing the fact that Galileo carried out observations from the tower. On the other side of the bridge are the **Carmine** church and its scuola (daily 8am–noon & 4–8pm); neither is desperately exciting, but the latter has some pleasing fifteenth-century frescoes (ask the church sacristan for access).

The Duomo and Baptistery

Close by is Padua's **Duomo** (daily 7am–noon & 4–7:30pm), an unlovely church whose architect cribbed his design from drawings by Michelangelo; the adjacent Romanesque **Baptistery**, though, is one of the unproclaimed delights of Padua (April–Sept Mon–Sat 9:30am–12:30pm & 3–6pm; Oct–March Mon–Sat 9:30am–noon & 2:30–5:30pm; Sun & hols 9:30am–noon all year; L2000). Built by the Carraresi in the thirteenth century, it's lined with frescoes by **Giusto de'Menabuoi** (c.1376), a cycle that makes a fascinating comparison with Giotto's in the Cappella degli Scrovegni. The influence of Giotto is plain, but in striving for greater naturalism Giusto has lost Giotto's monumentality and made some of his figures awkward and unconvincing. Yet many of the scenes are delightful—the *Marriage at Cana*, for instance—and the vibrancy of their colors, coupled with the size and relative quiet of the building, make the visit memorable. The polyptych **altarpiece**, also by Menabuoi, was stolen in 1972 but quickly recov-ered, minus some of the wooden framework. Don't overlook the **sepulcher of Finza Buzzaccharini**, one of the Carrara family's most assiduous artistic patrons; she's shown on the front being presented to the Virgin by John the Baptist.

Practicalities

A few years ago it was infinitely simpler to find an inexpensive room in Padua than in Venice; it's still the case that the average cost is lower, but availability can be a problem as more and more people use Padua as a base from which to visit its over-crowded neighbor. If you're visiting in high season, be prepared for a protracted search, but don't despair—Padua has thirty one-stars altogether. As in any university city, there's plenty of choice when it comes to unpretentious bars and restaurants, and the student population guarantees a pretty active after-dark scene.

The main **APT** is at the train station (Mon–Sat 8am–8pm, Sun 8am–noon; ☎049/8752077), with another branch at the coach station. Other useful addresses are: *Associazione Turistica Giovanile*, Via S. Biagio 28 (☎049/8750794), *Centro Turistico Giovanile*, Via A. Aleardi 30 (☎049/8752219) and the two offices of *Centro Turistico Studentesco*, Via S. Sofia 94 (☎049/26066) and Via Zabarella 84 (☎049/42843).

The central **post office** is at Corso Garibaldi 5 (Mon–Fri 8am–8pm, Sat 8am–noon) For **telephones**, best are the 24-hour *ASST* booths at Corso Garibaldi 7; alternatively there's the *SIP* office by the Caffè Pedrocchi (8am–9:30pm).

Padua's **markets** are a treat for the bargain-hunter and picnic-shopper alike. General markets are held every morning in Piazza delle Erbe, Piazza delle Frutta, Piazza dei Signori and Piazza Capitaniato. Other regular ones are held in Piazzale Azzurri d'Italia (Tues morning), Piazzale Cuoco-Guizza (Wed morning), Via Bajardi-Mortise (Fri morning) and Prato della Valle (all Sat).

Accommodation

The tourist offices have long lists of one-star hotels, with singles from L18,000 and doubles from L29,500 (without shower). A spacious, clean and friendly place is the *Albergo Pace*, near the Piazza della Frutta at Via Papafava 3 (☎049/8751566; doubles L30,000), and the centrally located *Verdi*, Via Dondi dell'Orologio 7 (☎049/663450) is in the same price range. Averaging at around L10,000 more expensive, as most of its rooms have showers, is the *Bellevue*, off the Prato della Valle at Via L. Belludi 11 (☎049/30434); it has a peaceful courtyard and well-tended rooms. All doubles have a bathroom in the similarly priced *Al Santo*, Via del Santo 147 (☎049/8752131), right by the Basilica. A couple of two-stars can be recommended: the large and efficiently run *Al Cason*, a few minutes from the station at Via Fra Paolo Sarpi 40 (☎049/662636), and the pleasant *Sant'Antonio*, not far from the Ponte Molino at Via San Fermo 118 (☎049/8751393); the latter has doubles from L42,000 to L68,000, but the former has them only at the upper range. If there's no space in any of these, try the area around the Piazza del Santo.

Budget alternatives are the two "holiday houses," which offer student-type rooms in the summer: *Antonianum*, Via Donatello 24 (☎049/651444; L12,000 per person; July 15–Sept 30) and *Missionary Verbiti*, Via Forcellini 172 (☎049/754411; July–Sept). **Women** looking for board and lodging in return for hospital assistance could try *Casa A. Angela Merici*, Via Falloppio 19 (☎049/39039) or *Instituto Missionarie Laiche*, Via Ospedale 69 (☎049/36833).

The **youth hostel** at Via A. Aleardi 30, a kilometer from the Basilica (☎049/8752219), is perfectly adequate and costs L11000 per night, including breakfast. The nearest **campground** is in Montegrotto Terme, Strada Romana Aponese 104 (☎049/793400; frequent trains from Padua take around 15min); a very upmarket site, it boasts not merely a swimming pool but thermal baths too.

Three national farm-workers' organizations promote **farm vacations** in the region. They are non-profit-making bodies, aiming to improve farm incomes while promoting protection of the environment and rural heritage. Offices to contact are: *Agritourist*, c/o Unione Provinciale Agricoltori, Via Martieri della Liberta 9 (☎049/35137); *Terra Nostra*, c/o Federazione Provinciale Coltivatori Diretti, Piazza Stazione 1 (☎049/8750366); and *Turismo Verde*, c/o Confcoltivatori, Via Scrovegni 2/a (☎049/32899).

Food and Drink

Padua's student population ensures that the city's **bars** have far longer opening hours than are common in Venice—many don't close until 2am—and that new places spring up as often as established ones revamp their image. Currently trendy are *Alla Ventura*, Via SS. Martino e Solferino or *Al Coccodrillo*, Riviera S. Benedetto 154. For something a bit more hip, try the devil's grotto ambience of *Lucifer Young*, in Via Altinate.

Catering for the midday stampede of ravenous students, Padua's bars generally produce weightier **snacks** than the routine *tremezzini*—slabs of pizza and sandwiches vast enough to satisfy a glutton are standard. A good variety of stand-up meals is offered at the *rosticceria* in Via Daniele Manin (daily 8:30am–1:30pm & 4–8:30pm), but for a more relaxed session at only slightly greater expense, one of the best cheap **restaurants** is *Al Traguardo*, Piazza Petrarca (closed Tues). Other places to check out include: *Alla Chiesetta*, Via Eremitani 16; *Da Giovanni*, Via De Cristoforis 1; *Evan's*, Via B. Pellegrino 21; *All'Anfora*, Via N. Tommaseo 13; *Self-Service Dopolavoro Ferroviaro*, Via J. d'Avanzo 7; *Vecia Padova*, Via Arco Valaresso 20; *7 Teste*, Via C. Battisti 44; and *Al Pero*, Via S. Lucia.

Nightlife and Entertainment

Being a major university city, Padua has a nightlife which fluctuates in synch with the academic year; check the posters up around the city, and particularly around the university, for details of music, theater and such like. Of the local newspapers, the most comprehensive for listings is *La Mattina*. During the summer vacation things tend to be a little sleepy.

There are eighteen **movie theaters** in Padua: check the local papers for listings. Look out for the *Associazione Cinemauno*, a club which screens art-house films in the *Esperia* cinema, Via Chiesanuova 112 (☎049/8714746).

Padua's half dozen regular **discos** are all fairly low-octane places: liveliest are *Ippopotamus*, Via Savonarola 149, and the flashier *Extra Extra*, Via Ciamician.

Transportation

Trains arrive every 30min from **Venice** (30min), hourly from **Vicenza** (25min), approximately hourly from **Verona** (50min), and every one or two hours from **Rovigo** (30min), **Bologna** (1hr 25min), and **Bassano del Grappa** (1hr 5min). There's also a through service to **Milan**, clustered in the early morning and through the afternoon and early evening (2hr 25min). The rail information office is open daily from 7am to 6:30pm (☎049/8751800).

The **bus station** is a few hundred yards from the train station at Piazzale Boschetti. **Local buses** for the city and nearby towns such as **Ábano** and **Montegrotto** leave outside the train station (though trains go to these two as well).

Padua's small **airport**, east of the city on Via Sorio, handles a few charters and domestic flights; bus links to the train station leave every fifteen minutes.

If you're looking for a long-distance **ride**, or can offer a place in your car, contact *Servizio Autostop*, c/o Associazione Studenti Universitari di Padova, Via Zabarella 19 (☎049/657730).

The Colli Euganei

A few kilometers to the southwest of Padua the **Colli Euganei** (Euganean Hills) rise abruptly out of the plains, their slopes patched with vineyards between scattered villages, villas and churches. Between Padua and the hills lie the spa towns of ÁBANO TERME and MONTEGROTTO TERME, which for much of the year are crowded with people looking for cures or beauty treatment from the radioactive waters and mud baths. It's been like this for centuries, as the names of the towns indicates: *Ábano* comes from Aponeus, a Roman god of healing, while *Montegrotto* is said to derive from "mons aegratorum," meaning "mountain of the infirm." Largely composed of big and expensive modern hotels, these really are places to avoid unless you're hell-bent on trying to poach yourself in the hot springs—the cruellest one bubbles away at 87°C.

A car is a great advantage for exploring the Colli Euganei proper, as buses are few and far between, even to somewhere reasonably popular such as Arquà Petrarca (see below). The **villas** of the region are its major architectural attractions, but many of them remain in private hands and can only be viewed from a distance. An exception is the **Villa Barbarigo**, at VALSANZIBIO, which is famous for its extraordinary gardens; laid out in 1699, they feature a maze and fantastical Baroque gateways (March 15–Oct 31 Tues–Sat 10am–noon & 2–7pm; Sun 2–7pm).

While touring the region, look out for the local wines with their own DOC seal: a red circle round an image of Donatello's *Gattamelata*. The range includes a Pinot Bianco and Tocai Italico (whites), a Cabernet and Merlot (reds), and a sparkling Moscato.

Arquà Petrarca

The gem of the Colli Euganei is the medieval village of **ARQUA PETRARCA**, most easily reached by bus from Este or Monsélice. The Carrara family gave the poet **Francesco Petrarca** (Petrarch) a piece of land here on which to realize his dream of a "delightful house surrounded by an olive grove and a vineyard." He spent the last summers of his life (1369–74) in his idyllic home, and this is where he died. Not only does the **house** still stand, but his desk and chair are still intact, as are various parts of the original fabric of the interior—though the frescoes, illustrating his works, were retouched in the seventeenth century. (April–Sept 9:30am–12:30pm & 3:30–7:30pm, Sun & hols 3–7pm; Oct–March 9:30am–12:30pm & 1:30–4:30pm, Sun & hols 10am–4pm; closed Mon, New Year, Christmas & Easter.) Petrarch's sarcophagus is in the center of the village, with one epitaph penned by him and another by his son-in-law, who placed it here. The church of **Santa Maria** (founded in the tenth century, altered in the sixteenth) and the **Oratorio della Santa Trinità**, farther down the hill, both have interesting fresco fragments.

Monsélice

In earlier times **MONSÉLICE** was perched on the pimple of volcanic rock round the foot of which it now winds. Five concentric walls that then protected it, though all that remains of them and their towers (thanks to nineteenth-century planning) is a small section of the outer ring and a citadel right on the hill's crest. The remnants make a powerful impression though, and the town possesses another fortress that is the equal of any in the Veneto.

From the train station, the route to the center of town crosses the Canale Bisato, from whose bridge you can look back to the **Villa Pisani** (sometimes open for exhibitions), which was a kind of stopover for the Pisani family as they traveled by water from Venice to their estates in Montagnana. The fragmentary town wall leads to the **Torre Civica**, built by Ezzelino da Romano in 1244 and

MONSÉLICE

To Padua

Train Station

Villa Pisani

City Walls

Rocca

S. Paolo

Ca'Marcello

Exedra

Villa Duodo

Loggetta

PIAZZA MAZZINI

Torre Civica

San Giorgio

Villa Nani

VIA SETTE CHIESE

VIA DEL SANTUARIO

Duomo Vecchio

PIAZZA OSSICELLA

VIA ROMA

VIA C. BATTISTI

VIA SAN STEFANO

PIAZZA S. MARCO

VIA S. LUIGI

San Martino

VIA PELLEGRINO

San Stefano

Villa Tortorini

Ca'Bertana

VIA GARIBALDI

Duomo Nuovo

VIA S. GIACOMO

Convento di San Giacomo

To Rovigo

repaired in 1504. Facing the Torre Civica across Piazza Mazzini, just beyond the wall, is the **Loggetta**, a seventeenth-century addition to the **Palazzo del Monte di Pietà**, the facade of which is on the road leading away from the square.

This road bends round and up the hill to the Castello di Ezzelino, or **Ca' Marcello** as it is more often known. (Guided tours only. April–Sept Tues, Thurs & Sat 9am, 10:30am, 3:30pm & 5pm, Sun 9am & 10:30am; Oct–Nov same weekdays 9am, 10:30am, 2:30pm & 4pm, Sun same hours; L3000.) Dating back to the eleventh century, the house was expanded in the thirteenth century by Ezzelino, who added the square tower across the courtyard (the coat of arms was appended after the town came under Venetian rule in 1405). The interior was altered by the Carraresi in the fourteenth century, and linking the two main sections is a fifteenth-century bit added by the Marcello family; a library (sixteenth century) and family chapel (eighteenth century) were the only later changes. The castle's immaculate appearance is down to **Count Vittorio Cini**, who inherited the derelict building after it had been in the tender care of the Italian army during World War I, and sank a fortune into restoring it and furnishing each section in the appropriate style.

The tour begins in the **armory**, three rooms of weaponry occupying the ground floor of Ezzelino's tower. Up from here are the **Marcello family apartments**, an adaption of part of Ezzelino's tower, furnished in sixteenth- and seventeenth-century fashion. The family restyled the **courtyard** in the seventeenth century—dripping with plants and with a well-head in the center, it looks like a Zeffirelli film set. Up the ramp, a gate leads to the upper story of the Marcello building, the **anteroom** of which was added to the external wall of Ezzelino's palace and retains the original windows as internal features. The **great hall** was formed by the Carraresi; its fireplace was originally from Ferrara, while the tapestries are from Brussels. The old part of the castle is quite domestic in feel: look for the fourteenth-century painted ceiling in the **Sala del Casteletto**. On the ground floor is the **kitchen**, set out with fifteenth-century furniture and copper plates up to 700 years old. The top part of this section contains the **council hall**, with delicate frescoes and fourteenth-century seating. The library, now minus its books, is used by the University of Padua and others as a conference room.

Continuing up the hill you see on the left the white, featureless **Palazzo Nani**: much more interesting than the palace itself are its steps up the garden (visible through the gate), flanked by mock Roman sculptures and leading to an imitation Roman temple.

The **Duomo Vecchio** is the next stop: fourteenth-century fresco fragments and a Romano-Gothic polyptych on the high altar are its principal attractions. Just beyond the Duomo a gateway guarded by two Venetian lions gives onto the *Via Sette Chiese*, a private road leading up to the **Villa Duodo** (grounds open Nov–Feb daily 9am–12:30pm & 1:30–7pm; March–May & Sept–Oct 8am–noon & 1:30–7pm; June–Aug 7am–12:30pm & 3:30–8pm). The seven churches of the road's name are a domesticated version of the seven pilgrimage churches of Rome, arranged as a line of six chapels leading up to the church of **San Giorgio** at the top. Sinners could earn pardon for their misdemeanours by praying their penitential way up the hill to San Giorgio, where rows of martyred saints are arranged in wood and glass cabinets not unlike old bookcases. The chapels, church, triumphal arch and the main part of the villa were all designed in the late sixteenth century by **Vincenzo Scamozzi**. Now an international center for the study of hydrology, the villa was commissioned by the son of Francesco Duodo, a hero of the battle of Lepanto; the land was donated by the Venetian state in thanks for services rendered.

It's not possible to go up the steps to the **Rocca**—Ezzelino's citadel right at the summit—as the area is now a nature reserve where rare birds breed.

An alley running round the back of the Duomo leads back to the center; the most interesting building you'll pass on the descent is the Gothic **Ca' Bertana** in Via M. Carron, which has elegant fourteenth-century windows. There's no need to traipse over to the **Duomo Nuovo**—you'll have seen as much as you need to from the walk up the hill: its only remarkable aspect is its size.

Practicalities

For **information**, the **Pro Loco** is in the Loggetta in Piazza Mazzini (Mon–Sat 8:30am–12:30pm & 5–8pm). Best option for **eating** is the *Caffè Grand Italia* in Piazza Mazzini (closed Sun); the little bar opposite the Ca' Marcello does food too (closed Mon). There's also a luscious *pasticceria* in Via Pellegrino (closed Tues).

Situated on a fork in the rail network and a little distance from a freeway, Monsélice is easily accessible. **Trains** from **Padua** run hourly and take twenty minutes; from **Venice** the service is equally regular, taking fifty minutes.

Este

If you're dependent on public transit, just about the best base from which to roam around the Colli Euganei is the ceramics-producing town of **ESTE**, on the southern edge of the outcrop. Sporadic buses run up into the hills from here and the central administration for all the *Pro Loco* offices of the Colli Eugenei is in the Piazza Maggiore (☎0429/3635).

From the train station a road runs straight to the central Piazza Maggiore, passing the blank-faced **Basilica di Santa Maria delle Grazie** (with a fourteenth-century Byzantine *Madonna*) and the Romanesque brick church of **San Martino**. The nearest thing to an alluring building in the Piazza itself is the tatty thirteenth-century home of the *Societa Gabinetto di Lettura*, a cultural organization and archive.

Turning to the right out of the Piazza you come face to face with the walls of the ruined **Castello dei Carraresi**, a fortress founded by the Este dynasty and rebuilt by the Carraresi in 1340. Material salvaged from the walls was used in the construction of the sixteenth-century palace that now houses the **Museo Nazionale Atestino** (April–Sept Tues–Sun 9am–1pm & 3–7pm; closes 6pm rest of year; L2000). The Veneto's outstanding collection of pre-Roman artifacts is installed on the upper floor (burial finds, Bronze Age tools and Iron Age pots), while much of the ground floor is given over to Roman remains. (Roman sites are still being excavated in the western part of the town.) The room devoted to medieval pieces includes a *Madonna and Child* by **Cima** which was once stolen from the church of Santa Maria della Consolazione and is now here for safe keeping. There's also a display of local pottery, a craft that Este has been famous for since before the Renaissance. The castle walls now enclose public gardens—useful on hot summer afternoons when everything is closed.

The privately-owned **Villa de Kunkler**, behind the castle, was the poet **Byron**'s residence in 1817–18, a stay commemorated by a plaque on the villa's wall. The house actually played a greater part in Shelley's life than Byron's—his daughter Clara fell ill while staying here, and died as a result of being carried by her father on an overnight gallop to see a doctor in Venice. When the Shelleys returned here a few days later, Percy wrote his poem of mourning for past splendor, "Lines Written Among the Euganean Hills."

Leading out of the Piazza Maggiore away from the castle, Via Matteotti passes under the **Torre Civica**, a restrained Baroque clock tower built on the site of a much earlier defensive tower. Over the river there's **Santa Maria Consolazione**, a homey church containing nothing of special interest since its Cima painting went to the museum. Turn right instead of going through the tower and you come to the dull sixteenth-century church of San Francesco, beyond which (in the *Quartiere Augusteo*) is the main Roman archaeological site in Este. The **Duomo** (turn right down Via Garibaldi) was rebuilt between between 1690 and 1708 after an earthquake, the oval plan of its Baroque interior anticipating the design of the Pietà in Venice by several decades. The only painting of note is the huge altarpiece of *St Thecla* by **G.B. Tiepolo**, and even that's not one of his best—maybe because it's set in a scene of pestilence and death, rather than one of his happier, light-filled heavens.

Practicalities

Este's **Pro Loco** is in the disused church of San Rocco (Mon–Sat 9am–noon & 4–6pm). The best one-star **hotel** in town is the *Leon d'Oro*, Viale Fiume 20 (☎0429/2955; singles from L14,000, doubles from L28,000); a good two-star hotel is *Beatrice d'Este*, Via Rimembranze 1 (☎0429/3681; singles L26,000, doubles L42,000). For **food**, try *Al Gambrero*, Via d'Azeglio 6 (closed Tues) or *Da Piero Ceschi*, Piazza Trento 16; both the above hotels have restaurants too. If you fancy some more energetic exploration, the second-hand **bicycle shop** in Via I. Alessi may be prepared to negotiate over renting machines.

To get to Este, change **trains** at **Monsélice**; connections usually involve only a twenty-minute wait, and the journey takes just eight minutes.

Montagnana

The pride of **MONTAGNANA** is its **medieval city walls**, raised by the ubiquitous Ezzelino da Romano after he had virtually flattened the town in 1242. They were later strengthened by the Carraresi as Padua's first line of defense against the Scaligeri to the west. It was not until the Wars of the League of Cambrai in the early sixteenth century that the battlements were called upon to fulfil their function, and when the hour came they were found wanting—controlled by the Venetians at the start of hostilities, Montagnana changed hands no fewer than thirteen times in the course of the war. After that the walls were not used again. With a circumference of nearly two kilometers and twenty-four polygonal towers spaced at regular intervals, these are among the best preserved medieval fortifications in the country, and the relatively sparse development around their perimeter makes them all the more impressive. (Appropriately enough, the town is the home of the *Instituto Internazionale dei Castelli*, a center for historical research on military architecture.)

Gates pierce the walls at the cardinal points of the compass, the entrances to the east and west being farther reinforced by fortresses. The **eastern** gate (Porta Padova) is protected by the **Castello di San Zeno**, built by Ezzelino in 1242, with a watchtower to survey the road to Padua. Nearby, the **Museo Civico e Archeologico** displays objects uncovered around the town (Tues–Fri 10am–noon

& 4–6pm; Sat 9am–noon & 3–6pm; Sun 4–7pm; L1000, under 18 free). On the **western** side, the **Rocca degli Alberi** was built by the Carraresi in 1362 to keep the roads from Mantua and Verona covered.

The center of Montagnana is the Piazza Vittorio Emanuele, dominated by the late Gothic **Duomo**. The most arresting feature of the exterior, its marble portal, was a later addition, possibly designed by Sansovino. **Veronese**'s altarpiece, a *Transfiguration*, is less engaging than the huge anonymous painting of the *Battle of Lepanto* on the left as you enter—it's said to represent accurately the ships and their positions at one point in the battle.

Outside the town, just beyond the Porta Padova, is the **Villa Pisani** by **Palladio** (closed to the public), its magnificent facade at a right angle to the road. It was built as a summer residence and administrative center for their mainland estates by a branch of the Pisani family of Venice. Also worth looking out for is the elegant facade of the **Palazzo Lombardesco** in Via Matteotti, with its five-lighted window.

Practicalities

The helpful **tourist office** is on the right-hand side of Piazza Vittorio Emanuele (Mon–Sat 10am–noon & 4:30–7pm). For **accommodation** *Locanda Baraldo*, Via San Zeno (☎0429/81673; singles L15,000, doubles L25,000), *Al Turismo*, Via San Antonio (☎0429/81143, singles L15,000, doubles L29,000) and *Ezzelino*, Via Praterie (☎0429/82035; singles L19,000, doubles L34,000) are all reasonable. The **youth hostel** is stunning, installed as it is in *Rocca degli Alberi* (April 1–Oct 15; reception 3–11pm, checkout at around 9am; ☎0429/81076; L7000); if you don't have an IYHF card, you can join on the spot.

All the hotels listed have **restaurants**; for the cheapest meal, try *Pizzeria al Palio*, Piazza Trieste. If you're stopping for a picnic in Montagnana, be sure to sample the local prosciutto, which is so delicious it's exported all over the world.

Come to Montagnana on the first Sunday in September and you'll see its **Palio**—it may be but a poor relative of the costumed horse races in Siena, but it's enthusiastically performed, and the day finishes with a splendid firework display.

The town is after Este on the **train** line from Monsélice (every 2–3hr; journey takes 25min from Monsélice).

Rovigo and Beyond

ROVIGO is the capital of the fertile and often-flooded zone between between the Adige and the Po, an area known as the *Polésine* (or "Little Mesopotamia"). Trains on their way to Ferrara and Bologna from Venice stop here hourly (average journey 90min), crossing another line running east to west—and frankly there's little reason for coming to the town except to change trains. (There's also a two-hourly connection to Chioggia, taking about an hour.) Should you be stuck for a couple of hours waiting for a connection, though, there are a couple of places you could visit. Maps are available from the **EPT** office, where they always look surprised to see visitors—it's at Via J.H. Dunant 10, to the right off Corso del Popolo as you walk from the station.

Two medieval towers in the center were part of a castle re-fortified in 954 by the Bishop of Adria when the region was threatened by barbarian invasions. The **Pinacoteca dei Concordi** in Piazza Vittore Emanuele is the city's pride and joy

(Mon–Fri 10am–noon & 4–6:30pm, Sat 10am–noon; free). Eminent artists of the Veneto in less than breathtaking form comprise the main part of the collection; Palma il Vecchio, G.B. Piazzetta and Rosalba Carriera are among those present.

About fifteen minutes' walk in the same direction is the **Museo Civico delle Civiltà in Polésine** in Piazza San Bartolomeo, the main archaeological institute for the area. This is more an assemblage of pieces unearthed by the researchers than a regular museum, and you're shown round by one of the staff, whose informed commentary makes up for the uninspiring display techniques. Items relating to the Polésine's disappearing rural life are exhibited as well—tools of various trades, agricultural implements and so forth.

The only other thing worth hunting out is **La Rotonda**, as La Tempio Beata Vergine del Soccorso, in Piazza XX Settembre, is generally known. An octagonal edifice built in 1594 by **Zamberlan**, a pupil of Palladio, it has a campanile by **Longhena** (1655) and a Baroque high altar of gilded wood.

Fratta Polésine

A trip to **FRATTA POLÉSINE**, 18km southwest of Rovigo, will appeal to the more ardent lovers of **Palladio**'s buildings. The **Villa Badoer** (Tues–Sun 3:30–7pm, plus 9am–noon on Thurs; check with the EPT at Rovigo for seasonal changes), designed in the 1560s, is one of his most eloquent flights of architectural rhetoric, with its distinctive curving colonnades linking the porticoed house to the storage spaces at the side. None of the original furnishings are left, but restorers have uncovered the villa's late sixteenth-century grotesque frescoes by **Giallo**, a Florentine. Two **trains** a day from Rovigo will get you there for the afternoon session.

Adria and the Po Delta

Heading **eastward** from Rovigo, trains leave every couple of hours for the Po Delta and Chioggia. **ADRIA**, a town of about 20,000 inhabitants, is all that is left of the city from which the Adriatic Sea got its name. It's a sleepy little town sitting on a tributary of the Po some 25km inland now, owing to heavy silting in the lagoon. The only sight is the **Museo Archeologico** in Piazzale degli Etruschi, which has a collection of Greek and Etruscan pieces dating from the time when Adria was a major port (daily 9am–1pm & 3–6pm).

It's difficult to explore the **Po Delta** properly unless you have a car, though bikes may be rented from *Vittorio Cacciatori* in PORTO TOLLE—to get there you have to take a bus from LOREO, a couple of train stops after Adria. *Cacciatori* also rents out canoes, but if you prefer a less strenuous investigation of the waterways and islets, companies in Porto Tolle and TAGLIO DI PO run half-day cruises for L10,000 per person—an excellent way to observe the waterfowl and other birds of the delta's nature reserve. The Po Delta's 300 square kilometers of water, swamps and mudflats constitute the finest birdwatching region in the country, with the prime sites being centered on COMACCHIO (buses from Venice) and the more southerly PUNTE ALBERETE, both of which lie outside the Veneto in Emilia Romagna. Migratory birds fly into the delta from both north and south, with several wintering species of ducks and waders giving way after April to magnificent herons and egrets—and even, rarely, the exotic glossy ibis.

A few villages around the Veneto sector of the delta tout themselves as beach resorts. Unfortunately the Po itself is the filthiest river in Italy, carrying an unspeakable brew of chemical fertilizers and industrial toxins into the northern reaches of the Adriatic. Its annual load of 234 tons of arsenic, 65 tons of mercury, 20,000 tons of phosphorous and 136,000 tons of nitrates is a major cause of the **algae slicks** that have plagued the resorts of Italy's east coast in recent summers (see "Conservation and Restoration" in *Contexts* for more). Faced with a drop in reservations as high as fifty percent, the tourist boards are telling everyone that the slime is harmless, blithely dismissing the ministry of health's warnings that children, old people, pregnant women, people with skin lesions—in fact, just about anyone who isn't in A1 health—should stay out of the water. The fact is that the precise biochemistry of the algae has still not been determined, as Professor Roberto Marchetti of Milan University observed—"I have been studying these phenomena for years, but what is occurring in the Adriatic is appalling. It is something we know nothing about." Even if it does turn out to be benign to humans, it still stinks and clings to the skin like glue. And if it were to disappear tomorrow, the water round here would still be foul.

CHAPTER TWELVE

VICENZA, VERONA, AND AROUND

L ying almost midway between Padua and Verona, the orderly and affluent city of **Vicenza** tends to be overlooked in favor of its more charismatic neighbors—passengers getting off at the train station are more likely to be personnel from the local US armed forces base than tourists. Yet the streets of Vicenza form one of the most impressive urban landscapes in Italy, owing largely to the activity of Andrea Palladio—the source of western Europe's most influential architectural style. Buildings by Palladio and his acolytes are plentiful not only inside the city itself, but also out in the surrounding country-side, where the Venetian and Vicentine nobility built up their farming estates from the sixteenth century onwards.

Some of these **villas** are of interest only to cognoscenti like those who overrun Vicenza every September for its architectural conference, but several—such as the **Villa Rotonda** and the Tiepolo-decorated **Villa Valmarana**, both on the outskirts—make an impact on the uninitiated and the expert alike. And while Palladianism is the region's distinctive style, it doesn't monopolise the scenery. Some of Vicenza's Gothic houses wouldn't look out of place in Venice, and the evocative **Palazzo Porto-Colleoni** at **Thiene** is as colorful a building as you'll find in the Veneto.

Verona is perhaps best known to English speakers as the setting for Shakespeares's *Romeo and Juliet*, and supposed sites of their courtship are scattered over the city. Authentic remnants of the city's long and varied past are what makes the place so memorable, though—in particular, the remains of the **Roman** period. Of these, the superb **Arena** is the most prominent, followed by the **Teatro Romano** and various archways and gates. Also high on the list of things to see are the monuments left by the **Scaligeri** family, the most celebrated rulers of medieval Verona. Their tombs are masterpieces of Gothic art, and scarcely less impressive is the **Castelvecchio**, once the Scaligeri fortress and now home of Verona's civic museum.

More good quality wine is produced in the Veneto than in any other area of Italy, and the region's most productive vineyards—**Soave**, **Valpolicella** and **Bardolino**—lie within the hinterland of Verona. Also easily reached from the city is **Lago di Garda**, on the western edge of the Veneto—a resort as popular with southern Austrians and Germans as it is with the Veronese.

Vicenza

Europe's largest center for the production of textiles, and the focus of Italy's "Silicon Valley," **VICENZA** is a very sleek city—by some estimates, one of the country's richest half-dozen. The wealth isn't as ostentatious as in Milan, but still it can seem that there are as many Mercs and BMWs in town as there are buses, and in one of its backstreets there's a showroom that has Ferraris the way others have Fiats. The discreet Vicentine obsession with style pervades even the local clergy, who recently invited Italy's designers to improve the look of their priestly attire—prompting entries from big-league names such as Krizia and Laura Biagiotti. Asked what sort of outfit he would be likely to approve, Monsignor Don Giancarlo Santi was anxious not to be too restrictive: "We certainly wouldn't want *Valentino* written on our chests, but anything that is beautiful, well-made and serves its purpose is a gift of God."

Industrial estates and factories form a girdle round the city, and yet modern prosperity hasn't ruined the look of central Vicenza—still partly enclosed by medieval walls, it's an amalgam of Gothic and classical buildings that today looks much as it did when the last major phase of construction came to an end at the close of the eighteenth century. This historic core is compact enough to be explored in a day, but the city and its environs really require a short stay to do them justice.

The early history of Vicenza follows a course familiar in this part of northern Italy—development under Imperial Rome, destruction by Attila, Lombard occupation, attainment of a degree of independence followed by struggles with neighboring towns, rule by the Scaligeri of Verona in the fourteenth century and finally absorption into the Venetian empire (1404). The fifteenth-century palaces of Vicenza reflect its status as a Venetian satellite, with facades reminiscent of the Canal Grande, but in the latter half of the sixteenth century the city was transformed by the work of an architect who owed nothing to Venice but a lot to ancient Rome, and whose rigorous but flexible style was to influence every succeeding generation—Andrea di Pietro della Gondola, alias **Palladio**.

Born in Padua in 1508, Palladio came to Vicenza at the age of sixteen to work as a stonecutter. At thirty he became the protegé of a local nobleman, Count Giangiorgio Trissino, who directed his architectural training, gave him his classicized name, and brought him into contact with the dominant class of Vicenza. Some of these men were landowners, recently enriched now that peace had returned to the mainland after the War of the League of Cambrai, many were wealthy soldiers, and a decent percentage were well-educated—it wasn't unknown for more than 40 of the 100 city councillors to possess doctorates. They turned to Palladio to design houses that would embody their financial and intellectual rank and their corporate superiority to their Venetian rulers. No architect in western history has been more influential than Palladio, and although much of that influence derives from his magisterial *I Quattro Libri dell'Architettura* (The Four Books of Architecture)—a survey of building techniques, classical structures and works (built and unbuilt) by himself—his buildings in and around Vicenza have been consistently studied by architects for the last four centuries. Between 1540 and his death in 1580 Palladio created around a dozen palaces and public buildings in Vicenza plus an even larger number of villas on the Vicentine and Venetian farming estates in the surrounding countryside, and the variety of his designs will surprise anyone who associates Palladianism with blandness. Even if you've been inclined to agree with Herbert Read's opinion that "In the back of every dying civilization there sticks a bloody Doric column," you may well leave Vicenza converted.

The City

The main street of Vicenza, the **Corso Andrea Palladio**, is a vestige of the Roman street-plan and cuts right through the old center from the Piazza Castello (overlooked by an eleventh-century tower, once part of the Scaligeri fort) down to the Piazza Matteotti. Cars are banned from the Corso, so the palaces that line it— now all occupied by shops, offices and banks—can be admired with no risk of being killed, although you should keep your ears open for mopeds.

The first major building comes just before the start of the Corso, on the far side of the Piazza Castello—it's the fragmentary **Palazzo Porto-Breganze**, Palladio's last palace in Vicenza. None of Palladio's town houses were completed to plan, but none of the others is as flagrantly unfinished as this one.

Particularly striking on the Corso itself are: no.13, the **Palazzo Thiene Bonin-Longhare** (by Palladio's follower Scamozzi); no. 38–40, **Palazzo Pagello** (1780); no. 47 **Palazzo Thiene** (fifteenth century); no. 67, **Palazzo Brunello** (fifteenth century—have a look at the courtyard); no. 98, **Palazzo Trissino** (now town hall, by Scamozzi); no. 147, **Palazzo da Schio** (fifteenth century, later restored), known as the *Ca' d'Oro* as it once had gilded decoration and bears a slight resemblance to the Ca' d'Oro in Venice); and no. 163, the **Casa Cogollo**, known as the Casa del Palladio even though he neither designed it (despite what the plaque says) nor lived there. None of the churches on the Corso repays the effort of pushing the door open.

The Museo Civico and Teatro Olimpico

The Corso Palladio ends with one of the architect's most imperious buildings, the **Palazzo Chiericati**. Begun in 1550 and completed about a hundred years later, this commission was a direct result of Palladio's success with the Basilica (see below), being a house for one of the Basilica's supervisors, Girolamo Chiericati. It's now the home of Vicenza's **Museo Civico**, many of whose pieces were gathered together in the 1810s to keep them out of the grasp of the marauding French (Tues–Sat 9:30am–noon & 2:30–5pm; closed Sun afternoon & hols; L3000, combined ticket for Museo & Teatro Olimpico L5000, reduced to L3000 on Sun).

The ground-floor archaeological collection of locally excavated pieces from the fifth century BC to the seventh AD is neither more nor less interesting than such provincial collections usually are, but the art galleries are more ambitious—especially the *Sezione d'Arte Medievale*, a hi-tech zone of automatic doors, hyper-sensitive environmental controls and ultra-sophisticated presentational techniques. The backbone of the picture collection is made up by Vicentine artists—eg Montagna, Buonconsiglio, Fogolino (all sixteenth century), Maffei and Carpioni (seventeenth century)—whose work throws up some pleasant surprises without actually knocking you flat on your back. It's the more celebrated names—Memling, Tintoretto, Veronese, G.B. Tiepolo, van Dyck—who'll probably make the visit memorable. Mind you, Carpione's bubble-blowing cherub (the most revolting painting in the Veneto?) does tend to stick in the mind, as does the ceiling fresco in one of the ground-floor rooms—a comically unflinching depiction of what you'd see if a group of horses steered by a stark naked charioteer flew overhead.

Across the Piazza Matteotti is the one building in Vicenza you shouldn't fail to go into—the **Teatro Olimpico**, the oldest indoor theater in Europe (March 16– Oct 15 Mon–Sat 9:30am–12:20pm & 3–5:30pm; Oct 16–March 15 9:30am– 12:20pm & 2–4:30pm; closed Sun afternoon, some hols and occasionally for rehearsals; L3000—for combined Teatro & Museo ticket, see Museo entry). Approached in 1579 by the members of the humanist Accademia Olimpica to produce a design for a permanent theater, Palladio devised a covered amphitheater derived from his reading of Vitruvius, architect to Augustus, and his studies of Roman structures in Italy and France. In terms of the development of theater design, the Teatro Olimpico was not a progressive enterprise—contemporary theaters in Florence, for example, were far closer to the modern proscenium arch—but it was the most comprehensive piece of classical reconstruction of its time, and the men responsible for it were suitably proud of their brainchild: the toga-clad figures above the stage are portraits of Palladio's clients. Palladio died soon after work commenced, and the scheme was then overseen by Scamozzi, whose contribution to the design—a backstage perspective of an idealized Thebes—is its most startling feature. As is demonstrated by the theater's guide (who'll give you a commentary in English on request), the illusion of long urban vistas is created by tilting the "streets" at an angle that demands chamois-like agility from the actors. The building was opened on March 3, 1585, with an extravagant production of *Oedipus Rex* that somehow had 108 performers on its roll-call, and although it later had to share the spotlight with the Teatro Eretenio, today it's once more the only permanent theater in Vicenza.

The Piazza dei Signori and Around

At the hub of the city, the Piazza dei Signori, stands the most awesome of Palladio's creations—the *Palazzo della Ragione*, known to all but the pedantic as the **Basilica**. Designed in the late 1540s (but not finished until the second decade of the next century), this was Palladio's first public project and secured his reputation. The architect himself, generally regarded as a mild and modest individual, had no doubt as to its merit: "this building can be compared to ancient ones and placed with the most beautiful of the major buildings that have been made by the ancients," he wrote in the *Quattro Libri*. The monumental regularity of the Basilica disguises the fact that the Palladian building is effectively a stupendous piece of buttressing—the Doric and Ionic colonnades, constructed in Istrian stone, enclose the fifteenth-century brick meeting-hall of the city council, an unstable structure which had defied a number of attempts to prop it up before Palladio's solution was put into effect. And if you look closely you'll see that the colonnades aren't quite as regular as they first appear—Palladio had to vary the spaces to accommodate the passageways that go through the lower level. The vast Gothic hall (entered from the upper gallery) is open to the public most days from 9:30am to noon and 2:30 to 5pm (closed Sun afternoon & all Mon; free). Discussions are taking place about the feasibility of converting the Basilica into an arts center, but it's early days yet; although exhibitions are put on in the hall from time to time, the only cultural institution in full-time residence is the *Centro Internazionale di Archittetura "A. Palladio,"* the keepers of the sacred flame and organizers of Vicenza's annual architectural conference.

Facing the Basilica across the Piazza dei Signori is a late Palladio building, the unfinished **Loggia del Capitaniato**. Built as accommodation for the Venetian military commander of the city (the *Capitano*), it's decorated with reliefs in celebration of the Venetian victory over the Turks at Lepanto in 1571. Had it been completed, the Loggia would have taken up much of the area now occupied by the terrace of the swish *Gran Caffè Garibaldi*; houses used to join onto the Loggia on that side, but they were demolished in the 1930s. Completing the enclosure of that side of the Piazza is the **Monte di Pietà**, put up in two instalments in the first half of the sixteenth century, which brackets the seventeenth-century church of **San Vincenzo**. The worryingly slender **Torre di Piazza** reached its present altitude in 1444, having been started in the twelfth century and raised in 1311; its clock is claimed to have been the first such public timepiece in Italy. The inescapable Lion of Saint Mark was deposited on top of its column in the mid-fifteenth century, not long after Venice took Vicenza into its bosom; the companion figure of the Redeemer dates from the mid-seventeenth century.

As in the sixteenth century, a daily fruit, vegetable and flower **market** is pitched at the back of the Basilica, in the Piazza dell'Erbe—glowered over by medieval **Torre del Tormento**, once the prison tower. If you're shopping for food, you'll save yourself quite a few lire by dropping down the slope to the shops over the river, where prices tend to be a notch or two lower than within the Basilica's shadow. On Tuesdays a vast general market hits town, spreading along the roads between the Basilica and the Duomo.

In Contrà Pigafetta, just a few yards down the slope from the Piazzetta Palladio, on the Duomo side of the Basilica, there's Vicenza's architectural oddity, the Spanish-influenced **Casa Pigafetta**. Built in 1481, it was the birthplace of Antonio Pigafetta, who set out with Magellan on his voyage of 1519 and kept a record of the expedition. Unlike his leader, Pigafetta lived to see his home town again. If you're puzzled by the street name, *contrà*—sometimes *contrada*—is the Vicentine dialect alternative to *via*.

The Duomo, Santa Corona, and Santo Stefano

The **Duomo**, founded before the eighth century but substantially rebuilt chiefly from the fourteenth to the sixteenth century, was bombed to bits in 1944 and carefully reconstructed after the war. It's a gloomy place, notable primarily as one of the few Italian cathedrals to be overwhelmed by its secular surroundings. A polyptych by **Lorenzo Veneziano** (fifth chapel on right) and a *Madonna* by **Montagna** (fourth chapel on left) are the best of its paintings. Excavations in the crypt have uncovered Roman sidewalks and parts of a pre-ninth-century basilica, but there's no admission to the public. You can, however, visit the **Criptoporticus**—probably part of a first-century palace—that was unearthed beneath the Palazzo Proti on the other side of the Piazza Duomo. Access is through the door at no. 6, but you first have to apply at the *Centro Touristico Giovanile*, at no. 2; the site's open Thursdays and Saturdays from 10 to 11:30am.

Far more interesting than the Duomo is the Dominican church of **Santa Corona**, on the other side of the Corso Palladio, at the Piazza Matteotti end (summer daily 9:30am–12:30pm & 3:30–6:30pm; winter 9:30am–12:30pm & 3–6pm). Begun in 1261 to house a thorn from Christ's crown, it has what's said to be the oldest Gothic interior in the Veneto; the thorn itself, a gift from the beatified King Louis IX of France, is sometimes displayed in its fourteenth-century gold reliquary in the chapel on the left of the chancel. Santa Corona is a church that positively welcomes visitors—everything is well-labeled and well-lit, the sacristan actually volunteers information about the place, and there's even piped Bach and Handel as background music. Here you'll find two of the three superlative church paintings in Vicenza—*The Baptism of Christ*, a late work by **Giovanni Bellini** (fifth altar on left), and *The Adoration of the Magi*, painted in 1573 by **Paolo Veronese** (fourth chapel on right). (For the third of the trio, see Santo Stefano, below.) Also well worth a look are the late fifteenth-century inlaid **choir stalls**, the simple and tranquil **Valmarana Chapel**, added to the crypt in 1576 by Palladio, and the anonymous *Madonna* near the Bellini picture, which includes at its base a **view of Vicenza** in c:1500, added by **Fogolino**. The cloisters of Santa Corona, recently restored, are often used for exhibitions.

The nearby church of **Santo Stefano** merits a call for its one outstanding painting—**Palma il Vecchio**'s typically stolid and fleshy *Madonna and Child with St George and St Lucy*. Getting into Santo Stefano is a bit hit-and-miss; you're likeliest to succeed from 9 to 11am and 4 to 6:30pm.

Palaces and Parks

The entrance to Santo Stefano faces the most powerful Gothic palace in the city, the **Casa Fontana**, and the immense **Palazzo Negri**—but more intimidating than either is Palladio's rugged **Palazzo Thiene**, on the Corso side of them. Had Palladio's plan been realized, the palace would have occupied the entire block down to Corso and back to Contrà Porti; in the end, work progressed no farther than the addition of this wing to the block built for the Thiene family at the end of the fifteenth century. The facade of the Gothic portion is in Contrà Porti. Palladio was not simply the most inventive architect in the Veneto, he was also the most cost-effective: his columns are usually made of brick covered with a skim of plaster, and as an inspection of the Thiene residence will reveal, his rough-hewn stonework is just cunningly worked brick as well.

There's no better example than the Contrà Porti of the way in which the builders of Vicenza skilfully grafted new houses onto old without doing violence to the line of the street: the palaces here span two centuries, yet the overall impression is one of cohesion. At no. 8 is the Gothic **Palazzo Cavalloni**; over the road at no. 11 is Palladio's **Palazzo Barbarano**, designed around 1570 and subsequently tarted up by others; the Thiene palace is followed by the Renaissance **Palazzo Trissino-Sperotti** (no. 14), opposite which is a sweep of Gothic houses (nos. 15–19), the best being the fourteenth-century **Palazzo Colleoni Porto** (19); next door is Palladio's **Palazzo Iseppo Porto**, designed a few years after the Thiene and a couple of decades before the Barbarano. Luigi da Porto, the author of the story of Romeo and Juliet, died at no. 15 in 1529.

Contrà Porti takes you towards the Pusterla bridge and the **Parco Querini**, the biggest expanse of green in the city; with its backdrop of trees, its avenue of statuary and its tiny decorative hill (populated by ducks, rabbits and peacocks), it reminds you of the picturesque grounds of an eighteenth-century English country house. For those intent on doing a comprehensive Palladian tour, there's a palace by him on this side of the Bacchiglione river too—the **Palazzo Schio-Angaran** at no. 39 Contrà San Marco. Vicenza's other refuge for the brick-wearied, the **Giardino Salvi** (at the beginning of Corso Santi Felice e

Fortunato—you pass it as you come up from the train station) is more compact with artificial fountains, ornamental canals, winding gravel paths punctuated by replicas of great sculptures and a pair of loggias (one by Longhena).

Along Corso Fogazzaro

Connected to Contrà Porti by Contrà Riale (itself not short of grand houses) is Corso A. Fogazzaro, a busy road with a spread of architectural attractions. At the Corso Palladio end is the **Palazzo Valmarana** (no. 16), where Palladio's use of overlapping planes makes the design of the facade legible in the narrow street and at the same time integrates the palace with the flanking buildings. Take a peep at the uncompleted courtyard—the finished section was no more than a third of the projected palace.

In the other direction you'll come across the Piazza San Lorenzo, on one side of which stands Francesco Muttoni's Palazzo Repeta (1701–11; now the Banca d'Italia), with the thirteenth-century Franciscan church of **San Lorenzo** opposite (daily 6:45am–noon & 3:30–7:30pm, but frequent masses). The fourteenth-century marble portal of the west front is the best feature of the church—the dimensions of the interior are impressive, but the church is rather barren in comparison with others of the same period in the Veneto, such as San Nicolò at Treviso or San Zanipolo and the Frari in Venice. **Montagna**'s fresco of the *Beheading of St Paul* (chapel on left side of chancel) may once have been stunning, but it's now looking pretty tattered. The cloister is worth a visit, though, even if the monastic calm has given way to the noise of traffic and the neighboring school.

Further along, where the arcades give out, is the church of **Santa Maria del Carmine**; founded in the fourteenth century but redone in the nineteenth, it has pictures by **Montagna**, **Veronese** and **Jacopo Bassano** which more than compensate for the peculiar decor—although you'll need infra-red vision to make them out on an overcast day.

The Fringes of the City

If the Museo Civico's collection has led to your acquiring a taste for **Francesco Maffei**'s superheated rehashes of Tintoretto, you'll not want to miss the **Oratorio di San Nicola** (July–Sept daily 9am–noon & 3–6pm) , which has more paintings by him and his contemporary **Carpioni** than the normal retina can take. Prolonged contemplation of Maffei's delirious altarpiece—*The Trinity*—is strictly for the strong-stomached, but if you want to know what happened to painting in the Veneto after the golden age of the late Renaissance, this is a quick way of finding out.

The Oratorio stands by the side of Vicenza's other river, the Retrone, at the foot of its most picturesque bridge, the hump-backed **Ponte San Michele** (built in 1620). You can follow a pleasant loop on the south side of the river by going straight ahead off the bridge to Piazzola dei Gualdi, then basically following your nose, so that you go past the thirteenth-century gate (**Portòn del Luzzo**) and recross the Retrone by the **Ponte Furo**, from where there's a good view of the Basilica and Torre di Piazza. The long building on the opposite bank is Palladio's unexceptional first project in the city, the **Casa Civena** (c:1540).

Another area just out of the center that's worth a look is on the other side of the Bacchiglione from the Teatro Olimpico. The bridge leads onto the major traffic confluence Piazza Venti Settembre: the building with porticoes on two facades is the **Palazzo Angaran** (fifteenth century but rebuilt). In Contrà Venti Settembre there's the house with the best preserved of Vicenza's exterior frescoes, the fifteenth-century **Palazzo Regaù**.

Don't miss the church of **Santi Felice e Fortunato** either. It's on the opposite side of town, about ten minutes' walk along the Corso of the same name. Dating back to immediately after the Edict of Constantine (313), the basilica is **the oldest church in Vicenza**, and is approached by a path littered with ancient sarcophagi and architectural fragments. Wrecked by barbarian invaders in 899 and then by earthquakes in 1117, it was largely reconstructed in the twelfth century, and recent restorations have stripped away later accretions to reveal the form of the church at around that period. Remnants of the earliest building have survived—portions of fourth-century and fifth-century **mosaics** have been uncovered in the nave and right aisle, and a door off the right aisle leads into a fourth-century **martyrs' shrine**. Almost as remarkable as the mosaics and *martyrion* is the twelfth-century **fortified campanile**, which now looks as if it might have problems standing up to the next high wind.

Practicalities

The **APT** is alongside the entrance to the Teatro Olimpico, at Piazza Matteotti 12 (Mon–Sat 9am–12:30pm & 3–6pm, Sun 9am–12:30pm); they hand out a map that gives the addresses of all Vicenza's movie theaters and sports halls plus details of local transport, a booklet seemingly written by the board of trade, and a very good leaflet on the Teatro. If you make a point of asking, they'll also provide lists and itineraries of the villas of the Veneto.

For **listings**, pick up a copy of the local papers—*Il Gazzettino* or *Il Giornale di Vicenza*. Culturally the busiest time of the year is from June to August, when there's a glut of concerts, opera productions and plays in town, many of the best being performed in the Teatro Olimpico.

The **post office** is in Piazza Garibaldi, between the Duomo and Basilica; the Corso Palladio is the place for **banks**. For telephones, the SIP offices are at Piazzetta Duomo 1 (daily 8:15am–9:30pm).

Accommodation

As you emerge from the train station a large map of the city confronts you, helpfully marking all Vicenza's **hotels**; ignore it, the information is years out of date. The best deal among the one-star hotels is the *Villa Marzia*, Via Mure Pallamaio 96 (✆0444/227055; reception open 8am–noon & 5–7pm; closed Sun; L26,000 double), a basic but centrally-placed *pensione*. The other one-stars are nearly all on very noisy roads, above bar/trattorias and some way out of the center—in this category there are two decent places close together on Corso Santi Felice e Fortunato: the *Marechiaro* at no. 255 (✆0444/563481; around L32,000) and the *Pechino* at no. 322 (✆0444/232041; around L30,000). The *Casa San Raffaele*, Viale X Giugno 10 (✆0444/235619), has the advantage of a beautiful position on the slope of Monte Bèrico, but will cost about the same as the cheaper rooms in some of the two-stars in the core of Vicenza—ie L37,000 and upwards. Of the two-stars within a few yards of the Piazza dei Signori, the following are worth trying—*Milano*, Stradella dei Servi 5 (✆0444/238643; L15,000 single, L25,000 double), *Due Mori*, Contrà Do Rode 26(✆0444/221886; L25,000 single, L30,000 double) and, friendliest of the bunch, *Palladio*, Via Oratorio dei Servi 25 (✆0444/221072;

L23,000 single, L35,000 double). Wherever you decide to stay, ring ahead to reserve a room if you're going in summer or early autumn—some places close down in August, and Vicenza's popularity as a conference center can make it tricky to find rooms, especially in September.

Eating and Drinking

First recommendation for **eating** goes to the *Antica Casa della Malvasia*, Contrà delle Morette 5 (closed Mon) a bustling, roomy inn just off the Piazza dei Signori. The food is variable but cheap, unpretentious, and genuinely regional; the menu is small but changes daily; it occasionally has live music; and the bar's excellent too. It's possible to eat more cheaply in central Vicenza—at *Al Bersagliere*, Contrà Pescaria 11 (closed Sun) and *Alla Bella Vicenza*, Contrà G. da Proti—but the *Malvasia* is the one where you'd be tempted to make an evening of it.

Equally popular, but a shade less basic at upwards of L20,000 for a hefty meal, is the *Vecchia Guardia*, at Contrà Pescheria Vecchia 11 (☎0444/21231; closed Thurs)—it's advisable to reserve at weekends. *Due Mori*, Contrà do Rode 26 (closed Wed), *Da Anna*, Contrà Porta Nova 41 (closed Tues) and *Giardini*, Via Giuriolo 10 (closed Wed) are big and busy pizzeria-restaurants—fine for pizzas and slightly more elaborate fare, as long as you don't want to linger over your food.

Drifting up-market a bit more, you might want to try *La Taverna*, in the ground floor of the Basilica (☎0444/22117; closed Mon), or, up another class, the much-praised *Tre Visi*, Contrà Porti 6 (☎0444/38677; closed Sun afternoon and all Mon). Local specialties include *baccalà alla Vicentina* (dried cod fried with anchovies and onion), *bigoli con l'arna* (spaghetti seasoned with gravy of roast duck) and *paeta col malgaragno* (turkey with pomegranates).

For a quick **snack**, *Paninoteca da Renato*, Stradella San Giacomo (between the Corso and Contrà Riale), provides lavish sandwiches for famished businessmen; the younger Vicentines prefer *La Cantinota*, Stradella del Garofalino (behind the *Corso* cinema), which offers sandwiches at lunchtimes and self-service meals in the evenings (open until 1am Mon–Fri, 2am on Sat). Another self-service place is *Righetti*, at Piazza del Duomo 3—but it closes at 9pm and is only open weekdays. If you want to buy your own food, the *alimentari* of the Corso are high on quality (especially *Il Ceppo* at no. 196) but correspondingly high on price; *Porro*, Contrà Orefice, is also good—but if you want to save money you should head out of the center across the Retrone, or try along the Corso Santi Felice e Fortunato (where there's a *Despar* supermarket at no. 109).

As for **bars** in the center of the city, the *Firenze*, Piazzetta A. Palladio, is always friendly, as is the *Borsa*, in one of the Basilica's passageways. *Lo Dolce* ... (the full name runs on for ever) in Contrà Fontana (beside the post office) is more atmospheric; and then of course there's the *Malvasia*. The *Big Ben*, in Contrà Castello, is very popular—partly because it stays open until 2am—but it's been the scene of a few flare-ups between the natives and the often resented personnel of the locally-based US armed forces.

There's a range of **cafés** and *pasticcerie* along the Corso and around the Basilica—try *Sorarù*, in the Piazzetta Andrea Palladio, or the *Offelleria della Meneghina*, in Contrà Cavour. You'll find some good ones on Corso Fogazzaro as well. Best **ice creams** in town are at the huge *Gran Caffè Garibaldi*, on the Piazza dei Signori, though *Tutto Gelato* in Contrà Frasche (between the Basilica and the Duomo) runs it close.

Transportation

Trains run regularly from Vicenza to **Venice** (approx. every 30min; journey 55min) through **Padua** (20min); to **Milan** (same frequency; 2hr) through **Verona** (30min), and to **Treviso** (approximately hourly; 1hr) through Castelfranco Véneto (40min). **Coaches** run all over the area, but as they're slower and more expensive than the trains, the only route you're likely to need, apart from the ones suggested for the villa trips, is the one that goes via **Maróstica** to **Bassano** (hourly; 1hr).

Around Vicenza

The countryside around Vicenza is dotted with hundreds of **villas**, many of them the result of Venice's diversion of money into agriculture in the mid-sixteenth century, as a way protecting the economy against the increasing uncertainties of shipping. For L8000 you can buy a map entitled *Ville Venete*, plotting the location of all of them, and if you have twenty times that sum to spare you can choose between a number of magnificently illustrated tomes on the subject. The trouble is, many of the villas are best seen as glossy photos, because some of the buildings are in the middle of nowhere, some are falling to bits and some of the better-kept specimens are closed to the public. And of those that are open, accessible and in fair condition, some probably won't make much impression on the untrained eye—such as Palladio's **Villa Thiene** at QUINTO VICENTINO (a short journey on the #10 bus) or his **Villa Pojana** at far-flung POJANA MAGGIORE (a coach trip). Yet a number of the villas of wider interest lie within the orbit of Vicenza's public transit network; two of the best, indeed, are to be found right on Vicenza's doorstep, beneath the pilgrimage church of Monte Bèrico, the other big attraction of Vicenza's immediate surroundings.

(Other villas of the Veneto are dealt with in the appropriate sections of this guide—for example, "The Brenta," "Masèr," "Castelfranco Véneto.")

Monte Bèrico, the Villa Valmarana, and La Rotonda

Rising behind the railroad, **Monte Bèrico** is seen by everyone who comes to Vicenza, but not actually visited by many, which is a pity as an expedition up the hill has a number of attractions: an amazing view (on a clear day the horizon beyond Vicenza is a switchback of mountain peaks), a clutch of excellent paintings and one of Europe's most famous and imitated buildings.

Buses for Monte Bèrico leave the coach station (beside the train station) on average every half hour; on foot it takes around 25 minutes from the center of town. If you decide to walk, the best route is to head for Viale X Giugno (ignoring the road sign that directs you up Viale Dante) and then follow the *Portici*, an eighteenth-century arcade built to shelter the pilgrims to the church, which takes you to the top. If you cross the road before the end of the climb, you'll see Palladio's Villa Capra, known to everyone as La Rotonda, perched on a hummock below.

In 1426–28 Vicenza was struck by an outbreak of bubonic plague, in the course of which the Virgin appeared twice at the summit of Monte Bèrico to announce the city's deliverance. A chapel was raised on the spot that the Virgin had obligingly marked out for its construction, and it duly became a place of pilgrimage. It was enlarged later in the century, altered again in the sixteenth century, and then, at the end of the seventeenth, replaced by the present **Basilica di Monte Bèrico**. (The facade of the enlarged fifteenth-century church is stuck on to the right side.) Pilgrims regularly arrive here by the coachload, and the glossy interior of the church, all gilding and fake marble, is immaculately maintained to receive them. A well-stocked shop in the cloister sells devotional trinkets to the faithful, close to a cash desk displaying the current rates for masses and other services.

The skeptical should nevertheless venture into the church for **Montagna**'s *Pietà* (1500; in chapel on right side of apse) and *The Supper of St Gregory the Great* by **Veronese** (1572; in the refectory, off the cloister). The latter, the proto-type of *The Feast in the House of Levi* in Venice's Accademia, was used for bayo-net practice by Austrian troops in 1848—the small reproduction outside the refectory shows what a thorough job they did on it.

The **Piazzale della Vittoria**, in front of the Basilica, was built to commemorate the dead of World War I; the local lads gather here to find out who's got the loud-est car radio, a virility ritual that only slightly detracts from the pleasure of the view across the city.

The Tiepolos at the Villa Valmarana

Ten minutes' walk away from the Basilica is the **Villa Valmarana ai Nani** (*Nani = Dwarves*, after the figures on the garden wall), an undistinguished eighteenth-century house made extraordinary by its decoration—a cycle of frescoes by **Giambattista and Giandomenico Tiepolo** which is one of the most gorgeous in the Veneto. To get there, go back to the elbow of the *Portici*, along the Via M. D'Azeglio for about 100m, then right into the cobbled Via S. Bastiano, which ends at the Villa Valmarana. There are two parts to the house: the *Palazzina*, contain-ing six rooms frescoed with brilliant virtuosity by Giambattista (scenes based on Virgil, Tasso and Ariosto—you're handed a brief guide to the paintings at the entrance); and the *Foresteria*, one room of which is frescoed by Giambattista and six by his son Giandomenico, whose predilections were a little less cerebral than his father's, but whose technique was very nearly as accomplished. (March 17–April 30 daily 2:30–5:30pm; May–Sept 3–6pm; Oct 1–Nov 15 2–5pm; plus Thurs, Sat, Sun & some hols 10am–noon; L4000, reductions L3000; if planning to visit on a holiday, check opening by ringing ☎0444/221803.)

Palladio's Rotonda

From the Valmarana house the narrow Strada Valmarana descends the slope to **La Rotonda**, unique among Palladio's villas in that it was designed not as the main building of a farming estate but as a pavilion in which entertainments could be held and the landscape enjoyed. The combination of the pure forms of the circle and square was a fundamental problem of Renaissance architecture (Leonardo, Bramante, Michelangelo and Serlio all worked at it), and the elegance of Palladio's solution led to innumerable imitations—for example Mereworth and Chiswick in England, and Jefferson's rejected plan for the official residence of the US President, a near facsimile of the Rotonda.

Only a tour of the lavishly decorated interior will fully reveal the subtleties of the Rotonda (the plan doesn't replicate the symmetry of the exterior), and you can get in each Wednesday from 10am to noon and from 3 to 6pm, from March

15 to October 15 (L5000). If you're here on a day when the interior's shut, try to get to see Losey's film of *Don Giovanni*—the Rotonda was used as the remorseless seducer's residence. The grounds alone are open during this period on Tuesdays and Thursdays (and occasionally on other days when the staff can be found), same times, entry L2000 but unless you're an architecture student and really want to scrutinize the place from point-blank range, the grounds can be given a miss, as they're not much more than a belt of grass round the villa.

Sant'Agostino

Vocational students of Vicenza's ecclesiastical heritage might want to visit the abbey of **Sant'Agostino**, 4km out of the city, southwest of Monte Bèrico. (Take the #4 bus from the train station.) Built in 1322-57, on the site of an eighth-century foundation, the abbey has a polyptych painted in 1404 by **Battista da Vicenza**, as well as frescoes painted in the fourteenth-century by itinerant artists of the school of Vitale da Bologna. It's worth seeing, but for most people not worth going to see.

The Villa Cordellina-Lombardi—and on to Bagnolo

A must for Tiepolo fans is the eighteenth-century **Villa Cordellina-Lombardi**, on the outskirts of the small town of **MONTECCHIO MAGGIORE**, 13km to the southwest of Vicenza. Giambattista's frescoes in the entrance hall—*The Clemency of Scipio*, *The Clemency of Alexander* and, on the ceiling, *The Light of Reason Driving out the Fog of Ignorance*—are a touch less exuberant than the later ones at the Villa Valmarana, and show his debt to Paolo Veronese more plainly, but they'll still make you feel better about life for the rest of the day. You have to work for your pleasure, though: the Valdagno-Recoaro and Arzignano-Crespadoro **coaches** from Vicenza go through Montecchio Maggiore (very regular service), but it's best to get off at ALTE CECCATO, just before the coach turns right into Montecchio (get off when you see the huge *Bertozzo* clothes supermarket)—then follow the signs for the villa, which is about ten minutes' walk from the road. The journey takes about thirty minutes, through an unrelentingly grim landscape of shops, factories and commercial estates.

The house is now owned by the province of Vicenza and used as a conference center, but from April 13 to October 15 it's open to the public on Wednesdays, Saturdays and Sundays from 9am to noon and 3 to 6pm (except for April 29–May 3 & July 19–Aug 16; L2000). Montecchio's other attractions, a pair of rebuilt fourteenth-century Scaliger forts erected on a ridge overlooking the town, look their best from afar. They were made the strongholds of the Montague clan in Luigi da Porto's *Romeo and Juliet*.

The Villa Pisani

About 20km to the south of Montecchio Maggiore, at **BAGNOLO**, is Palladio's **Villa Pisani**. Dating from the early 1540s, the Villa Pisani is one of his less sophisticated designs, marking a transition from the traditional fortified villa (see "Thiene," below) and the fully classicized projects of the later sixteenth century. The division of the rooms follows a pattern found all over the Veneto: kitchens in the basement, highly decorated living quarters on the next level, and granary space on the upper storey.

Only specialists will get a great deal out of the Villa Pisani, but if you've got a car, or if you've made the effort of getting to Montecchio by public transit and fancy spending the afternoon out of the city, you might want to give it a look. From the Alte Ceccato stop (see above) you can get a connection to LONIGO—at the moment it leaves at 12:30pm. (There's also a direct Vicenza–Lonigo service— useful for the return leg.) Once at Lonigo you need the school bus that leaves for COLOGNA shortly after 1pm, which drops you in Bagnolo around half an hour before the house opens. The alternative to the school bus is to walk or hitch the 4km to Bagnolo—coming back from Bagnolo these are the only options. (The return walk does at least offer the diversion of a good view of Scamozzi's **Villa Rocca-Pisani**, a lineal descendant of the Rotonda.) From time to time the terrace is packed with upper-crust tourists who've paid even more than the customary L5000 whack to secure the honor of sipping wine with the boss—so it's wisest to ring ahead to check that the gates aren't chained against the plebs (☎0444/831104; official opening hours Wed & Fri 9–11am & 2–6pm).

Thiene and Lugo di Vicenza

It was only with the ending of the War of the League of Cambrai in 1516 that the landowners of the Veneto were able to disregard defensive considerations when building homes out of the urban centers—prior to that, the great houses of the *terra firma* were a sort of cross-breed between a castle and a palace, and the most imposing example of this genre still standing is the **Villa** (or **Castello**) **Porto-Colleoni**, built in the 1470s at **THIENE**, a bland textile town 20km to the north of Vicenza.

The crenellated corner towers, large central block and the encircling protective wall are all features that would have been common in this area in the fifteenth century, although this house, with its facade decorations and ornate Gothic windows, was probably more precious than most. Nowadays the buildings that most closely resemble it are to be found along Venice's Canal Grande (for example the Fondaco dei Turchi)—which is not as strange as it first seems, as they belong to the same family tree, springing from the long-ruined provincial villas of the late Roman Empire. The interior has sixteenth-century frescoes by G.B. Zelotti and G.A. Fasolo, and a plethora of equine portraits—the Colleoni had a tradition of service in the Venetian cavalry. The advertised opening hours are Tuesday to Sunday 9:30am to noon and 3 to 6pm between March 15 and October 15, but adherence to these times seems to become optional as the days grow shorter, so you'd best ring to check—☎0445/32121. To get to Thiene from Vicenza, take the Schio train; it leaves virtually every hour, and takes 25 minutes.

Lugo di Vicenza

The next rung up the evolutionary ladder of the villas of the Veneto is represented 8km to the north of Thiene, on the edge of **LUGO DI VICENZA** (aka Lonedo di Lugo), where you'll find Palladio's first villa—the **Villa Godi Malinverni**, built in 1537–42 (open Tues, Sat, Sun & hols: March 19–May 31 2–6pm; June–Aug 3–7pm; Sept–Oct 2–6pm; L5000). The plan of the Villa Godi Malinverni isn't all that different from that of the Villa Porto-Colleoni, but it's been shorn of fortified trappings and is clearly more of a country house than a castle; on the other hand, there's not a feature on the building that refers to the architecture of ancient Rome, and so it could be seen as occupying a space between the Gothic and Renaissance villas.

Professor Remo Malinverni restored the house in the early 1960s, and installed his collection of nineteenth-century Italian paintings in some of the rooms; elsewhere in the building you'll find a fossil museum—neither display can really compete with the sixteenth-century frescoes, some of which show our old friend **G.B. Zelotti** on top form.

Just above the Godi Malinverni stands the **Villa Piovene**, the central block of which was also built by Palladio around 1540; the Ionic portico was added later in the sixteenth century, and the external staircase and portal came in the eighteenth. Only the nineteenth-century landscaped garden is open to the public—best settle for a remote inspection. An infrequent bus service runs from Thiene to Lugo, on its way to CALVENE—there's a stop by the Porto-Colleoni.

Verona

With its wealth of Roman sites and streets of pink-hued medieval buildings, the easy-going city of **VERONA** has more in the way of sights than any other place in the Veneto except Venice itself. Unlike Venice, though, it's not a city overwhelmed by the tourist industry, important though that is to the local economy. Verona is the largest city of the mainland Veneto, its economic success largely due to its position at the crossing of the major routes from Germany and Austria to central Italy and from the west to Venice and Trieste.

Verona's initial development as a **Roman** settlement was similarly due to its straddling the main east–west and north–south lines of communication. A period of decline in the wake of the disintegration of the Roman empire was followed by revival under the Ostrogoths, who in turn were succeeded by the Franks— Charlemagne's son, Pepin, ruled his kingdom from here. By the twelfth century Verona had become a city state, and in the following century approached the zenith of its independent existence with the rise of the **Scaligeri** family. Ruthless in the exercise of power—they once hired Werner of Urlingea, self-styled "enemy of God and of compassion"—the Scaligeri were at the same time energetic patrons of the arts, and many of Verona's finest buildings date from the century of their rule. Both Giotto and Dante were guests of the Scaligeri, the latter dedicating his *Paradiso* to Cangrande I, the head of the family at the time.

With the fall of their dynasty a time of upheaval ensued, Gian Galeazzo Visconti of Milan emerging with control of the city. Absorption into the Venetian empire came in 1405, and Venice continued to govern Verona down to the arrival of Napoleon. Verona's history then shadowed that of Venice: a prolonged interlude of Austrian rule, brought to an end by the unification of Italy in 1866.

The City

The first impression of Verona is of a city with space. The big lazy curve of the Adige river has carved a wide amphitheater out of the hills that gives room to look down on the city from within its boundaries, and walking around the city walls, the embankments of the river, and in parts of the very center, the sense of spaciousness persists. Even in areas where the city is more cramped, the banning of cars from many of the central roads makes Verona a less pressurized place than Padua, for instance, which is a city of comparable size.

S. Giorgio in Braida
S. Stefano
Castel San Pietro
Museo Archeologico
Duomo
Teatro Romano
PONTE PIETRA
BIG BORROTONI
S. Anastasia
VIA PONTE PIETRA
VIA SOTTORIVA
VIA SAN MAMASO
CORSO S. ANASTASIA
Palazzo Maffei
Loggia
Palazzo dei Scaligeri
Arche Scaligeri
PIAZZA DEI SIGNORI
Casa Mazzanti
S. Maria Antica
PIAZZA ERBE
Domus Mercatorium
CORSO PORTA BORSARI
Palazzo del Capitano
PONTE NUOVO
Arco della Costa
VIA PELLICCIAI
Casa di Giulietta
VIA NIZZA
Palazzo del Commune
VIA MAZZINI
VIA CATTELSPACE
VIA DELLA STELLA
VIA CAPPELLO
River Adige
To Vicenza
VIA A.G. CARDUCCI
VIA DEL PONTIERE
VIA DEL 190 ANTITEATRO
VIA LEONCINO
S. Fermo Maggiore
PONTE NAVI
Palazzo Municipale
STRADONE S. FERMO
VIA CAMPO FIORE
VIA PALLONE
LUNGA PTA. VITTORIA
VIC. ADIGETTO
PIAZZA D'ARM. D. CAMPO FIORE
PONTE ALEARDI
Cimitero Monumentale
CAMPO DI FIERA
Tomba di Giulietta

Traffic restrictions make walking the most efficient way of exploring Verona, and the center is concentrated enough to make this no great hardship. The only buses you're likely to need are the frequent #1 or #8 services (#51 or #58 in the evening) from the train station to the Piazza Brà; buy your ticket before you get on board, from just outside the station.

To Piazza Brà

Coming from the station or the Verona Sud motorway exit, you pass the Verona's south gate, the **Porta Nuova**, built in the sixteenth century by **Michele Sanmicheli** (though messed around by the Austrians in the nineteenth century). From Corso Porta Nuova, which begins here, the red roofs and towers of the city stand out against the backdrop of the Torricelle and the Lessini mountains. At the other end of the Corso, battlemented arches of the **Portoni della Brà** (1389), formerly part of the city walls, marks the entrance to the historic center. Built by the Visconti family, the Portoni once carried a covered walk from the Castelvecchio (left down Via Roma; see below) to their residence, of which only the **Torre Pentagona** remains, behind the the **Gran Guardia** (1610) on the right.

Through these arches the mildly chaotic **Piazza Brà** opens up, bordered on the south side by the Gran Guardia (now an exhibition and conference venue), on the east by the nineteenth-century **Palazzo Municipale**, on the west by the *Liston*—the starting point for the Veronese *passeggiata*—and at the far end by the mightiest of Verona's Roman monuments, the **Arena**. Dating from the first century AD, the Arena has survived in remarkable condition, despite the twelfth-century earthquake which destroyed all but four of the arches of the outer wall. The interior (Tues–Sun 8am–6:45pm; L3000, free on holidays) was scarcely damaged by the tremor, and nowadays audiences come here to watch gargantuan opera productions where once crowds of around 20,000 packed the benches for gladiatorial contests, mock naval battles and the like. Originally measuring 152m by 123m overall, and thus the third largest of all Roman amphitheaters (after the Colosseum and the amphitheater at Capua), the Arena is still an awesome sight—and as an added treat offers a tremendous urban panorama from the topmost of the 44 pink marble tiers.

To the Casa di Giulietta and San Fermo

Going north from the Arena, Via Mazzini is a narrow traffic-free street lined with generally expensive clothes, shoes and jewelry shops. A left turn at the end leads to the Piazza delle Erbe (see below), while a right takes you into Via Cappello, a street named after the family that Shakespeare turned into the Capulets—and there on the left, at no. 23, is the **Casa di Giulietta** (Juliet's House). Sadly for romantics, the association of the house with Juliet is based on nothing more than its picturesque courtyard and balcony, and even this latter feature is placed, as Arnold Bennett wrote, "too high for love, unless Juliet was a trapeze acrobat, accustomed to hanging downwards by her toes." In fact, although the "Capulets" and the "Montagues" (Montecchi) did exist, Romeo and Juliet were entirely fictional creations; and although bloody feuds were common (the head of one family invited his enemy to a truce-making meal, informing him afterwards that he'd just dined off the liver of his son), there's no record of these two clans being at loggerheads. The cheerless facts notwithstanding, a bronze Juliet has been shoved into a corner of the courtyard, her right breast polished bright by groping hands. (A second spurious shrine—the **Tomba di Giulietta**—is maintained in the southwest of the city, in the cloister of the disbanded San Francesco al Corso.) The house itself, constructed at the start of the fourteenth century and in a fine state of preservation, is open to the public (Tues–Sun 8am–6:45pm; L3000).

Via Cappello leads into Via Leone with its Roman gate, the **Porta Leone**, and segment of excavated Roman street, exposed three meters below today's street level. At the end of Via Leone and across the road stands the red-brick **Basilica di San Fermo**, a church whose inconsistent exterior betrays the fact that it consists of two churches combined. The Benedictines built the original church in the eighth century, then rebuilt it in the eleventh to honor the relics of Saint Fermo and Saint Roch (both supposedly martyred on this site); very soon after, flooding forced them to superimpose another church for day-to-day use, a structure greatly altered in the early fourteenth century by the Minorites. The Gothic upper church may have no outstanding works of art (though the *Annunciation* by Pisanello at the west end is the earliest surviving fresco by the artist), but the numerous fourteenth-century frescoes and the fine wooden keel vault (1314—the oldest such ceiling left in the Veneto) compose a graceful interior. The Romanesque lower church can be entered from the left of the choir; its low vaulting is sometimes obscured by exhibitions.

Piazza delle Erbe and Piazza dei Signori

Originally a major Roman crossroads and the site of the forum, **Piazza delle Erbe** is still the heart of the city, a place where people come to meet friends and see who's around. As the name suggests, the market used to sell mainly vegetables; nowadays the range has widened to include clothes, souvenirs, antiques and fast food.

Lined along the square's central axis, and camouflaged by the stalls, are the **Colonna Antica** (a fifteenth-century lantern on a marble pillar), the **Capitello** (a fourteenth-century pavilion where public servants were invested with their office), the fountain of **Madonna Verona** (built in 1368 by Cansignorio della Scala) and finally the column of the lion of Saint Mark, demonstrating Verona's past allegiance to Venice. This specimen is a nineteenth-century copy of one destroyed during the *Pasqua Veronese* (Veronese Easter), as the city's 1797 uprising against the French is known.

On the left as you look from the Via Cappello end, past the tall houses of the old Jewish ghetto, is the **Domus Mercatorium**, which was founded in 1301 as a merchants' warehouse and exchange and is now a bank and chamber of commerce. At the far end, the Baroque **Palazzo Maffei** has been taken over by shops, luxury apartments and an expensive restaurant; to its left is the fourteenth-century **Torre del Gardello** (1370) and to its right the **Casa Mazzanti**, whose sixteenth-century murals are best seen after dark, under enhancing spotlights.

Moving along this side of the piazza, the **Palazzo del Comune** (twelfth century, with Renaissance additions and nineteenth-century alterations) flanks the **Arco della Costa** (Arch of the Rib), the passageway to the Piazza dei Signori. Cynical folklore has it that the whale's rib suspended under the arch will fall if an adult virgin passes underneath.

Piazza dei Signori, sometimes known as Piazza Dante after the grimly pensive statue of the poet in the center, used to be the chief public square of Verona. Much of the right side is taken up by the **Palazzo del Capitano** (with a splendid gateway by Sanmicheli), which is separated from the Palazzo del

Comune by a stretch of excavated Roman street. Facing you as you come into the square is the **Palazzo degli Scaligeri**, residence of the Scaligeri; a monument to more democratic times extends from it at a right angle—the late fifteenth-century **Loggia del Consiglio**, former assembly hall of the city council and Verona's outstanding early Renaissance building. The rank of Roman notables along the roof includes Verona's most illustrious native poet, Catullus. For a dizzying view of the city, take a sharp right as soon as you come into the square, and go up the twelfth-century **Torre de Lamberti** (Tues–Sun 8am–6:45pm; L2500 by lift, L1500 on foot); 83m tall, it's the highest tower in Verona. The beautiful Gothic staircase alongside leads to the magistrates' chambers.

The Arche Scaligere

Passing under the arch linking the Palazzo degli Scaligeri to the Palazzo del Capitano, you come to the little Romanesque church of **Santa Maria Antica**, in front of which are ranged the **Arche Scaligere**, among the most elaborate Gothic funerary monuments in Italy. Over the side entrance to the church, an equestrian statue of **Cangrande I** ("Big Dog"; d.1329) grins on the summit of his tomb's pyramidal roof; the statue is a copy, the original being displayed in the Castelvecchio (see below). The canopied tombs of the rest of the clan are enclosed within a wrought iron palisade decorated with ladder motifs, the emblem of the Scaligeri—the family name was della Scala, "scala" meaning ladder. **Mastino I** ("Mastiff"; d.1277), founder of the dynasty, is buried in the simple tomb against the wall of the church; **Mastino II** (d.1351) is to the left of the entrance, opposite the most florid of the tombs, that of **Cansignorio** ("Top Dog"; d.1375); the two who didn't take canine names, **Giovanni** (d.1359) and **Bartolomeo** (d.1304), are at the back. (Enclosure open Tues–Sun 9am–noon & 2:30–6pm.)

Sant'Anastasia and the Duomo

Going on past the Arche Scaligere, and turning left along Via San Pietro, you come to **Sant'Anastasia**, Verona's largest church. Started in 1290 and completed in 1481, it's mainly Gothic, with undertones of the Romanesque. The early-fourteenth-century carvings of New Testament scenes around the doors are the most arresting feature of its bare exterior; the interior's highlight is **Pisanello's** delicately colored fresco of *St George and the Princess* (in the sacristy), a work in which the normally martial saint appears as something of a dandy.

Via Sottoriva, one of Verona's oldest streets, runs parallel to the Adige beyond Sant'Anastasia; the majority of the houses here date from the Middle Ages, making this one of Verona's most atmospheric areas. Spanning the river and leading over to the Roman theater, the Roman **Ponte Pietra** was destroyed in 1945 by the retreating Germans, but rebuilt using mostly the original stones and bricks.

Verona's red and white striped **Duomo** lies just round the river's bend. Consecrated in 1187, it has been worked on constantly over the centuries and the campanile is still said to be incomplete, even though the bell-chamber wasn't added until 1927. As a whole it's Romanesque in its lower parts, developing into Gothic as it goes up; the two doorways are twelfth-century—look for the story of Jonah and the whale on the south porch, and the figures of statues of Roland and Oliver, two of Charlemagne's paladins, on the west. The interior has a splendid organ, and fascinating architectural details around each chapel and on the columns—particularly fine is the **Cappella Mazzanti** (last on the right). In the first chapel on the left, an *Assumption* by **Titian** occupies an architectural frame by **Sansovino**, who also designed the choir.

Just to the north of the Duomo is a Romanesque cloister, with fragments of sixth-century mosaic sidewalk, and the church of Sant'Elena, under which have been uncovered parts of the eighth-century precursor of the Duomo.

To the Castelvecchio and San Zeno

After the Arena, Verona's most impressive Roman remnant is the **Porta dei Borsari** (on the junction of Via Diaz and Corso Porta Borsari), a structure which was as great an influence on the city's Renaissance architects as the amphitheater. Now reduced to a monumental screen straddling the road, it used to be Verona's largest Roman gate; the inscription dates it at 265, but it's almost certainly older than that.

Along Corso Cavour, which stretches away from the gate, you'll find a couple of minor churches including the Romanesque **San Lorenzo**; the **Palazzo Bevilacqua**, opposite, is an uncharacteristically ornate building by **Sanmicheli**. A short distance farther, set back from the road on the right, stands the **Archo dei Gavi**, a first-century Roman triumphal arch; originally raised in the middle of the Corso, it was shifted to its present site overlooking the Adige in 1932. This is your best vantage point from which to admire the **Ponte Scaligero**; built by Cangrande II between 1355 and 1375, the bridge was blown up by the Germans in 1945—the salvaged material was used for the plausible reconstruction.

The fortress from which the bridge springs, the **Castelvecchio**, was commissioned by Cangrande II at around the same time, and became the stronghold for Verona's subsequent rulers, all of whom altered it in some way—for example, there's a small fort in the inner courtyard which was built by Napoleon. Opened as the city museum in 1925, it was damaged by bombing in World War II, but opened again after scrupulous restoration in 1964 (daily 8am–8pm; L5000).

The Castelvecchio's collection of paintings, jewelry, weapons and other artifacts flows through a labyrinth of chambers, courtyards and passages that is fascinating to explore in itself. Halfway through the itinerary, you'll come face to face with the equestrian figure **Cangrande I**, removed from his tomb and strikingly displayed on an outdoor pedestal; his expression is disconcerting from close range, his simpleton's grin difficult to reconcile with the image of the ruthless warlord. Outstanding among the paintings are two works by **Jacopo Bellini**, two *Madonnas* by **Giovanni Bellini**, another *Madonna* by **Pisanello**, **Veronese**'s *Descent from the Cross*, a **Tintoretto** *Nativity*, a **Lotto** portrait and works by **G.B. and G.D. Tiepolo**. The real joy of the museum, however, is in wandering round the fourteenth- and fifteenth-century pieces—beautiful sculptures and frescoes by the often nameless artists of the late Middle Ages.

San Zeno Maggiore

A little over a kilometer northwest of the Castelvecchio is the **Basilica di San Zeno Maggiore**, one of the most significant Romanesque churches in northern Italy. A church was founded here, above the tomb of the city's patron saint, as early as the fifth century, but the present building and its campanile were put up in the first half of the twelfth century, with additions continuing up to the end of the fourteenth century. Its large **rose window**, representing the Wheel of Fortune, dates from the early twelfth century, as does the magnificent portal, whose lintels bear relief sculptures representing the months—look also for Saint Zeno trampling the Devil. Extraordinary bronze panels on the **doors** depict scenes from the Bible and the Miracles of San Zeno, their style influenced by Byzantine and Ottoman art; most of those on the left are from c.1100, most of the right-hand panels dating from a century later.

Areas of the lofty and simple **interior** are covered with frescoes, some super-imposed upon others, some defaced by ancient graffiti. Diverting though these are, the one compulsive image in the church is the high altar's luminous *Madonna and Saints* by **Mantegna**. In the apse of the left aisle is a disarming fourteenth-century wooden figure of San Zeno, smiling even more broadly than Cangrande; the saint's tomb is in the beautifully colonnaded crypt beneath the raised choir.

North of the Adige

On the other side of Ponte Garibaldi, and right along the embankments or through the public gardens, is **San Giorgio in Braida**, in terms of its art-works the richest of Verona's churches. A *Baptism* by **Jacopo Tintoretto** hangs over the door, while the third chapel on the right contains a *Descent of the Holy Ghost* by **Domenico Tintoretto**. The main altar, designed by **Sanmicheli**, incorporates a marvelous *Martyrdom of St George* by **Paolo Veronese**. If you're in need of place to recuperate or picnic, the piazza in front of the church is your spot, providing a view along the river that must be the most photographed and painted scene in Verona.

It's a short walk along the embankments, past the twelfth-century church of **Santo Stefano** and the Ponte Pietra, to the first-century BC **Teatro Romano** (Tues–Sun 9am–noon & 2:30–6pm); much restored, the theater is now used for concerts and plays. When the restorers set to work clearing later buildings away from the theater, the only one allowed to remain was the tiny church of **Santi Siro e Libera** (tenth century but altered in the fourteenth). Higher still, and reached by a rickety-looking lift, the **Museo Archeologico** occupies the buildings of an old convent; its well-arranged collection features a number of Greek, Roman and Etruscan finds.

Steps to the side of the theater lead to the **Castel San Pietro**, built by the Austrians on the site of a Visconti castle which had been destroyed by Napoleon. An uningratiating building, its sole appeal is the view away from it.

Practicalities

In Verona limited financial resources are not the disadvantage they are in Venice. Cheap and comfortable accommodation is easily found, and numerous trattorias offer full meals for under L15,000. On almost every street corner there's a bar where a glass of house wine costs as little as L300—and only a little more for a classy local vintage. (Bardolino or Valpolicella for fans of red wine, Custoza or Soave if white is your predilection). Night life here is more varied than in Venice, and genuinely goes on into the night, in contrast to Venice's general late-evening shutdown.

The two main **tourist offices** are the **APT** at Via Dietro Anfiteatro 6 (Mon–Fri 9am–noon & 3:30–6pm, Sat 9am–noon; ☎045/592828) and their new office at Piazza delle Erbe 42 (same hours; ☎045/30086). There's also a small office at the train station.

Accommodation

The *Locanda Catullo*, Via V. Catullo 1, just off Via Mazzini (☎045/8002786; singles L7500–15,000, doubles L14,000–16,500) and the *Albergo Rosa*, Vicolo Raggiri 9, just off Piazza delle Erbe (☎045/8005693 singles L18,500, doubles L30,000), are clean and centrally placed **hotels**—and you could probably negotiate cheaper rates for longer stays out of season. With many of its rooms overlooking the Piazza delle Erbe, the *Hotel Aurora*, Via Pellicciai 2 (☎045/594717; singles L25,000, doubles L40,000 and upwards), is recommended if money's not too much of a problem.

Verona's **youth hostel**, the *Ostello della Gioventù*, is at Salita Fontana del Ferro 15, a beautiful old building in a back street behind the Teatro Romano (☎045/590360). It has 100 beds, plus some overspill accommodation, at L10,000 per night including breakfast; there's a 10:30pm curfew. The #20 bus goes nearest to the hostel, but by so circuitous a route that it's easier to walk from the center. Along similar lines are the *Casa del Giovane "Don Bosco,"* Via Provolo 16 (☎045/591300) and the *Casa della Giovane*, Via Pigna 7 (☎045/596880). The latter is run by nuns and is for women only; both are in the old center, have a midnight curfew and cost in the region of L13,000 per night, excluding breakfast.

For **campers**, *Camping Giulietta e Romeo*, about 10km from the center on the road to Bussolengo and Peschiera, is really only an option if you have your own transport; it's open all year round, has a swimming pool, and operates a midnight curfew. More convenient and pleasant summer campgrounds are *Campeggio Castel San Pietro*, up behind the Teatro Romano, and the small site right by the *Ostello*.

Eating and Drinking

A sandwich or a snack in a bar is the cheapest way of keeping hunger at bay, but if you require something more substantial, a **pizza**, as ever, is the most filling low-cost meal. Verona's best are served at *Da Salvatore*, Corso Porta Borsari 39 (closed Mon); other central places worth trying (for simple pasta dishes as well as pizzas) are the *Pizzeria Corte Farina*, Corte Farina 4 (closed Mon) and the *Pizzeria Arena*, Vicolo Tre Marchetti 1 (closed Mon), both of which stay open until 1am. A little out of the center *Il Posto*, Via Fincato (closed Tues and all July & Aug), also does excellent pizzas and often has live music. The pizzerias along the side of Piazza Brà are all pretty good, but avoid the expensive and unappetizing specimens dished up around Piazza delle Erbe and Piazza Dante.

In the center of the city, the best value among the **restaurants** is at the *Osteria Cucina al Cristo*, Piazza Pescheria (closed Sun), where a genuine, no-frills meal will cost around L12,000 with wine. Although it is possible to find cheapish places within the historic center, they're far more plentiful over the river. Especially good is the *Trattoria Ropeton*, Piazza Cisterna, below the youth hostel (closed Tues)—around L17,000 for three courses. On the other side of the Teatro Romano, the *Osteria Fontanina*, Via Madonna Terraglio, is excellent but usually crowded. In the Veronetta district, over the Adige from San Fermo, *Circolo Perbacco*, Via Carducci 48 (closed Wed) specializes in fish and traditional dishes, and *Capitan Trinchetto*, Lungadige Porta Vittoria (closed Mon) prides itself on its *risotto* and *crostini* starter. If you want to economise and have just a first course, there's no problem at either of these places. *Al Cacciatore*, Via Seminario 4, off Via Carducci (closed Sun) has a decent *menu turistico* at L11,000, including wine.

Bars

Two old **bars** with a selection of wines from all over Italy are the *Bottega dei Vini* in Vicolo Scudo di Francia, just off the north end of Via Mazzini (10:30am–3pm & 6pm–midnight; closed Tues), and the *Osteria delle Vecete* in Via Pellicciai, also near Piazza delle Erbe (Mon–Sat 10am–2:30pm & 5–9:30pm). The bars in Piazza Brà and Piazza delle Erbe are a little more expensive, but the city-life spectacle is worth the extra few lire. For a marvelous view of Ponte Pietra and the Teatro Romano, sip a glass in the garden of the *Al Ponte* bar in Via Ponte Pietra (8am–3pm & 5pm–2am; closed Wed). A bar little changed by twentieth-century fashion is the *Osteria de Duomo* at Via Duomo 7a (7am–8pm, but reopens Fri 9pm till late), which is enlivened on Wednesday afternoons and Friday nights by an enthusiastic troupe of folk musicians.

Night-hawks should head for the *Corto Maltese* in Lungadige Porta Vittoria (Mon–Sat 11am–2am) and the *Campofiore* in Via Campofiore, near the university (Mon–Sat 8am–3pm & 5pm–2am). The former gets livelier as the night wears on and sometimes has live music downstairs, while the latter is a favorite with Verona's gay population and many heterosexuals—drawn by a relaxed, unoppressive atmosphere which even allows women on their own to drink without being hassled.

If you're pining for a pint of Guinness and are willing to pay L4500 a shot, make for the mock-Irish *Celtic Pub* in Via Regaste Redentore (Tues–Fri 11:30am–2:30pm & 7pm–2am; Sat & Sun 7pm–2am); it tends to attract a yuppie clientele, but is handy for the hostel and serves a range of UK beers. The bars up in the hills to the north of the city can be investigated if you've independent transport. Probably the nicest one is *San Mattia*, the first bar on the left past the Sanctuary (9am–midnight, with 2:30–5pm siesta in summer); occupying the grounds of an old farmhouse, it has a marvelous view across part of the city.

Entertainment

After the early evening *passeggiata* up and down Via Mazzini, the typical Veronese takes a couple of hours for the day's main meal and then hits the streets again some time after 9pm, for a session of open-air socialising. Even for a stranger there are few more pleasurable ways to end the day than wandering through the city, stopping now and then for a glass of local wine in a remote bar or at a table in the bustle of Piazza Brà. For a non-alcoholic indulgence, sit outside one of the *gelaterie* in Piazza delle Erbe and give a few minutes to an incredible concoction of fruit, cream and ice cream. (Though if you want to follow the current trend, the place to make for is *Gelateria Pompanin*, by Ponte Garibaldi.)

Music and **theater** are the dominant art-forms in the cultural life of Verona. In July and August an opera festival takes place in the **Arena**, often featuring a no-expense-spared production of *Aida*; **big rock events** crop up on the Arena's calendar too—Bob Dylan, Sting, Tina Turner and Joe Cocker have all played it in recent years. (The booking office is in arch 6 of the Arena;—tickets can only be reserved by post or in person.) A season of Shakespeare in Italian is the principal summer fare at the **Teatro Romano**; plays by other dramatists are performed here as well, with **jazz**, **blues** and **rock** festivals as frequent additional attractions. Some of the Teatro events are free; for the rest, cheapskates who don't mind inferior acoustics can always park themselves on the steps going up the hill alongside the theater. The Teatro's box office (☎045/594363) also sells tickets for the

Arena and vice versa. Additional open-air concerts and other entertainments are staged sporadically throughout the summer in **Piazza Dante**.

From October to May **English language films** are shown every Wednesday at the *Cinema Stimate*, Piazza Cittadella (☎045/8000878). The **disco** scene is much more lively than in Venice, with venues coming and going; look in the local paper—*L'Arena*—under *Ritrovi* to find out where they are and what days they're open. For one-off events, check the *Spettacoli* section of *L'Arena* (you needn't buy it, as there's a copy in every bar); alternatively, get a copy of *Verona For You* from the tourist office—though the times and prices are not always dependable.

As the Veneto produces more DOC (*Denominazione di Origine Controllata*) wine than any other region in Italy, it's not surprising that Italy's main wine fair, *Vinitaly*, is held in Verona; it takes place in April, and offers infinite sampling opportunities.

Transportation

Situated on the main Turin–Trieste line, Verona is ninety minutes by **train** from both **Venice** (every 30min) and **Milan** (ditto). Direct services also run to Bologna, Rome (6 daily), Brennero, Munich and Paris (3 daily). The station is in front of Piazzale XXV Aprile, by the Porta Nuova; the information desk operates from 7am to 10pm every day (☎045/590688). There's an *Albergo Diurno* here, for toilets, showers and hairdressers.

Access by **road** is equally straightforward, with the north–south Brenner to Modena motorway intersecting the motorway from Trieste to Turin a few miles outside the city. The main **coach and bus station** is on Piazzale XXV Aprile (information ☎045/8004129).

The **airport** at Villafranca, with flights to many major European cities, is about 16km from the city center, and linked by regular bus and coach services.

Around Verona

Of all the major centers of the Veneto, Verona affords the easiest access to rural isolation, with the magnificent Lessini mountains a short bus ride or an easy cycle north of the city. To the west, there's Lago di Garda, the healthiest expanse of water in the region, while in the opposite direction lies the Soave district, which, with the Bardolino and Valpolicella regions, plays a major part in making the Veneto the country's largest producer of DOC wine.

Lago di Garda

Arriving in summer at the shore of **Lago di Garda** (Lake Garda), 40km from Verona, you might well think you've crossed the border, as the Brenner motorway brings so many visitors down from the north that German and Austrian cars outnumber Italian by about three to one. For swimming and sunbathing, **Punto San Vigilio** is probably the nicest spot on the Verona side; **buses** run from Verona to this and other towns along the water, but unless you're desperate for the feel of sun on bare flesh, give them a miss in summer. Spring and autumn are far more pleasant, bringing days on which the lake's usual haze lifts to reveal the far shore and the mountains around it. Wine buffs will get a lot out of a harvest-time trip to **BARDOLINO**, on the eastern shore; the vineyards around here are well-known abroad for their rosé (Chiaretto) and ruby-red wines, but much of the best stuff doesn't get farther than a few dozen kilmotres from the presses.

Lessinia

The area north of Verona, **Lessinia**, is hilly verging on the mountainous, offering fertile valleys of vineyards and cherry orchards, a number of villages and small towns, and opportunities for both casual and serious walking. Should you want to walk all the way from the city, the Verona APT can provide maps and advice on the well-marked trails (*sentiere*); a good map is essential to get the best from the expedition. Alternatively, bikes can be hired from the shop next to *Bar Brà* in Piazza Brà, and there are frequent buses from the train station and Corso Porta Nuova. All the places mentioned below are within a brief hike of bus-stop; the last return bus is usually at around 8pm.

Snow can lie meters-deep for months in the Lessini hills, and the hardship of the winter is leading to increased migration from the close-knit, conservative communities farther up the valleys. Whole villages have been abandoned, but the old way of life still endures in places, with woodcutting and cowherding the main livelihoods.

Amateur geologists and palaeontologists will find this part of the Veneto especially rewarding—particularly around **BOLCA**, in the eastern **Alpone** valley. Fifty million years ago this was a coral atoll surrounded by the sea; a succession of earthquakes and eruptions left it stranded, fossilizing over 150 species of fish and 250 species of plants. Specimens can be bought in the local **museum**, or you can look for your own: turn left below the village and follow the road to the *Osteria Nuova*, where a right turn brings you to **Monte Pastale**—PESCIAIA, at its base, is the prime fossil site.

Northwest of here is the village of GIAZZA, isolated at the narrow head of the Val d'Illasi. Its inhabitants probably originated in Bavaria, and certainly their strange Germanic dialect and folkloric tales of giants and orcs have scarcely changed over the centuries.

Another place of geological interest is the chasm at CAMPOSILVANO, a short way southwest of Giazza. From here, it's 10km to **BOSCO CHIESANUOVA**, the area's largest town and a busy resort. The open-air ice rink is open every night (disco on Sat), and there's a museum of ethnography near the church (Sat & Sun 4:30–6:30pm). Most Sundays the *Club Alpino Italiano* organizes walks in the extraordinary karst terrain of the surrounding **Val di Squarento**; details of these trips, which are free, are available at the tourist office.

The westernmost valley of Lessinia is **Valpolicella**, which rises to the attractive alpine village of **SANT'ANNA D'ALFAEDO**. People have been living around heresince at least 2000 BC, and the local museum displays ancient tools and jewelry, as well as finds from the limestone caves of nearby Monte Loffa—including a six-meter-long shark and a seventy-million-year-old turtle. Mule paths run north to the fine vantage point of the **Corno di Aquilio**, passing the abyss called the **Spluga della Preta**, where a network of tunnels descends to a depth of 985 meters—for experienced potholers only. If you have nerves of steel, you might check out the **Ponte di Veja**, southeast of Sant'Anna between VAGGIMAL and GIARE. This fifty-meter span of rock arches nearly thirty meters over a stream and waterfall, and is said to have been the inspiration for the bridge of Malebolge, in Dante's *Inferno*. Forming part of the entrance to a vast cavern in which palaeolithic human remains have been found, it is reputed to be the meeting place for local witches.

Valpolicella is of course renowned for its red **wine**: produce from the various growers can be sampled at the well-signposted *cantine*, where you'll be expected to buy a few bottles for the pleasure. While you're in the valley, you could also try the port-like Recioto and the drier Amarone, both made from grapes that have been left to dry before fermentation. They're very strong, so take care.

East of Verona

Moving east from Verona, buses bound for SAN BONIFACIO will get you to **CALDIERO**, 15km away, where thermal swimming pools provide an unusual means of abating the tensions of urban sightseeing. The water bubbles up from the spring at 28°C, and possesses medicinal properties which have been exploited for a long time: the oldest of the pools dates back to the Roman era. Now there's a modern Olympic-size pool plus a small one for the kids, all set in a pleasant lawn with trees for shade.

A short distance farther east is **SOAVE**, its center encircled by walls built by the Scaligeri in the fourteenth century, and protected by a castle and twenty-four towers from the same period. Outside the walls, the renovated twelfth-century church of San Giorgio is worth a look for its spindly tower and bas-relief of Saint George and the dragon over the door. But **wine** is the chief attraction of the town, and there are plenty of bars in which to sample the delicate, dry product of the local vineyards: *Enoteca San Giorgio*, near the path up to the castle, is a nice place to sit outside. Best of all, come here for the *Festa del Vino* (first Sun in March), or the *festa* to celebrate the harvest (first Sun in Sept).

CHAPTER THIRTEEN

THE NORTHERN VENETO

L acking a city of Verona or Padua's appeal, the area extending from the lagoon to the southern edge of the Dolomites is the least visited part of the Veneto—most of those who pass through it are simply hurrying through to the ski-slopes of resorts like Cortina d'Ampezzo. It doesn't deserve such neglect: its attractions might be generally on a smaller scale than those of the better-known Veneto towns, but they are well worth sampling.

The northern Veneto's only real city is **Treviso**, whose medieval buildings and frescoes merit at least an afternoon's expedition from nearby Venice, and whose centrality to the rail network makes it a good base from which to wander into the crannies of the region. A direct line connects with **Conegliano**, a town where life revolves around the production of wine, and of the sparkling Prosecco in particular. From there a service continues up through **Vittório Véneto** (with remarkably preserved Renaissance streets) and on to **Belluno**, in effect the mountains' border post. A short way beyond Belluno, lodged on a ridge overlooking the valley of the Piave, **Feltre** boasts another historic center almost untouched by the last four centuries.

To the west of Treviso, **Castelfranco Véneto**—the birthplace of Giorgione – also sits in the middle of a web of rail lines that runs south to Venice. A hop in one direction brings you to **Cittadella**, an ancient walled town (like Castelfranco itself), while to the north is **Bassano del Grappa**, source of the fiery grappa spirit. Two other remarkable old towns lie within a short radius of Bassano: **Maróstica**, famous for its ceremonial chess-game played with human "pieces," and **Ásolo**, historically a rural retreat for the Venetian aristocracy. Finally, just a few kilometers from Ásolo, there's arguably the finest country house in all of Italy—the **Villa Barbaro** at **Masèr**.

Treviso

The local tourist board are pitching it a bit high when they suggest that the water-ways of **TREVISO** may remind you of Venice, but you can't blame them for trying. To most people, Treviso is just the place the cheap flights go to, and it does deserve more respect than that—the old center of the town is far more allur-ing than you might imagine from the modern suburbs you pass through on your way to or from the airport.

Treviso today is a brisk commercial center and the capital of a province that extends to the north almost as far as Belluno. As with every settlement in the area, it used to be under Venetian control, but it was an important town long before its assimilation by Venice in 1389. As early as the eighth century it was minting its own coins, and by the end of the thirteenth century, when it was ruled by the da Camino family, Treviso was renowned as a refuge for artists and poets, and a model of good government. (Dante, in the *Purgatorio*, praises Gherardo da Camino as a man "left from a vanished race in reproof to these unruly times.") Plenty of evidence of the town's early stature survives in the form of Gothic churches, public buildings and, most dramatically of all, the paintings of **Tomaso da Modena** (1325–79), the dominant artist in north Italy in the years immedi-ately after Giotto's death. The general townscape within Treviso's sixteenth-century walls is often appealing too. A lack of local dressing stone led in thir-teenth century to the use of frescoes to decorate the houses, and these painted facades (often overhanging the road on corbels), along with the lengthy porticoes that shelter the sidewalks, give many of the streets an appearance quite distinct from those of other towns in the region.

The City

Some of the best of these arcades and frescoes are in the main street of the center, **Calmaggiore**, where modern commerce (epitomized by the locally-based and omnipresent Benetton) has reached the sort of compromise with the past that the Italians seem to arrange better than anyone else. Modern construction techniques have played a larger part than you might think in shaping that compromise—Treviso was pounded during both World Wars, and on Good Friday 1944 around half its buildings were destroyed in a single bombing raid.

The early thirteenth-century **Palazzo dei Trecento** (hall of the town council), at the side of the **Piazza dei Signori**, was one casualty of '44—a line round the exterior shows where the restoration began. Exhibitions are sometimes held in the main hall, which is generally open to the public each weekday from 8:30am to 12:30pm (free entry). The adjoining **Palazzo del Podestà**, with its high tower, is a late nineteenth-century structure, concocted in the appropriate style.

Incorporated into the back of this block are three buildings you could easily overlook: the Monte di Pietà (municipal pawnshop) and the churches of San Vito and Santa Lucia. The **Monte di Pietà** (Mon–Fri 8:30am–noon), at the end of the small piazza of the same name, is worth a visit for the Cappella dei Rettori, a chapel decorated in the sixteenth century with frescoes, panel paintings and gilded leather. In adjacent rooms you can see the scales used to assess the loans, and pictures by Luca Giordano and Sebastiano Ricci, plus one labeled "attrib. Giorgione," to the understandable embarrassment of the custodians. To get into it, ask at the Cassa di Risparmio della Marca Trivigiana—ring the bell at no. 2, or just go straight up the staircase at no. 5 and ask at one of the counters. The joined medieval churches of **San Vito** and **Santa Lucia** (9am–noon and late afternoon) are tucked behind the Monte di Pietà, on the edge of the Piazza San Vito. The latter is the more interesting—a tiny, dark chapel with extensive frescoes by **Tomaso da Modena** and his followers; San Vito has even earlier paintings (twelfth- and thirteenth-century) in the alcove through which you enter from Santa Lucia, but they're not in a good state.

Another one of Treviso's ancient landmarks, the patricians' meeting-place known as the **Loggia dei Cavalieri**, is close to the Palazzo dei Trecento, down Via Martiri della Libertà. Built in the early thirteenth century and pieced back together after the 1944 air raid, it was decorated first with a brick pattern and grotesque figures, and then with romanticized scenes from the Trojan wars, scraps of which you might be able to make out if you've got hawk-like vision. It's remarkable more for the fact of its survival than for its appearance, but keep your eyes open for it if you're strolling down that way towards the Santa Caterina side of town (see below).

The Duomo

The Duomo of Treviso, **San Pietro** (daily 7am–noon & 3–7pm), stands at the end of Calmaggiore, rising above the squall of mopeds on the Piazza del Duomo. Founded in the twelfth century, as were the **campanile** and perpetually closed **Baptistery** alongside, San Pietro was much altered between the fifteenth and nineteenth centuries (when the huge portico was added), and then rebuilt to

CENTRAL TREVISO

rectify the damage of 1944. The oldest clearly distinguishable feature of the exterior is the pair of eroded Romanesque lions at the base of the portico; fragments of Romanesque wall are embedded in the side walls too.

The interior is chiefly notable for the **crypt**—a thicket of twelfth century columns with scraps of fourteenth and fifteenth century mosaics (if locked ask sacristan)—and the **Malchiostro Chapel**—with frescoes by **Pordenone** and a much restored *Annunciation* by Titian. Although Pordenone and Titian were the bitterest of rivals, their pictures were commissioned as part of a unified scheme, representing the conception and birth of Christ; bombs of 1944 annihilated the crowning piece of the ensemble—a fresco by Pordenone on the chapel dome, representing *God the Father*. Paintings by **Paris Bordone**, the most famous Treviso-born artist, hang in the vestibule of the chapel and in the sacristy. Other things to search out are the *Monument to Bishop Zanetti* by **Pietro Lombardo** (1486; on left wall of chancel—not easy to see), the *Tomb of Bishop Nicolò Franco* by **Lorenzo and Giambattista Bregno** (1501; in chapel to left of chancel), and **Lorenzo Bregno**'s figure of *St Sebastian* (west pillar of left aisle).

San Nicolò and the Paintings of Tomaso da Modena

The severe Dominican church of **San Nicolò**, dominating the corner of the old town just over the Sile river from the railroad station, upstages the Duomo in every department. Wrapped round several of its massive pillars are delicate frescoes by **Tomaso da Modena** and his school, of which the freshest are the *St Jerome* and *St Agnes* by Tomaso himself, on the first column on your right as you enter. The towering *St Christopher* on the wall of the right aisle, with feet the size of canoes, was painted around 1410, probably by **Antonio da Treviso**. Equally striking, but considerably more graceful, is the composite *Tomb of Agostino d'Onigo* on the left wall of the chancel, created in 1500 by **Antonio Rizzo** (who did the sculpture) and **Lorenzo Lotto** (who painted the attendant pages). Another collaborative work stands on the altar of the Monigo chapel, on the right of the chancel—**Sebastiano del Piombo** painted the upper section, and **Lotto** the lower gallery of portraits; the frescoes on the side walls are by fourteenth-century Sienese and Riminese artists. If it's not a sunny day you'll have problems seeing these pictures—on the last visit the church authorities had fitted intruder alarms, but still hadn't got round to any form of illumination.

The figures of Agnes and Jerome are an excellent introduction to Tomaso da Modena, but for a comprehensive demonstration of his talent you should visit the neighboring **Seminario**, where the **chapter house** is decorated with a series of portraits of members of the Dominican order, executed by the artist in 1352. Although these are not portraits in the modern sense of the term, in that they don't attempt to reproduce the appearance of the men whose names they bear, these paintings are astonishingly advanced in their observation of idiosyncratic reality. Each shows a monk at study in his cell, but there is never a hint of the merely formulaic: one man is shown sharpening a quill, another checks a text through a magnifier, a third starts back from his desk as if in surprise, and so on. (Mon–Fri 9am–noon; arrange a visit either at the caretaker's office—no. 3 in the courtyard at the west end of the church—or by phoning ☎0422/542322.)

Treviso has another brilliant fresco cycle by Tomaso da Modena—*The Story of the Life of Sant'Ursula*—but getting to see it is a bit more of a test. Painted for the now extinct church of Santa Margherita sul Sile, the frescoes were detached from the walls in the late nineteenth century and transported to the Museo Civico.

From there they were dispatched in 1979 to **Santa Caterina**, on the other side of town from San Nicolò, a deconsecrated church maintained for the display of the frescoes in its Cappella degli Innocenti, by Tomaso and his school. To get into the church you have to make an appointment at the Museo Civico (stop by in person or phone ☎0422/51337 Tues–Sat 9am–11:30pm & 2–4:30pm; L1000). So, if you're coming to Treviso for the day and you want to see this extraordinary series, make sure you phone at least one day in advance.

The East Side

Two other churches in the Santa Caterina quarter are also worth a look. To the north of Santa Caterina is the thirteenth-century church of **San Francesco**, which was reopened and restored early this century after years as a military depot. It's an airy building with a high ship's-keel ceiling and patches of fresco, including another vast *St Christopher* and a *Madonna and Saints* by **Tomaso da Modena** in the chapel to the left of the chancel. Close to the door on the right side is the tomb of **Francesca, daughter of Petrarch**, who died in 1384, twenty years after **Dante's son, Pietro**, whose tomb is in the left transept.

To the south, at the end of one of the most attractive streets in Treviso—Via Carlo Alberto—stands the **Basilica di Santa Maria Maggiore** (largely fifteenth century), which houses the most venerated image in Treviso, a fresco of the Madonna, originally painted by Tomaso da Modena but subsequently retouched.

This is the workshop and market stall area, a district in which Treviso has the feel of a smaller town. The antique sellers and furniture restorers of Treviso even outnumber the Benetton outlets, and it's over this side that you'll see most evidence of them. Trevisans once characterized their town as "gioiosa e amorosa" (happy and amorous), and still insist that there's a "certain sweetness" to life here, to quote the tourist leaflet. You can best appraise the extent to which this sweetness has pervaded the local character by hanging round the stalls in and around the **Pescheria**, which occupies an island in the middle of Treviso's biggest canal. (As in Venice, health regulations dictated the siting of the fish-market by a waterway.) For a full-blown display of Trevisan mercantile skills, be here on a Saturday or Tuesday morning, when the the northern part of this quarter, along Viale Bartolomeo Burchiellati and Borgo Mazzini, is overrun by a gigantic market.

The Museums and City Walls

From the historic center around the Duomo, the recommended route to the **Museo Civico** (Tues–Sat 9am–noon & 2–5pm, Sun & hols 9am–noon; closed Mon; L1000) is along Via Riccati, which has a number of fine old houses—and cycle-fetishists can drool at the window of Colnago, makers of racing machines to the elite of professional road cycling and sponsors of a team in the Tour de France. The ground floor of the museum is taken up by the archaeological collection, predominantly late Bronze Age and Roman relics; the picture collection, on the upper floor, is typical of provincial collections all over Italy—acres of hackwork interrupted by a few paintings for which any gallery director would give a year's salary. In this second category are three paintings hanging cheek by jowl in room 9—a *Crucifixion* by **Jacopo Bassano**, *Portrait of Sperone Speroni* by **Titian** and **Lorenzo Lotto's** psychologically acute *Portrait of a Dominican*. Comparing the Titian and Lotto portraits, you can see some justice in Bernard Berenson's contrast between the two—"we might imagine

Titian asking of every person he was going to paint: Who are you? What is your position in society? while Lotto would put the question: What sort of person are you? How do you take life?"

Treviso's other public collection, the **Museo della Casa Trevigiana** (same hours as Museo Civico), is only a couple of minutes away, in Via Antonio Canova. Housed in the fourteenth- to sixteenth-century Casa da Noal, a building that would merit a visit even if it were empty, this is the town's museum of the applied arts—furniture, dolls, architectural decorations, armor, musical instruments and, most impressive of all, wrought iron work (a local specialty). Not the first place to head for in Treviso, but a definite if you're around for a couple of days.

The longest unbroken stretch of the **city walls** is in the vicinity of the Museo and Casa Trevigiana, between the Porta dei Santi Quaranta and Porta San Tomaso. The fortification of Treviso was undertaken in 1509, at the start of the War of the League of Cambrai, and the work was finished around 1517, with the construction of these two monumental gates. If you fancy a walk away from the traffic, albeit only ten meters away, there's a path along the walls.

Practicalities

The **EPT** is in the Palazzo Scotti, Via Toniolo 41 (☎0422/547632); their free *Carnet del Turista* lists all hotels, restaurants and museums in the province of Treviso, with prices and opening hours (but not, in the case of restaurants, addresses), and their fold-out guide to the town features a list of Treviso's frescoed houses. The **post office** is in the Piazzale della Vittoria, over to your left shortly after crossing the river from the train station; for **banks** keep going straight along Corso del Popolo towards Calmaggiore—you'll pass most of them along this stretch.

Accommodation

Although Treviso itself isn't likely to tempt you to stay, you might want to use it as a base from which to strike out into the mainland, or as a back-up if accommodation in Venice is hard to find. There are two one-star hotels in the old town: *Vittoria*, Via San Nicolo 3/B (☎0422/52285; L27,000 double) and *Alla Colomba*, Via Ortazzo 25 (☎0422/542284; closed Fri; L18,000 double). It's a good idea to phone ahead in both cases, as *Alla Colomba* has only four rooms, being a trattoria with lodgings, and the Vittoria has a knack of closing down "for restoration." Of the central two-stars, the cheapest is *Al Cuor*, Piazzale Duca d'Aosta 1 (☎0422/546275; L34,000 double), as it's right on top of the main road and rail convergences, to the side of the train station. After that, your best bet is the *Becchiere*, Piazza Ancillotto 11 (☎0422/540871)—which will be about L40,000 for a double, L22,000 for a single.

Eating and Drinking

Treviso has a number of restaurants with very high reputations and prices to match—the leader of the pack being *Alfredo el Toulà*, at Via Collalto 26 (☎0422/540275, for the benefit of Gold Card holders). For a good range of local dishes, at around L30,000 with wine, try the restaurant of the *Becchiere* (see above; closed Thurs). If that's still too steep, the homey *Toni del Spin*, not far from the Duomo at Via Inferiore 7 (☎0422/543829), is almost as good and around L5000 cheaper; try their risotto with *luganega*, a soft sausage produced only in the Veneto. Also good value, in descending order of cost and quality, are: *All' Oca Bianca*, Vicolo della Torre 7 (☎0422/541850; closed Wed); *Al Morer*, Via Riccati 28 (☎0422/533224; closed Sun); *Al Cavallino*, Borgo Cavour 54 (☎0422/548322; closed Sun); and the very plain and very cheap *Alla Colomba* (see above, closed Fri).

The most popular **bars and cafés** in Treviso are those clustered underneath the Palazzo dei Trecento; also lively, and only a few yards from the Piazza dei Signori, is the bar of *San Vito*, Piazza San Vito 40, where a knowledge of the fortunes of AC Milan and Ruud Gullit's knee injuries will do wonders for your credibility. Two other decent bars are the *Osteria dalla Elsa*, Vicolo San Gregorio, just to the south of the Piazza dei Signori, and the *Osteria Gioiosa* in Via Inferiore. The polished chrome cafés of Calmaggiore serve some delicious pastries, but are a bit too slick and not the friendliest places in the Veneto. *Casellato*, Via della Campana 2, just off Piazza San Vito, is the chosen *pasticceria* of Treviso's school-kids and a fair number of more senior Trevisans.

Transportation

Trains run regularly from Treviso to **Venice** (on average every 30min; journey 30min), **Vicenza** (approximately hourly; 1hr) via Castelfranco and Cittadella, **Udine** (hourly; 90min) and **Montebelluna** (hourly; 30min). One train a day goes to Rome (6hr) and one runs to Milan (3hr 30min). **Coaches** depart from the station in Lungosile Antonio Mattei, just before you cross the river going from the railroad station. As usual, there's little point taking a bus where the route duplicates the train's, so the only services you might need are the direct services to **Padua** (every 30min), **Asolo** (hourly) and **Bassano** (every 2hr).

The #6 **bus** for **Treviso airport** goes twice an hour from a stop over the road from the train station. Tickets cost L600, and you can buy them at the *ACTT* booth inside the train station or at any shop showing the *ACTT* sign. Allow half an hour for the journey.

Conegliano

Traveling north from Treviso, it's at the amiable town of **CONEGLIANO**, as the terrain rises towards the mountains, that the landscape ceases to be boring. The surrounding hills are patched with vineyards, and the production of wine is central to the economy of the district. Italy's first wine-growers' college was set up in Conegliano in 1876, and today there are a couple of well-established **wine routes** for the tourist to explore: the **Strada del Vino Rosso**, which follows a looping 68-kilometer course southeast to ODERZO, and the more rewarding **Strada del Vino Bianco**, a straighter 42-kilometer journey west to VALDOBBIÁDENE. The former takes you through Merlot, Cabernet and Raboso country; the latter passes the Bianco dei Colli, Prosecco and Cartizze producers—the last, a more refined version of Prosecco, could be mistaken for champagne with a small effort of will.

The old center of Conegliano, adhering to the slope of the Colle di Giano and presided over by the Castello on its summit (founded in tenth century), is right in front of you as you come out of the station. After crossing the principal street of the modern town (Corso V. Emanuele–Corso G. Mazzini) you pass through a portico and into the original high street—**Via XX Settembre**. Lined with fifteenth- to eighteenth-century houses, this is an attractive street on any day, but to see it at its best you should turn up on a Friday morning, when the weekly **market** sets up camp.

The most decorative feature of Via XX Settembre is the unusual facade of the **Duomo**—a fourteenth-century portico, frescoed at the end of the sixteenth century by **Ludovico Pozzoserrato**, which joins seamlessly the buildings on each side. The interior of the church has been rebuilt, but retains fragments of fifteenth-century frescoes; the major adornment of the church, though, is the magnificent altarpiece of *The Madonna and Child with Saints and Angels*, painted in 1493 by **Giambattista Cima** (c.1459–c.1517), the most famous native of Conegliano.

Alongside the Duomo, at the top of the steps facing the door off the right-hand aisle of the church, is the **Sala dei Battuti** (Hall of the Flagellants), the frescoed meeting place of a local confraternity. (Ask the sacristan for admission.) The pictures are mostly sixteenth century and depict scenes from the Creation to the Last Judgement, incorporating the weirdest *Ascension* you'll ever see, with Christ half out of the frame and a pair of footprints left behind at the point of lift-off. Individually the frescoes are nothing much to write home about, but the room as a whole is quite striking.

Cima's birthplace, no. 24 Via G.B. Cima, at rear of Duomo, has been restored and converted into the **Casa Museo di G.B. Cima** (Sat & Sun 4–6pm; free). Formally unadventurous, Cima exemplifies the conservative strand in Venetian painting of the early sixteenth century, but at their best his paintings have something of the elegiac tone of Giovanni Bellini's later works. The museum's pictures present clearly his strengths and his weaknesses; not one of them, though, is a painting by Cima—they're all high-class reproductions.

The **Museo Civico** (summer Tues–Sun 9am–noon & 3:30–7pm; winter Tues–Sun 9am–noon & 2–5:30pm; L1500) is housed in the main tower of the reconstructed Castello on top of the hill—reached quickest by the steep Calle Madonna della Neve, which begins at the end of Via Accademia, the street beside the enormous *Accademia* cinema. There are no masterpieces among the paintings (largely workshop of . . . , school of . . ., etc) and the displays of medals, maps, war memorabilia, armor and so forth are no more fascinating than you'd expect. But two aspects of the museum lift it out of the rut: the exhibition on the upper floors devoted to "The Grape in Art"—a maniacally diligent investigation of the grape motif in painting, furniture and jewelry design, glass and silverware, and any other applied art you care to think of; and the view from the roof, after which you'll never look at a Cima painting the same way again.

Practicalities—and Prosecco

Via Settembre XX has all you'll need in the way of cafés, bars and food shops; if you're planning to stay, the *Canon d'Oro* at no. 129 is a good **hotel** with an excellent **restaurant** (☎0438/22173; doubles from L46,200). Cheaper trattorias are easy to find in the immediate vicinity. Double rooms in the *Stadio*, behind the train station at Via Istria 51 (☎0438/22320), are around L20,000 cheaper—so if money's a bit tight, stay here and put the difference towards a treat from the kitchen of the *Canon d'Oro*.

Prosecco is the chief wine of the Conegliano district, and its producers compile a list of recommended outlets: two authorized bars to try in the town itself are the *Giardini* café in Piazza Duca d'Aosta and the *Al Montegan Enoteca* in Via Istria. If you want to sample the nectar at source, exploration of the Strada del Vino Bianco by public transit isn't a problem—**buses** run frequently from Conegliano to Valdobbiádene, leaving from Piazzale Santa Caterina (turn left out of train station along Via C. Colombo). For details of both the wine routes, ask at the extremely helpful **AAST**—Viale Carducci 32, in front of railroad station (☎0438/21230). They also have a very good tourist map of the Veneto, packed with information on matters recreational, gastronomic and architectural.

Getting to Conegliano from Venice is easy—all the Venice to Udine **trains** stop there. The journey from Venice takes fifty minutes and the service is hourly (except around 9–11am, when there's a gap in the schedule). There are nine northward connections a day from Conegliano to Vittório Véneto (13min)—sometimes (not often) these connections are by *Autocorsa*, a bus service on which rail tickets alone are valid. From Vittório Véneto four carry on to Belluno (60–90min), and four connect with the Belluno shuttle at PONTE DELLE ALPI. The remaining one chugs north from Ponte delle Alpi to Calalzo, in the heart of the eastern Dolomites.

Vittório Véneto

The name **VITTÓRIO VÉNETO** first appeared on the map in 1866 when, to mark the unification of Italy and honor the first king of the new country (Vittorio Emanuele II), the neighboring towns of Cèneda and Serravalle, who hadn't previously been the best of friends, were knotted together and rechristened. A new town hall was built midway along the avenue connecting the two towns, and the railroad station constructed opposite, thus ensuring that the visitor steps straight from the train into a sort of no-man's-land.

Cèneda

CÈNEDA, overlooked by the seventh-century Lombard castle of San Martino (now the bishop's residence), is the less appealing of the halves; having a more open situation than Serravalle it has inevitably developed as the commercial center of Vittório Véneto. It is, nonetheless, worth a visit for the **Museo della Battaglia** in the sixteenth-century Loggia Cenedese, which is possibly by Sansovino (May–Sept Tues–Sun 10am–noon & 4–6:30pm; Oct–April Tues–Sun 10am–noon & 2–5pm; combined L2000 ticket for the Museo della Battaglia and the Museo and San Lorenzo in Serravalle). It's next to the cathedral, which you get to by turning right out of the station and keeping going until you see the sign for the center (15min). The Battle of Vittório, which lasted from October 24 to November 3, 1918, was the final engagement of World War I for the Italian army—which is why most towns in Italy have a Via Vittório Véneto—and the museum is dedicated to the climactic engagement.

The only other building that merits a look in Cèneda is the church of **Santa Maria del Meschio**, where you'll find a luscious *Annunciation* by **Andrea Previtali** (c.1470–1528), a pupil of Giovanni Bellini. If you turn left off the Cèneda–Serravalle road instead going right for the cathedral square, you'll find it quickly.

Serravalle

The Romanesque church of **Sant'Andrea di Bigonzo** will catch your attention as you trudge from Cèneda to Serravalle, at the end of an avenue to the right; it's decorated with Renaissance frescoes, but unless you've a bit of time to spare, content yourself with the view from a distance.

SERRAVALLE, wedged in the neck of the gorge between the Col Visentin and the Cansiglio, is an entirely different proposition from its partner. Once through its southern gate—to the left of which the ruined walls disappear into the trees on the valley side—you are into a town that has scarcely seen a demolition since the sixteenth century. Franco Zeffirelli exploited the place's charm to the full when he used it as one of the locations for his soft-focus *Romeo and Juliet*. Most of the buildings along Via Martiri della Libertà, Via Roma and Via Mazzini, and around the stage-like Piazza Marcantonio Flaminio date from the fifteenth and sixteenth centuries—the handsomest being the finely-painted and shield-encrusted *Loggia Serravallese* (rebuilt c.1460). This is now the home of the **Museo del Cenedese**, a jumble of sculptural and archaeological bits and pieces, detached frescoes and minor paintings (May–Sept 10am–noon & 4:30–6:30pm; Oct–April 10am–noon & 3–5pm; closed Tues).

Time is more profitably spent in the churches of Serravalle than in its museum. One of the best preserved fresco cycles in the Veneto covers the interior of **San Lorenzo dei Battuti**, immediately inside the south gate (3:30–4:30pm; closed Tues; visit arranged at the Museo). Painted in c.1450, the frescoes were damaged when Napoleon's troops used the chapel as a kitchen, but restoration subsequent to the uncovering of the cycle in 1953 has rectified the situation.

The **Duomo**, across the Meschio river on the far side of the Piazza Flaminio from the Museo, is a dull eighteenth-century building with a medieval campanile (good view of the gorge from the back)—an altarpiece of *The Virgin with St Peter and St Andrew*, produced in 1547 by **Titian** and his workshop, is the sole reason to go inside.

Behind the apse of the Duomo a flight of steps leads to a path that winds through the woods to the **Sanctuary of Santa Augusta**—go for the walk, not for the building. If you're in town on August 21, the festival of Saint Augusta's martyrdom, you'll be treated to a huge firework display and all-night party. Carry on up the Via Roma instead of veering across the Piazza Flaminio, and you'll pass the remnant of the Castello and, eventually, the little church of **San Giovanni Battista** (outside the walls), which has beautiful cloisters. Further on still, and a few yards over the river (take the first right after San Giovanni), is **Santa Giustina**, which contains one of the best funerary monuments in the region—the **tomb** erected in 1336 by Verde della Scala (ie Scaliger) for her husband, Rizzardo VI da Camino, who had been killed in battle. The four praying warriors that support the Gothic sarcophagus were probably purloined from an older pulpit or other such structure.

Practicalities

The **AAST** is on Piazza del Popolo (☎0438/57243). It's best for information on the ski resorts and walking terrain around the town; the fold-out guide to Vittório Véneto is printed in Italian only, and includes one of the most useless street maps ever committed to paper.

The cheapest **accommodation** in Vittório Véneto is at Serravalle's miniscule *Alla Giraffa*, Piazza Fontana 10 (☎0438/550269)—doubles start at L20,000, and there's a single for L10,000. If that's full, you could try the *Leon d'Oro*, at Via Cavour 39 (☎0438/53327), or *Al Postiglione*, a few doors away at no. 39 (☎0438/556924)—both cost about L20,000 for a single, L34,000 for a double. For **food** in Serravalle, there's the *Trattoria alla Cerve* on Piazza Flaminio, or the bar-pizzeria *Al 128* in Via Roma. If you can afford to spend L30,000, the restaurant of the

Terme hotel is excellent; it's at Via delle Terme 4, on the Serravalle–Cèneda road (☎0438/554345).

Three **trains** a day call at Vittório Véneto from Venice; an additional six trains take you to **Conegliano**, where you change for the fifteen-minute hop to Vittório Véneto: the quickest journey lasts one hour, the slowest lasts two. Read the timetable carefully when checking your connection back to Vittório Véneto—if it's marked as an *Autocorsa* (a bus on which you use your train ticket), you'll have to skip over to the bus station. For northward services from Vittório Véneto, see the Conegliano entry. **Buses** leave from the station behind Piazza del Popolo (facing the train station), and scatter in all directions over the foothills of the Dolomites.

Around Vittório Véneto

The environs of Vittório Véneto offer plenty of opportunities for activities more energetic than church crawling. From the center of the town there are paths leading up into the hills, such as the one that takes you up to Monte Altare, immediately to the west. Further out, there are ski centers on both sides of the gorge to the north of the town, on the ALPAGO and NEVEGÀL slopes. These are the nearest ski resorts to Venice, but are best approached from Belluno, to the north. The **Lago di Santa Croce**, the reservoir which occupies much of the valley floor, is a center for water-sports. The Vittório Véneto–Belluno bus skirts the lake.

Progressing up the valley to the west of Vittório Véneto, the area around the two small lakes of **REVÌNE** is good walking country; the town of Revine Lago has a campground with 140 places and a number of inexpensive hotels, and access by public transit from Vittório Véneto is straightforward. Doughtier individuals can climb up to the head of the valley, past the huge castle of CISÒN DI VALMARINO, to the thirteenth-century Cistercian abbey at FOLLINA (two one-star hotels).

A walker's paradise is to be found to the northeast of Vittório Véneto—the **Bosco del Cansiglio**, a plateau forested with beech and pine which once was husbanded by the Venetian state as a source of timber for oars. Although the area has been developed as a vacation resort, you can still roam here for hours without seeing a soul. A good base from which to explore this vast expanse of woodland is FREGONA—it has three one-star hotels, is connected by bus to Vittório Véneto and is close to **Le Grotte del Calieron**, a network of narrow caves scoured out of the rock by an underground torrent.

Belluno

The most northerly of the major towns of the Veneto, **BELLUNO** stands at the point where the tiny Ardo river flows into the Piave, in the shadow of the eastern Dolomites. Once a strategically important ally of Venice, which took the town under its wing in 1404, it is today a provincial capital, and attached more firmly to the mountainous region to the north than to the urban centers to the south—the network of the *Dolomiti-Bus* company radiates out from Belluno, trains run fairly regularly to CALALZO (where the line comes to an end), and the tourist office's handouts are geared mostly to hikers and skiers. Unfortunately, many visitors to the town use the place simply for its access to the mountains, and miss out on its attractions—of which there are quite a few, besides its breathtaking position.

The Town

Belluno has two quite separate, but adjacent, centers. The hub of the modern town, the spot where you'll find its most popular bars and cafés, is the wide **Piazza dei Martiri** (named after a group of partisans executed in the square by the Nazis in 1944). Off the south side, a road leads to the **Piazza del Duomo**, the kernel of the old town. The sixteenth-century **Duomo** (or Santa Maria Assunta), a Gothic-classical amalgam built in the pale yellow stone that's a distinctive feature of Belluno, was designed by **Tullio Lombardo**; it has had to be reconstructed twice after earthquake damage, in 1873 and 1936. The elegant interior—a long barrel vault ending in a single dome, with flanking aisles—has a couple of good paintings: one by **Andrea Schiavone** (first altar on right), and one by **Jacopo Bassano** (third altar on right). From the bell-chamber of the stately **campanile** you get a view that'll have you reeling off the Fujicolor like there's no tomorrow; the tower was designed in 1743 by **Filippo Juvarra**, best known for his rebuilding of chunks of eighteenth-century Turin.

Occupying one complete side of the Piazza del Duomo, at a right-angle to the Duomo itself, is the residence of the Venetian adminstrators of the town, the **Palazzo dei Rettori**, a frilly late fifteenth-century building dolled up with Baroque trimmings. A relic of more independent times stands on the right—the twelfth-century **Torre Civica**, all that's left of Belluno's medieval castle. Continuing round the Piazza, in Via Duomo, along the side of the nineteenth-century town hall, you'll find the **Museo Civico** (Tues–Sat 10am–noon & 3–6pm, Sun & hols 10am–noon). It's strongest on the work of Belluno's three best-known artists: the painters Sebastiano and Marco Ricci (1659–1734 and 1673–1736) and the brilliant sculptor-woodcarver Andrea Brustolon (1662–1732), who features prominently in Venice's Ca' Rezzonico. For those who prefer less agitation in their art, Bartolomeo Montagna (see "Vicenza") is here as well.

Via Duomo ends at the **Piazza del Mercato**, a tiny square hemmed in by porticoed Renaissance buildings. Until the Venetians shifted the administrative offices to the Piazza del Duomo, this was the nerve-center of Belluno, and even after the Venetian alterations it remained the commercial center. Its fountain dates from 1410 and the **Monte di Pietà** (no. 26) from 1501, making it one of the oldest pawnshops in Italy. One of the prime claimants to the honor of being the originator of pawnshops is Francesco Terrile (aka Saint Bernardino), a Franciscan monk from the village of Tomo, in the vicinity of nearby Feltre. The principal street of the old town, **Via Mezzaterra**, goes down from the Piazza del Mercato to the fourteenth-century Porta Ruga (veer left along the cobbled road about 50m from the end), from where the view along the Piave gorge will provide some compensation if you haven't managed to find the campanile open. The unprepossessing church of **San Pietro**, just off Via Mezzaterra at the end of Vicolo San Pietro, is worth looking into for pieces by **Sebastiano Ricci** (main altarpiece), **Brustolon** (carved altarpieces on 2nd altars on both sides, and angels over baldachin) and **Andrea Schiavone** (paintings over door and to sides of high altar).

Leaving the Piazza del Mercato in the other direction, you pass through the sixteenth-century **Porta Dojona** and into Piazza Vittorio Emanuele, an extension of the main square of the modern town. Belluno's other major church, **Santo Stefano**, is to the right, on Via Roma. A bright Gothic building (1486) with banded arches and alternating brown and white columns, it has yet more carvings by **Brustolon** (candelabra by the main altar and, in the left aisle, a Crucifix resting on figures in Purgatory) and restored frescoes by **Jacopo da Montagnana**, painted within a year or so of the church's construction.

Practicalities—and Mountain Excursions

Accommodation in Belluno is pitched at the skiing fraternity, who generally aren't the type to suffer cash-flow problems. There's a clutch of **hotels** on and just behind the north side of the Piazza dei Martiri, but they are not inexpensive. Cheapest in town, at around L10,000 for a single and L20,000 for a double, is the Taverna, Via Cipro 7 (☎0437/25192). It's followed by *Da Mares*, Via F. Pellegrini 4 (☎0437/22860; L18,000 single, L27,000 double), and *Da Carlo*, Via Cordevole 27 (296488; L16,000 single, L32,000 double). If you are staying, the best **restaurant** at a moderate price is *Al Sasso*, Via del Cansiglio 12 (☎0437/22424; closed Mon and late July); it serves local specialties at around L20,000 for a full meal, with excellent homemade *gnocchi*.

For **tourist information** go to the AAST at Via Matteotti 3 or *ASVI Viaggi* at Piazza dei Martiri 27e (both Mon–Fri 9:30am–12:30pm & 3:30–7pm, Sat 9:30am–12:30pm). Apart from *Dolomiti Neve* leaflets on the ski resorts of the area, they can supply you with details of the **Alte Vie** (High Trails) of the eastern Dolomites—these are six mountain-top routes, up to nearly 200km in length, punctuated by alpine refuges.

Most popular is the **Alta Via** no. 1, a north–south route right across the Dolomites from Braies to Belluno. The **Italian Alpine Club** (*CAI*; at Via Ricci 1) runs several of the refuges, and is another good source of information for intrepid hikers. If a two-week trek across the vertiginous peaks of northern Italy doesn't appeal, but you feel like a quick burst of alpine exertion, it's best to head south, to the ski center of NEVEGÀL (11km), easily reached by bus. From there you can take a chairlift up to the *Rifugio Brigata Alpina Cadore*, and then embark on the climb up the mountain ridge to the refuge of **Col Visentin** (1761m—allow at least two and a half hours), from where you can survey the crags of the Dolomites in one direction, and the waters of Venice in the other.

At present there's just one **train** a day that connects Venice and Belluno directly, but it's just as quick anyway to go to Conegliano and change (see "Conegliano" for details). Via Conegliano the complete expedition takes just over two hours. (If you do take the direct train, you'll have to pay a supplement, because the direct route actually covers more kilometers than the routine Venice–Conegliano–Belluno route.) For those with bottomless reserves of stamina, Belluno and Feltre can just about be taken in on a single day's train excursion from Venice: Venice–Feltre / Feltre–Belluno / Belluno–Venice via Conegliano is an exhilarating expedition, but it does require very careful study of the timetable.

If you're pressing on into the mountains from Belluno, the train will only take you up the Piave to Calalzo (6 daily; journey takes about 1hr), so you'll probably find the **buses** more useful. All the *Dolomiti-Bus* services depart from the railroad station forecourt, and there's an information office there too.

Feltre

The historic center of **FELTRE**, spread along a narrow ridge overlooking the modern town, owes its beguiling appearance to a disaster. At the outbreak of the War of the League of Cambrai, Feltre declared its allegiance to Venice—and so, when the army of Emperor Maximilian I swept into town in 1509, it was decided to punish Feltre by wiping its buildings and a hefty number of its inhabitants from the face of the planet. The Venetians took care of the reconstruction, and within a few decades the streets had been rebuilt. They still look pretty much as they did when the scaffolding came down. You're not going to find the town crawling with students making notes on the architecture of the Renaissance, but you'll have to travel a long way to get a better idea of how an ordinary town looked in sixteenth-century Italy. And on top of that, there's the beauty of Feltre's position—the Dolomites in one direction, the valley of the Piave in the other. The last stretch of the train journey from the south, along the Piave from Valdobbiádene, is on its own worth the price of the ticket.

The Old Town

From the station the shortest route to the old town is to cross straight over into Viale del Piave, over Via Garibaldi (where there's a decent range of bars, restaurants and hotels) and along Via Castaldi, which brings you to the **Duomo** and **Baptistery**, at the foot of the ridge. The oldest section of the much-altered duomo is the fifteenth-century apse; its main objects of interest are a sixth-century Byzantine cross in boxwood—incorporating 52 New Testament scenes—and a tomb by Tullio Lombardo. At the top of the steps going past the side of the baptistery, on the other side of the road, is the painted south gate (1494), from under which a long covered flight of steps rises into the heart of the old town.

You come out by the sixteenth-century **Municipio**, with a portico by Palladio; Goldoni's first plays were performed here in 1730, in a wooden theater that was redesigned at the start of the nineteenth century and has recently been restored (ask custodian for admission, weekday mornings). Behind the stage-like **Piazza Maggiore** rises the keep of the medieval Castello, just below which is the church of **San Rocco** – go round the back for a good view of the mountains. And take a closer look at the carved wall between the steps going up to the church: it's actually a fountain by Tullio Lombardo.

The two Feltrian luminaries facing each other across the square are **Panfilo Castaldi** and Vittorino de' Rambaldoni, usually known as **Vittorino da Feltre**—both unsung heroes of the Renaissance. The former was instrumental in the development of printing in Italy, and according to some he beat Gutenberg to the invention of movable type; the latter ran a school in Mantua in the first half of the fifteenth century, under the financial patronage of the Gonzaga family, which took in pupils from aristocratic families and unprivileged backgrounds alike, and put them through a regime in which, for the first time, a broad liberal arts education was combined with a program of physical training.

To the left as you look across at San Rocco, the main street of Feltre, **Via Mezzaterra**, slopes down to the fifteenth-century Porta Imperiale. Nearly all the houses here are sixteenth-century, and several are decorated with external frescoes by **Lorenzo Luzzo** (1467–1512) and his pupils. Feltre's most important artistic figure, Luzzo is more widely known **Il Morto da Feltre** (The Dead Man ...), a nickname prompted by the pallor of his complexion. Having begun with spells in Rome and Florence, Il Morto's career received something of a boost when he was called in to help Giorgione on the Fondaco dei Tedeschi in Venice.

The impact Giorgione made on him can be gauged from the *Madonna with St Vitus and St Modestus* in the **Museo Civico**, which is at the end of Via L. Luzzo, the equally decorous continuation of Via Mezzaterra on the other side of the piazza (Tues–Fri 10am–1pm, Sat 10am–1pm & 4–6pm, Sun & hols 11am–1pm & 4–6pm; L2000). Apart from this and other pieces by Il Morto, the Museo has paintings by **Cima** and **Gentile Bellini**, and a display of Roman and Etruscan finds. Il Morto's finest work is generally held to be the fresco of the *Transfiguration* in the **Ognissanti** church; this building is unlikely to be open in the foreseeable future, but if you want to try your luck, you go out of the Porta Oria, right by the Museo, down the dip and then along Borgo Ruga for a couple of hundred meters.

Feltre has another, more unusual museum—the **Museo Rizzarda** at Via del Paradiso 8, parallel to Via Mezzaterra (June–Sept Tues–Sun 10am–1pm & 4–7pm). This doubles as the town's collection of modern art and an exhibition of wrought iron work, most of it by **Carlo Rizzarda** (1883–1931), the former owner of the house. It might not sound appetizing, but the finesse of Rizzarda's pieces is remarkable. The frescoed building at the piazza end of Via del Paradiso is the **Monte di Pietà**, one of the few fifteenth-century buildings to escape the wrath of the Imperial hordes.

Walks, Buses, and Trains

If you fancy roaming out of the town, two undemanding **walks** can be recommended. The village of PEDAVENA, famous for its brewery (with beer garden and attached restaurant), is only 3km to the northwest; it stands at the base of the Feltrino peaks, where the terrain gets tougher but not dauntingly so. About 5km southeast, on MONTE MIESNA, stands the Romanesque church of **Santi Vittore e Corona**; founded in 1096, it's decorated inside with medieval frescoes, and has a beautiful fifteenth-century cloister attached.

Getting to Feltre from Venice is a long-winded business: only one **train** a day goes directly to Feltre (it's the Venice–Belluno service), so the journey normally involves changing at Padua, from where the service is rather more regular and takes ninety minutes. The trains from Padua go on to Belluno (30min).

Buses strike out from Feltre to the busiest resort of the southern Dolomites, SAN MARTINO DI CASTROZZA (48km; 90min); the route goes up the Cismòn valley, through the winter sports center of FIERA DI PRIMIERO (35km).

Castelfranco Véneto

In the twelfth century **CASTELFRANCO VÉNETO** stood on the western edge of Treviso's territory, and from the outside the old town—or **Castello**—looks much as it must have done when the Trevisans had finished fortifying the place against the Paduans. The battlemented and moated bricks walls, raised in 1199, run almost right round the center, and five of their towers still stand (the largest being the Torrione, the clock tower over the north gate). Of all the walled towns of the Véneto, only Cittadella and Montagnana bear comparison with Castelfranco, and the place would merit a call just for its brickwork, even though the Castello is so small that you can walk in through one gate and out through the opposite in three minutes flat. But the place has one other attraction: it was the birthplace of Giorgio da Castelfranco—**Giorgione**—and possesses a painting which on its own is enough to vindicate Vasari's judgement that Giorgione's place in Venetian art is equivalent to Leonardo da Vinci's in that of Florence.

The Castelfranco Madonna

The painting in question—*The Madonna and Child with St Francis and St Liberale*, usually known simply as the **Castelfranco Madonna**—hangs in the eighteenth-century **Duomo** (daily 9am–noon & 3–6pm), in a chapel to the right of the chancel; the bars of the iron grill across its entrance are far enough apart for you to be able to see the picture clearly, and there's a light switch to the side (leave discretionary donation in nearby box).

Giorgione is the most elusive of all the great figures of the Renaissance: including the Castelfranco Madonna, only six surviving paintings can indisputably be attributed to him; and so little is known for certain about his life that legends have proliferated to fill the gaps—for instance, the story that his premature death in 1510, aged not more than 34, was caused by his catching bubonic plague from a mistress. The paintings themselves have compounded the enigma, and none is more mysterious than this one, in which formal abstraction is combined with an extraordinary fidelity to physical texture, while the demeanour of the figures suggests, in the forgiveably lush words of one writer—"withdrawal . . . as if their spirit were preoccupied with a remembered dream." Even the identity of the saint acompanying Saint Francis is far from clear: candidates other than Liberale include Saint Nicasio, Saint George and Saint Theodore.

But some facts are known about the picture's origin. It was commissioned by Tuzio Costanza, probably in 1505, to honor his son, Matteo, who had been killed in battle the previous year. The church for which the piece was painted was demolished long ago, and the present arrangement (dating from 1935) differs crucially from that devised by Giorgione's patron, in that the painting was originally placed so that the three figures were looking down at the tomb of Matteo Costanza. Matteo's tombstone is now set into the wall to the left.

After the Giorgione, the only other paintings in the Duomo likely to hold your attention are in the **sacristy**—fragments of allegorical frescoes by **Veronese**, removed from the Villa Soranza in the nineteenth century, when the villa was knocked down. The interior of the building itself was designed by the local architect **Francesco Maria Preti**, whose major contribution to the landscape of the Véneto is to be seen at the Villa Pisani at Stra (see Chapter Eleven); the facade is a late nineteenth-century botch job.

The Rest of the Town

Next to the Duomo is the **Casa Giorgione**, which contains nothing of note except a chiaroscuro **frieze** in one the first floor rooms which has been hopefully attributed to Giorgione. (Tues–Fri 9am–12:30pm & 3–6pm, Sat & Sun 9am–12:30pm & 2:30–6pm; often closed weekday mornings in winter; free.) In Via Garibaldi, opposite the duomo, is the freshly restored **Teatro Accademico**, designed in the mid-eighteenth century by **Preti**; the auditorium, which is less modest than you might think from the sober look of the outside, can be visited on appointment (Tues–Thurs 9am–12:30am & 2–6pm, plus Mon & Fri mornings); either ask at the theater or phone ☎0423/494500—the visit is free.

The palaces facing the Torrione across the road ringing the Castello are worth a moment's perusal, but beyond them, the only part of Castelfranco that you might find interesting are the grounds of the nineteenth-century **Villa Rivedin-Bolasco**, a park that covers as big an area as the old town. It's on Borgo Treviso—walk straight down Viale Brigata Battisti from the railroad station and you'll find yourself in front of it—and is open every Saturday and on the first Sunday of each month (June–Sept 4–7pm; Oct–May 2–5pm; L1000).

Staying and eating in Castelfranco

The cheapest **rooms** in the immediate vicinity of central Castelfranco are at *Alla Speranza*, a few yards beyond the walls at Borgo Vicenza 13 (☎0423/494480)—singles from L16,000, doubles from L26,000. (Borgo Vicenza is the continuation of the main street, Via F. M. Preti, on the opposite side of the Castello from the train station.) Cheaper still, but farther outside the Castello than *Alla Speranza*, is *All'Antica Priora*, at Borgo Padova 55 (☎0423/491764).

There are a number of excellent **restaurants** in the town, the best value being *Ai due Mori*, an *osteria* specializing in local dishes; it's inside the walls, in Vicolo Montebelluna, close to the Torrione (☎0423/497174; closed Wed). A feast at *Ai due Mori* should set you back around L20,000; if this is too much for your budget, there are a few trattorias in Borgo Padova, including one attached to the *Antica Priora* hotel. *Alla Torre*, a large restaurant-pizzeria at the foot of the Torrione, is as good a place as any for pizza, although its restaurant menu is not cheap (closed Tues).

Transportation and Information

Castelfranco is well connected by **rail** with all parts of the Véneto, but it's most easily approached from Treviso (25min) or Vicenza (40min)—trains run along this line on average once an hour. Connections to Venice (50min) are more sporadic—during working hours it averages out at around one every two hours. In addition there are hourly links to Padua and Trento (through Bassano), and a train to Belluno every ninety minutes. **Buses** leave from Via Podgora (north side of Borgo Vicenza) and Corso XXIX Aprile (which you cross to go into the Castello when coming from the station)—best get on at Via Podgora, because the buses are often packed with schoolkids by the time they get to the Corso. The most useful lines, apart from the one for Fanzolo (see below), are the *ACTM* routes to Asolo and Possagno.

Tourist information is handled by the **Pro Loco**, at Via Garibaldi 2 (☎0423/495000); their new tourist guide, glossier than those produced by many larger towns, covers places of interest in the surrounding area as well as in Castelfranco, and has a restaurants and food section that might tempt the gastronome to stay longer than intended—but it's available only in Italian, and you have to pay L2000 for it.

Around Castelfranco—Cittadella and Palladio's Villas

When Treviso turned Castelfranco into a garrison, the Paduans promptly retaliated by reinforcing the defenses of **CITTADELLA**, 15km to the west. (Easily reached by train—it's on the same Treviso–Vicenza line as Castelfranco.) The **fortified walls** of Cittadella were built in the first quarter of the thirteenth century, and are even more impressive than those of its neighbor, forming an almost unbroken oval round the town.

You enter the town through one of four rugged brick gateways, built on the cardinal points of the compass; if you're coming from the train station it'll be the **Porta Padova**, the most daunting of the four, flanked as it is by the Torre di Malta. The tower was built as a prison and torture chamber by **Ezzelino da Romano III**, known to those he terrorized in this region in the mid-thirteenth century as the "Son of Satan." Basing his claim to power not on any dynastic or legalistic argument, but solely on the exercise of unrestrained military might,

Ezzelino was the prototype of the despotic rulers of Renaissance Italy, and his atrocities earned him a place in the seventh circle of Dante's *Inferno*, where he's condemned to boil eternally in a river of blood. (See "Ásolo," below.)

There's not much else to Cittadella—unless you're entranced by the deer, swans, emus and llamas that constitute the Parco Zoo, under one section of the walls—but it's definitely worth hopping off the train for a quick circuit.

The Villa Emo

Just 8km northeast of Castelfranco is **FANZOLO**, where you'll find one of the best maintained and most sumptuous of **Palladio**'s villas—the **Villa Emo** (Sat, Sun & hols except Easter, Christmas and New Year: May–Sept 3–6pm; Oct–April 2–5pm). In 1556 the Venetian government set up a department called the Board of Uncultivated Properties, to promote agricultural development on the *terra firma* and control subsidies to the landowners. One of the first to take advantage of this campaign was Leonardo Emo, who commissioned the villa from Palladio around 1564, when he switched his financial interests to farming.

With its central accommodation and administration block, and its arcaded wings for storage, stables, dovecotes and so on, the building belongs to the same type as the earlier Villa Barbaro at Masèr, and as at Masèr the main living rooms are richly frescoed. Nobody would make out that **G.B. Zelotti**'s scenes are a match for Veronese's in the Barbaro house, but neither would anyone complain at having to stare at them every morning over breakfast either.

But the trip does have its minus points. For a start, the entrance fee is an inexcusable L5000, and you're shadowed through the rooms by a scowling custodian, just in case you should take it into your head to improve Zelotti's handiwork—which admittedly is a temptation in the case of his rubber-necked grotesques. And getting there isn't easy without a car; some trains from Castelfranco stop at Fanzolo, but so few that the #5 bus is the better option. The return service is so fitful, though, that you either have to zip through the building in twenty minutes or kill three hours there. Hitching could entail a long wait. In other words, if you're coming from farther afield than Castelfranco, and you're dependent on public transit, the cons will probably outweigh the pros.

The Villa Cornaro

Palladio's villas fall into two broad types: the first is the type designed to be the focus of a large, cohesive farm, and takes the form of a low central block with attached lateral buildings; the second is designed to be the living quarters of an estate which is scattered or where the farming land is unsuitable for building, and takes the form of a tall single building with a freestanding pedimented porch. The Emo and Barbaro houses belong to the first category, and to the second belong the Villa Pisani at Montagnana, the Villa Foscari at Malcontenta and the **Villa Cornaro** (May–Sept Sat 3:30–6pm; L3000), built in the 1550s at **PIOMBINO DESE**, 9km southeast of Castelfranco. (The local Venice–Castelfranco train stops at the village, and there's a bus from Castelfranco.) The majestic double-decker portico is the most striking element of the exterior, and when Palladian style was imported into America, this became one of his most frequently copied devices. Unfortunately, the villa's decoration—frescoes by the obscure eighteenth-century artist Mattia Bortoloni—isn't anything to get excited about.

Bassano del Grappa

Situated on the Brenta river where it widens on its emergence from the hills, **BASSANO DEL GRAPPA** has expanded rapidly this century, though its historic center remains largely unspoiled by twentieth-century mistakes. It's better known for its manufactures and produce, and for the events of the two World Wars (see below), than for any outstanding architecture or monuments. For centuries a major producer of ceramics and wrought iron, Bassano is also renowned for its **grappa** distilleries and delicacies such as *porcini* (dried mushrooms), white asparagus and honey.

The Town

Almost all of Bassano's sights lie between the Brenta and the train station; go much farther in either direction and you'll quickly come to recently developed suburbs. Walking away from the station, the orbital Viale delle Fosse stands between you and the town center, following the line of the fourteenth-century outer walls. Cross the road, turn right then left to get to Via Da Ponte, which forms a main axis through the center. The statue is of **Jacopo da Ponte**, leader of the dynasty of Renaissance painters more commonly known simply as the Bassano family.

On the left of **Piazza Garibaldi**, one of the center's two main squares, the four-teenth-century church of **San Francesco** carries a gold medal plaque in honor of the resistance fighters of World War II; a few fresco fragments remain inside, including an *Annunciation* of 1400 (in the porch). The cloister now houses the **Museo Civico** (Tues–Sat 10am–12:30pm & 2:30–6:30pm, Sun & hols opens 30min later in afternoon; L1000; free guided tour Sun 10:15am). Downstairs the rooms are devoted to ceramics, printing (for a long time one of Bassano's chief crafts), and Roman and other archaeological finds. Upstairs is a collection of sixteenth- to eighteenth-century work, including paintings by the **Bassano** family, and a number of plaster works by **Canova**, 2000 of whose drawings are owned by the museum. Most extraordinary are the huge frescoes from a palace in Piazzetta Montevecchio, moved here while the palace roof was being restored. There's also a room devoted to the great operatic baritone **Tito Gobbi**, who was born in Bassano.

Overlooking the other side of the piazza is the **Torre Civica**, once a lookout tower for the twelfth-century inner walls, now a clock tower with spurious nine-teenth-century battlements and windows. Further in the same direction is **Piazza Libertà**, with its seventeenth-century sculpture of San Bassiano, the patron saint of Bassano, and the all-too-familiar winged lion of Venice. Dominating the left hand side of the piazza, the church of **San Giovanni** was founded in 1308 but is now overbearingly Baroque in this relatively delicate city center; the style continues within. Under the arches of the fifteenth-century **Loggia** on the other side are the frescoed coats of arms of the various Venetian governors of Bassano.

From the far right-hand corner, Piazzetta Montevecchio (the original core of the town), its frescoes now faded or removed, leads to a little jumble of streets and stairways running down to the river and the **Ponte degli Alpini**. The river was first bridged at this point in the late twelfth century, and replacements or repairs have been needed at regular intervals ever since, mostly because of flooding; the present structure was designed by **Palladio** in 1568, and built in wood (at the council's insistence) in order to make the bridge as flexible as possible. Mined by the resistance during the last war, and badly damaged by the retreating German army, it was restored in accordance with Palladio's design, as has been the case with every repair since the day of its completion.

Nardini, a grappa distillery founded in 1779, stands at this end of the bridge; cross over to reach the **Taverna al Ponte**, which contains the **Museo degli Alpini** (8am–8pm; closed Mon; free), which also gives a good view of the underside of the bridge. The Alpine soldiers, who crossed the bridge many times during World War I on their way to Monte Grappa and Asiago, saw the bridge as a symbol of their tenacity, and so adopted it as their emblem. They still have strong associations with Bassano, and take part in parades here, looking as though they've just stepped out of some nineteenth-century adventure yarn.

Back over the bridge again, and Via Gamba takes you up to the remnants of the **castle**; the huge, blank and none too safe looking tower was built in the twelfth century by the Ezzelini. The campanile of **Santa Maria in Colle** is a conversion of another tower, while the church itself dates from around 1000; it contains two paintings by **Leandro da Ponte**.

Go out of the castle enclosure and round to the right, and spreading round to the right is the **Viale dei Martieri**, named after the resistance fighters who were rounded up in the hills and hanged from trees along here in September 1944. A telescope enables you to get the most out of the views of the Dolomites. To one end is the **Piazzale Generale Giardino**, with its fascist-style memorial to the General, who died 1935; a World War I monument in similar vein stands in the **Parco Ragazzi del'99** below.

If you cut across the town, through Piazza Libertà and south down Via Marinelli or Via Roma, then outside the city walls and right, you can't miss the vast **Tempio Ossario**. Begun in 1908 as a church, its function was changed in 1934, when it became repository of over 5400 tombs, each containing the ashes of a soldier.

The major **war memorial**, however, is out of town on **Monte Grappa**. A vast, circular, tiered edifice with a "Via Eroica" leading to a war museum, it holds 12,000 Italian and Austro-Hungarian dead; less a symbol of mourning and repentance than a declaration of future collaboration, it was built by the fascists in 1935. Buses go up there from Bassano during the summer months.

Practicalities

The **APT** is at Viale delle Fosse 9 (Mon–Sat 9am–12:30pm & 3–6:45pm; ☎0424/24351 or 26651); from the train station go straight ahead then turn right. A free magazine called *Bassano Mese* gives up-to-date information about the city's facilities and special events. The main **post office** is in Via G.B. Verci (Mon–Fri 8:10am–7:40pm; Sat 8:10am–1:35pm).

For budget **accommodation**, it comes down to a choice between two places: *Bassanello*, at Via P. Fontana 2 (☎0424/35347) or *Castello*, at Piazza Terraglio 20 (☎0424/23462)—both have singles at around L18,000 and doubles at L28,000. After that it's a steep jump to the likes of the *Victoria*, Viale Diaz 33 (☎0424/22300), with singles at L30,000 and doubles at L45,000.

As for **food**, the *Antica Osteria*, Via Matteotti 5 (7:30am–10pm; closed Mon) has good bars snacks, while *Combattini*, Via Gamba 22 (closed Sat) is recommended for a full meal. *Ottocento*, Via San Giorgio 2, is a welcoming *birreria*. Of all Bassano's *alimentari*, the one with the fullest range of local delicacies is on the corner of Salita B. Ferracina and Via B. Ferracina; for **grappa**, go to the distillery on the Ponte degli Alpini (8am–8pm; closed Mon)—it sells the best quality stuff (cheaper than malt whisky), and has a bar so you can sample before you select your bottle.

Trains run from Venice to Bassano every one or two hours; the journey takes an hour. There's a useful train timetable in the center of town on the corner of Via Guiseppi Barbieri and the piazza; more details and tickets are available nearby in the *Monte Grappa* travel agency, Via Giuseppi Barbieri 40.

Buses leave from Piazzale Trento, at other end of Viale delle Fosse from the APT; the *Bar Trevisani*, on the Piazzale, deals with tickets and information (Mon–Sat 6:30am–8:30pm, Sun & hols 8am–noon & 3–7:15pm). Buses run to Masèr (every 3hr), Possagno (every 1–2hr), Maróstica (every 2–3hr) and Ásolo (every 1–2hr).

Maróstica

Seven kilometers to the west of Bassano, the walled town of **MARÓSTICA** was yet another stronghold of Ezzelino da Romano III, whose fortress glowers down on the old center from the crest of the hill of Pausolino. The fortress, the lower castle and the almost intact ramparts that connect them make a dramatic scene, but Maróstica's main claim to fame is the **Partita a Scacchi**—a chess game played every other September with human "pieces."

The Ezzelini controlled Maróstica for quite a while (Ezzelino III was preceded by Ezzelino the Stutterer and Ezzelino the Monk), but it was another despotic dynasty, the Scaligeri of Verona, who constructed the **town walls** and the **Castello Inferiore** (lower castle)—the castle being built by Cangrande della Scala, and the walls by his successor, Cansignorio, in the 1370s. An exhibition of costumes for the *Partita a Scacchi* is now housed in the castle (Sun 2–6pm; L500—group visits at other times are arranged by the Pro Loco).

Beyond the castle is **Piazza Castello**, the central square of the town, onto which is painted the board for the **Partita a Scacchi**. The game's origin was an everyday chivalric story of rival suitors, the only unusual aspect being that the matter was decided with chess pieces rather than swords. In 1454 two men, Vieri da Vallonara and Rinaldo d'Angarano, both petitioned the *podestà* of Maróstica, Taddeo Parisio, for the hand of his daughter. Parisio decreed that the matter should be decided by a chess match, with the winner marrying Lionora and the loser being consoled with the prize of Parisio's younger sister—who seems to have had as little say in the proceedings as Parisio's daughter. The game was played with live pieces here in the square, and is re-enacted biennially with great pomp—500 people in the costume of the time, with music, dancing and fireworks.

The **Doglione**, behind the inevitable lion of Saint Mark, is a much-altered fifteenth-century building; once the castle armory, it now contains the town library. To the left of it, Via San Antonio runs past the church of the same name to the forgettable church of the **Carmine**, looking for all the world like a Baroque palace with the windows missing. A path round to the left of the Carmine winds up through an olive grove to the **Castello Superiore** (upper castle), which was built by Ezzelino III and later expanded by the Scaligeri. Most of it is closed for restoration, but the view is marvelous, and the fort does contain a bar. It's only when you're at the top that you realize there's a road up, much less steep than the stony path but longer; if you take this route back down, look out for the cyclists who train on the hill—they whizz through the hair-pins with scarcely a sound to warn of their approach. Near the bottom a little junk shop sells war memorabilia scavenged from the mountains around.

The oldest church in Maróstica, **Santa Maria**, is outside the city walls on the other side—go through the eastern gate, turn left, then second right. Unfortunately it was rebuilt in the eighteenth century, but it has some quirky attractions: modern votive paintings on the ceiling, for instance, and an altarpiece that's a copy of the top half of Titian's *Assumption* in Venice's Frari.

Practicalities

Tourist information is available from the **Pro Loco** in the lower castle (Mon–Sat 10am–noon & 4–7pm). There is one relatively cheap place **to stay**: the *Bar Taverna* at Via Piazza Castello 16 (☎0424/72165; L17,400 single, L28,000 double). For **food**, the *Pizzeria, Trattoria e Bar all'Alfiere*, Piazza Castello 42 (Tues–Sun

10:30am–3pm & 5:30pm–1am) should fit the bill; alternatively, drop in on the *Trattoria al Cappello* at Via Stazione 8 (Tues–Sun 8am–10pm), a friendly no-nonsense bar which serves food at the appropriate times. The misnamed *Caffè Centrale*, in the courtyard of the upper castle, does good ice cream and at night functions as a chic piano bar (11am–2am; closed Fri and Mon).

Regular events include first and foremost the **Partita a Scacchi**, played in the second weekend of September on even-numbered years. An exhibition of **cartoonists** specializing in political and social comment takes place in May and June, followed in July and August by a **crafts fair**. An **antiques market** is held the first Sunday of every month.

A frequent **bus** service runs between Maróstica and **Bassano** (30min); the stop is outside the lower castle.

Possagno

As you approach **POSSAGNO**, a small town lodged at the base of Monte Grappa, one of the strangest sights in the Veneto hits you: a huge temple that rises above the houses like a displaced chunk of ancient Rome. It was built by **Antonio Canova**, one of the dominant figures of Neoclassicism and the last Italian sculptor to be generally regarded as the most accomplished living practitioner of his art. He was born here in 1757, and his family home now houses a magnificent museum of his work. Just as you can't come to grips with Tintoretto until you've been to Venice, so an excursion to Possagno is essential to an understanding of Canova. You can reach Possagno by **bus** from Bassano or Castelfranco Véneto; the first is easier—a fairly regular service that takes an hour.

Shortly after Canova's death in 1822, all the working models that had accumulated in his studio in Rome were transported to Possagno, and here, from 1831–36, an annexe (the **Gypsoteca**) was built onto the Canova house for the display of the bulk of the collection. A second addition was built in the 1950s, and the Gypsoteca is now one of only two complete displays of an artist's working models in Europe—the other being Copenhagen's collection of pieces by Thorvaldsen.

The Gypsoteca e Casa Canova

The process by which Canova worked towards the final form of his sculptures was a painstaking one, involving the creation of a series of rough clay models (*bozzetti*) in which the general shape would be refined, then a full-scale figure in plaster, and finally the replication of the plaster figure in marble. Preparatory works from all stages of Canova's career are shown in the Gipsoteca (Oct–April Tues–Sun 9am–noon & 2–5pm; May–Sept Tues–Sun 9am–noon & 3–6pm; closed Christmas, New Year & Easter; L2500), and even if you're repelled by the polish of the finished pieces, you'll be won over by the energy and spontaneity of the first versions—such as the tiny terracotta model for the tomb of Pope Clement XIV, or the miniature group of Adam and Eve weeping over the body of Abel.

Canova's range will probably be as much of a surprise as his technique. Among the works collected in the vast main hall, for example, you'll find portraits, images of classical deities, the funerary monument for Maria Christina of Austria (adapted by Canova's pupils for his own tomb in Venice), and a large *Deposition*, a bronze version of which is to be found in the Tempio (see below). Notions of Canova as a bloodless pedant are dispelled by two overpowering tableaux of violence, each over ten feet high—*Hercules and Lichas* and *Theseus and the*

Centaur. More models are kept in the house, but the pleasure of this section of the museum is weakened by Canova's paintings—a parade of winsome Venuses and frolicking nymphs, which will not dispose you to disagree with the artist's own low opinion of his pictorial talents.

The Tempio

Donated to the town to serve as its new parish church, the **Tempio** (Oct–April daily 8am–noon & 1:30–5pm; May–Sept 8am–noon & 2–7pm) was designed by Canova with assistance from **Giannantonio Selva** (architect of La Fenice in Venice) and constructed from 1819–30. Both Roman and Greek classical sources were plundered for its composition—the body of the building is derived from the Pantheon, but its portico comes from the Parthenon. The cool precision of the interior is disrupted by a sequence of dreadful paintings of the Apostles, and an appalling altarpiece for which Canova himself was the culprit. To the right is the bronze version of the *Deposition* in the Gypsoteca (cast posthumously in 1829), and opposite is the **tomb of Canova** and his half-brother Monsignor G.B. Sartori, with a self-portrait bust to the right. Designed by Canova for a different occupant, this tomb is not the Veneto's only memorial to the sculptor– the other one is in the Frari in Venice. If the sacristan is around, ask him to let you up to the top of the dome—the view of the Asolean hills and the plain of the Piave is marvelous.

Ásolo

Known as "la Città dai cento orizzonti" (the city with a hundred horizons), the medieval walled town of ÁSOLO presides over a tightly-grouped range of twenty-seven gentle peaks in the foothills of the Dolomites. Fruit trees and pastures cover the lower slopes of the Asolean hills, and a feature of life in the town itself are the festivals that take place at the various harvest times.

Paleolithic settlements have been found in the region, but the earliest documented settlement was the Roman town called *Acelum*, which thrived from the second century BC until its destruction by Attila. Following resettlement, a succession of feudal lords ruled Ásolo, culminating with the vile **Ezzelino da Romano III**, whose parents were born in the town. Ezzelino wrested Ásolo from the Bishop of Treviso in 1234, and a network of castles over much of the Véneto shows the extent of his conquests in the years that followed. On his death in 1259 the townspeople of Ásolo ensured that the dynasty died with him by butchering the rest of his family, who were at that time in nearby San Zenone.

The end of the fifteenth century was marked by the arrival of **Caterina Cornaro** (see below); her celebrated court was attended by the likes of Cardinal Bembo, one of the most eminent literary figures of his day, who coined the verb *Asolare* to describe the experience of spending one's time in pleasurable aimlessness. Later writers and artists found the atmosphere equally convivial: Gabriele d'Annunzio wrote about the town, and Robert Browning's last published work—*Asolando*—was written here.

The Town

The main road into town from Bassano enters the southern Porta Loreggia, with a fifteenth-century fountain on the left and on the right **Casa Freia**, home of the traveler and writer Freya Stark. Via Browning continues up the hill; no. 151, formerly the house of Pen Browning, bears a plaque recording his father's stay in 1889. At the top is the hub of the town, **Piazza Garibaldi**, to the south of which, on the Piazza Maggiore, stands the **Duomo**—not an attraction itself, but containing a couple of good pictures by Jacopo Bassano and Lorenzo Lotto.

Also on the Piazza Maggiore, in the fifteenth-century Loggia del Capitano, is the **Museo Civico** (Tues–Sun 8am–noon & 4–8pm; L1500). The main interest of the art collection is provided by a pair of dubiously attributed Bellinis, a portrait of Ezzelino painted a good couple of centuries after his death and a brace of large sculptures by **Canova**. More diverting are the memorabilia of Ásolo's residents, especially the portraits, photos and personal effects of **Elenora Duse**. An actress in the Sarah Bernhardt mold, Duse was almost as well known for her tempestuous love-life as for her roles in Shakespeare, Hugo and Ibsen, and she came to Ásolo to seek refuge from public gossip. Although she died in Pittsburgh while on tour in 1924, her wish was to be buried in Ásolo, and so her body was transported back here, to the church of Sant'Anna.

The Teatro Duse occupies part of the **Castello**, most of which is currently being restored. From 1489 to 1509 this was the home of **Caterina Cornaro**, one of the very few women to have played a decisive part in Venetian history. Born into one of Venice's most powerful families, Caterina was betrothed at the age of 14 to the philandering Jacques II, king of the strategically vital island of Cyprus. The prospective groom then prevaricated for a while, until the scheming of his half-sister (who wanted him overthrown) and the Venetian promises of help against the belligerent Turks finally pushed him into marriage. Within a year Jacques was dead, in all likelihood poisoned by Marco Venier, the Venetian governor of Famagusta harbor. A few weeks later Caterina gave birth to a son, after whose christening the Venetian fleet set sail for home. No sooner had the detested Venetians left than the city was taken over by men of the Royal Council, Caterina jailed, and her son handed over to her mother-in-law, Marietta. (Marietta's hatred of Caterina was to an extent due to resentment of the latter's beauty: when Marietta was the mistress of Jacques' father she had been caught making love to him by the king's wife, who bit her nose off in the ensuing melée.)

While Caterina refused to surrender Famagusta to the rebels, news of the insurrection reached the Venetian galleys, who promptly returned and overpowered the city. Their reappearance was a mixed blessing. The death of her son at the age of one was taken by Venier as a cue to propose marriage; spurned, he plotted to kill her instead, but was discovered and hanged. For nine years Caterina resisted Venice's political pressure until at last, in 1489, she was forced to abdicate in order to gain much-needed weapons and ships against a new Turkish attack. Brought back to Venice to sign a deed "freely giving" Cyprus to the Republic, she was given the region of Ásolo as a sign of Venice's indebtedness, and a joust was held on the frozen Canal Grande in her honor. In Ásolo her court was constantly under the eye of the Council of Ten, who dispatched any man rumored to be her lover for fear that a new dynasty should be started. Eventually Ásolo too was taken away from her by the Emperor Maximilian, and she returned to seek asylum in Venice, where she died soon after, in 1510.

Ásolo's ruined medieval fortress, the **Rocca**, is reached by taking Via Collegio up the hill from the back of Piazza Brugnoli (right by Piazza Garibaldi) and going through the Porta Colmarian. You have to be fairly fit to tackle it in the heat of the midday sun, but the views on both sides are worth the sweat. Built on Roman foundations, the Rocca stands 350m above sea level.

Via Canova leads west away from the town center past Elenora Duse's house (no. 306), near the Porta Santa Caterina. The church of **Santa Caterina** next to the Carabinieri is deconsecrated but open to allow visitors to see its fifteenth-century frescoes. Some way farther on, at the junction of the road, is the enchanting fifteenth-century **Lombard house** with allegorical figures carved in soft stone; the architect was Francesco Graziolo, who worked for Caterina Cornaro. Taking the central of the three roads at this junction you will arrive at the pedestrian Franciscan church of **Sant'Anna**; the **cemetery** on the right, from which there are splendid views, is where Elenora Duse and Pen Browning are buried.

Practicalities

Tourist information is handled by the Pro Loco in Via Regina Cornaro, close to the Museo (☎0423/55045); if it's closed, you might find the boss in the bar opposite. They give out a map of the town which is quite handy, even if it isn't exactly a model of clarity.

Accommodation is impossible—two luxury hotels and no *pensioni*. Ásolo does have a handful of **bars and restaurants**, though. The large and popular *Caffè Centrale* on Piazza Garibaldi is okay (closed Tues), but not as friendly as the *Enoteca Marcello Agnoletto*, an excellent wine bar in Via Browning (Tues–Sun 8am–12:30pm & 3–8pm). *La Papessa* in Via Pietro Bembo (10:30am–3pm & 6pm–1am; closed Thurs morning & all Wed) has a good range of pizzas plus a few other interesting dishes.

To get to Ásolo from Venice, take a **train** to Bassano, then a **bus**, which runs about every hour or so and takes 45 minutes. The Bassano bus drops you at the foot of the hill, a connecting minibus taking you up into the town. Bus information in Ásolo is posted on the wall of the gift shop and bar on the corner of Piazza Garibaldi; the times are for the buses on the main road—the minibus leaves Ásolo about 15 minutes earlier. Tickets are sold in the bar, where they can also give precise schedule information.

The Villa Barbaro at Masèr

Of all the villas of the Veneto, the one that's most likely to make you forget the effort of getting to it is the **Villa Barbaro** at **MASÈR** (7km east of Ásolo), a building that gets onto any shortlist of Europe's most beautiful houses. Touring the villas of the mainland, you become used to discrepancies between the quality of the architecture and the quality of the decoration, but at Masèr you'll see the best of two of the central figures of Italian civilization in the sixteenth century—**Palladio** and **Paolo Veronese**, whose careers crossed here and nowhere else.

The villa was built in 1557–58 for Daniele and Marcantonio Barbaro, men whose humanist training and diverse cultural interests set them apart from most of the other wealthy Venetians who were then beginning to farm the Veneto. Both were prominent figures in the society of Venice. Marcantonio served as the Republic's ambassador to Constantinople and became one of the Procurators of San Marco, a position that enabled him to promote Palladio's scheme for the church of the Redentore. Daniele, the more scholarly of the pair, edited the writings of Vitruvius, wrote on mathematics and perspective, and founded the botanical gardens in Padua; he was also Venice's representative in London and was later elected Patriarch of Acquileia, as well as becoming the official historian of Venice. The association between Palladio and the brothers was very close by the time the villa was built—in 1554 Daniele and Palladio had visited Rome, and they'd worked together on Barbaro's edition of Vitruvius—and the process of designing the house was far more of a collaborative venture than were most of Palladio's other projects.

The Interior and the Tempietto

The Villa Barbaro was a working farm in which was embodied a classical vision, derived from writers such as Livy, of the harmony of architectural form and the well-ordered pastoral life. The entire ground floor was given over to farm functions—dovecotes in the end pavilions, stables and storage space under the arcades, administrative offices on the lower floor of the central block.

It's in the living quarters of the *piano nobile* that the more rarified aspect of the brothers' world is expressed, in a series of **frescoes** by Veronese (1566–68) that has no equal anywhere in northern Italy. You need to be a student of Renaissance iconography to decode unassisted the allegorical figures in the amazing trompe l'oeil ceiling of the *Hall of Olympus*—the scheme was devised by Daniele Barbaro and centers on the figure of Eternal Wisdom—but an excellent guidebook is on sale in the villa, and most of the other paintings require no footnotes. The walls of the Villa Barbaro are the most resourceful display of visual trickery you'll ever see—servants peer round painted doors, a dog sniffs along the base of a flat balustrade in front of a landscape of ruins, illusory statues throw counterfeit shadows, flagstaffs lean in alcoves that aren't there, a huntsman (probably Veronese himself) steps into the house through an entrance that's a solid wall. (Inevitably it's speculated that the woman facing the hunter at the other end of the house was Veronese's mistress.) On top of all this, there's some remarkable architectural sculpture by **Alessandro Vittoria**: chimneypieces in the living rooms, figures in the tympanum of the main block, and an ornate **nymphaeum** in the garden at the back. The last incorporates a pond that used to be the house's fish tank, and whose waters were channelled through the kitchens and out into the orchards.

In the grounds in front of the villa stands Palladio's **Tempietto**, the only church by him outside Venice and one of his last projects—commissioned by Marcantonio a decade after his brother's death, it was built in 1580, the year Palladio himself died. From the outside it's clear that the circular domed temple is based on the Pantheon, but when you get inside you find that the tiny side-chapels give the building a modified Greek Cross plan, thus combining the mathematically pure form of the circle with the liturgically perfect form of the cross. The other surprise of the interior is the richness of the stucco decoration, much of which is again by Vittoria.

There's also a **carriage museum** in the grounds, for which there's an extra entrance charge; it contains a few curiosities—such as a boat-shaped nineteenth-century ice-cream cart with a voluptuous mermaid on its prow—but you'd be better advised giving every spare minute to the villa and Veronese.

The Villa Barbaro is open Tuesdays (except Jan & Feb), Saturdays and Sundays, from 3 to 6pm from June to September, and from 2 to 5pm for the rest of the year (closed hols; L5000). The only way to get to Masèr and back in a day from Venice is to take the train to Bassano and then catch one of the two lunchtime school buses from Bassano to CORNUDA via Masèr, a round trip that'll set you back around L10,000.

A HISTORY OF VENICE

"In the midst of the waters, free, indigent, laborious, and inaccessible, they gradually coalesced into a Republic."
Edward Gibbon.

BEGINNINGS

Though the Venetian lagoon supported small groups of fishermen and hunters at the start of the Christian era, it was only with the barbarian invasions of the fifth century and later that sizable communities began to settle on the mudbanks. The first mass migration was provoked by the arrival in the Veneto of **Attila the Hun**'s hordes in **453**, but a large number of the refugees struck camp and returned to dry land once the danger seemed to be past. Permanent settlement was accelerated a century later, when, in **568**, the Germanic **Lombards** (or Longobards), led by **Alboin**, swept into northern Italy.

A loose conglomeration of island communes arose, each cluster of islands drawing its population from one or two clearly defined areas of the Veneto: the fugitives from Padua went to **Malamocco** and **Chioggia**; the inhabitants of **Grado** mainly came from Aquileia; and Altino supplied many of the pioneers of **Torcello**, **Burano** and **Murano**. Distinct economic, ecclesiastical and administrative centers quickly evolved: Torcello was the focal point of trading activity; Grado, the new home of the Bishop of Aquileia, was the church's base; and Heraclea

(now extinct) was the seat of government. The lagoon confederation was not autonomous, though—it owed **political allegiance to Byzantium**, and until the end of the seventh century its senior officials were the **maritime tribunes**, who were effectively controlled by the imperial hierarchy of Ravenna.

The refugee population of the islands increased steeply as the Lombard grip on the Veneto strengthened under the leadership of **Grimoald** (667–71), and shortly after this influx the confederation took a big step towards independence. This is one of the many points at which Venetian folklore has acquired the status of fact: tradition has it that a conference was convened at Heraclea in 697 by the Patriarch of Grado, and from this meeting sprang the election of the **first doge**, to unify the islands in the face of the Lombard threat. (John Julius Norwich adroitly disentangles the myth in his history of Venice—see *Books*.) In fact, it was not until **726** that the lagoon settlers chose their first leader, when a wave of dissent against Emperor Leo III throughout the Byzantine Empire spurred them to elect **Orso Ipato** as the head of their provincial council.

After a period during which the old system of government was briefly reinstituted, Orso Ipato's son **Teodato** became the second doge in 742. Yet the lagoon administration—which was now moved from Heraclea to **Malamocco**—was still not autonomous. Teodato's relationship to the emperor was less subservient than his father's had been, yet he nonetheless took orders from the capital, and the fall of Ravenna to the Lombards in 751 did not alter the constitutional relationship between Byzantium and the confederation.

At the close of the eighth century, the Lombards were overrun by the Frankish army of **Charlemagne**, and in **810** the emperor's son **Pepin** sailed into action against the proto-Venetians. Malamocco was quickly taken, but Pepin's fleet failed in its attempt to pursue the settlers when they withdrew to the better-protected islands of **Rivoalto**, and retreated with heavy losses. Now the seat of government in the lagoon was shifted for the second and last time, to Rivoalto, the name by which the central cluster of islands was known until the late twelfth century, when it became generally known as **Venice**. The **Rialto** district, in the core of the city, perpetuates the old name.

FROM INDEPENDENCE TO EMPIRE

In the **Treaty of Aix-la-Chapelle**, signed by Charlemagne and the Byzantine emperor shortly after Pepin's defeat, Venice was declared to be a dukedom within the Eastern Empire, despite the fact that by now the control of Byzantium was little more than nominal. The traders and boatmen of the lagoon were less and less inclined to acknowledge the precedence of the emperor, and they signalled their recalcitrance through one great symbolic act—**the theft of the body of Saint Mark from Alexandria in 828**. Saint Mark, whose posthumous arrival in Venice was held to be divinely ordained (see the "Basilica di San Marco" entry), was made the patron saint of the city in place of the Byzantine patron, Saint Theodore, and a basilica was built alongside the doge's castle to accommodate the holy relics. These two buildings—the **Basilica di San Marco** and the **Palazzo Ducale**—were to remain the emblems of the Venetian state and the repository of power within the city for almost one thousand years.

By the end of the ninth century the population of the islands of central Venice was increasing steadily. The city was comprehensively protected against attack, with chains slung across the entrance to the major channels and fortified walls shielding the waterfront between the Palazzo Ducale and the area in which the church of Santa Maria Zobenigo now stands. Before the close of the following century, the Venetian **trading networks** were well established—military assistance given to their former masters in Byzantium had earned concessions in the markets of the East, and the Venetian economy was now prospering from the distribution of eastern goods along the waterways of northern Italy .

Slav pirates, operating from the shelter of the Dalmatian coast, were the greatest hindrance to Venetian trade in the northern Adriatic, and in the year **1000** a fleet set out under the command of **Doge Pietro Orseolo II** to subjugate the troublemakers. The successful expedition was commemorated each subsequent year in the ceremony of the **Marriage of Venice to the Sea**, in which the city's lordship of the Adriatic was ritually confirmed. (See the "Lido" entry.) However, although the Doge of Venice could now legitimately claim the title "Duke of Dalmatia," there remained the problem of the **Normans** of southern Italy, whose navy threatened to confine the Venetians to the upper part of the Adriatic. The breakthrough came in the 1080s. In **1081** the Byzantine emperor Alexius Comnenus, himself endangered by Norman expansion, appealed to Venice for aid. The result was a series of naval battles costing thousands of lives, at the end of which Venice had strengthened its shipping lanes, established itself as the protector of the Eastern Empire's seaboard, and earned invaluable commercial rights for its traders. In a charter of 1082, known as the *Crisobolo* (Golden Bull), the emperor declared Venetian merchants to be exempt from all tolls and taxes within his lands. In the words of one historian—"On that day Venetian world trade began."

VENICE AND THE CRUSADES

In 1095 Pope Urban II called for a Christian army to repossess the Holy Land from the Muslims, and within four years Jerusalem had been retaken by the **First Crusade**. Decades of chaos ensued, which the Venetians, typically, managed to turn to their commercial advantage. Offering to transport armies and supplies to the East in return for grants of property and financial bonuses, Venice extended its foothold in the Aegean, the Black Sea and Syria, battling all the time (sometimes literally) against its two chief maritime rivals in Italy—Pisa and Genoa. While it was consolidating its overseas bases, Venice was also embroiled in the political maneuverings between the papacy, the Western Emperor and the cities of northern Italy, the conclusion of which was one of Venice's greatest diplomatic successes: **the reconciliation of Emperor Frederick Barbarossa and Pope Alexander III** in 1177, in Venice.

Now a major European power, Venice was about to acquire an empire. In November 1199 Count Tibald of Champagne proposed a **Fourth Crusade** to regain Jerusalem, which twelve years earlier had fallen to Saladin. It came about that Venice was commissioned, for a huge fee, to provide the ships for the army. In 1202 the forces gathered in Venice, only to find that they couldn't raise the agreed sum. In the negotiations that followed, the doge obtained a promise from the French commanders that the Crusade would stop off to reconquer the colony of Zara, recently captured from Venice by the King of Hungary. No sooner was that accomplished than the expedition was diverted, after Venetian persuasion, to Constantinople, where the succession to the imperial throne was causing problems. The eventual upshot was the **Sack of Constantinople in 1204**, one of the most disgusting episodes in European history. Thousands were massacred by the Christian soldiers and virtually every precious object that could be lifted was stolen from the city, mainly by the Venetians. So vast was the scale of the destruction and murder that a contemporary historian regretted that the city had not fallen instead to the Infidel. Ultimately its consequences were disastrous—not only did no help reach the forces in the Holy Land, but the Eastern Empire was fatally divided between the native Greeks and the barbaric westerners. The Ottoman conquest of Constantinople in 1453, and the consequent peril of western Europe, were distant but direct results of the Fourth Crusade. Venice got what it wanted, though—"one quarter and half a quarter" of the Roman Empire was now under its sway, with an almost uninterrupted chain of ports stretching from the lagoon to the Black Sea.

THE FOURTEENTH CENTURY

The enmities created within the Eastern Empire by the Fourth Crusade were soon to rebound on Venice. The Genoese were now the main opposition in the eastern markets, maintaining a rivalry so violent that some Venetian historians refer to their succession of conflicts as the **Five Genoese Wars**. Genoa's hatred of Venice led to an alliance with the dethroned Byzantine dynasty, whose loathing of the Venetians was no less intense; within months of the Pact of Ninfeo (1261), **Michael Palaeologus VIII** was installed as emperor in Constantinople. Venice now faced a struggle to hold onto their commercial interests against the favored Genoese.

For the rest of the century, and almost all the fourteenth century, the defeat of Genoa was the primary aim of Venice's rulers. Both sides suffered terrible defeats: at the battle of **Curzola** (1298) 65 ships out of a Venetian fleet of 95 were lost, and 5000 Venetians taken captive; at the Sardinian port of **Alghero** (1353) the Genoese navy lost a similar propor-

tion of its vessels. The climax came with the Fourth War of Genoa, better known as the **War of Chioggia**. Following a victory over the Venetians at Zara in 1379, the Genoese fleet sailed on to Venice, supported by the Paduans and the Austrians, and quickly took Chioggia. This was the zenith of Genoa's power—in August **1380** the invaders were driven off, and although the treaty signed between the two cities seemed inconclusive, within a few decades it was clear that Venice had at last won the battle for economic and political supremacy.

POLITICAL UPHEAVAL

It was during the Genoese campaigns that the **constitution** of Venice arrived at a state that was to endure until the fall of the Republic, the most significant step in this evolution being the **Serrata del Maggior Consiglio** of **1297**, a measure which basically allowed a role in the government of the city only to those families already involved in it. (See the "Palazzo Ducale" entry.) Not surprisingly, many of those disenfranchised by the *Serrata* resented its instigator, **Doge Pietro Gradenigo**, and when Venice lost its tussle with the papacy for possession of Ferrara in 1309, it seemed that Gradenigo had scarcely a single supporter in the city. Yet the insurrection that came the following year was a revolt of a patrician clique, not an uprising of the people; its leader—**Bajamonte Tiepolo**—had personal reasons for opposing the doge and appears to have wanted to replace the new system not with a more democratic one but with a despotic regime headed by himself. Tiepolo's private army was routed in a battle in the center of the city, but his rebellion had a permanent effect upon the history of Venice, in that it led to the creation in 1310 of the **Council of Ten**, a committee empowered to supervise matters of internal security. Though the Council was intended to be an emergency measure, its tenure was repeatedly extended until, in 1334, it was made a permanent institution.

The most celebrated attempt to subvert the Venetian government followed a few years later, in **1355**, and this time the malefactor was the doge himself—**Marin Falier**, who ironically had played a large part in the sentencing of Bajamonte Tiepolo. Falier's plot to overthrow the councils of Venice and install himself as absolute ruler seems to have been prompted by his fury at the lenient treatment given to a young nobleman who had insulted him. Exploiting the grievances felt against certain noble families by, among others, the director of the Arsenale, Falier gathered together a group of conspirators, many of whom were drawn from the working class, a section of Venetian society which was particularly affected by the economic demands of the rivalry with Genoa. (Open war had recently broken out again after a long but tense period of truce, and to make the situation worse, the **Black Death of 1348–49** had killed around 60 percent of the city's population.) Details of the planned coup leaked out, Falier was arrested, and on April 17, eight months after becoming doge, he was beheaded on the steps of the Palazzo Ducale.

TERRA FIRMA EXPANSION

The sea lanes of the eastern Mediterranean were the basis of Venice's wealth, but its dominance as a trading center clearly depended on free access to the rivers and mountain passes of northern Italy. Thus, although Venetian foreign policy was predominantly eastward-looking from the start, a degree of intervention on the mainland was inevitable, especially with the rise in the fourteenth century of ambitious dynasties such as the **Scaligeri** in Verona and the **Visconti** in Milan. Equally inevitable was the shift from a strategy to preserve Venice's commercial interests, to a scheme that was blatantly imperialistic.

The unsuccessful battle for Ferrara was Venice's first territorial campaign; the first victory came thirty years later, when the combined forces of Venice, Florence and a league of Lombard cities defeated the Scaligeri, allowing Venice to incorporate **Castelfranco**, **Conegliano**, **Sacile**, **Oderzo** and, most importantly, **Treviso** into the domain of the Republic. Having thus made safe the roads to Germany, the Venetians set about securing the territory to the west. The political and military machinations of northern Italy in this period are extremely complicated, with alliances regularly made and betrayed, and cities changing hands with bewildering frequency— Treviso, for example, was lost and won back before the close of the fourteenth century. The

bare outline of the story is that by **1405** Venice had eradicated the most powerful neighboring dynasty, the **Carrara** family of Padua, and had a firm hold on **Bassano**, **Belluno**, **Feltre**, **Vicenza**, **Verona** and **Padua** itself. The annexation in **1420** of **the Friuli** and **Udine**, formerly ruled by the King of Hungary, virtually doubled the area of the *terra firma* under Venetian control, and brought the border of the empire right up to the Alps.

Many Venetians thought that any farther expansion would be foolish. Certainly this was the view of **Doge Tommaso Mocenigo**, who on his deathbed urged his compatriots to "refrain ... from taking what belongs to others or making unjust wars." Specifically, he warned them against the ambitions of **Francesco Fóscari**—"If he becomes doge, you will be constantly at war ... you will become the slaves of your masters-at-arms and their captains." Within a fortnight of Mocenigo's funeral in 1423, Fóscari was elected as his successor, and Venice was soon on the offensive against the mightiest prince of northern Italy—**Filippo Maria Visconti** of Milan. In the first phase of the campaign nothing except a tenuous ownership of Bergamo and Brescia was gained, a failure for which the Venetian mercenary captain, **Carmagnola**, served as the scapegoat. He was executed in 1432 for treason, and his place taken by Erasmo da Narni, better known as **Il Gattamelata**. The **Treaty of Cremona** (1441) confirmed Venetian control of **Peschiera**, **Brescia**, **Bergamo** and part of the territory of **Cremona**, and by now **Ravenna** was also officially part of the Venetian dominion, but still the fighting did not stop. Peace on the mainland finally came in **1454**, with the signing of a treaty between Venice and the new ruler of Milan, **Francesco Sforza**, Venice's erstwhile ally against the Visconti. Ravenna didn't stay Venetian for long; the rest of its mainland empire, though, remained intact until the coming of Napoleon.

THE TURKISH THREAT

The other Italian states might have taken concerted action against Venice had it not been for the fact that the entire peninsula now faced the common threat of the Ottoman Turks, as was acknowledged in the pact drawn up at

Lodi later in 1454 between Venice, Milan, Naples, Florence and the Papal States. Open conflict between Venice and the Turks had broken out early in the century—the Republic winning the naval battle of Gallipoli in 1416—but the policy of *terra firma* expansion kept the majority of Venice's warships on the rivers of the north, so reliance had to be placed in diplomatic measures to contain the Turkish advance. They were ineffective. Reports of a Turkish military build-up under the command of the young **Sultan Mahomet II** were not treated with the necessary urgency, and the consequence was that western troops sent to defend **Constantinople** against the Sultan's army were insufficient to prevent the fall of the city in **1453**.

The trade agreement which the Venetians managed to negotiate with the Sultan could not arrest the erosion of its commercial empire in the east. The Turkish fleets penetrated into the northern Aegean and many times in the last years of the century its cavalry came so close to Venice that the fires from the villages it destroyed could be seen from the top of the Campanile of San Marco. In **1479** Venice was forced to sign away the vital port of **Negroponte** and a batch of other Aegean islands; the defeat of the Venetian navy at **Sapienza** in 1499 led to the loss of the main fortresses of the **Morea** (Peloponnese), which meant that the Turks now controlled the so-called "door to the Adriatic." Virtually the only bright spot in all the gloom came about through the marriage of the Venetian **Caterina Cornaro** to the King of **Cyprus** in 1468. In 1473 the king died, and the ensuing political pressure on the widow paid off in **1489**, when Caterina handed over the island to the government of Venice.

THE ECONOMIC DOWNTURN

In **1494** Italy was invaded by **Louis XII of France**, an intervention which Venice lost no time in exploiting. By playing the various territorial contenders off against each other (mainly France and the Habsburgs), Venice succeeded in adding bits and pieces to the *terra firma* empire, and in 1503 signed a disadvantageous treaty with the Turks so as to be able to concentrate its resources on the mainland. Given the accumulated hostility to Venice, it

was a dangerous game, and when the Republic began to encroach on the papal domain in Romagna, it at last provoked a unified response from its opponents. The **League of Cambrai**, formed in **1508** with Pope Julius II, Louis XII, Emperor Maximilian and the King of Spain at its head, pitted almost every power in Europe against the Venetians, in a pact that explicitly declared its intention of destroying Venice's empire as a prelude to conquering the Turks.

The ensuing war began calamitously for Venice—its army was crushed by the French at **Agnadello**, city after city defected to the League, and Venice prepared for a siege. The siege never came, and in the end the conflicting interests of the League enabled the Venetians, through subtle diplomacy, to repossess nearly everything they had held at the start of the war. Nonetheless, when the fighting finished in **1516** many of the cities of the Veneto had been sacked, great swathes of the countryside ruined, and the Venetian treasury bled almost dry.

Worse was to come. Clearly **the discovery of the New World** was going to have significant repercussions for Venice, but the most catastrophic of the voyages of discovery from Venice's point of view was that of **Vasco da Gama**. In September **1499**, da Gama arrived back in Lisbon having reached India by the Cape of Good Hope. The slow and expensive land routes across Asia to the markets and docks of Venice could now be bypassed by the merchants of northern Europe—from the moment of da Gama's return the economic balance of Europe began to tilt in favor of the Portuguese, the English and the Dutch.

In **1519**, with the accession of the 19-year-old **Charles V**, the Habsburg Empire absorbed the massive territories of the Spanish kingdom, and after the **sack of Rome in 1527** the whole Italian peninsula, with the sole exception of Venice, was under the young emperor's domination. Meanwhile, the **Turks** were on the move again—**Syria** and **Egypt** had been taken in **1517**; **Rhodes** had fallen to **Suleiman the Magnificent** in **1522**; and by 1529 the Ottoman Empire had spread right along the southern Mediterranean to Morocco. To survive, Venice had to steer a path between these two empires and France, the other superpower of the period. It did survive, but at a cost. When a combined Christian fleet took on the Turks at **Prevesa** in **1538**, the supreme commander, acting under Charles V's instructions, was so concerned to prevent the Venetians profiting from an allied victory that his tactics ensured a Turkish victory; the Venetians were obliged to accept a punitive treaty shortly after. Even the great allied success at **Lepanto** in **1571** didn't work to Venice's advantage, as the Habsburg commander of the fleet, Don John of Austria, refused to consolidate the Venetian position by sailing east after the victory. In the subsequent negotiations, Venice was forced formally to surrender **Cyprus**, the brutal capture of which by the Turks had been the reason for the allied offensive in the first place.

THE SEVENTEENTH CENTURY

Relations between Rome and Venice were always fractious. Venice's expansion on the mainland was a source of aggravation, especially when it turned its attention to areas over which the Vatican claimed sovereignty, but papal animosity was also caused by the restrictions imposed on the pope's authority within the Republic's boundaries, which led to Venice's being regarded in some quarters as a crypto-Protestant state. The pope was Venice's spiritual overlord, the Venetians agreed, but the doge and his officers were the masters in temporal affairs. The problem for the papacy was that the doge's notion of what constituted temporal affairs was far too broad, and at the start of the seventeenth century, **Pope Paul V** and the Republic came to a head-on clash.

Two incidents provoked the fight: Venice's insistence that the pope should routinely approve its candidate for the office of Patriarch; and its determination not to hand over to papal jurisdiction two clerics it had decided to prosecute. Matters came to a head with the **Papal Interdict of 1606** and the excommunication of the whole city. Venice's resistance, orchestrated by the scholar-priest **Paolo Sarpi**, was fierce—the Jesuits were expelled, priests within Venetian territory ordered to continue in their duties, and pamphlets printed putting the Venetian case. One year later the Interdict was lifted, damaging the prestige of the papacy throughout Europe.

No sooner was the Interdict out of the way than the Spanish and Austrian **Habsburgs**

entered the fray again. The Austrian branch was the first to cause trouble, by encouraging the piratical raids of the **Uskoks**, a loosely-defined and regularly obstreperous community living along the Dalmatian coast. Venice took retaliatory action, Archduke Ferdinand objected, and a half-hearted war dragged on until **1617**, when, under the peace terms, the benighted Uskoks were removed completely from their sea-ports.

The Spanish wing was more devious, attempting, in **1618**, to subvert the Venetian state with a wildly ambitious scheme that has always been known as **The Spanish Conspiracy**. Masterminded by the Spanish Viceroy of Naples, the **Duke of Osuna**, and the Spanish Ambassador to Venice, the **Duke of Bedmar**, the plot involved smuggling a Spanish army into the city in disguised groups of two or three, and then inciting a mutiny among a contingent of Dutch mercenaries already lodged there. Just how convoluted the conspiracy was can be gathered from the fact that its betrayal resulted in the execution of around 300 people.

And then, after half a century of ceasefire, the **Turks** renewed their harassment of the Venetian colonies, concentrating their attention now on the one remaining stronghold in the eastern Mediterranean, **Crete**. The campaign lasted for 25 years, ending in **1669** with the inevitable fall of the island. Even then the war with the Turks was not over—in **1699**, under the military command of **Doge Francesco Morosini**, the Venetians embarked on a retaliatory action in the **Morea** (Peloponnese), and succeeded in retaking the islands. By 1715, however, all the gains had been turned to losses once more, and in the **Treaty of Passarowitz** of **1718** Venice was forced to accept the definition of its Mediterranean empire drawn up by the Austrians and the Turks. It was left with just the Ionian islands and the Dalmatian coast, and its power in those colonies was little more than hypothetical.

COLLAPSE

Venice in the eighteenth century became a political nonentity, pursuing a foreign policy of unarmed neutrality of which one historian wrote "she sacrifices everything with the single object of giving no offence to other states." When the **Treaty of Aix-la-Chapelle** in **1748** confirmed Austrian control of the neighboring areas of the mainland, the Venetians felt compelled to send ambassadors to the Austrian court in a humiliating attempt to wheedle guarantees of their possessions on the *terra firma.* At home, the economy remained strong, but the division between the upper stratum of the aristocracy and the ever-increasing poorer section was widening, and all attempts to dampen discontent within the city by democratizing its government were stifled by the conservative elite.

Politically trivial and constitutionally ossified, Venice was now renowned not as one of the great powers of Europe, but rather as its playground. Hester Thrale observed in 1789 that no other place was "so subservient to the purposes of pleasure," and William Beckford recorded the effects of a life spent between the ballroom and casino—"Their nerves unstrung by disease and the consequence of early debaucheries, allow no natural flow of lively spirits . . . they pass their lives in one perpetual doze."

The conflict between Austria and post-revolutionary France quickly brought about the end of the Venetian Republic. Having mollified the Austrians by handing over the Veneto to them, **Napoleon** waited for a pretext to polish off the Republic itself. On 20 April 1797 the Venetians duly provided him with one, by attacking a French naval patrol off the Lido. "I will have no more Inquisitors. I will have no more Senate; I shall be an Attila to the state of Venice," Bonaparte proclaimed; war was declared on Venice, and on May 9 an ultimatum was sent to the city's government, demanding the dissolution of its constitution.

On Friday **12 May 1797**, the Maggior Consiglio met for the last time. By 512 votes to 20, with 5 abstentions, the Council voted to accede to every one of Napoleon's demands; the vote cast, the last Doge of Venice, **Lodovico Manin**, handed to his valet the linen cap worn beneath the ducal crown, saying— "Take it, I shall not be needing it again." The Venetian Republic was dead.

Within days a provisional democratic council had been formed and there were French troops in the city, many of them occupied with wrecking the Arsenale or stripping the place of its art treasures and shipping them off to Paris. On this occasion, the French didn't stay long, because in the **Treaty of Campo Formio**, signed in October, Napoleon relinquished Venice to the Austrians. They were soon back, though—in **1805** Napoleon joined the city to his Kingdom of Italy, and it stayed under French domination until the aftermath of Waterloo, ten years later. It then passed back to the Austrians again, and remained a Habsburg province for the next half-century, the only break in Austrian rule coming with the **revolt of March 1848**, when the city was reinstituted as a republic under the leadership of **Daniele Manin**, the last heroic figure in Venetian history. The rebellion lasted until **August 1849**, when a combination of starvation, disease and relentless bombardment forced the Venetians to surrender. Liberation finally arrived in the wake of Prussia's defeat of the Austrians at Sadowa in **1866**. Soon after, Venice was absorbed into the Kingdom of United Italy.

TO THE PRESENT

In many respects the Austrians were better for Venice than the French had been. Although the French initiated modernization schemes such as the creation of public gardens and the cemetery of San Michele, not all of the fifty or so religious buildings and forty palaces which they demolished were destroyed in a good cause; in addition to which, they also wrecked the ship-yards and confiscated hundreds of works of art. The Austrians' urban improvements were less ruthless: they filled in some of the less hygienic canals (the origin of the *rio terrà*), built a rail link with the mainland, and undertook two major, albeit controversial, restoration projects—the Fondaco dei Turchi and the church of Santi Maria e Donato on Murano.

Yet Venice went through most of the nineteenth century in a state of destitution. There were no more government jobs to provide a source of income, and Trieste was the Austrians' preferred port on the Adriatic. By 1820 begging was the main means of support for about one quarter of its population. Families that had once been among the city's wealthiest were obliged to sell their most treasured possessions; the Barbarigo family sold seventeen paintings by Titian to the Czar, for example. Later in the century, even the churches were selling their property to pay for their upkeep. It's been calculated that of the movable works of art that were to be found in Venice at the fall of the Republic, only four percent remains.

Manufacturing activity within the city revived towards the end of the nineteenth century: there were flour mills on Giudecca, glass factories on Murano, lace workshops on Burano, and the 1913 edition of Baedeker described Venice as a "shipbuilding, cotton spinning and iron working center." The opening of the Suez Canal in 1869 brought a muted revival to the Arsenale docks. Already, though, **tourism** had emerged as the main area of economic expansion, with the development of the **Lido** as Europe's most fashionable resort. It was the need for a more substantial economic base than bathing huts, hotels and a few pockets of industrial production that led, in the wake of World War I, to the development of the industrial complex on the marshland across the lagoon from Venice, at **Porto Marghera**.

By the end of World War I, Venice itself was finished as a maritime center—battleships had been built in the Arsenale, but the proximity of the enemy forces persuaded the navy to dismantle the docks in 1917 and switch its yards to Genoa and Naples. The new port of Marghera was not a shipyard but a processing and refining center to which raw materials would be brought by sea. In 1933 a **road link** was built to carry the workforce between Venice and the steadily expanding port, whose progress was a special concern of Mussolini's government. (Venice was the second city in Italy in which organized Fascism appeared; as early as 1919 the local newspaper published an appeal for the formation of fascist squads.) After World War II (from which Venice emerged undamaged) Marghera's growth accelerated even more rapidly. The consequences were not those that had been predicted.

What happened was that the factory workers of Marghera, instead of commuting each day from Venice, simply decamped to the mainland. Housing in Marghera's neighbor, **Mestre**, is drier, roomier, warmer and cheaper to maintain than the apartments in Venice, and as a result the population of Mestre-Marghera is today more than three times that of the historic center of Venice, which is now around the

80,000 mark. (Immediately after World War II it was around 170,000.) Apart from polluting the environment of the lagoon, Mestre has siphoned so many people of working age from the islands that the average age of Venice's population is now the highest of any major European city. Moreover, the percentage of native Venetians in the city is declining as the place becomes a favorite base or retirement home for the wealthy of Milan, Turin and other more prosperous Italian cities—and only the wealthy can afford to maintain the fragile fabric of many of the city's houses. When an apartment is sold in Venice, the odds are around 2/1 that the buyer will not be a Venetian.

VENICE'S REVIVAL?

No city has suffered more from the tourist industry than Venice—nearly twenty million people visit the city each year, and around half of those don't even stay a night. Yet the fact is that no city needs its tourists more than Venice. This dependency is understandably irksome to the city's inhabitants, and every year proposals are put forward to restore a degree of autonomy to Venice. A science park, a national library, a conservation and marine technology center, a national institute for restoration research—all have been suggested as projects which could give Venice a more active role in the life of twentieth-century Italy. Some dismiss such ideas as mere gestures, and prefer to see the recent political shifts in Yugoslavia and Hungary as the harbingers of Venice's revival. Should political realignment lead to the development of a market economy in these countries, Venice will once again be sitting on a major European trade route – or so the argument runs.

Perhaps the craziest scheme for the renewal of Venice was the proposal that it should be the venue for **Expo 2000**, the trade jamboree that will usher in the new millennium. The project envisioned the drainage of a large part of the lagoon to build the Expo site, and it was anticipated that 45 million people would come to the city over the four months of the show—in other words, four times the city's population daily. Despite the environmental idiocy of the idea, and the fact that it was of no conceivable long-term benefit to Venice, it was vociferously championed by Venice-born Foreign Minister Gianni de Michelis—who, quite coincidentally, owns a lot of property in the city and has ambitions to be the mayor of Venice (he could hold both jobs simultaneously). By a combination of blatant threats and bribery, de Michelis secured the backing of a majority among the 43 member states of the *Bureau International des Expositions*, and it seemed that the *BIE*'s meeting on June 14, 1990, would be nothing more than a formal ratification of Venice's disastrous application.

But the forces of reason were making themselves heard in the upper reaches of the Italian government. Environmentalists from all over the world lobbied the Italians to reconsider and

the upper house of the Italian parliament passed a motion deploring the scheme—as did the European Parliament, by 195 to 14. The near-unanimity of this latter vote seems to have been decisive. Two days' before the *BIE* meeting the Italian government cancelled the city's application.

Expo 2000 will be held in Hanover, and Gianni de Michelis will not be Venice's next mayor. The news of his decision to withdraw from the mayoral contest was cheered when it was announced over loudspeakers to the crowd gathered in the Piazza to celebrate the scuppering of Expo.

VENETIAN PAINTING AND SCULPTURE

After just a day in Venice you notice that the light is softer than that on the mainland and changes more during the course of a day. Reflecting off the water and the white stone facades, it gives shifting impressions of places that would otherwise be shadowed, and adds shimmering highlights to solid brickwork. In view of the specific qualities of Venetian light, it's scarcely surprising that the city's painters emphasized color and texture rather than structure and perspective. The political and social peculiarities of Venice were equally influential on the development of its art, as will become apparent in the following thumbnail account.

BYZANTINE VENICE

The close political and commercial ties between the early Venetian state and the Byzantine empire (see the "History" section) led to a steady exchange of works of art between the two, and to the creation of the most important work of art from that period—the **Pala d'Oro** on the high altar of San Marco. Begun as a collaboration between Venetian and Byzantine craftsmen, it epitomizes the Venetian taste for elaborate decoration and creates the impression of a complex content unified by a dazzlingly rich surface. The *Pala* was later expanded with panels stolen from Constantinople during the sack of 1204, a wholesale plundering which provided Venice with a hoard of artifacts that was to nourish its craftsmen and artists for centuries.

It is notable that the earliest Venetian painter of renown, **Paolo Veneziano** (working from the 1330s to at least 1358), shows far stronger affinities with Byzantine work than with the frescoes created by Giotto at the start of the century in nearby Padua. He generally employs a flat, gold background and symmetrical arrangements of symbolic figures, rather than attempting a more emotional representation of individuals. Two paintings in the Accademia show these characteristics: a *Madonna and Child Enthroned* and a polyptych which achieves the same overall effect as that of the Pala d'Oro—and indeed it was he who was commissioned to paint the **cover of the Pala d'Oro**, now in San Marco's museum.

The first room of the Accademia is full of work displaying this Byzantine indebtedness, and Byzantium remained a living influence in the city up to the seventeenth and eighteenth centuries, sustained in part by the influx of refugees following the **fall of Constantinople** in 1453. The neo-Byzantine *Madoneri* (the main school of the Greek community) are represented in the **Museo Dipinti Sacri Bizantini**, where the paintings show a complete indifference to the post-Renaissance cult of the artist and to notions of aesthetic novelty. The young Cretan **El Greco** (1545–1614) worked with the *Madoneri* for a while, before setting out for fame and fortune in Spain.

GOTHIC PAINTING AND SCULPTURE

Deemed to be relics of a barbaric age, a huge number of Gothic paintings and sculptures were destroyed in the seventeenth and eighteenth centuries. The reinstatement of the Gothic is in large part due to the determination of John Ruskin, whose particular preoccupation was the Gothic architecture and sculpture of Venice. His meticulous work in **San Zanipolo**, mapping the change from Gothic to Renaissance through a study of the **funerary sculpture**, is still a useful analysis.

San Zanipolo's main apse contains the **tomb of Doge Michele Morosini** (d.1382), described by Ruskin as "the richest monument of the Gothic period in Venice," although its figures (apart from those at the head and foot of the doge) have an awkward, un-Gothic stiffness. More interesting sculpturally is the **tomb of Doge Marco Corner** (d.1368) opposite, which was carved in the workshop of the non-Venetian **Nino Pisano**. Slightly later is San Marco's **rood screen**, by the two brothers **Pierpaolo and Jacobello Dalle Masegne**, who made a study of the work of Pisano and northern European Gothic sculpture. The other high points of Gothic sculpture in Venice are also architecturally related—the **Palazzo Ducale's capitals**, **corner sculptures** and **Porta della Carta** (though the main figures on the *Porta* are nineteenth-century replicas of fifteenth-century originals).

Paulo Veneziano's unrelated namesake, **Lorenzo Veneziano** (working 1356–72) marries a distinctly Gothic element to the Byzantine elements in Venetian painting. The large polyptych in the Accademia is a fine example of his work, showing a roundedness in the face and hands and in the fall of the drapery, and a sinuousness of pose in the figures that suggests the influence of Gothic painters such as Simone Martini of Siena.

Around 1409 **Gentile de Fabriano**, the exemplar of the style known as **International Gothic**, frescoed parts of the Palazzo Ducale with the help of his pupil **Pisanello**. These frescoes are all now destroyed, and the nearest example of Pisanello's work is his *St George* (1438–42) in Verona's church of Sant'Anastasia. Even in this one piece it's possible to see what the Venetians would have found congenial in his art: chiefly an all-over patterning that ties the content of the painting to the picture plane and eschews the illusion of receding space.

The work of Gentile and Pisanello was most closely studied in Venice by **Michele Giambono** (working 1420–62), represented in the Accademia by a *Coronation of the Madonna in Paradise* (1447) and in the church of San Trovaso by *St Chrysogonus* (c.1450). These claustrophobic paintings are of the same date as Padua's frescoes by Mantegna and sculptures by Donatello—Giambono and others in

Venice were happily working in a sophisticated high Gothic style at a time when the Renaissance was elsewhere into its maturity.

EARLY RENAISSANCE PAINTING

Petrarch, who lived in Venice in the 1360s, described the Republic as "a world apart" and nothing illustrates this insularity better than the reception of Renaissance ideas in the city. Venetians were wary of over-emphasizing the individual, a tendency implicit in the one-point perspective of Renaissance painting; in addition, the use of abstract mathematical formulas in the depiction of form was alien to the pragmatic Venetian temperament. When the principles of the Florentine Renaissance did belatedly filter into the art of Venice, they were transformed into a way of seeing that was uniquely Venetian.

Key figures in this period of absorption were the **Vivarini** family—**Antonio** (c.1419–c.80), his brother **Bartolomeo** (c.1430–c.91) and son **Alvise** (c.1445–1505). Antonio's work, though still part of the Gothic tradition, marks a shift away from it, with his more angular line and construction of pictorial spaces consistent with the rules of one-point perspective—as in the *Madonna and Child* tryptych in the Accademia, painted in collaboration with Giovanni d'Alemagna. A more humanistic temperament is embodied in the paintings of **Alvise**, manifested less through his depiction of space than through his representation of people. He individualises his figures, giving an emotional charge to narratives which had to that point functioned symbolically. The *St Clare* in the Accademia is an excellent example of his work, establishing an unprecedentedly intimate contact between the saint and the viewer.

The preeminent artistic dynasty of this transitional period was that of **Jacopo Bellini** (c.1400–70), once a pupil of Gentile da Fabriano, and his sons **Gentile** (c.1429–1507) and **Giovanni** (c.1430–1516). Jacopo suffered from the anti-Gothic zealotry of later years, and his two major cycles of paintings—at the Scuola di San Marco and the Scuola di San Giovanni Evangelista—were destroyed. From descriptions of these works, it would appear that the two *Madonnas* in the Accademia are rather restrained in their decoration; other pieces by him can be seen in the Museo Cor, er.

Giovanni is the one that people mean when they refer simply to "Bellini." In the Accademia he's represented by a number of *Madonnas*, a series of allegorical panels, and a couple of large altarpieces. Other works around Venice include altarpieces in San Zaccaria, San Pietro (Murano), the Frari, Madonna dell'Orto and San Zanipolo. In the majority of these paintings the attention is concentrated on the foreground, where the arrangement of the figures or a device such as a screen or throne turns the background into another plane parallel to the surface, rather than a receding landscape. That this was a conscious choice which had nothing to do with his perspectival skills is demonstrated by the **San Giobbe altarpiece** (in the Accademia), in which a meticulously worked out illusionistic space would have suggested the presence of an extra chapel. A fundamental humanism pervades much of Giovanni's output—although these *Madonnas* show an idealized version of motherhood, each possesses an immediacy which suggests to the viewer that this ideal could be attainable.

Meanwhile, **Gentile** was pursuing a form of painting that was also a specifically Venetian Renaissance phenomenon—the *istoria* or narrative painting cycle. At least ten of these were commissioned by public bodies between around 1475 and 1525: the three remaining cycles in Venice are the *Miracles of the Relic of the True Cross* (Accademia), by five artists including Gentile and **Carpaccio**, and the *St Ursula* cycle (Accademia) and the *St George and St Jerome* cycle (Scuola di San Giorgio degli Schiavoni), which are both by Carpaccio. To the modern observer the story line of the *Relic* and *St Ursula* cycles in particular can seem to be naive pretexts for precise renditions of the pageant of Venetian social life and a wealth of domestic minutiae. The details of the paintings were not mere incidentals to the narrative, however—a person hanging out washing or mending a roof would have been perceived as enhancements of the miracle's physical reality of the miracle, and not as distractions from the central event.

HIGH RENAISSANCE PAINTING

While these narrative cycles were being produced Giovanni Bellini was beginning to experiment with oil paint, then beginning to displace tempera (pigment in egg yolk) as the preferred medium. Whereas tempera had to be applied in layers, the long drying time of oil allowed colors to be mixed and softened, while its thick consistency enabled artists to simulate the texture of the objects depicted. Close examination of later paintings by Bellini shows he used his fingers to merge colors and soften light, and two of his young assistants at the time—**Giorgione** and **Titian**—were to explore even further the potential of the new material, developing a specifically Venetian High Renaissance style.

Giorgione (1475–1510) seems custom-built for myth: little is known about him other than he was tall and handsome and he died young (possibly of plague). The handful of enigmatic works he created were innovative in their imaginative self-sufficiency—for instance the Venetian collector Michiel, writing in 1530, was unable to say precisely what the subject was of *The Tempest* (Accademia), perhaps Giorgione's most famous image. His only altarpiece, still in the cathedral at Castelfranco (his home town), isolates the Madonna and the two saints from each other by manipulating perspective and by placing the Madonna against a landscape while the attendant saints stand against a man-made background. Despite the serenity of the individual figures, the painting instills in the viewer a disquieting sense of elusiveness.

Given his long life and huge output, **Titian** (c.1485-1576) is very badly represented in his home town: a *Presentation in the Temple*, a *Pietà* left unfinished at his death, and a couple of minor works in the Accademia; a handful in the Salute; the *Assumption* and *Pésaro Altarpiece* in the Frari, and that's more or less it. (Napoleon made off with a good crop of Titians, including a *Venus* which he hung in his tent; the Louvre now has a fine collection.)

Titian, like Giorgione, used the qualities of oils to evoke a diffuse light and soften contours—in contrast with the contemporaneous art of Rome, the city of Michelangelo, where the emphasis was on the solidity and sculptural aspects of the objects depicted. Artists in Florence were answerable to an imperious ruling family, in Rome they had to comply with the wishes of successive popes, but Titian's success was so great that he could virtually pick and choose from a host of clients from all over the continent, and the diversity of works he produced—portraits, allegories, devotional paintings, mythologies—remains unsurpassed in western art. The technical range is as impressive as the range of subject matter; the earliest works are highly polished and precisely drawn, but in the later pieces he tested the possibilities of oil paint to their very limit, using his bare hands to scrape the canvas and add great gobbets of paint (see the Accademia *Pietà*).

Giorgionesque is an adjective used to describe a number of early sixteenth-century Venetian painters, in reference to the richening of color popular at the time and to the increasingly "poetic" approach to content. **Sebastiano del Piombo**, who studied under Giovanni Bellini with Titian and Giorgione before moving to Rome in 1611, is one of the artists to whom the term is applied. His altarpiece of **San Giovanni Crisostomo** in the eponymous church is his best work still in Venice. Another is **Palma il Vecchio** (1480-1582); although he was often frivolous in a way that Giorgione and Titian rarely were—ponds of frothy nymphs and the like—his strongest work in Venice is a redoubtable *St Barbara* in Santa Maria Formosa. The most interesting painter of this period and type is **Lorenzo Lotto** (c.1480–1556), represented in the Accademia by the almost metaphysical *Portrait of a Young Man*. The rivalries of other painters eventually drove Lotto from Venice, and it's not too fanciful to see a reflection of the artist's anxieties in his restless, wistful paintings.

RENAISSANCE SCULPTURE

Venetian **sculpture** in the Renaissance was conditioned by the society's ingrained aversion to the over-glorification of the individual and by the specific restrictions of the city's landscape. Freestanding monumental work of the sort that was being commissioned all over Italy is conspicuous by its absence. The exception to prove the rule, the **monument to Colleoni**, was made by the Florentine artist **Verrocchio**. Venetian sculptors worked mainly to decorate tombs or the walls of churches, and up to the late Renaissance no clear distinction was made between sculptors, masons and architects. Beyond the Renaissance, sculpture was generally commissioned as part of an architectural project, and it's usually futile to try to disentangle the sculpture from its architectural function.

Pietro Lombardo (c.1438–1515) was born in Cremona and went to Rome before arriving in Venice c.1460. His development can be charted in the church of San Zanipolo: his first major monument, the **tomb of Doge Pasquale Malipiero**, is pictorially flat and smothered with carved decoration, but the **monument to Doge Pietro Mocenigo**, with its classicized architectural elements and figures, is a fully Renaissance piece. In true Venetian style the latter glorifies the State through the man, rather than stressing his individual salvation—the image of Christ is easily overlooked. Pietro's sons **Antonio** (c.1458–c:1516) and **Tullio** (c.1460–1532) were also sculptors and assisted him on the Mocenigo monument. Tullio's independent work is less pictorial: his **monument to Doge Andrea Vendramin** (also in San Zanipolo) is a complex architectural evocation of a Roman triumphal arch, though again the whole is encrusted with decorative figures.

Jacopo Sansovino, who went on to become the Republic's principal architect, was known as a sculptor when he arrived in Venice from Rome in 1527. More of a classicist than his predecessors, he nonetheless produced work remarkably in tune with Venetian sensibilities—his figures on the *logetta* of the Campanile, for example, animate the surface of the building rather than draw attention to themselves. **Alessandro Vittoria** was the major sculptor of the middle and later part of the century; originally a member of Sansovino's workshop, Vittoria developed a more rhetorical style, well demonstrated in the figures of *St Jerome* in the Frari and San Zanipolo.

TINTORETTO AND VERONESE

Born in 1518, two years after Bellini's death and eight years after that of Giorgione, **Tintoretto** grew up during the period in which the ascendancy of Titian became established. Princes were sending agents to Venice to buy the latest Titian, no matter what the subject, and every visiting dignitary would want to be painted by him. Titian's exploratory attitude to paint and the increasing Venetian receptivity to individual style were both exploited by the energetic and competitive younger artist. The painting that made his reputation, the *Miracle of the Slave* (Accademia; 1548) shows how he learned from Titian's experiments and distanced himself from them. Tintoretto's palette is as rich as Titian's, but is aggressively vivid rather than sensuous, and uses far stronger lighting. And while Titian is concerned with the inner drama of an event, Tintoretto's attention is given to the drama of gesture.

Tintoretto's dynamic style was not universally acclaimed. Pietro Aretino, Titian's close friend and most vociferous champion, disparaged the speed and relative carelessness of his technique, and one member of the **Scuola di San Rocco** said he would give his money towards the decoration of the Scuola's building as long as anyone except Tintoretto got the commission. He didn't get his way, and San Rocco's cycle is the most comprehensive collection of paintings by the artist. Dramatic perspectival effects, bizarre juxtapositions of images and extraordinarily fluid brushwork here make the substantial world seem otherworldly—the converse of the earlier *istorie* cycles.

In contrast, the art of **Paolo Veronese** (1528–88), who moved to Venice from Verona in his twenties, conveys worldly harmony rather than spiritual turbulence. This is particularly evident in his work for architectural settings (San Sebastiano in Venice and the Villa Barbaro at Masèr), where he constructed logical spaces which complement the form of the buildings. More urbane than Tintoretto, he nonetheless attracted controversy: in his *Christ in the House of Levi* (Accademia) the naturalistic representation of German soldiers was interpreted as a gesture of support for Protestantism. Veronese's response to his accusers revealed a lot about the changing attitude towards the status of the artist: claiming licence to depict what he wanted, he simply changed the title of the work from *The Last Supper* to the title by which it's now known.

SEVENTEENTH AND EIGHTEENTH CENTURIES

The High Baroque style in painting and sculpture was largely a Roman phenomenon and the Venetians, whose distrust of Rome led in 1606 to a Papal Interdict (see "History" section), remained largely untouched by it. Suitably enough, the only Venetian interior that relates to Roman Baroque is the **Gesuiti**.

After the hyper-productive **Palma il Giovane,** who seems to have contributed something to the majority of the city's church interiors, it was up to foreign painters—**Johann Lyss** for instance—to keep painting alive in the city. Much the same is true of sculpture: the Venetian **Baldassare Longhena** early in his career turned from sculpture to architecture, leaving the field to the Bolognese **Giuseppe Mazza** (bronze reliefs in San Zanipolo) and the Flemish **Juste Le Court** (high altar of the Salute), although Le Court's Venetian pupil **Orazio Marinelli** (portrait busts in the Querini-Stampalia) did achieve a measure of celebrity. A particularly successful artist towards the end of the seventeenth century was **Andrea Brustolon** of Belluno, best known for his sculptural furniture (Ca' Rezzonico).

The last efflorescence of Venetian art began around the start of the eighteenth century, as Venice was degenerating into the playground of Europe. The highly illusionistic decorative paintings of **GB Piazzetta** (1682–1752) mark the first step and foreshadow the work of **Giambattista Tiepolo** (1696–1777), whose ever-lightening colors and elegant, slightly disdainful Madonnas typified the climate of the frivolous Republic. There's a similarity of mood to most of Tiepolo's work—from the dizzying tromp l'oeil ceiling painted in the Ca' Rezzonico to celebrate a marriage, to the airy *Virgin in Glory* painted for the Carmini.

Another major figure of the period was **Rosalba Carriera** (1675–1758), the first artist to use pastel as a medium in its own right. She was known chiefly as a portraitist, and the Ca' Rezzonico and the Accademia both contain fine selections of her work—the latter featuring a *Self-Portrait in Old Age* which expresses a melancholy temperament usually suppressed from her pictures. (Incidentally, Carriera was not Venice's only woman artist: **Marietta Robusti**, Tintoretto's daughter, was known as a fine portraitist and the Carriera's contemporary **Giulia Lama** has a *Judith and Holofernes* in the Accademia.)

By this time, Venetian art was in the export market, with people such as the English Consul Joseph Smith sending pictures home in large quantities. Aristocrats on the Grand Tour were particularly interested in topographical work—

kind of up-market postcards—and in this area the preeminent artist was **Canaletto** (1695–1768), whose work was copied and engraved to make farther saleable items. Don't be misled into believing he showed the "real" Venice—he idealized the city, changing spatial arrangements in order to suit a harmonious composition and sometimes even altering individual buildings. Canaletto's work in Venice is as sparse as Titian's—there's one painting by him in the Accademia and a couple in the Ca' Rezzonico.

More somber is the work of **Francesco Guardi** (1712–93), whose images of the lagoon and imaginary architectural scenes are frequently swathed in atmospheric mist and dotted with a few prophetic ruins. Genre painters were also popular at this time, none more so than **Pietro Longhi** (1708–-85), whose wonderful illustrations of Venetian life (painted with a technique that is at best adequate) can also be seen in the Accademia and the Ca' Rezzonico. Longhi's production line was as busy as Canaletto's, as his workshop churned out copies of his most popular paintings to meet demand.

The last word on the painting of the Venetian Republic should be devoted to **Giandomenico Tiepolo** (1727–1804), seen at his best in the cycle of frescoes painted for his home and now installed in the Ca' Rezzonico. Freed from the whims of clients, he produced here a series of images that can with hindsight be seen as symbolic of the end of an era, with Sunday crowds gawping at a peepshow and clowns frittering away their time flirting and playing.

NINETEENTH AND TWENTIETH CENTURIES

After the fall of the Republic, art in Venice became the domain of outsiders. **Turner**, who visited the city three times, was its supreme painter in the nineteenth century, but as Ruskin said, you'd only have to stay in Venice for a few days to learn about it what Turner had learned. **Whistler**, **Monet** and **Sargent** were among other visitors. The only Venetian nineteenth-century artist of note is **Frederico Zandomeneghi** (1841–1917), and he decamped for Paris in 1874 to join the Impressionists' circle.

This century the story of art in Venice is no more cheerful. The internationally known artists who stayed as guests of **Peggy Guggenheim** between 1949 and 1979 came and left without making an impact on its cultural life. Every two years the **Biennale** brings in the hot-shots of the international art world, but does little to help young Venetian artists. The few Italian artists who have worked here have not exactly galvanized the city: the painter **Lucio Fontana** lived in Venice in the 50s, and **Emilio Vedova**—a founder member of the avant-garde groups *Fronte Nuovo* and *Gruppo degli Otto*—taught at the Accademia until his death in the mid-80s. Today the best-known artists at work in Venice are the video/installation artist **Fabrizzio Plessi** and the American painter **Judith Harvest**.

AN OUTLINE OF VENETIAN ARCHITECTURE

This is just a brief chronology of Venetian architectural styles, intended simply as a means of giving some sense of order to the city's jumble of buildings. For more detailed accounts, refer to the "Books" section—Deborah Howard's **The Architectural History of Venice** is the best starting point.

BYZANTINE VENICE

Although settlement of the lagoon began as far back as the fifth century, no building has survived intact from earlier than the start of the eleventh century. The very first houses raised on the mudflats were "built like birds' nests, half on sea and half on land .. the solidity of the earth ... secured only by wattle-work," according to a letter written in 523 by a Roman official named Cassiodorus. Many of the earliest shelters were only temporary, constructed as refuges from the Barbarian hordes of the mainland and abandoned as soon as the threat had receded, but with the Lombard invasions of the second half of the sixth century, communities uprooted from northern Italy began to construct more durable buildings on the islands. Some of the materials for these buildings were scavenged from Roman temples and dwellings, and a few of these fragments— used over and over again in succeeding centu-

ries—can still be seen embedded in the walls of some of Venice's oldest structures. The great majority of the lagoon buildings were still made of wood, however, and of these nothing is left.

From the twelfth century onwards the houses of the richest families were made from brick and stone; before then, such materials were reserved for the most important public buildings, and so it is that the **oldest structure in the lagoon** is a church—the **cathedral at Torcello**. Founded in 639 but altered in 864 and again, comprehensively, in **1008**, it takes its form from such early Christian basilicas as Sant'Apollinare in Ravenna. The prototypes of the Western Empire influenced other lagoon churches either founded or rebuilt in the eleventh and twelfth centuries—for example **Sant'Eufamia** on Giudecca, **Santi Maria e Donato** on Murano, and **San Giovanni Decollato** and **San Nicolò dei Mendicoli** in central Venice—but the predominant cultural influence on the emergent city was **Byzantium**, on which the lagoon confederation was originally dependent.

Santa Fosca on Torcello and **San Giovanni di Rialto**, traditionally the oldest church in Venice, are Byzantine in their adherence to a Greek Cross plan, but the building in which the Byzantine ancestry of Venice is most completely displayed is the **Basilica di San Marco**. Like the cathedral of Torcello, San Marco was extensively rebuilt in the eleventh century, but the basic layout—an elongated version of the five-domed Greek Cross design of Constantinople's Church of the Apostles— didn't change much between the consecration of the first Basilica in 832 and the completion of the final version in 1094. As much as its architectural form, the mosaic decoration of San Marco betrays the young city's eastern affiliations—and it was in fact begun, as soon as the shell of the church was completed, by artists from Constantinople.

Byzantium has also left its mark on the **domestic architecture** of Venice, even though the oldest specimens still standing date from the late twelfth century or early thirteenth, by which time the political ties between the two cities had been severed. The high and rounded Byzantine arch can be seen in a number of Canal Grande palaces—the **Ca' da Mosto**, the **Donà** houses, the neighboring

Palazzo Loredan and **Palazzo Farsetti**, and the **Fondaco dei Turchi**. All of these buildings have been altered greatly over the years, but paradoxically it's the one that's been most drastically reconstructed—the Fondaco dei Turchi—which bears the closest resemblance to the earliest merchants' houses. Descended from the Roman villas of the mainland, they had an arcade at water level to permit the unloading of cargo, a long gallery on the upper storey, and lower towers at each end of the facade. Frequently they were embellished with relief panels (*paterae*) and insets of multicolored marble—another Byzantine inheritance, and one that was to last, in modified form, for hundreds of years (for example in the predilection for heraldic devices on the fronts of houses).

GOTHIC

Building land is scarce in Venice, and the consequent density of housing imposed certain restrictions on architectural inventiveness—ground plans had to make the fullest possible use of the available space (hence the rarity of internal courtyards and the uniformly flat facades) and elevations had to maximize the window areas, to make the most of the often limited natural light. Thus architectural evolution in the domestic buildings of Venice is to be observed not so much in the development of overall forms but rather in the mutations of surface detail, and in particular in the arches of the main facades. Nearly all the rich families of Venice derived their wealth from trade, and the predominant shipping lanes from Venice ran to the east—so it was inevitable that **Islamic features** would show through in Venetian architecture. As the thirteenth century progressed, the pure curve of the Byzantine arch first developed an upper peak and then grew into a type of ogival arch—as at the **Palazzo Falier** near Santi Apostoli, and the **Porta dei Fiori** on the north side of the Basilica. This Islamicized Byzantine shape was in turn influenced in the fourteenth century by contact with the Gothic style of the mainland, so producing a repertoire that was uniquely Venetian.

The masterpiece Venetian Gothic is also the city's greatest civic structure—the **Palazzo Ducale**. Begun in 1340, possibly to designs by

Filippo Calendario, the present building was extended in a second phase of work from 1423 onwards, culminating in the construction of the most elaborate Gothic edifice in Venice—the **Porta della Carta**, by **Giovanni and Bartolomeo Bon**.

Imitations and variations of the Palazzo Ducale's complex tracery can be seen all over the city, most strikingly in the **Ca' d'Oro**, begun by Giovanni Bon at much the same time as work began on the extension of the Palazzo Ducale. The Ca' d'Oro represents the apex of Gothic refinement in Venice's domestic architecture; for monumental grandeur, on the other hand, none can match the adjoining Gothic palaces on the *Volta del Canal*—the **Palazzi Giustinian** and the **Ca' Fóscari**.

Ecclesiastical architecture in fourteenth- and fifteenth-century Venice is not as idiosyncratic as its secular counterpart—the religious communities who built the churches, affiliated to orders on the mainland, tended to follow the architectural conventions that had been established by those orders. In some of Venice's Gothic churches the old basilical plan prevailed over the cruciform (eg at **Madonna dell'Orto**), but the two most important churches of the period, the immense **San Zanipolo** (Dominican) and the **Frari** (Franciscan), display many of the basic features of contemporaneous churches in the Veneto: the Latin Cross plan, the pointed arches, the high nave with flanking aisles, and the chapels leading off from the transepts. Yet even these churches have distinctively Venetian characteristics, such as the use of tie-beams and the substitution of lath and plaster vaulting for vaults of stone—both necessary measures in a place with no bedrock for its foundations to rest on. In a few Gothic churches the builders capitalized on the availability of skilled naval carpenters to produce elegant and lightweight ceilings in the shape of an inverted **ship's keel**—for example at **Santo Stefano** and **San Giacomo dell'Orio**.

EARLY RENAISSSANCE

The complicated hybrid of Venetian Gothic remained the city's preferred style well into the second half of the fifteenth century, long after the classical precepts of Renaissance architecture had gained currency elsewhere in Italy.

The late work of **Bartolomeo Bon** contains classical elements mixed with Gothic features (for example the portal of **San Zanipolo** and the incomplete **Ca' del Duca**, both from c.1460), but the first architect in Venice to produce something that could be called a classical design was **Antonio Gambello**, with his land gate for the **Arsenale** (1460). Gambello was not a committed proponent of the new ideas, however, and had work on his church of **San Zaccaria** not been interrupted by his death in 1481, it would have resembled a north European Gothic church more closely than any other in Venice.

In the 1470s another dynasty of stonemason-architects succeeded the Bon family as the leading builders in Venice—**Pietro Solari** and his sons **Antonio and Tullio**, otherwise known as the **Lombardi**. Having worked with followers of Donatello in Padua in the 1460s, Pietro Lombardo was familiar with the latest principles of Tuscan architecture, but the chief characteristics of his own work—the elaborately carved pilasters and friezes, and the inlaid marble panels of various shapes and sizes—are not so much architectonic as decorative. The chancel of **San Giobbe**, the courtyard screen of the **Scuola di San Giovanni Evangelista**, the tiny church of **Santa Maria dei Miracoli** and the facade of the **Scuola di San Marco** represent the best of the Lombardi's architecture. Over-ornate though much of their building projects were, their style was closely imitated by numerous Venetian architects: nobody is certain, for example, whether the **Palazzo Dario** (on the Canal Grande) was designed by Pietro Lombardo or one of his "Lombardesque" acolytes.

Antonio Rizzo, a contemporary of Pietro Lombardo, was similarly esteemed as both a sculptor and architect. After the fire of 1483, Rizzo was put in charge of the rebuilding of the entire **east wing of the Palazzo Ducale**, and it was he who designed the **Scala dei Giganti**, a work which displays a typically Venetian delight in heavy ornamentation.

CODUCCI AND HIS SUCCESSORS

The most rigorous and inventive Venetian architect of the early Renaissance was the man who took over the design and supervision of San Zaccaria after the death of Gambello—**Mauro Coducci** (sometimes spelled "Codussi"). His first commission in the city, the church of **San Michele in Isola** (1469), is not purely classical—the huge lunette and inset roundels are specifically Venetian features—but its proportions and clarity, and the use of classical detail to emphasize the structure of the building, entitle it to be known as the **first Renaissance church in Venice**. Coducci reintroduced the traditional Greek Cross plan in his other church designs (**Santa Maria Formosa** and **San Giovanni Crisostomo**), his impetus coming in part from a scholarly revival of interest in the culture of Byzantium and in part from the work of Renaissance theorists such as Alberti, whose *De Re Aedificatoria* proclaimed the superiority of centrally-planned temples. In his secular buildings the influence of Alberti is even more pronounced, especially in his **Palazzo Vendramin-Calergi**, which is strongly reminiscent of Alberti's Palazzo Rucellai in Florence. Coducci was employed by the Venetian nobility, the Scuole (he designed staircases for both the **Scuola di San Giovanni Evangelista** and the **Scuola di San Marco**) and the religious foundations, yet despite his preeminence it was only after archive research in the nineteenth century that he was identified as the author of all these buildings—a fact indicative of the difference between the status of the architect in Renaissance Florence and his standing in Venice.

The economic effects of the War of the League of Cambrai limited the amount of building work in Venice at the start of the sixteenth century, yet it was nonetheless a period of rapid transformation in the center of the city: the **Campanile** of San Marco was completed, and the **Torre dell'Orologio** and **Procuratie Vecchie** were built—the last two being commenced to designs by Coducci. In the aftermath of serious fires, major projects were undertaken in the Rialto district as well—notably the **Fabbriche Vecchie** and the **Fondaco dei Tedeschi**—but the architects of the generation after Coducci (who died in 1504) were generally undistinguished. **Guglielmo dei Grigi** designed the **Palazzo dei Camerlenghi** at the foot of the Ponte di Rialto and went on to add the **Cappella Emiliana** to Coducci's San Michele in Isola. **Bartolomeo Bon the Younger** took over the supervision of the Procuratie Vecchie after Coducci's death, and began the **Scuola di San Rocco** in 1515—a project that was completed by **Scarpagnino** (Antonio Abbondi), the man in charge of the rebuilding of the Rialto markets after the fire of 1514. **Giorgio Spavento**, described by the diarist Marin Sanudo as "a man of great genius," was the most talented architect of this period, and with **San Salvatore** he produced its best church design. By joining together three Greek Cross plans, Spavento created a building which reconciled the long open nave required by modern liturgy with the traditional Byzantine centralized plan.

HIGH RENAISSANCE

The definitive classical authority for the architectural theorists of Renaissance Italy was **Vitruvius**, architect to the Emperor Augustus, and it was in Venice in 1511 that the first printed edition of his *De Architectura* was produced. However, the consistent application of classical models was not seen in Venice until after the sack of Rome by the Imperial army in 1527. A large number of Roman artists then sought refuge in Venice, and it was with this influx that the advances of such figures as Raphael, Michelangelo and Bramante were absorbed into the practice of Venice's architects.

Of all the exiles, the one who made the greatest impact was **Jacopo Sansovino**. Despite his limited architectural experience—he was known mainly as a sculptor when he arrived in Venice—Sansovino was appointed *Proto* of San Marco on the death of Bartolomeo Bon in 1529, a position which made him the most powerful architect in the city, and which he was to hold for the next forty years. From 1537 onwards a group of buildings by Sansovino went up around the Piazzetta, completely changing the appearance of the area: the **Zecca** (Mint) was the first, then the **Loggetta** at the base of the Campanile, and then the most celebrated of all his designs—the **Libreria Sansoviniana**. Showing a familiarity with the architecture of ancient Rome that was unprecedented in Venice, the Libreria is still unmistakeably Venetian in its wealth of surface detail, and the rest of Sansovino's buildings similarly effect a compromise between classical precision and

Venetian convention. Thus his palace designs—**Palazzo Dolfin-Manin** (1538) and **Palazzo Corner della Ca' Grande** (1545)—are clearly related to the houses of the Roman Renaissance, but perpetuate the traditional Venetian division of the facade into a central bay with symmetrically flanking windows. Though principally a secular architect, Sansovino did also design churches; the religious buildings by him that still stand are **San Francesco della Vigna**, **San Martino di Castello**, **San Giuliano** and the apse of **San Fantin**.

Of Sansovino's contemporaries, the only one of comparable stature was **Michele Sanmicheli**. More proficient as an engineer than Sansovino, he was employed early in his career by Pope Clement VII to improve the military defenses of Parma and Piacenza, and in 1535 was taken on as Venice's military architect. The **Fortezza di Sant'Angelo** (1543), protecting the Lido entrance to the lagoon, was his largest public project, and in addition to this he built two of the most grandiose palaces in the city—the **Palazzo Corner Mocenigo** at San Polo (1545) and the **Palazzo Grimani** (c.1559) on the Canal Grande.

Andrea Palladio, Italy's dominant architect in the second half of the sixteenth century, was based in nearby Vicenza yet found it difficult to break into Venice's circle of patronage. In the 1550s his application for the position of *Proto* to the Salt Office (supervisor of public buildings) was turned down, and his project for the Palazzo Ducale's Scala d'Oro rejected; later schemes for the Ponte di Rialto and the rebuilding of the entire Palazzo Ducale were no more successful. He was never asked to undertake a private commission in the city. The facade of **San Pietro in Castello** was his first contract (eventually built in a much altered form), and it was the religious foundations who were to provide him with virtually all his subsequent work in Venice. Palladio's churches of **San Giorgio Maggiore** (1565) and the **Redentore** (1576) are the summit of Renaissance classicism in Venice: the scale on which they were composed, the restraint of their decoration, the stylistic unity of exterior and interior, the subtlety with which the successive spaces were combined, and the correctness of their quotations from the architecture of imperial Rome—all these factors distinguished them from all previous designs and established them as reference points for later churches.

Once Palladio's churches had been finished, the islands of San Giorgio Maggiore and Giudecca presented much the same face to the main part of the city as they do today. The work of his closest follower, **Vincenzo Scamozzi**, brought the landscape of the Piazza very close to its present-day state—it was Scamozzi who completed the Campanile end of the Libreria Sansoviniana and began the construction of the **Procuratie Nuove** in 1582. Another Venetian landmark, the **Ponte di Rialto**, was built at this time; its creator, **Antonio da Ponte**, was also in charge of the repair and redesign of the Palazzo Ducale after the fire of 1577, and designed the new **Prisons** on the opposite bank of the Rio di Palazzo. The bridge connecting the prisons to the Palazzo Ducale—the **Ponte dei Sospiri** (Bridge of Sighs)—was the work of **Antonio Contino** (1600).

BAROQUE

Although there are a few sixteenth-century Venetian buildings that could be described as proto-Baroque—**Alessandro Vittoria**'s **Palazzo Balbi** (1582), with its encrusted decoration and broken pediments, is one example—the classical idiom remained entrenched for some time as the stylistic orthodoxy in Venice, as is demonstrated by the appointment of the unadventurous **Bartolomeo Monopola** to complete the final stages of the **Palazzo Ducale** in first decades of the seventeenth century. The colossal **Palazzo Pisani** at Santo Stefano, possibly by Monopola, is further evidence of the city's aesthetic conservatism.

It was not until the maturity of Venice's finest native architect **Baldassare Longhena**, that the innovations of the Baroque made themselves fully felt. Longhena's early work—for example the **Palazzo Giustinian-Lolin** and the **Duomo** at **Chioggia** (both 1624)—continues the Palladianism of the previous century, but with his design for the votive church of **Santa Maria della Salute** (1631) he gave the city its first Baroque masterpiece. In its plan the Salute is indebted to Palladio's Redentore, but in its use of multiple vistas and devices such as the huge volutes round the

base of the dome, it introduces a dynamism that was completely alien to Palladio's architecture. In 1640 Longhena became the *Proto* of San Marco, and between then and his death in 1682 he occupied a position in Venetian architectural circles as commanding as Sansovino's had been. Among his major projects were the completion of the **Procuratie Nuove**, the addition of a grand staircase and library to the monastic complex of **San Giorgio Maggiore**, and the design of two of the Canal Grande's most spectacular palces—the **Ca' Pésaro** and the **Ca' Rezzonico**.

When compared to much of the work being produced in other parts of Italy at this time, Longhena's brand of Baroque was quite sober. Yet it was the chief exception in his output—the grotesque facade of the **Ospedaletto**—that proved in the short term to be specially influential. Its most direct descendant was **Alessandro Tremignon**'s facade for the church of **San Moisè** (1668), which is choked with sculpture by Heinrich Meyring. **Giuseppe Sardi**'s church of **Santa Maria Zobenigo** (1680) can also be traced back to the Ospedaletto, but on the other hand Sardi's work is equally redolent of the architecture of the sixteenth century—his facade for Scamozzi's **San Lazzaro dei Mendicanti** could be seen as a deliberate rejection of the excesses of the Baroque. His other prominent designs are the **Scuola di San Teodoro** and the facades of **San Salvatore** and **Santa Maria di Nazareth** (the Scalzi), all of them rather routine efforts.

THE EIGHTEENTH CENTURY

The concerted reaction against Baroque began with the work of Sardi's nephew, **Domenico Rossi**. Rossi's facade for the church of **San Stae** (1709) is essentially a neo-Palladian design enlivened by the addition of some exuberant pieces of sculpture, and his rebuilding of the **Palazzo Corner della Regina** is closer to the palace projects of Sansovino than to such works as Longhena's nearby Ca' Pésaro. **Andrea Tirali**, Rossi's exact contemporary (1657–1737), was an even more faithful adherent to the principles of the sixteenth century—the portico he added to the church of **San Nicolò da Tolentino** is strictly classical, and his facade for **San Vitale** is a straight plagiarism of San Giorgio Maggiore. Another church of this period—**San Simeone Piccolo**—is one of the most conspicuous in Venice, standing as it does right opposite the train station. Designed in 1718 by **Giovanni Scalfarotto** (Rossi's son-in-law), its facade and plan are derived from the Pantheon, but the vertical exaggeration of its dome makes it closer in spirit to Longhena's Salute.

The most significant architect of the period was **Giorgio Massari** (1687–1766), whose church of the **Gesuati**, begun in 1726, combines Palladian forms (for example the facade and the arrangement of the interior bays) with understated Rococo details (the ceiling frames). His later church of the **Pietà**, based on Sansovino's destroyed Incurabili church, is more sober in its use of decoration, and his design for the last of the great palaces of the Canal Grande, the **Palazzo Grassi** (1748) is the severest of all his buildings.

The Palladian creed was kept alive in late eighteenth-century Venice through innumerable academic and polemical publications. Two of the leading figures in this movement were **Antonio Visentini** (1688-1782) and Scalfarotto's nephew, **Tomaso Temanza** (1705-89), both of whom taught architecture at the Accademia. Temanza was the more important architect, and his **Santà Maria Maddalena** was the first uncompromisingly Neoclassical building in Venice.

TO THE PRESENT

With the work of **Giannantonio Selva**, a pupil of Visentini and Temanza, Neoclassicism entered its most spare and fastidious phase. His first large scheme was **La Fenice** opera house (1790), where exterior adornment was reduced to the minimum necessary to signify the building's function and importance. Selva's career was undisturbed by the subsequent collapse of the Venetian Republic, and his other main works—the churches of **San Maurizio** (1806) and **Nome del Gesù** (1815)—were created under French rule.

During the second period of French occupation (1806–15) a large number of buildings were demolished to facilitate urban improvement schemes. Four churches were knocked down to make space for the **Giardini Pubblici**, for instance, and by the time the

French were ejected by the Austrians a total of nearly 50 religious buildings had been demolished. The most celebrated loss was that of Sansovino's **San Geminiano**, pulled down in 1807 to make room for the construction of the **Ala Napoleonica**, a ballroom wing added to the Procuratie Nuove, which was then serving as a royal palace. In the 1830s the designer of the ballroom, **Lorenzo Santi**, went on to build the now abandoned coffee house (**Palazzetto Bucintoro**) by the Giardinetti Reali, and the **Palazzo Patriarcale**, alongside the Basilica.

Alterations to Venice's network of canals and streets, which had been started by the French with schemes such as the creation of **Via Garibaldi**, were accelerated under Austrian rule. Most of Venice's *rii terrà* (infilled canals) originated in the period of Austrian occupation, and a number of new bridges were constructed at this time too—including the ones at the **Accademia** and **Scalzi**, the first bridges to be put across the Canal Grande since the Ponte di Rialto. It was the Austrians who connected Venice by rail with the mainland (1846), and in 1860 they expanded the train station, demolishing Palladio's church of **Santa Lucia** in the process. The first major **restoration projects** were also carried out under Austrian supervision—at the **Fondaco dei Turchi**, at **Santi Maria e Donato** on **Murano**, and on the north facade of **San Marco**.

Major city planning schemes continued after Venice joined the unified kingdom of Italy. In the 1870s two wide thoroughfares were completed—the **Strada Nova** in Cannaregio and **Calle Larga XXII Marzo** between San Moisè and Santa Maria Zobenigo and **Campo Manin** was opened up in 1871. The brief industrialization of central Venice in the late nineteenth century has left behind one prominent hulk—the **Mulino Stucky**, built on Giudecca in 1895. The hotels and middle-class housing developments of the **Lido**—which became a fashionable resort in this period—have outlived the city's industrial sites.

In 1933 Venice was joined by road to the mainland, and five years later the Rio Nuovo was cut from the recently created Piazzale Roma towards the Canal Grande. The chief buildings of the Fascist era are the **fire station** on the Rio di Ca' Fóscari (which continues the Rio Nuovo), and the **Palazzo del Casinò** and

Palazzo del Cinema on the Lido. Few buildings worth a mention have been put up in Venice since then—the least objectionable are, perhaps, the **train station** (1954) and the **Cassa di Risparmio di Venezia** in Campo Manin, designed in 1964 by **Pier Luigi Nervi** and **Angelo Scattolin**. The density and antiquity of most of Venice's urban fabric makes intervention particularly problematic for the modern architect. Understandable Venetian resistance to new developments, hardened by such insensitive twentieth-century efforts as the extension to the **Hotel Bauer-Grünwald**, adds further difficulties, and accounts for the fact that the two most interesting modern schemes, **Frank Lloyd Wright**'s **Ca' Masieri** and **Le Corbusier**'s plan for a civic hospital in Cannaregio, never left the drawing board.

CONSERVATION AND RESTORATION

In 1818 Byron published the fourth section of Childe Harold's Pilgrimage, in which is encapsulated the Romantic notion that if Venice isn't actually sinking, then it ought to be:

Venice, lost and won,
Her thirteen hundred years of freedom done
Sinks, like a sea-weed into whence she rose!

Ever since, it's been a commonplace that Venice is doomed to an aquatic extinction. In reality, Venice as an entity was not sinking in Byron's day and is not sinking today—but this is not to say that alarmists have no reason to panic.

The city is threatened by water, by salt, by air pollution and by local subsidence, and faces massive problems of conservation and restoration. The scale of the projects to which this situation gives rise shifts dizzyingly from the restoration of a single painting or architectural detail through to schemes to control the industrialization of the mainland and the encroachments of the Adriatic. In addition to the intrinsic difficulties of each project, the major interventions prompt interminable arguments about the very purpose of restoration—should Venice be turned into even more of a museum piece, its buildings preserved in the aspic of contemporary restoration techniques, or should parts of the city be razed and rebuilt, reintroducing industry and modern housing? On the one hand, Venice desperately needs the income from tourism, and on the other its population has halved since the war and its houses are in such a state that 45 percent of them don't have adequate bathrooms.

FLOODING

On November 4, 1966 the waters of the Adriatic, already dangerously high after two successive high tides had been prevented from receding by gale-force south-easterly winds,

were disturbed by an earth tremor. The resulting tidal wave breached Venice's Murazzi (the sea walls), and for the next 48 hours the sea level remained an average of six feet above mean high tide—in other words, nearly four feet above the sidewalk of the Piazza, the lowest point of the city. Venice was left with no power or telephone lines, and buildings were awash with filthy water, mud and oil from broken storage tanks.

Outside Venice, the flooding did not immediately cause extreme concern, partly because floods in Venice were nothing new—at the height of the crisis national radio simply announced "high water in the Piazza San Marco"—and partly because attention was focussed on the same day's disaster in Florence. (A reservoir above Florence had become swollen by a month of heavy rain, and in order to relieve pressure on the dam the reservoir gates had been opened, causing a flash-flood that killed several people and caused serious damage—some of it irreparable—to numerous works of art.) Nobody was hurt in the Venice flood and no artifacts were lost, but the photographs of water swirling through the doors of San Marco and around the courtyard of the Palazzo Ducale did highlight the perilous condition of the city. When floods almost as bad occurred in the following year, the international campaign to save Venice was already gathering strength, and similarly severe floods in 1979 and 1986 kept the situation in the public eye.

Called the aqua alta (high water), the winter flooding of the lower parts of the city is caused by a combination of seasonal tides and persistent south-easterly winds, and has always been a feature of Venetian life. However, in recent years there has been a marked increase in the frequency. Between 1931 and 1945 there were 8 serious aque alte; in the 14 years following 1971 there were 49. This may in part be due to slight shifts in global weather conditions, or to the effect of any melting of the polar ice cap, but at least one independent study points the finger firmly at avoidable factors. In a nutshell, the argument is as follows. At the ancient port of Aquileia, at the head of the Adriatic, the height of the Roman wharves relative to the water seems to indicate that there has been no major change in sea level since they were built. Excavations of building foundations in various parts of the city indicate that the notion of a general subsidence is unfounded. Therefore the increased flooding is a local phenomenon related to recent changes in the balance of the lagoon.

It is certainly a fact that the workings of the lagoon have been interfered with in an unprecedented way this century. Land has been reclaimed, both for industrial sites on the mainland and in central Venice itself—around the docks, for instance. At the same time, channels have been deepened to allow modern industrial and commercial vessels to pass through the lagoon, and smaller motor boats within the city also churn up the sea bed and cause erosion. Consequently, both the speed and depth of the tides have been affected.

Bodies such as the centuries-old *Magistrato alle Acque* and the *Consiglio di Nazionale Ricerca Venezia* have studied the workings of the lagoon in detail, and the construction of a tidal barrier across the three entrances to the lagoon has often emerged as a possible solution to the problem. In early November 1988 the first component of just such a barrier was towed into place. Nicknamed *Moisè* (Moses) after the first great manipulator of the waters, it has been put together by a consortium of engineering companies, all eager for international publicity. Around £3.5 billion have been set aside for the project, which basically involves laying three gigantic steel flaps on the floor of the lagoon; when the water level rises, the ballast is released from the flaps and the barrier rises to protect the city, not unlike the Thames Barrier.

Predictably enough, the relationship between the government and the various companies in the consortium has run into difficulties. The original deadline for the completion of Moisè was 1995; latest predictions suggest that 2020 is a more realistic estimate. And many conservationists think that the abandonment of the barrier would be more beneficial to Venice than its completion. *Italia Nostra*, Italy's national heritage group, insists that the alteration of the shipping channels and the cessation of land reclamation would be cheaper and more effective responses to the situation, and concludes that "the barrage system will not really solve the basic problems of Venice with its dwindling population and dying lagoon."

WATER POLLUTION

A major objection to the barrier is that it will further inhibit the cleansing effects of the tides, already diminished in parts of the lagoon by the creation of firm land out of mudflats. Twice-daily tidal movements and the activity of waste-digesting marine life were enough until fairly recently to keep the water relatively fresh—fresh enough until the 1980s for fastidious Venetians to swim in certain deep spots at high tides.

Much of the pollution is the fault of the industrial complexes of Mestre/Marghera, which have dumped thousands of tons of zinc, copper, iron, lead and chrome into the lagoon, creating a toxic sludge so dangerous that nobody has yet devised a safe way of dredging the stuff out. Chemical fertilizers seeping into the water from the mainland add to the accumulation of phosphates in the water, a situation exacerbated by the heavy use of phosphate-rich detergents in Venetian homes. (Although Venice treats its sewage in sumps before emptying it into the sea, all household sinks and baths drain straight into the canals.) Plants, fishes and other forms of marine life are being suffocated by algae that thrive on these phosphates, forming a foul-smelling scum that is thickened by the rotting animal and vegetable matter. When photographs of gondoliers and tourists in face masks brought adverse publicity abroad, it was finally acknowledged that a crisis had been reached, and in 1988 the Ministry of the Environment earmarked £175million to clean up the lagoon—though this too is to be delivered into the hands of a private consortium. Moreover, the center-left coalition (including the Greens) that now rules city hall has banned the sale of phosphate-enriched detergents. (Venice's boat-restorers will be pleased about this too: their work has steadily diminished as the bottoms of boats have stayed ever cleaner.)

But local action such as this will still not be enough. Venice's lagoon is threatened by the grossly polluted water of the whole upper Adriatic, into which the Po and numerous other waterways disgorge their effluents. In 1989 the Italian government assigned a sum of $800 million to the cleansing of the Adriatic, but the complexity of the problem is terrifying. It has even been proposed that the techniques used to purify sewage may be actually contributing to the proliferation of the algae by feeding them with vitamin-saturated fluids on which to feed.

In the 1950s and 1960s Lake Erie was threatened with the same sort of marine disaster as now faces the Venice region; regulations imposed in the 1970s seem to have redeemed the lake. At the most optimistic estimate, if drastic action is taken now, the Po might be a moderately clean river by the end of this century.

AIR POLLUTION

The other environmental problem facing Venice is that of air pollution, which worsened in phase with the growing industrial complexes on the mainland. Sulphur dioxide combines with the salty and humid air of the lagoon to make a particularly vicious corrosive which eats at brick, stone and bronze alike. An experiment carried out in the 1970s showed that stone covered with pigeon droppings stayed in better condition than stone exposed to the Venetian air. The conversion of domestic heating systems from oil to gas has helped to cut down the amount of sulphur dioxide in the atmosphere, and expenditure on industrial filtration has had an effect too, but Marghera's factories still pump around 50,000 tons of the gas into the atmosphere each year. Some observers point out that the prevailing winds carry the plumes from the Marghera stacks inland, but even though the bulk of the emissions are someone else's problem, the ambient air of Venice was one of the factors the Italian trades union congress had in mind when they recently christened the city "the capital of pollution."

In the years immediately after the 1966 flood, as Venice attracted ever more attention from outside the country, the city authorities were often criticized for their tardiness in commissioning restoration work on Venice's crumbling stonework. Their cautiousness was to an extent vindicated when it became apparent that the restoration work on Sansovino's Loggetta—initially hailed as an unqualified success—had in fact done as much damage as it had repaired. The resins used to protect the restored marble have now begun to discolor the building, and it may prove impossible to sluice the resins out. A major restoration of the Miracoli church has turned out to be similarly ill-advised, with salt eating at the walls from inside and excreting white crusts onto the marble cladding. The cleaning and strengthening of the Porta della Carta was undertaken with far greater circumspection, and so far it sems that all is well; the lessons learned on that project are being employed on the continuous restoration of the Basilica di San Marco and the Palazzo Ducale.

SUBSIDENCE

The industries at Marghera used to threaten Venice from below as well as from above. Drawing millions of gallons of water directly from the ground, they caused a dramatic fall in the water table and threatened to cause the subsidence of the entire city. Calamity was averted in 1973 when the national government built two aquaducts to pipe water from inland rivers to the refineries and factories of Marghera and the houses of Venice.

Local subsidence will continue to be a problem, though. Thirteen major sites are currently being consolidated against erosion by the water, including the Lido's Fortezza di Sant'Andrea, which has been lurching forwards owing to the undermining action of the current at its base. There are countless instances of *ad hoc* measures to counteract smaller scale collapses. The majority of buildings in Venice are built on wooden pilings driven deep into the mudbanks of the lagoon. Interference with the lagoon's equilibrium has resulted in an increase in the number of extremely low tides as well as the number of floods, and occasionally the water falls so far that air gets at the pilings, causing them to decay. Furthermore, those people unable to afford proper wood-piled foundations would have used rubbish and rubble instead, which through the years slowly compresses. Projects to consolidate the houses and churches of Venice will never cease to be necessary.

AID GROUPS

Resoration in Venice is principally a collaborative venture between UNESCO and the city's Superintendancies of Art and of Monuments. The former co-ordinates the fund-raising and restoration proposals from the multitude of aid groups set up in various countries after the 1966 floods; the latter pair oversee the restoration centers in Venice, the cataloguing of endangered buildings and objects and the deployment of restoration teams.

The first complete makeover for a Venetian building was the restoration of Madonna dell'Orto, undertaken by the British *Italian Art and Archives Rescue Fund* (transformed in 1971 into *Venice in Peril*). The church's facade statue of Saint Christopher was the first Istrian stone sculpture to be cleaned in Venice, and the techniques used were taken up by later restorers. Since then, the organization has completely restored San Nicolò dei Mendicoli, the Loggetta at the base of the Campanile di San Marco and the Porta della Carta (the ceremonial gateway of the Palazzo Ducale); it's also been a major partner in the restoration of Santa Maria Assunta on Torcello and the Oratorio dei Crociferi, and is at present working on the Sala della Musica in the church of the Ospedaletto.

Over thirty groups worldwide are now devoted to the rescue of Venice, all of them open to offers of financial help. If you're interested, contact John Millerchip at the British Center, Campo San Luca, San Marco 4267/a. (Please note: the British Center is a school for English-speaking children, emphatically not an information source or drop-in center for Anglophiles.)

UNESCO's office in Venice (Piazza San Marco 63) is also used by *Amici dei Musei*, which began as an organization running cultural courses and guided tours during the winter, and is now also one of the city's main groups for collecting funds and initiating restoration projects. For the most up-to-date information on the state of restoration in Venice, this is the address to approach.

BOOKS

A comprehensive Venetian reading-list would run on for dozens of pages, and would include a vast number of out-of-print titles. Most of our recommendations are in print, and those that aren't shouldn't be too difficult to track down.

VENICE IN FICTION

Italo Calvino, *Invisible Cities* (Harcourt, Brace, Jovanovich, 1978, $5.95). Characteristically subtle variations on the idea of the City, presented in the form of tales told by Marco Polo to Kublai Khan. No explicit reference to Venice until well past half-way, when Polo remarks—"Every time I describe a city I am saying something about Venice."

Ernest Hemingway, *Across the River and into the Trees* (1950; Macmillan, 1988, $5.95). Hemingway at his most square-jawed and most mannered: our hero fights good, drinks good, loves good, and could shoot a duck out of the skies from the hip at a range of half a mile. Target of one of the funniest parodies ever written: EB White's *Across the Street and into the Grill*—"'I love you,' he said, "and we are going to lunch together for the first and only time, and I love you very much.''

ETA Hoffman, *Doge and Dogaressa* (1817; in *Tales of Hoffman*, Penguin, 1982, $4.95). Fanciful reconstruction of events surrounding the treason of Marin Falier, by one of the pivotal figures of German Romanticism. Lots of passion and pathos, narrated at headlong pace.

Henry James, *The Aspern Papers* (1888; OUP, 1984, $3.95) & *The Wings of the Dove* (1902; OUP, 1983, $2.95). The first, a 100-page

nouvelle about the manipulative attempts of a biographer to get at the personal papers of a deceased writer, is one of James's most tautly constructed longer tales. The latter, one of the three vast and circumspect late novels, was likened to caviar by Ezra Pound, and is likely to put you off Henry James for life if you come to it without acclimatizing yourself with the earlier stuff.

Erica Jong, *Serenissima* (Houghton Mifflin, 1989, $3.98). Actress named Jessica, in Venice for the Film Festival, stays on to play the part of her namesake in a film of *The Merchant of Venice*; a mysterious admirer sends her flowers, signing himself "W.S." (geddit?). A daft tale of lives mingling across the centuries, which nobody could possibly take seriously—but it might pass an hour or two while you're waiting for air traffic control to find you a slot.

Jonathan Keates, *Allegro Postillions* (Braziller, 1985, $6.95). The Fenice is the setting for the longest piece in this highly-praised first collection of short stories, all of which take place in nineteenth-century Italy. Wears its erudition on its sleeve, and the artfully old-fashioned narrative style won't be to everyone's taste.

Thomas Mann, *Death in Venice* (1912; McGraw, 1970, $3.95). Profound study of the demands of art and the claims of the flesh, with the city itself thematically significant rather than a mere exotic backdrop. Richer than most stories five times its length and infinitely more complex than Visconti's sentimentalizing film.

Ian McEwan, *The Comfort of Strangers* (Penguin, 1989, $6.95). Ordinary young English couple fall foul of sexually ambiguous predator. Venice is never named as the locality, but evoked by means of arch little devices such as quotes from Ruskin. A thin Gothic yarn, and extremely predictable.

Marcel Proust, *Albertine Disparue* (1925; Schoenhof, 1984, $7.95). The Venetian interlude, occurring in the penultimate novel of the sequence, can be sampled in isolation for its acute dissection of the sensory experience of the city—but to get the most from it, you've got to knuckle down and commit yourself to the preceding ten parts.

Frederick Rolfe (Baron Corvo), *The Desire and Pursuit of the Whole* (1909; Da Capo, 1986, $9.95). Transparent exercise in self-justification, much of it taken up with venomous ridicule of the English community in Venice, whom Rolfe moved among while writing the book in 1909. (Its libellous streak kept it unpublished for 25 years.) Snobbish and incoherent, redeemed by hilarious character-assassinations and gorgeous descriptive passages. One of the few books by an Anglophone to be saturated with a knowledge of the place.

Muriel Spark, *Territorial Rights* (Putnam, 1984, $6.95). Examination of the wealthy, cultured and venal of Venice. Not one that's going to convince the skeptics that Spark has hidden depths, and even her most devoted admirers wouldn't rate it as one her best.

Barry Unsworth, *Stone Virgin* (Houghton Mifflin, o/p). Yet another story of the uncanny repetitions of history—this time an English expert in stone conservation begins to suspect that his emotional entanglement with a sculptor's wife is a recapitulation of a past liaison. The gobbets of scholarly detail sit uncomfortably alongside the melodrama of the plot.

Jeanette Winterson, *The Passion* (Random, 1989, $7.95). Intertwined lives of a member of Napoleon's personal catering corps and a female gondolier. At once fantastical and plausible, it's perceptive about the city itself and passions of all sorts. Although a bit too sweet and whimsical for some tastes, it'll never give you the feeling that you've read it all before.

GUIDEBOOKS

Milton Grundy, *Venice: A Guidebook and Anthology* (A & C Black UK edition available in libraries). A series of itineraries of the city fleshed out with appropriate excerpts from a huge range of travelers and scholars. Doesn't cover every major sight in Venice, but the choice of quotations couldn't be bettered.

Sheila Hale, *The American Express Pocket Guide to Venice* (Simon & Schuster, 1984, $8.95). More reliable when dealing with the up-market hotels, restaurants and shops of Venice

than when tackling the cultural side of the place. Its one advantage over most of the opposition is the section on the mainland, though here again the entries are pretty flimsy and a high disposable income is taken for granted.

Hugh Honor, *The Companion Guide to Venice* (Harper & Row, o/p). One of the best guides for an unhurried exploration—Honor is as knowledgeable as any writer on Venice, but carries his learning lightly. The weaknesses are in the practical information and observations about daily life in present-day Venice, where the book shows its age.

John Kent, *John Kent's Venice* (Grossman, 1988, $15.95). Minimal information teased out with comic-strip pictures. A kids' book for adults.

JG Links, *Venice for Pleasure* (Farrar, Straus & Giroux, 1985, $10.95). Contains a fair amount of anecdotal detail, but in places degenerates into well-bred English philistinism—Venice as a sequence of eye-baths and coffee-stops. The imaginative illustrations are the best feature, and the "Books about Venice" section is pretty good, despite eccentricities such as seven recommendations for farther reading on Canaletto yet not a mention of Titian, Tintoretto or Veronese.

Giulio Lorenzetti, *Venice and its Lagoon* (Lint, L40,000). The most thorough cultural guide ever written to any European city—Lorenzetti seems to have researched the history of every brick and every canvas. Though completely unmanageable as a guidebook (it even has an index to the indexes), it's indispensible for all those besotted with the place. Almost impossible to find outside Venice.

Alta Macadam, *Venice* (Blue Guide, Norton, 1986, $15.95). If you want to know the date of what you're looking at, and who did it, this is the best one to get. As with nearly all this series, as an inventory it's virtually infallible.

ART AND ARCHITECTURE

James S. Ackerman, *Palladio* (Penguin, 1974, $7.95). Concise introduction to the life, works and cultural background of the Veneto's greatest architect. Especially useful if you're visiting Vicenza or any of the villas.

Patricia Fortini Brown, *Venetian Narrative Painting in the Age of Carpaccio* (Yale, 1988, $45). Rigorously researched study of a subject central to Venetian culture yet often overlooked in more general accounts. Fresh reactions to the works discussed are combined with penetrating analysis of the ways they reflect the ideals of the Republic at the time. Worth every penny.

Deborah Howard, *The Architectural History of Venice* (Holmes & Meier, 1981, $24.50) and *Jacopo Sansovino: Architecture and Patronage in Renaissance Venice* (Yale, 1987, $13.95). The first is by far the best available introduction to the subject in English—a good first acquisition for any serious Venetian library. The analysis of the environment within which Sansovino operated makes the second book of wider interest than you might think—a logical next step after Howard's general survey.

Peter Lauritzen and Reinhart Wolf, *Villas of the Veneto* (Abrams, 1988, $49.50). More of a coffee-table job than the palaces book (see below), with a skimpier text and glossy, full-page color pictures. Still, it's the best book on the subject available in English, and the photos are a treat.

Peter Lauritzen and Alexander Zielcke, *The Palaces of Venice* (Viling, o/p). Lauritzen lives in Venice and knows the place as intimately as anyone currently writing. This is a fascinating blend of social and architectural history, and Zielcke's photographs are uniformly good.

Ralph Lieberman, *Renaissance Architecture in Venice* (Abbeville Press, 1982, $45). Lieberman illustrates the complex development of architecture in fifteenth- and sixteenth-century Venice through a chronological survey of key buildings, but annoyingly calls a halt at 1540. Authoritative without being pedantic.

J McAndrew, *Venetian Architecture of the Early Renaissance* (MIT, o/p). Definitive study of its subject by the only writer to have studied Venice's buildings with anything like Ruskin's concentration. It's one of the most beautiful books you'll ever see, and at this price it should be.

David Rosand, *Painting in Cinquecento Venice* (Yale, 1986, $25.95). Covers the century of Giorgione, Titian, Tintoretto and Veronese as thoroughly as most readers will want; especially good on the social networks and artistic conventions within which the painters worked.

John Ruskin, *The Stones of Venice* (1853; Moyer Bell, 1989, $34.95). Enchanting and infuriating in about equal measure, this is still the most stimulating book written about Venice by a non-Venetian.

John Steer, *Venetian Painting* (Thames & Hudson, 1980, $9.95). Whistle-stop tour of Venetian art from the fourteenth to the eighteenth century. Undemanding, but a useful aid to sorting your thoughts out after the visual deluge of Venice's churches and museums, and the plentiful pictures come in handy when your memory needs a prod.

John Unrau, *Ruskin and St Mark's* (Thames & Hudson, 1984, $19.95). Ruskin discarded around 600 pages of notes and drawings of San Marco when he came to prepare the text of *The Stones of Venice*; using this material, Unrau has produced a book that is as illuminating about Ruskin as it is about the building. A brilliant selection of watercolors, paintings and photographs (both nineteenth-century and modern) complements the text.

HISTORY

Fernand Braudel, *The Mediterranean and the Mediterranean World in the Age of Philip II* (Harper & Row, 1976, 2 vols: $12.95 & $13.95). Vast, magisterial analysis of the economics and politics of the Mediterranean in the second half of the sixteenth century, with Venice rarely off the stage. Braudel's deployment of masses of raw material (population statistics, contemporary chronicles, trade documents) requires the reader's prolonged and unwavering attention.

D.S. Chambers, *The Imperial Age of Venice* (HBJ o/p). Concise and fluent account of Venice's heyday and the beginnings of decline, spanning the years 1380-1580. Informative and well illustrated.

Robert Finlay, *Politics in Renaissance Venice* (Rutgers, 1980, $45). Subverts a few received ideas about the political tranquillity of La Serenissima, and is laced with anecdotes about the squabbling, scheming aristocracy. Though not the first book you'd read after your holiday, it explains the mechanics of power in Venice with great clarity.

Christopher Hibbert, *Venice, The Biography of a City* (Norton, 1989, $39.95). The usual highly proficient Hibbert synthesis of a vast range of secondary material. Very good on the changing social fabric of the city, and has more on twentieth-century Venice than most others. Excellent illustrations too.

Frederic C. Lane, *Venice, A Maritime Republic* (Johns Hopkins, 1973, $14.95). The best one-volume history of the city in English, based on decades of research. Excellent on the economic infrastructure of the city and the changing texture of everyday life, and in its overview of Venice's military and political history.

Jan Morris, *The Venetian Empire: A Sea Voyage* (Penguin, 1990, $7.95). Anecdotal survey of the Republic's Mediterranean empire, with excursions on the evidence left behind. More a sketch than an attempt to give the full picture, it bears Morris's usual stylistic imprint.

John Julius Norwich, *A History of Venice* (McKay, $14.95). Although it's far more reliant on secondary sources than Lane, and nowhere near as compendious—you won't learn much, for example, about Venice's finances—this is unbeatable for its grand narrative sweep, and very elegantly written.

VENETIAN MISCELLANY

Pietro Aretino, *Selected Letters* (Italian edition only). Edited highlights from the voluminous correspondence of a man who could be described as the world's first professional journalist. Recipients include Titian, Michelangelo, Charles V, Francis I, the pope, the doge, Cosimo de' Medici—virtually anybody who was anybody in sixteenth-century Europe.

Henry James, *Italian Hours* (1909; Ecco Press, 1987, $10.50). Urbane travel pieces from the young Henry James, including five essays on Venice. Perceptive observations on the paintings and architecture of the city, but mainly of interest in its evocation of the tone of Venice in the 1860s and 70s.

Peter Lauritzen, *Venice Preserved* (Adler & Adler, 1986, $29.95). Generally optimistic report on the restoration of Venice's paintings and monuments, and the outlook for the future; sometimes contentious too—Lauritzen doesn't mince his words about Olivetti's part in the "rescue" of the San Marco horses. As with all Lauritzen's books, the pictures are splendid.

HV Morton, *A Traveler in Italy* (Dodd, o/p). A mellower book than his earlier *In Search of Ireland* and *In Search of Scotland*, mixing anecdote, observation and history. Concentrates on northern Italy, with a chapter on Verona and two on Venice.

Mary McCarthy, *Venice Observed* (Harcourt, Brace, Jovanovich, 1963, $4.95). Entertaining, incisive report, originally written for the *New Yorker*, the briskness is a refreshing antidote to the gushing enthusiasm of most first-hand accounts.

James Morris, *The World of Venice* (Harcourt, Brace, Jovanovich, 1985, $8.95). To some people this is the most brilliant book ever written about Venice; to others it's appallingly fey and self-regarding. But even if you can't stomach the style, Morris's encyclopedic knowledge of Venice's folklore provides some compensation.

Stella M. Newton, *The Dress of the Venetians 1495–1525* (Gower Publishing, 1986, $36.90). Specialized academic book accessible to anyone with an interest in fashion, Venetian social history or the art of the period. Official costume, festive costume, the apparel of the visiting foreigners—nothing is missed out except, sadly, the dress of the city's working class.

Jeanette Nance Nordio, *A Taste of Venice: Traditional Venetian Cooking* (Salem House, 1989, $18.95). Written by a former chef at the *Cipriani* and full of delicious recipes. Getting hold of some of the ingredients might pose problems, but a fair proportion of them can be done if you've a decent supermarket or delicatessen.

A.J.A. Symons, *The Quest for Corvo* (1934; Macmillan, o/p). Misanthropic, devious and solitary, Frederick Rolfe was a tricky subject for a biographer to tackle, and Symons's book, subtitled *An Experiment in Biography*, makes the difficult process of writing Rolfe's life the focus of its narrative. An engrossing piece of literary detective work, and a perfect introduction to Rolfe's Venetian novel, *The Desire and Pursuit of the Whole*.

LANGUAGE

Although it's not uncommon for the staff of Venetian hotels and restaurants to speak some English, you'll make a lot more friends by attempting the vernacular. Outside the city, you might by able to get by in English at tourist offices, but life will be considerably easier if you can master at least a few of the phrases below.

SOME TIPS

You'd do well to master at least a little **Italian**, a task made more enjoyable by the fact that your halting efforts will often be rewarded by smiles and genuine surprise that an English-speaker should stoop to learn Italian. In any case, it's one of the easiest European languages to learn, especially if you already have a smattering of French or Spanish, both extremely similar grammatically.

Easiest of all is the **pronunciation**, since every word is spoken as it's written, and usually enunciated with exaggerated, open-mouthed clarity. The only difficulties you're likely to encounter are the few **consonants** that are different from English:

c before e or i is pronounced as in **ch**urch, while **ch** before the same vowels is hard, as in **c**at.
sci or **sce** are pronounced as in **sh**eet and **sh**elter respectively. The same goes with **g**— soft before **e** and **i**, as in **g**eranium; hard when followed by h, as in **g**arlic.
gn has the ni sound of our "o**ni**on'.
gl in Italian is softened to something like li in English, as in stal**li**on.
h is not aspirated, as in **h**onor.

When **speaking** to strangers, the third person is the polite form (ie *Lei* instead of *Tu* for "you"); using the second person is a mark of disrespect or stupidity. Also remember that Italians don't use "please" and "thank you" half as much as we do: it's all implied in the tone, though if you're in any doubt, err on the polite side.

All Italian words are **stressed** on the penultimate syllable unless an **accent** (´ or `) denotes otherwise, although accents are often left out in practice. Note that the ending **-ia** or **-ie** counts as two syllables, hence *trattoria* is stressed on the i. We've put accents in, throughout the text and below, wherever it isn't immediately obvious how a word should be pronounced: for example, in *Maríttima*, the accent is on the first **i**; similarly the stress in *Pésaro* is not on the **a**, where you'd expect it, but on the **e**. We've omitted accents on some of the more common exceptions (like *Isola*, stressed on the I), some names (*Domenico*), and words that are stressed similarly in English, such as *archeologico* and *Repubblica*.

The **Venetian dialect** virtually qualifies as a separate language, with its own rules of spelling and grammar, and distinctive pronunciation. However, you'll probably encounter it only in the form of the words given in the Glossary below, dialect proper names (which are deciphered in the text) or the occasional shop sign—eg *Venexiana* rather than *Veneziana* .

ITALIAN NUMBERS

1	uno	9	nove	17	diciassette	50	cinquanta	200	duecento
2	due	10	dieci	18	diciotto	60	sessanta	500	cinquecento
3	tre	11	undici	19	diciannove	70	settanta	1000	mille
4	quattro	12	dodici	20	venti	80	ottanta	5000	cinquemila
5	cinque	13	tredici	21	ventuno	90	novanta	10,000	diecimila
6	sei	14	quattordici	22	ventidue	100	cento	50,000	cinquanta mila
7	sette	15	quindici	30	trenta	101	centuno		
8	otto	16	sedici	40	quaranta	110	centodieci		

BASIC WORDS AND PHRASES

Good morning	*Buon giorno*	I live in…	*Abito a…*
Good afternoon/ evening	*Buona sera*	I'm American/ Canadian	*Sono Americano/ Canadese*
Good night	*Buona notte*	Today	*Oggi*
Hello/goodbye	*Ciao* (informal; when speaking to strangers use the phrases above)	Tomorrow	*Domani*
		Day after tomorrow	*Dopodomani*
		Yesterday	*Ieri*
Goodbye	*Arrivederci* (formal)	Now	*Adesso*
Yes	*Sì*	Later	*Più tardi*
No	*No*	Wait a minute!	*Aspetta!*
Please	*Per favore*	In the morning	*di mattina*
Thank you (very much)	*Grázie (molte/mille grazie)*	In the afternoon	*nel pomeriggio*
		In the evening	*di sera*
You're welcome	*Prego*	Here (there)	*Qui/Là*
Alright/that's OK	*Va bene*	Good/bad	*Buono/Cattivo*
How are you?	*Come stai/sta?* (informal/ formal)	Big/small	*Grande/Píccolo*
		Cheap/expensive	*Económico/Caro*
I'm fine	*Bene*	Early/late	*Presto/Ritardo*
Do you speak English?	*Parla inglese?*	Hot/cold	*Caldo/Freddo*
		Near/far	*Vicino/Lontano*
I don't understand	*Non capisco*	Vacant/occupied	*Libero/Occupato*
I haven't understood	*Non ho capito*	Quickly/slowly	*Velocemente/Lentamente*
I don't know	*Non lo so*	Slowly/quietly	*Piano*
Excuse me/sorry (informal)	*Scusa*	With/without	*Con/Senza*
		More/less	*Più/Meno*
Excuse me/sorry (formal)	*Mi scusi/Prego*	Enough, no more	*Basta*
		Mr…	*Signor…*
Excuse me (in a crowd)	*Permesso*	Mrs…	*Signora…*
		Miss…	*Signorina…(il Signor, la Signora, la Signorina*
I'm sorry	*Mi dispiace*		when speaking about
I'm here on vacation	*Sono qui in vacanza*		someone else)

FINDING THE WAY

Airplane	*Aeroplano*	What time does it leave?	*A che ora parte?*
Bus	*Autobus/pullman*	When is the next bus/ train to…?	*Quando parte il próssimo pullman/treno per…?*
Train	*Treno*		
Car	*Mácchina*	Where does it leave from?	*Da dove parte?*
Taxi	*Taxi*		
Bicycle	*Bicicletta*	Which platform does it leave from?	*Da quale binario parte?*
Hitch-hiking	*Autostop*		
On foot	*A piedi*	Do I have to change?	*Devo cambiare?*
Bus station	*Autostazione*	How many kilometers is it?	*Quanti chilómetri sono?*
Railroad station	*Stazione ferroviaria*		
Port	*Porto*	How long does it take?	*Quanto ci vuole?*
A ticket to…	*Un biglietto a…*	What number bus is it to…?	*Que número di autobus per…?*
One-way/ round-trip	*Solo andata/andata e ritorno*		
		Where's the road to…?	*Dov'è la strada a …?*
Can I reserve a seat?	*Posso prenotare un posto?*	Next stop please	*La próssima fermata, per favore*

QUESTIONS AND DIRECTIONS

Where? (where is/ are…?)	Dove? (Dov'è/Dove sono)	Can you tell me when to get off?	Mi può dire scendere alla fermata giusta?
When?	Quando?	What time does it open?	A che ora apre?
What? (what is it?)	Cosa? (Cos'è?)		
How much/many?	Quanto/Quanti?	What time does it close?	A che ora chiude?
Why?	Perché?		
It is/there is (is it/is there…?)	È/C'è (È/C'è…?)	How much does it cost (…do they cost?)	Quanto costa? (Quanto costano?)
What time is it?	Che ora è/Che ore sono?	What's it called in Italian?	Come si chiama in italiano?
How do I get to…?	Come arrivo a…?	Left/right	Sinistra/Destra
How far is it to…?	Cuant'è lontano a…?	Go straight ahead	Sempre diritto
Can you give me a lift to…?	Mi può dare un passaggio a…?	Turn to the right/left	Gira a destra/sinistra

SOME SIGNS

Entrance/exit	Entrata/Uscita	To let	Affitasi
Free entrance	Ingresso líbero	Platform	Binario
Gentlemen/ladies	Signori/Signore	Cash desk	Cassa
Toilet	Gabinetto, bagno	Go/walk	Avanti
Vacant/engaged	Líbero/Occupato	Stop/halt	Alt
Open/closed	Aperto/Chiuso	Customs	Dogana
Arrivals/departures	Arrivi/Partenze	Do not touch	Non toccare
Closed for restoration	Chiuso per restauro	Danger	Perícolo
Closed for holiday	Chiuso per ferie	Beware	Attenzione
Pull/push	Tirare/Spingere	First aid	Pronto soccorso
Out of order	Guasto	Ring the bell	Suonare il campanello
Drinking water	Acqua potabile	No smoking	Vietato fumare

ACCOMMODATION

Hotel	Albergo	Do you have anything cheaper?	Ha niente che costa di meno?
Is there a hotel nearby?	C'è un albergo qui vicino?	Full/half board	Pensione completa/ mezza pensione
Do you have a room…	Ha una cámera…		
		Can I see the room?	Posso vedere la cámera?
for one/two/three people	per una/due/tre person(a/ e)	I'll take it	La prendo
for one/two/three nights	per una/due/tre nott(e/i)	I'd like to reserve a room	Vorrei prenotare una cámera
for one/two weeks	per una/due settiman(a/e)	I have a reservation	Ho una prenotazione
with a double bed	con un letto matrimoniale	Can we camp here?	Possiamo fare il campeggio qui?
with a shower/bath	con una doccia/un bagno		
with a balcony	con una terrazza	Is there a campground nearby?	C'è un camping qui vicino?
hot/cold water	acqua calda/fredda		
How much is it?	Quanto costa?	Tent	Tenda
It's expensive	È caro	Cabin	Cabina
Is breakfast included?	È compresa la prima colazione?	Youth hostel	Ostello per la gioventù

DRIVING

Parking	*Parcheggio*	Slow down	*Rallentare*	Intersection	*Incrocio*
No parking	*Divieto di sosta/ Sosta vietata*	Road closed/up	*Strada chiusa/ guasta*	Speed limit	*Límite di Velocità*
One way street	*Senso único*	No through road	*Vietato il transito*	Traffic light	*Semáforo*
No entry	*Senso vietato*	No passing	*Vietato il sorpasso*		

PHRASEBOOKS

Best of the **phrasebooks** is Prentice Hall's Italian Phrase book (Prentice Hall; $4.95), which has useful vocabulary sections and menu readers. Prentice Hall also publish a Mini Dictionary ($3.95), which is an excellent pocket reference.

A GLOSSARY OF ITALIAN WORDS AND ACRONYMS

ITALIAN WORDS

ANFITEATRO Amphitheater.
AUTOSTAZIONE Bus station.
AUTOSTRADA Freeway.
BELVEDERE A view point.
CAPPELLA Chapel.
CASTELLO Castle.
CENTRO Center.
CHIESA Church
COMUNE An administrative area; also, the local government or the city hall.
CORSO Avenue/boulevard.
DUOMO/CATTEDRALE Cathedral.
ENTRATA Entrance.
FESTA Festival, carnival.
FIUME River.
LAGO Lake.
MARE Sea.
MERCATO Market.
MUNICIPIO City Hall.
PALAZZO Palace, mansion or apartment block.
PARCO Park.
PASSEGGIATA The customary early evening walk.
PIAZZA Square.
PONTE Bridge.
SANTUARIO Sanctuary.
SENSO ÚNICO One-way street.
SOTTOPASSAGGIO Subway.
SPIAGGIA Beach.
STAZIONE Station (Railroad Station, Stazione Ferroviaria; Ferry Terminal, Stazione Maríttima).
STRADA Road/street.
TEATRO Theater.
TEMPIO Temple.
TORRE Tower.
TRAGHETTO Ferry.
USCITA Exit.
VIA Road (always used with name; as Via Garibaldi).

VENETIAN WORDS

CALLE Main alleyway.
CAMPO Square, generally named after a church.
CAMPIELLO Small square.
CORTE Courtyard.
FONDACO (or *Fontego*) Warehouse/hostel used by foreign traders.
FONDAMENTA Pavement along a stretch of water.
PISCINA Former site of a pool.
PUNTA Point, the extremity of an island—eg Punta della Dogana.
RAMO Small side street.
RIO (pl. *Rii*) Canal.
RIO TERRÀ Infilled canal.
RIVA A major *fondamenta*.
RUGA Usually a main shopping street.
SACCA Body of water into which two or more canals flow.
SALIZZADA (sometimes *Salizada*) Main street of a parish. Means "paved street"—originally only main thoroughfares were paved.
SOTTOPORTICO (or *Sottoportego*) Small alleyway running under a building.

ACRONYMS

AAST Azienda Autonoma di Soggiorno e Turismo (local tourist office).
ACI Italian Automobile Club.
APT Azienda Promozionale Turismo; equivalent to the AAST.
DC Democrazia Cristiana; the Christian Democrat party.
EPT Ente Provinciale di Turismo (provincial tourist office).
FS Italian State Railroads
IVA Imposta Valore Aggiunto (sales tax).
MSI Movimento Sociale d'Italia; the Italian Fascist party.
PCI Partito Comunista d'Italia; the Italian Communist Party.
PSI Partito Socialista d'Italia; the Italian Socialist Party.
RAI The Italian state TV and radio network.
SIP Italian state telephone company.
SS Strada Statale.

A GLOSSARY OF ARTISTIC AND ARCHITECTURAL TERMS

AMBULATORY Corridor round the back of the altar formed by a continuation of the aisles

APSE Recess at the altar end of a church.

ARCHITRAVE The lowest part of the entablature.

BALDACHIN Canopy over an altar or tomb.

BAPTISTERY Chapel for baptisms, often detached from church.

BAROQUE Dynamic architectural and sculptural style of seventeenth century and early eighteenth century.

CAMPANILE Bell-tower, sometimes detached.

CAPITAL Top of a column.

CHANCEL Part of church containing the altar and sanctuary.

CHOIR Part of church in which the service is sung; often raised or screened, usually near the altar.

CRYPT Burial place, usually under the choir.

CUPOLA A dome.

ENTABLATURE The part above the capital on a classical building.

EX-VOTO Painting or some other object presented as thanksgiving to a saint.

FRESCO Painting applied to wet plaster so that pigments are absorbed into the wall.

FRIEZE Decorative strip along top of wall or on an entablature.

ICONOSTASIS Screen between the sanctuary and nave in Eastern churches.

LUNETTE Semicircular panel above a door or window.

NAVE Central space in a church, usually flanked by aisles.

PANTOCRATOR An image of Christ, portrayed with outstretched arms in the act of blessing

PIANO NOBILE Main floor, usually the first.

POLYPTYCH Painting or carving on several joined wooden panels.

PORTICO The covered entrance to a building.

ROCOCO Florid eighteenth century style.

RELIQUARY Receptacle for a saint's relics.

ROMANESQUE General term for plain architectural style of eleventh century to latethirteenth century.

ROOD SCREEN Screen between sanctuary and nave, bearing a rood (crucifix).

RUSTICATION Large blocks of stone with deep joints, or brick designed to simulate them.

SANCTUARY Area immediately surrounding the high altar.

STELE Inscribed stone slab.

STUCCO Plaster made from water, sand, lime and powdered marble, used for decorative work.

TESSERA Small square pice of stone or glass used in mosaics.

TRACERY Geometrical or patterned stonework.

TRANSEPT Part of church at ninety degrees to the nave.

TROMPE L'OEIL Painting designed to trick the viewer into seeing a three-dimensional image.

TRIPTYCH Painting or carving on three joined panels.

TYMPANUM Panel enclosed by lintel of a door and the arch above it.

INDEX OF NAMES

GENERAL INDEX